THE INTERNATIONAL ASSOCIATION FOR COPTIC STUDIES

ACTS OF THE
FIFTH INTERNATIONAL CONGRESS
OF COPTIC STUDIES

WASHINGTON, 12–15 AUGUST 1992

VOLUME 2

PAPERS FROM THE SECTIONS
PART 1

Edited by David W. Johnson

ROMA — C.I.M. — 1993

ISBN 88-85354-03-3

Centro Italiano Microfiches
Piazzale di Ponte Milvio 28
I-00191 Roma (Italia)

TABLE OF CONTENTS

PART ONE

PART TWO

PROGRAM FOR THE FIFTH INTERNATIONAL CONGRESS OF COPTIC STUDIES
12-15 AUGUST 1992

12 August, 1992
PLENARY SESSION

Presidential Address
Peter Nagel

Report on Research in Coptic Art (section I)
Marguerite Rassart-Debergh

Report on Research in Coptic Literature (section IIIa)
Tito Orlandi *(in absentia)*

Les salles coptes dans le futur Grand Louvre
Marie-Hélène Rutschowscaya

L'informatisation des collections coptes du Musée du Louvre
Jean-Luc Bovot

SECTION I.   COPTIC ART
Presider: Marguerite Rassart-Debergh

Constitution of an International Working Group about Textiles from Antinoë
Loretta del Francia

Jonasdarstellungen in koptischen Kunst
Cäcilia Wietheger

A Vision of Paradise: On the Origin and Significance of Textiles with Tree Motifs
Annemarie Stauffer

Die Ikonographie der Geburt Christi in der Tekla Haymanot Kapelle der al-Mu'allaqah Kirche in Alt-Kairo
Katarzyna Urbaniak-Walczak *(in absentia)*

Some Remarks on False Coptic Monuments
Alexander Kakovkin *(in absentia)*

The Crucifixion: A Coptic Textile of the Benaki Museum Collection
Lila de Chaves *(in absentia)*

LIST OF PARTICIPANTS
FIFTH INTERNATIONAL CONGRESS
OF COPTIC STUDIES

Samiha ABD EL-SHAHEED
Cairo, Egypt

Lola ATIYA
Salt Lake City, Utah

Roger S. BAGNALL
New York, New York

Daniel BARAZ
Jerusalem, Israel

George BASSALY
Ridgefield Park, New Jersey

Constantine BELISARIUS
Heliopolis, Egypt

Dominique BENAZETH
Paris, France

Hans-Gebhard BETHGE
Mühlenbeck, Germany

Monica J. BLANCHARD
Washington, D.C.

Anka BLÖBAUM
Münster (Westf.), Germany

Noss-hi A.-S. BOTROS
Cairo, Egypt

Anne BOUD'HORS
Paris, France

Wassif BOUTROS-GHALI
Cairo, Egypt

Jean-Luc BOVOT
Paris, France

Heinzgerd BRAKMANN
Bonn, Germany

S. Kent BROWN
Provo, Utah

Karl-Heinz BRUNE
Münster (Westf.), Germany

Alberto CAMPLANI
Rome, Italy

Régine CHARRON
Québec, Canada

Sarah CLACKSON
Cambridge, England

Aelred CODY, O.S.B.
St. Meinrad, Indiana

Jacques DEBERGH
Brussels, Belgium

Loretta DEL FRANCIA
Rome, Italy

Anna DI BITONTO-KASSER
Yverdon, Switzerland

Stephen EMMEL
New Haven, Connecticut

Luisa FERRETTI-CUOMO
Jerusalem, Israel

Andreas FLUCK
Münster (Westf.), Germany

Wolf-Peter FUNK
Québec, Canada

Gawdat GABRA (Abdel-Sayed)
Cairo, Egypt

Salah E. Mohamed GALAL
Alexandria, Egypt

Michael GHATTAS
Marburg, Germany

Claudio GIANOTTO
Ivrea, Italy

Wlodzimierz GODLEWSKI
Warsaw, Poland

James E. GOEHRING
Fredericksburg, Virginia

Peter GROSSMANN
Cairo, Egypt

Johannes DEN HEIJER
Leiden, The Netherlands

Suzana HODAK
Münster (Westf.), Germany

Jürgen HORN
Göttingen, Germany

William Makram ISHAK
Port Said, Egypt

Kamal Farid ISHAQ
Heliopolis, Egypt

Atef R. JACOUB
Centerville, Virginia

David W. JOHNSON
Washington, DC

Kurt KARLSSON
Washington, D.C.

Rodolphe KASSER
Yverdon, Switzerland

A. Fouad KHOUZAM
Courbevoie, France

Hoda KHOUZAM
Toronto, Canada

Karen L. KING
Los Angeles, California

Anitra Bingham KOLENKOW
Berkeley, California

Klaus KOSCHORKE
Worb, Switzerland

Brigitte KRAUSE
Münster (Westf.), Germany

Martin KRAUSE
Münster (Westf.), Germany

Rebecca KRAWIEC
New Haven, Connecticut

Ginette LACAZE
Pau, France

Bentley LAYTON
New Haven, Connecticut

Guy LECUYOT
Paris, France

Gerard P. LUTTIKHUIZEN
Groningen, The Netherlands

Leslie S.B. MACCOULL
Washington, D.C.

Fatma MAHMOUD
Cairo, Egypt

Nabil A. MALEK
Québec, Canada

Ann MARTONE
Alexandria, Virginia

Claire S.G. EL-MASRY
Heliopolis, Egypt

Paul Allan MIRECKI
Lawrence, Kansas

C. Detlef G. MÜLLER
Remagen/Rhein, Germany

Christa MÜLLER
Göttingen, Germany

Peter NAGEL
Halle (Saale), Germany

Wolf B. OERTER
Prague, Czechoslovakia

Louis PAINCHAUD
Québec, Canada

Lucia PAPINI
Florence, Italy

Birger A. PEARSON
Santa Barbara, California

Susanne PETSCHEL
Münster (Westf.), Germany

Paul-Hubert POIRIER
Québec, Canada

Delio Vania PROVERBIO
Rome, Italy

Marguerite RASSART-
  DEBERGH
Brussels, Belgium

Magnus REISINGER
Münster (Westf.), Germany

Siegfried RICHTER
Münster (Westf.), Germany

Mary RIZK
Morris Plains, New Jersey

Samy F. RIZK
Morris Plains, New Jersey

Marian ROBERTSON-
WILSON
Salt Lake City, Utah

Gesine ROBINSON
Claremont, California

James M. ROBINSON
Claremont, California

Marie-Hélène
RUTSCHOWSCAYA
Paris, France

Ashraf Alexandre SADEK
Limoges, France

Ann SALISBURY
Stillwater, Minneapolis

Sofia SCHATEN
Münster (Westf.), Germany

Hans-Martin SCHENKE
Berlin, Germany

John Lawrence SHARPE III
Durham, North Carolina

William SHEHATA
Washington, D.C.

Mark SHERIDAN, O.S.B.
Rome, Italy

Ariel SHISHA-HALEVY
Jerusalem, Israel

Stephen SHOEMAKER
Chapel Hill, North Carolina

Rachad M. SHOUCRI
Ontario, Canada

Galina SHRON
Russia

Adel Y. SIDARUS
Evora, Portugal

Joseph SKEFFINGTON
Washington, D.C.

Jay SMITH
New Haven, Connecticut

Annemarie STAUFFER
Bern, Switzerland

Bishop Samuel AL-SURYANY
Cairo, Egypt

Hany N. TAKLA
Los Angeles, California

Thelma K. THOMAS
Ann Arbor, Michigan

Janet TIMBIE
Chevy Chase, Maryland

Gonnie VAN DEN BERG-
 ONSTWEDDER
Gouda, The Netherlands

J. VAN DER VLIET
Leiden, The Netherlands

Gertrud J.M. VAN LOON
Leiden, The Netherlands

Peter VAN MINNEN
Ann Arbor, Michigan

Armand VEILLEUX
Rome, Italy

Petra VOMBERG
Münster (Westf.), Germany

Zakaria WAHBA
Gaithersburg, Maryland

Ramses M. WASSIF
San Gabriel, California

F. WEIDMAN
New Haven, Connecticut

Cäcilia WIETHEGER
Münster (Westf.), Germany

Terry G. WILFONG
Chicago, Illinois

Gregor WURST
Münster (Westf.), Germany

Silvia WURST
Münster (Westf.), Germany

Nawara YACOUB
Port Said, Egypt

Dwight W. YOUNG
Chicago, Illinois

Fouad N. YOUSSEF
Washington, D.C.

Ewa D. ZAKRZEWSKA
Leiden, The Netherlands

PRESIDENTIAL ADDRESS

PETER NAGEL

President of the IACS, 1988–1992

Ladies and Gentlemen,
Dear Colleagues,

It is a great honor, and, still more, a cause for deep gratitude, to welcome you on behalf of the International Association for Coptic Studies on the occasion of the Fifth International Congress of Coptic Studies at the Catholic University of America in Washington, D.C.

Our special greetings to Wassif Boutros Ghali, president of the Société d'archéologie copte, the "sister society" of our association, and to our other Egyptian colleagues.

At the same time, we express our deep feeling of thanks to the authorities of the illustrious host of the congress, the Catholic University of America, its president, Brother Patrick Ellis, and especially to the tireless congress secretary, Father David W. Johnson S.J., Professor in the Department of Semitic and Egyptian Languages and Literatures, whose labor in preparation of our congress is hardly to be overestimated.

Since the last congress in Louvain-la-Neuve, 1988, we have lost forever three honorary presidents of our association:

> Pierre du Bourguet († 1988)
> Hans Jakob Polotsky († 1991)
> Mirrit Boutros Ghali († 1992)

They will last in our hearts and in our memory:

> ϵⲣϵ ⲡⲛⲟⲩⲧϵ † ⲛⲁⲩ ⲙⲡϵⲙⲧⲟⲛ ϩⲛ ⲧϵϥⲙⲛⲧⲣⲣⲟ
> May God give them rest in His kingdom

Looking backward to the beginnings and the history of our association and the preceding congresses, we can say that the first pentad is in a good way completed—not only in the simple sense that we have reached congress no. 5 after Cairo 1976, Rome 1980, Warsaw 1984, and Louvain-la-Neuve 1988; besides that, we can see a deeper sense in the location of the 5th congress.

The founding congress, at that time under the designation "Colloquium on the Future of Coptic Studies," was convened in the very homeland of the Copts, but it should never be forgotten that it was a scholar from the United States, James M. Robinson, in collaboration with his then young staff, who was among the moving forces for the inauguration of our association and for the organization of periodic congresses.

Very soon, the association went its own way. That is due, on the one hand, to the well-balanced statutes of our association, which are based on and directed to scientific programs and tasks, independent of great names and leading personalities.

If I am allowed to quote from our "Magna Charta," the first issue of the association's *Newsletter* (issued in March 1977), we learn that

> the Association shall be a non-profit organization designed to encourage and contribute to the progress of all aspects of Coptic Studies. It shall promote international cooperation among individuals as well as among organizations and institutions. It shall advance the dissemination of information about work in progress, new discoveries and new results, organize periodic Congresses on Coptic Studies, facilitate full access to and the rapid publication of source materials, identify priorities for research at a given time, bring to the attention of younger scholars the whole range of Coptic Studies, etc.

Sentences such as these should be the criterion for any evaluation of advantage or disadvantage in the work of the association and its congresses—whether it be the fine *Journal of Coptic Studies*, founded at the congress in Louvain-la-Neuve, or the eminently practical *International Directory of Institutions Holding Collections of Coptic Antiquities outside of Egypt*, edited by Stephen Emmel on the basis of information collected by a team of IACS members (1990), or whether it be the less successful publication of the proceedings of our congresses.

With some hesitation I name the admirable completion of the *Coptic Encyclopedia*, because it was not published under the auspices of our association, but it should be mentioned here, because the idea for this monumental work was born during the congress in Rome, 1980, and the responsible editors as well as many contributors are members of our association. The great scholar who inspired the work from the very beginning, Aziz Surial Atiya, deceased only two years before it was finished. Our warmest felicitations to Madame Lola Atiya for the completion of the work.

On the other hand, the independence of the association from dominant personalities is due to its members. Thanks to the activity of our association, Coptic studies in its manifold branches are disseminated over five continents. It was you, the members, fellows and friends of the IACS, who filled the statutes with life.

Sixteen years since the foundation is a short time in history; five congresses is not so great a number. However, years and events should not only be numbered, but they should be pondered.

From 1976 until the 4th congress in Louvain-la-Neuve, 1988, the world seemed to be at a standstill. There was a rigid borderline between East and West, Moscow and Washington, the Kremlin and the White House. Only one year and some months after the congress in 1988, the world has changed more than since the end of World War II. The iron curtain has broken down, democracy has begun to rise in the eastern countries. We can meet without any political permission or prohibition, and I would add that state permission or prohibition to attend a congress are but two sides of a single coin, which means oppression.

As for the time before, it should never be forgotten that American and West European scholars acknowledged the eastern members and scholars as colleagues with equal rights from the very beginning. Again and again they searched for ways to enable at least a small number of eastern Coptologists to attend the conferences in western countries. By exchange and sending of letters, offprints, books, and photocopies, they broke off our not so splendid isolation.

On the other hand, scholars from the United States and West Europe accepted willingly the invitation of the Polish Academy of Sciences to hold the Third International Congress of Coptic Studies in Warsaw, in 1984. So they gave the eastern members the feeling of being not only boarders, but also landlords. Therefore, it makes good sense, beyond the already mentioned pentad, that the 5th congress be held in Washington, D.C. From this town, two centuries ago, was issued the declaration of human rights. Not least is it due to this declaration that we can meet here.

Let us turn to some practical questions. If we compare the programs of the five congresses from Cairo until Washington, the last two are more closely linked by arrangement than the preceding ones. At the first congresses, there was a gap between archeology and the history of Coptic art, on the one side, and the bulk of philological disciplines on the other. Therefore, after the Warsaw congress, by initiative of our former president, Rodolphe Kasser, the IACS board proposed an arrangement in sections covering almost all branches of Coptology. In order to promote the exchange of information among the neighboring disciplines, a main report on work in progress in the respective field since the preceding congress was scheduled for the plenary sessions, whereas the special communications were placed in the sections. This arrangement held good in Louvain-la-Neuve, and it is applied to the present congress with some slight variations in favor of more concentration. The arrangement into sections and the nomination of reporters was decided at the board meeting of the IACS in Copenhagen, 1990, and the board takes the responsibility. It is a reason for gratitude that no one of the reporters nominated by the board refused this task.

Two of the nominated reporters and leaders of sections, Søren Giversen and Tito Orlandi, have to be absent from the congress because of heavy illness in their families. Our best wishes for recovery to Copenhagen and to Rome. Now, Professor Kasser will preside over the section on Coptic literature (section IIIa), and Dr. Wolf-Peter Funk over the section on Manichaeism (section IX).

In our Eon of Darkness, there is nothing above criticism. Offer your proposals for amendments to the next board and its congress secretary, but meanwhile let us begin our work in the sense of the little "Magna Charta" of Coptologists, in the spirit of communication and not of excommunication, in Call and Hearing, in order to promote once again "the future of Coptic studies."

Thank you.

THE EAST BASILICA OF PELUSIUM

MOHAMED ABD EL-SAMIE

The East Basilica of Pelusium is one of the most important discoveries in the region of Pelusium (today "Tall al-Farama"). The traditional
name of the complex among the Bedouins is "Tall al-Makhzan" (Hill of
the magazines) which probably refers to its many semi-circular chambers.
It is an impressive isolated hill situated to the east of the main center of
Pelusium and it was excavated by the Egyptian Antiquities Organization
during the years 1988-92[1]. According to its location, the church might be
identified with the memorial church of St. Epimachus, which is said to be
situated at the east of Pelusium[2].

The church is a huge basilica, one of the biggest examples ever
found in Egypt, with an atrium (until now not fully excavated), a narthex, a
three-aisled nave, an apse with an inner *synthronon*, a slightly raised *bema*
in front of the latter, and rows of different rooms on all sides. At the west
end of the northern side even a double row of rooms is extant, the outer
rooms are, however, of later date.

The main entrance was surely from the west. But there are lateral
entrances also from the north and south. At both ends of the narthex two
square rooms are extant which might have been two tower-like structures
as are often found in Early Christian church buildings[3]. Inside the church
proper and contrary to the usual rule in Egypt, there is no return aisle at
the western end of the nave. The *bema* is clearly detectable at the eastern
end, raised by two steps above the general level of the floor. Some little
remains of masonry a few meters to the west of the bema might be
explained as the vestiges of the pulpit. Among the rooms on both sides is a
staircase to the south, and a small additional chapel to the north. This
chapel has an apse with two tiny little side-chambers inserted into the
curve. The emplacement of an altar is not traceable.

---

[1] See our preliminary report: Le monastère de Tell Makhzan à Péluse, *CRIPEL* 14,
1992, (in press), which refers to the first three seasons.

[2] St. Timm, *Das christlich-koptische Ägypten in arabischer Zeit*. II (Wiesbaden 1984)
926-935, esp. 928 with references.

[3] One of the closest parallels is the church in the famous monastery at Mount
Moses in South Sinai, recently P. Grossmann, in: K.A. Manafis (ed.), *Sinai. Treasures of the
monastery of Saint Catherine* (Athens 1990) 29-39 with new plans and a discussion of the
developement of the church.

Much more complicated are the additional rooms to the east, on both sides of the apse. The spacial programm is very different from the ordinary pastophoria usually to be found at the sides of the apses in eastern ecclesiastical architecture[4]. However, although there are several joints detectable and even some changes in the stone material used for the masonry, there is no doubt that this eastern group of rooms belongs - as a whole - to the original building programme of the church.

Immediately to the left of the apse a long east-west elongated room is extant, accessible through a *tribelon* from the northern aisle of the church. At the eastern end a block of limestone masonry is attached against the wall. Its surface is not preserved. It might have been a support for a *mensa* or even a podium of an *aedicula*[5]. To the south a door, subsequently narrowed, gives access to a small court situated behind the apse of the church. Its floor is one step higher than the neighbouring rooms. At the eastern end are some secondary rooms and a two aisled underground cistern.

The neighbouring room to the north attracts special attention. It is entered from the south through a very wide opening which was apparently subdivided with at least two, possibly four columns. Attached to the eastern wall, but considerably off the east-west axis of the room, stands a rather high block of masonry containing a small cross-shaped deepening, which appears *prima facie* as a baptistry and was apparently designed to be filled with water. But, the dimensions of this deepening are so small, only 27 cm wide, and ca. 45 cm deep, while the block itself is 80 cm high, that it is very doubtful whether it could really serve for baptisms. The distances from the sides are such that would be physically very difficult to dip a little child into this basin. It seems therefore more likely that this basin was used for other purposes, probably as a *colybion* for consecration services only.

Nevertheless, it is quite remarkable how this basin was set to one side. This could only mean that the center of the wall was kept free for something else. Since the wall itself is not thick enough for a central niche of normal depth, perhaps a picture of a saint could have been extant here

---

[4] On a functional discussion of these rooms see G. Descoeudres, *Die Pastophorien im syro-byzantinischen Osten* (Wiesbaden 1983).

[5] A similar podium combined with a niche in the eastern wall is extant in the northwest corner room of the episcopal church of Pharan in South Sinai, see P. Grossmann, *Excavations in Wadi Fayran 1985 and 1986.* ASAE 72, 1987 (in press); and in the south pastophorium of the little church in the Late Roman army camp of Taposiris Magna, see J.B. Ward Perkins, *The monastery of Taposiris Magna.* BSAA 36, 1943-1944, 48-53 Pl. 4; there is no reference in the text on this feature, but in the plan, ibid. Pl. 4, it is clearly indicated as "altar".

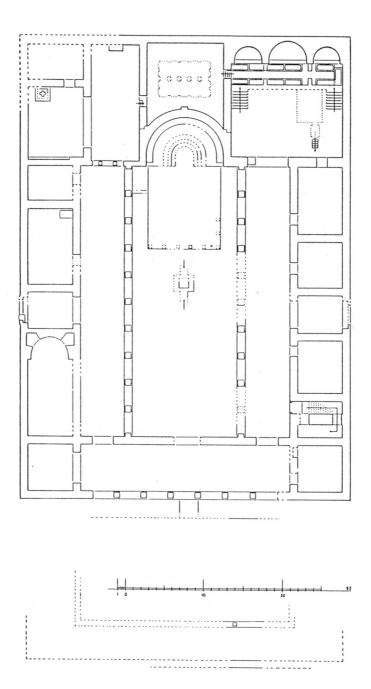

Fig. 1. Ground plan of the church of Tall al-Makhzan

painted in a rather flat recess and framed probably with pilasters and a pediment of stucco.

But, the most interesting feature of this church are the installations to the south of the apse, which are unfortunately not well enough preserved to gain an immediately clear idea of how they should be interpreted. At first there is a broad hall accessible from the south aisle of the nave through another large, probably *tribelon*-like entrance. In the southern half of the hall, below the floor a vaulted underground burial chamber is extant to which a flight of stairs descends from the western end of the hall. On the eastern side of the hall is a raised platform, which opens eastwards to three semicircular apses of unequal sizes. The largest is placed in the middle. To ascend to the level of the platform two stairs were erected at the two ends left and right, in front of it.

The space below the platform was used for a vaulted corridor running north-south. The access to it was provided from the north, out of the already mentioned little court to the east of the apse. An entrance from the south-east hall does not exist. Inside this corridor a sequence of burials was found, that had obviously been added later. These were lined up along both lateral walls. Thus, with the single exception of the first burial at the southern end, all of them are orientated north-south, which contradicts the usual east-west orientation of Christian burials[6]. The reason for this exception is, however, rather simple. Only in the middle of the corridor could an adult person stand in an upright position. Consequently, one may assume that in all probability, the corridor below the platform was originally not intended for use as a burial place.

The whole arrangement of the south-eastern hall, with the raised platform, the two stairs, and the three eastern apses, seems to be a *martyrium*, basically corresponding to similar arrangements, of course usually of much smaller size, in Syria and Palestine where in one of the side chambers of the apse two or even three shrines with relics of different saints were sometimes placed[7]. The three apses in our case would just be a more monumental way of displaing such shrines, each for the relics of an indivi-

---

[6] There are also other exceptions to the strict east-west orientation of Christian burials. The Princeton University expedition to North Syria describes at least three monasteries where the burial grounds are provided with several, in a strict sense, "wrongly" orientated burial places, see H.C. Butler, *Syria. Publications of the Princeton University archaeological expeditions to Syria in 1904-5 and 1909. II Architecture B. Northern Syria* (Leyden 1920) 222 fig. 218. 224 sect. E-F (= Qaṣr al-Banat); 245 fig 247 (= Dair Tall 'Adah); 274f. fig. 286 (= West monastery of Dair Siman, "campo santo").

[7] Some examples from North Syria are mentioned in: G. Tchalenko, *Villages antiques de la Syrie du Nord. I-II* (Paris 1953) I 315f. Pl. 99 (Bamūqqa); I 347ff. 354ff. Pl. 111ff. (East and West church of Behyo).

dual saint. The two stairs left and right at the eastern side of the hall, one for going up the other for descending, were presumably erected to create a kind of order in the movement of the faithfull when they come to obtain the *eulogia* of the saints, a ceremony which is often carried out at the end of the liturgy in eastern churches[8]. The *eulogia* offered here were probably, small amounts of oil, placed on the relics of the day's saint, and dispensed into small vessels brought by the daithfull for this purpose[9].

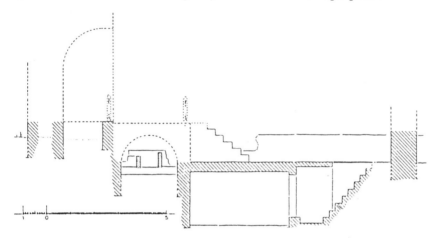

Fig. 2. Section (east-west) through the *martyrium*

The technical construction of the church consists - as all buildings in Pelusium - mainly of fired bricks laid in ordinary clay mortar. Only for the more heavily loaded parts of the building, such as the outer corners, the abutments of the triumphal arch, the burial chamber and the vault below the platform in the *martyrium*, were regularly cut limestone blocks set in lime-mortar used. The brick masonry of the rest was reinforced by an extensive armature of parallell and transversely distributed planks of wood, as often occurs in buildings of Late Antiquity in Egypt[10]. The average distances of the transverse planks are ca. 2 m. Marble slabs, of which

---

[8] H. Brakmann (Bonn) pointed out to me that the reception of the *eulogia* could also have taken place on other occasions.

[9] A characteristically similar example, with, however, only one level structure, represents the martyrium at the Church of the Holy Cross in Ruṣāfa (ancient Sergiopolis), cf. Th. Ulbert, *Resafa II. Die Basilika des Heiligen Kreuzes in Resafa-Sergiupolis* (Mainz 1986) 43ff. 137ff. fig. 25ff.

[10] P. Grossmann, *Holzbewehrung im römischen und spätantiken Mauerwerk in Ägypten*, in: *Bautechnik der Antike. Int. Kolloqium in Berlin vom 15.-17. Febr. 1990* [Diskussion zur Archäologischen Bauforschung 5, 1991] 56-62.

traces survived at many instances, were used for finishing the walls of the church proper and of the *martyrium*. The other walls were simply plastered. In the same sense the church proper and the *martyrium* were paved with marble. For the majority of the other rooms ordinary lime plastered floors or pavements with fired bricks were used. Fragments of columns did not survive, except for a few attic bases, too small to be those employed in the colonnades of the nave. Extant is, however, a small pedestal which, according to its vertical grooves on two adjoining sides, served as a corner post for the *cancelli* of the *bema*. On the northern side of the *bema* lies a fragment of a column shaft of corresponding size.

Fig. 3. a) General view from the West; b) General view from the South

12

Fig. 4. a) The martyrium from the South;   b) North-Eastern rooms
from the North

EPACT NUMERALS

Samiha Abd El-Shaheed Abd El-Nour

I. INTRODUCTION

Definition

The "epact numerals" are a late form of the Greek numerals developed by Egyptian scribes, consisting of the letters of the Greek alphabet but with distinctive forms which Marcus Simaika called "cursive letters" in the list at the end of his catalogue.[1] These "cursive letters" are written with a line above them to denote units, tens, and hundreds, and with an additional short sloping line underneath them to denote thousands. A sloping stroke to the upper right of a figure denotes a fraction.

The Greek word ἐπακτή (which comes into Arabic as *abuqtī*)[2] applied to these figures means "brought in from abroad." This use of the word "epact" is to be distinguished from its application to the Coptic calculation of the date of Easter and its preceding fast — the *ḥisāb al-abuqtī* or "epact computation" -- attributed to Demetrius, the twelfth patriarch of Alexandria (A.D. 189–231).[3]

---

1. Marcus SIMAIKA Pasha, *Catalogue of the Coptic and Arabic Manuscripts in the Coptic Museum, the Patriarchate, the Principal Churches of Cairo and Alexandria and the Monasteries of Egypt*, vols. I–II,1, Cairo: 1939–42 [hereafter cited as SIMAIKA], II,1:509.

2. See, for example, Coptic Patriarchate MS 177 Liturgy (Serial No. 1005), 2 (listed in SIMAIKA, II,1:449).

3. See George SOBHY Bey, "The Coptic Calendrical Computation and the System of Epacts," *Bulletin de la Société d'Archéologie Copte* 8 (1942) 169–99; and Khalil SAMIR, "Book of Epact," *The Coptic Encyclopedia*, 409–11.

The Development and Use of the Epact Numerals

Early evidence for the use of the "epact numerals" is provided by Egyptian documents of the eighth and ninth centuries, many of which have been catalogued in this century. Margoliouth published a catalogue of the Arabic papyri in the John Rylands Library, dating back to the seventh through the ninth centuries.[4] Grohmann published a collection of Arabic papyri from the eighth and ninth centuries preserved in the Egyptian Library,[5] including tax lists and other economic and administrative texts. In these papyri the scribe, writing in a rapid hand, gives lists of items in Arabic and, opposite each item, a cursive Coptic numeral corresponding to the production of a particular crop,[6] or the payment of tax.[7] From the ninth century comes the "Coptic Calculation Manual" published by Drescher, who provided plates of two specimen pages in order to illustrate the various numerical symbols used therein. He observed that numbers are represented by Greek letters having the later form common in the Arabic papyri.[8]

It is well known that from the beginning of the eighth century the Arabic language began gradually to displace Coptic, due in part to the order of the caliph 'Abd al-Malik Ibn Marwān (A.D. 685-705), and in part simply to the intimate relations existing in Egypt between Copts and Muslims. In the twelfth century the Coptic patriarch Gabriel II (A.D. 1131-45) ordered the bishops to explain the church's prayers and beliefs in Arabic, even though

---

4. D. S. MARGOLIOUTH, *Catalogue of the Arabic Papyri in the John Rylands Library*, Manchester: 1933, pp. 131-32 (Plate XII.2).

5. A. GROHMANN, *Arabic Papyri in the Egyptian Library*, I-VI, Cairo: 1934-62.

6. Ibid., IV:354, Plate II (MS No. 217).

7. Ibid., I:189 (MS No. 200).

8. J. DRESCHER, "A Coptic Calculation Manual," *Bulletin de la Société d'Archéologie Copte* 13 (1951) 137-60.

Coptic continued to be used in the liturgy.[9] In a preface
to a thirteenth-century Copto-Arabic manuscript of the
four gospels,[10] this literary evolution is explained as
follows:[11]

إنّه لمّا كان القصد بنقل الإنجيل المجيد
إلى اللسان العربيّ بدئاً إمّا لتغلّبه على قوم،
كما صار لنا؛ وإمّا لحذق مَن أخرجه باللغتين؛
وإمّا لقصد غير هذين. ولثقتهم بأنّ لا يُمكن
أن يُتلى في بيعهم إلّا لغاتهم الّتي ما يعرفون
غيرها، بلغوا في نقله حدّ الطاقة، ولم يوقفهم
التماس التحرير البالغ عن ترجمة ما شرعوا
فيه. فلهذا، وُجد بينه وبين اللغات تفاوت ما.

Translation:

The purpose of translating the Holy
Gospel into the Arabic language was originally
only because of its coming to predominate in a
community, such as happened among us; or
because of the proficiency of the person who
produced the book in the two languages; or for
some purpose other than these two. And
because of their certainty that [the Gospel]
must not be read in their churches except in
their own languages, apart from which they
know no other, they went to the limit of their
capacity in its translation, and the demands of
effective composition did not stop them from

---

9. See Raouf HABIB, *The Coptic Museum*, Cairo: 1967, p. 44, note 1.
10. Coptic Museum MS 93 Bible (Serial No. 5), SIMAIKA, I:6. The
      manuscript is dated (f. 346ᵛ): end of Baūnah 973 A.M. and
      Ğumādā l-āḫirah 655 A.H. (= early July 1257 A.D.).
11. f. 347ʳ.

the translation of what they had begun. Therefore, a certain degree of disparity is found between [the Gospel] and the languages [of its translations].

Scribes came to paginate and to date their Copto-Arabic or Arabic manuscripts with those cursive letters which, written rapidly, took on the characteristic form known as "epact."

A Table of Numerals

A Copto-Arabic *Psalmodia* dated A.M. 1597 (= A.D. 1881) and preserved in the Coptic Museum[12] contains a table giving equivalents in different systems of numeration: the names of the Coptic letters written in the Bohairic dialect; the epact numerals; Indian serial numerals, and finally the *al-ǧummal* numerals (i.e., the Arabic *abǧadiyyah* letters). This last system of numeration became popular in the 18th century, when Muslim artists used it to fix the date of their manual works.

II. EXAMPLES

Many examples of the use of epact numerals are to be found in the collections of manuscripts and artifacts in the Coptic Museum. These include:

(1) Coptic Museum MS 33 Liturgy (Serial No. 156),[13] containing "*Ṭurūḥāt* of the four odes and the seven *theotokias* and the evening offices for the month of Kîhak" (in Coptic and Arabic) and an Arabic *mîmar* "On the presentation of the Virgin Mary" by Anba Cyril, archbishop of Jerusalem. The pagination and the date on the final page of the *mîmar* is written in epact numerals: A.M. 1144 (= A.D. 1427), while the Copto-Arabic portion of the

---

12. Coptic Museum MS 13 Liturgy (Serial No. 284); SIMAIKA I:128. See Plate I below.
13. SIMAIKA, I:78-79.

manuscript is paginated with Coptic letters in an elegant, educated hand. This section is dated, at f. 33^V, A.M. 1139 (= A.D. 1422).

(2) A unique steelyard ornamented with a cross, set off with silver (no. 1570). This piece, which probably comes from Akhmim, is dated in epact numerals: A.M. 1036 (= A.D. 1302).

(3) An icon showing the archangel Michael shod in decorative sandals (no. 3433). In his right hand he holds the sceptre with three signs fixed at the top in the form of the heiroglyph Djed, symbolising Osiris and eternity. In his left hand he holds the balance by means of which human acts upon earth are to be weighed. The artist's name and the date of the work in both epact and Arabic numerals are given at the bottom of the icon: Ibrāhīm al-Nāsiḫ, A.M. 1493 (= A.D. 1777).

(4) A sleeve of red silk embroidered in silver-gilt decorated with floral patters of a very fine and delicate craftsmanship (no. 2242; see Plate II). Its date is embroidered in both epact and Arabic numerals: A.M. 1466 and A.H. 1163 (= A.D. 1750).

The preceding examples of the use of epact numerals are confined to *Coptic* art. However, after the Arab conquest of Egypt (A.D. 641), Muslim governors of Egypt used local craftsmen to carry out their projects. The works that these governors commissioned reflect both their own specifications and certain features which had been traditional before the conquest. Coins, for example, continued to be stamped with the epact numerals iota and beta traditionally used to define their weight, even though the figure of the emperor was replaced by other, specifically Islamic motifs.[14]

At the Islamic Museum in Cairo we find a unique masterpiece, a fragment of a lustre-painted glass vessel (Plate III). While the name of the workshop is given in Kufic letters around its edge, the date is given in epact numerals: A.H. 163 (= A.D. 779).[15]

It is clear from the foregoing examples that the Copts used epact numerals not only in manuscripts, but in various kinds of artifacts. Evidence for the use of epact numerals can be found at least as early as the eighth century, and their use is commonplace in the Arabic Christian manuscripts from Egypt that we possess from the thirteenth century onwards.[16]

We hope that further studies will further elucidate this interesting subject.

---

14. 'ABD AL-RAḤMĀN Fahmī Muḥammad, "Christian Signs and Coptic Symbols on Islamic Coinage" [Arabic], in the *Acta* of the Third International Congress on Islamic Antiquities in the Arab Nations, Fās, 8-18 November, 1959, p. 355.

15. HASSAN el Pasha, ABD EL-RAOUF Ali Yousef *et al*, *Cairo and its Monuments*, Cairo: 1969, pp. 331-32.

16. Earlier Egyptian Christian Arabic manuscripts are lacking, according to Khalil SAMIR, "Arabic Sources for Early Egyptian Christianity," in Birger A. PEARSON and James E. GOEHRING (eds.), *The Roots of Egyptian Christianity*, Philadelphia: 1986, p. 87, note 5.

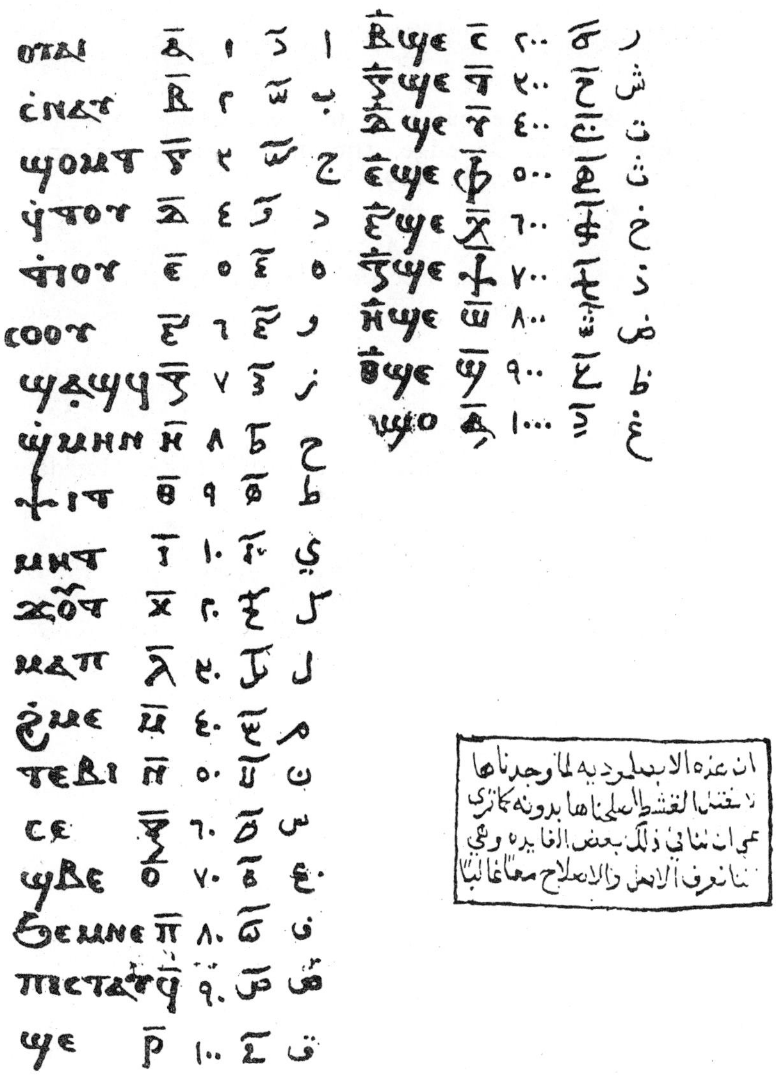

PLATE I: Table of numerals, giving the names of the Coptic numerals in Bohairic, followed by the Coptic, Arabic, epact, and *al-ǧummal* numerals. (Coptic Museum MS 13 Liturgy (Serial No. 284))

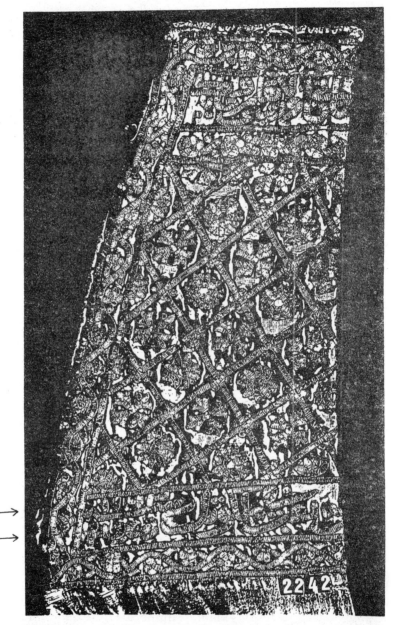

PLATE II: A sleeve of red silk dated in epact numerals, ⳍⲥⲇⲉ (A.M. 1466), and in Arabic numerals, ١١٦٣ (A.H. 1163). (Coptic Museum no. 2242)

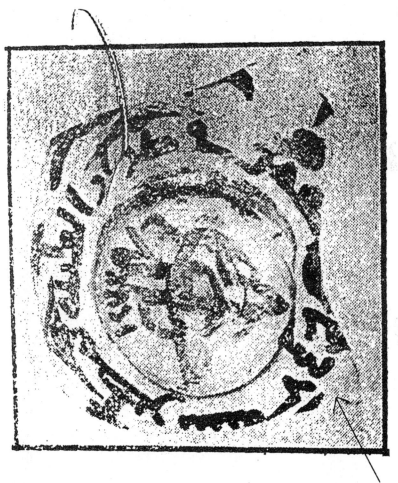

PLATE III: Bottom of a lustre-painted glass vessel with inscription around its edge:

(A.H. 163 =) ٢٦٣ سنة بمصر الفيله طراز في عمل «مما

(Islamic Museum 12739-6)

Coptic-Arabic Collections of Western Marian Legends

The Reception of a Western Text in the East – A Case of Intercultural Relations in the Late Middle Ages*

Daniel Baraz

Around the beginning of the 12th century a new type of popular religious literature emerged in Western Europe: collections of Marian legends. The novelty was not in the stories they contained, some of which were centuries old, but in the formation of the new genre. During the 12th century it rapidly became widespread in Europe. The growing size of the collections, the formation of vernacular ones, and the number of surviving manuscripts, all attest to the growing popularity of the genre in Europe in the 12th and 13th centuries[1].

The content of these stories is rather repetitive: most of them present instances of the Virgin Mary's aid and protection to people who worship her, and particularly to sinners whose only virtue was their devotion to her. A typical story is the one known as the tale of "The Drowned Sacristan". A monk drowns, while reciting the Ave Maria, on his way across the river to his mistress. Mary prevents the devils from dragging his soul to hell, claiming that the monk was in her service. He is given a second chance and is restored to life, after which he lives virtuously until his death.

In the period between the 13th and the 15th centuries this new genre appeared in the popular religious literature of the Coptic and Ethiopian churches. The Coptic collections, in Arabic, appeared at the beginning of this period, and the first Ethiopian ones at its end. The whole corpus of Coptic-Arabic collections of Marian legends until the 17th

---

*   This paper is a part of an M.A. thesis presented at the Hebrew University of Jerusalem. I would like to thank my advisor Prof. B.Z. Kedar and Prof. H. Lazarus-Yafeh for many helpful comments.

[1]   For a detailed survey of the Western Marian miracles literature see: Adolfo Mussafia (1886-1898), Studien zu den mittelaelterlichen Marienlegenden, in Sitzungsberichte der k. Akademie der Wissenschaften, Wien, Phil.-Hist. Kl., 113(1886), 115(1888), 119(1889), 123(1891), 139(1898); and H.L.D. Ward (1962[1893]), Catalogue of Romances in the Department of Manuscripts in the British Museum, London.

century consists of a collection of 74 stories[2]. All known mss. of the complete collection are late ones, from the 17th century onwards. There are earlier mss. of smaller collections, the earliest of which bears the date 1289, but they are fragments of the 74 story collection, and do not contain any additional material[3]. These texts have been studied intermittently by Louis Villecourt and Enrico Cerulli, who concentrated on the identification of sources and influences[4]. Villecourt has already shown in 1924 that most of the material in the Arabic collection is of Western origin; however, no <u>direct</u> source of the Arabic collection was found.

The proximity in time between the formation of these collections in the West and in the East, in conjunction with the fact that most of the stories in the Arabic collection are, in fact, of Western origin, affected the way in which the reception of the Western texts was perceived. The accepted view about the reception of these legends in the East, as initially presented by Wallis Budge, is that the 74 story collection is the product of a centralized Coptic effort to produce a uniform collection for liturgical purposes. This view was accepted and elaborated by E. Cerulli in <u>Il libro etiopico dei Miracoli di Maria</u>, which is still the most detailed study of the Arabic collection, and it was reiterated more

---

[2]   In the 17th century a Greek collection of Agapios Landos was translated into Arabic (L. Villecourt (1924), "Les collections arabes des miracles de la Sainte Vierge", in <u>Analecta Bollandiana</u> 42(1924), p. 21. This article will be referred to hereafter as **Villecourt**).

[3]   The main manuscripts of the Arabic collections are (in chronological order):
> BN ar. 177 (1289) - 12 legends.
> BN ar. 69 (1334) - 14 legends.
> *Dayr Abū Maqār* 381 (14th cent.) - 32 legends.
> BN ar. 155 (1486) - 42 legends.
> *Dayr Mārī Mīnā* 123 (15th-16th cent.) - 32 legends.
> *Dayr Abū Maqār* 480 (1580) - 33 legends.
> *Dayr Marī Mīnā* 13 (1697) - 74 legends.
> Vat. ar. 170 (1718) - 75 legends.
> Vat. ar. 821 (18th cent.) - 63 legends.
> BN ar. 4771 (19th cent.) - 74 legends.

[4]   Villecourt; E. Cerulli (1943), <u>Il libro etiopico dei Miracoli di Maria</u>, Rome, 1943 (hereafter **Cerulli**); Cerulli (1969), "'Il suicidio della peccatrice' nelle versioni araba ed etiopica del Libro dei Miracoli di Maria", in <u>Annali dell'Istituto Orientale di Napoli</u>, n.s. 19(1969:2):147-179.

recently in a study by Giamberardini. Cerulli dated the formation of this collection between 1237-1289[5].

The emergence of this Western genre in the East, and the fact that most of the Arabic legends have Western sources, are intriguing, given the usual lack of receptivity of these Eastern churches to Western influences. However, the view presented above concerning the reception of these texts is problematic. Its most questionable aspect is why would the Western texts, which probably had no liturgical function in Europe, be adopted so uncritically and be accorded a more official and elevated status than they had in their places of origin? And, furthermore, why would such an activity take place at the same period in which the Synaxary, an official Coptic hagiographic collection for liturgical purposes, was compiled.

The plausibility of this liturgical function of the Western texts in the Coptic church is weakened even further as it hinges on a late Ethiopian text of doubtful authenticity, the Canon of al-Mu^{c}allaqa. It is found only in a single 18th century Ethiopian manuscript, and there is no Arabic Coptic version of the canon.

A manuscript discovered in 1950 by Paltrinieri and Sangalli - University of Bologna 1794 - helps to solve some of the problems concerning the formation of the Arabic collection, and the reception of the Western texts. This is a Latin collection of Marian legends by the Dominican Bartolomeo da Trento, who died in 1251[6]. This ms. supports the view that the 74 story Arabic collection was formed during the second half of the 13th century. However, there is no evidence that it was a product of a centralized Coptic activity, or that these collections had a liturgical function.

Paltrinieri and Sangalli, who discovered Bartolomeo da Trento's collection, realized that it supplies the source of 4 stories in the Arabic collection, for which no Western source was found previously. But the importance of Bartolomeo's collection is even greater than has been

---

[5]   E.A. Wallis Budge (1933), One Hundred and Ten Miracles of Our Lady Mary, London, p. liv; Cerulli, p. 534; Cerulli 1969: pp. 151,179; Gabriele Giamberardini (1978), Il culto mariano in Egitto, Jerusalem, vol. III, p. 407.

[6]   I. Paltrinieri and G. Sangalli (1950), "Il 'Liber miraculorum B.M.V.' di fra Bartolomeo Tridentino, in Salesianum 12(1950):372-297; Antoine Dondaine (1975), "Fra Bartolomeo da Trento e alcuni codici a lui attribuiti", in Archivum Fratrum Praedicatorum 45(1975):79-105.

recognized, as these 4 stories are the <u>direct</u> source of their Arabic parallels. No direct source of any story in the Arabic collection was known previously, and this offers, for the first time, an opportunity to study in detail the reception of a sample of the Western texts within the Coptic tradition. Using this manuscript and the sources it supplies for stories in the Arabic collection, I would like to concentrate here on the reception of the Western legends in terms of their content, by referring to the following 3 issues:

1. Do the Arabic versions of the Western texts show any characteristic editorial changes?

2. If so, what religious attitudes do such changes reflect?

3. And finally, what can such tendentious changes indicate about the Coptic attitude towards the Western texts?

I would like to argue here that on the textual level there is a tendency to "Copticize" the legends, that is to adapt them to local religious attitudes. In a broader perspective, the Coptic reception of the Western Marian legends was limited, since central aspects of the Western legends were rejected.

A parallel reading of the Arabic versions and the Western sources shows 2 prominent tendencies:

One is the mitigated presentation of sinners and their actions. Thus, for instance, one of the stories in Bartolomeo's collection (no. 10) deals with a bishop who is rebuked by Mary for a too rigorous penance he imposed on a man who came to be confessed. In the Arabic version the erring bishop is introduced with an additional list of virtues, absent from the Latin collection. The penitent who is presented as a sinner (criminal - <u>sceleratus</u>) in the Latin version is presented here merely as a man (<i>rajul</i>). Another story tells of a sinner, who was assaulted by his enemies, and was rewarded for his devotion to Mary, by being kept alive until he was confessed by a priest. The Latin version presents his devotion to Mary as motivated by interest:

> Hic ob spem ne impenitens moreretur ad honorem christianorum spei Matris Dei nativitatis, annunciationis, purificationis et assumptionis vigilias arcto jejunio observabat et in aliis virginem honorabat (University of Bologna 1794, f. 71v).

(With the hope of not dying impenitent, this [man] observed the vigils of the mother of God's Nativity, Annunciation, Purification, and Assumption with a strict fast and honoured the Virgin with other things [as well]).

In the Arabic version his devotion to the Virgin is presented as pure:

wahuwa kāna muḥibban lilsayyida umm al-raḥma min kull qalbihi

wakāna yaṣūmu laha ṣiyāmaha biqalb ṭayyib waniyya ṣāliḥa (Vat. ar. 170, f. 14r)[7].

(And he loved the Lady with all his heart, and observed her fasts with a willing heart and pure intention).

In addition to such a presentation of the sinners, the other prominent characteristic of the Arabic version is the added emphasis on the remorse and penitence of the sinners at the end of the stories. Another one of the 4 stories for which Bartolomeo's collection supplies the direct source (no. 136), tells of a woman who is not allowed by her husband to fast on one of Mary's feast days. When the woman accidentally opens a coffer kept in the house she finds it full of gold, and understands that this is an earthly compensation for the reward she will no longer receive in the other world. Her husband, seeing her desolate, but ignorant of the coffer, allows her to fast. Later, the woman discovers that the coffer is empty and rejoices. She tells her husband, who, consequently, also begins to observe the Virgin's fasts. In the Latin version it is merely stated that he followed his wife's example in fasting:

```
et qui prius inhibuerat, ieiunio devotissime
sequitur uxorem (University of Bologna 1794,
f. 91r).
```

(And he who has formerly forbidden, [now] followed his wife most devoutly in fasting).

The Arabic version elaborates, and states explicitly that he repented his former behaviour:

---

7   The language of the Arabic collections is a mixture of half-classical and colloquial Arabic. Therefore I transcribed the text as classical Arabic wherever the text permitted, without, however pointing out the numerous deviations.

fanadima wawāẓaba huwa ayḍan al-ṣiyām wakhidmatihi lilṣitt al-sayyida bikull qudratihi waᶜāshū ᶜalā dhālika (BN ar. 177, f. 117r).

(And he repented, and he, too, strictly observed the fasts and served the Lady to the best of his ability, and they [continued] to do so [all] their lives).

Up to this point Bartolomeo's texts were confronted with the earliest, almost contemporary, Arabic versions, which despite the varying emphases follow the European original rather closely. The later Arabic versions are based on the early Arabic ones, and not on the European originals, and therefore provide us with the next link in the chain of reception of the Western legends[8]. The aforementioned tendencies concerning the characterization of the protagonists and the ending of the stories become even more prominent in the later Arabic versions, thus demonstrating that the changes observed between the Latin and the early Arabic versions are meaningful and not accidental. These later versions make it clear that there is a persistent effort to extract, or at least tone down, one of the central elements of the European stories - the reference to the sin of the protagonist.

Thus, for example, one of the stories in the Arabic collection (no. 52[9]) tells of a robber devoted to Mary, who is caught and hanged, but even at the point of death continues to recite the <u>Ave Maria</u>. Mary appears to the bishop of the town in a dream, ordering him to take the body down from the gallows, and bury it in the cemetery among the faithful. The bishop ignores Mary's instructions for two consecutive nights, and obeys only after she threatens him, on the third night, with a severe punishment. Four days after the burial, a beautiful flower springs from the grave, and it is discovered that it springs from the thief's tongue. The early Arabic version introduces the thief in the following manner:

kāna ʾinsān liṣṣ mā yaᶜīsh ʾillā min al-sirqa lakinna kāna kull yawm yusallim ᶜalā al-sitt al-sayyida (Vat. ar. 170, f. 80v).

---

[8] From the manuscripts of the <u>complete</u> collection I consulted, Vat. ar. 170 reflects the earliest stage of the Arabic texts; Vat. ar. 821, although based on the earlier versions, reflects a later stage of the text.

[9] The numbering of the stories is that of Vat. ar. 170, which is the one used by Villecourt and Cerulli.

(There was a robber who lived by theft alone, but every
day used to greet Mary [with the <u>Ave Maria</u>]).

In a later version of the text, he is presented not as a sinner whose
redeeming quality is the devotion to Mary, but as a virtuous man who fell
prey to the Devil's snares:

> <u>dh</u>ukira ^can ba^cḍ al-luṣus ʾannahu kullamā aqbala ^calā al-ṭawba
> yujāhiduhu al-<u>sh</u>ayṭan bil-fiqr wal-maskana wayad^cūhu ʾila al-
> ḥarām daf^ca ba^cda daf^ca liʾannahu kāna liṣṣan muqtaṣiran lā
> yasriqu ʾilla mā yaqūma bikifāyatihi min waqt ʾila waqt wakāna
> ma^ca <u>dh</u>ālika fīhi ^cāda ʾu<u>kh</u>rā jamīla (Vat. ar. 821, f. 98r).

(It was told about a certain robber, that whenever he decided to
repent the devil afflicted him with poverty and misery, and caused
him to sin time after time, since he was robbing only because of
deprivation, and only as much as he needed from time to time.
Nevertheless, he had one nice habit ...)

and the text goes on describing his devotion to Mary.

The tendency to charge the Devil with the responsibility for the sin
committed by the protagonist is characteristic of the later Arabic versions.
And it is significant even if it is a mere figure of speech; in the final effect
it does reduce the protagonist's culpability.

Complementary to this tendency we see in the later Arabic
versions, as in the earlier ones, an effort to supply the stories with an
idealized "happy end", which is supposed to compensate for the evil
actions committed in the story. One of the stories tells of a farmer who
exploited and cheated his neighbours, and is saved from hell only by
virtue of his devotion to Mary. In the early version he appears to his wife
eight days after his death and informs her of what happened to him in the
other world. In the later version he also orders her to return those of his
possessions which were wrongfully acquired to their rightful owners.

These tendencies of a positively biased characterization of the
sinner-protagonist, and an emphasis on his penitence, seem to suggest that
there is a·basic divergence between the Western conception of sin and
redemption and the Coptic one. Mary's help to various types of sinners is
the principal theme of the Western Marian miraeles, while in the Coptic

treatment of these texts one can see an objection to their lenient, and even sympathetic, treatment of sinners[10].

An examination of the Synaxary, the main indigenous Coptic hagiographic collection, suggests similar tendencies. The comparison with the Synaxary is pertinent, as the beginning of its compilation is contemporaneous to the translation of the Western legends into Arabic[11].

The Synaxary differs significantly from its contemporary European hagiography. The typical protagonists of the Synaxary stories are martyrs or hermits. In either case it idealizes the saint's willingness to undergo tortures, whether self inflicted or not, and evokes an ideal of strict asceticism. The protagonists in the Synaxary stories are always people whose virtuousness is beyond doubt. Their sins, if committed, go back to the period before their conversion; and then the state of sin is described as total, in order to accentuate the contrast with their subsequent virtuous behaviour. The life of Martha the Egyptian is emblematic of this attitude. In her youth "she liked to lead an impure life, and the sons of the honourable and of the noble people used to come to her in secret. When this became known she hid it no more, and fornicated publicly"[12]. One Christmas she decides to go to church, and is prevented from entering. She declares her intention to repent, and the bishop orders her to bring all her clothes and jewelry. He burns them publicly, shaves her, and clothes her as a male monk. She enters a monastery, and never leaves it until her death.

In the Coptic Synaxary stories there is no half way between sin and saintliness. Sin and purity are two different worlds, which cannot be reconciled, and the transition between them is difficult. There are no virtuous people who give in to temptation, and there are no sinners who have a redeeming quality (as the devotion to Mary, for instance). The

---

[10]   Opposition to the stories on this ground in Ethiopia is explicit; see Cerulli, p. 18ff.

[11]   Nevertheless, one has to bear in mind that some of the difference may be attributed to the fact that the Synaxary is an official compilation, intended for liturgical reading; while the status of the Western Marian collections in Europe was much less "official", and it is not clear if they had even a minor liturgical function.

[12]   Synaxary, 3 Ba'ūna Patrologia Orientalis (hereafter PO) XVII: 533-535. The edition used is Le synaxaire arabe jacobite. Rédaction copte, ed. by Rene Basset, published in PO I,3; III,3; XI,5; XVI,2; XVII,3; XX,5; Turnholt 1922-1929.

Western texts, in comparison, show a different set of religious attitudes. They present an attitude which is ambivalent to sin. Sin is, of course, condemned, but it is also suggested that special devotion to one aspect of the faith, in conjunction with true repentance and divine grace, can absolve every sin and even lead to spiritual elevation. Crossing the borderline between sin and purity is much easier, and is more frequent. In the Marian stories ordinary people and sinners are also eligible to revelation or miracle, and these are not reserved for an "aristocracy of holiness" as in the Eastern texts.

This marked contrast is reflected in the attitude towards repentance and absolution. In the Western stories contrition is a sufficient condition for the remission of sins, which is always granted if the sinner repents sincerely. In the Synaxary sin has an aspect of irreversibility: sinning priests or monks are tainted forever even if they are forgiven. True contrition is no guarantee of absolution, and nor does the saint's mediation provide such an assurance.

The difference between the Western stories and the Synaxary is best seen when they deal with similar initial situations. The Synaxary tells of a young woman who committed incest, became pregnant and aborted with the aid of a magician. She comes to ask for Anba Mattheus's help, and he instructs her to confess her sins publicly. She does so, and afterwards the saint prays. The end of the story is surprising, for whoever expects the Western model of contrition and absolution:

> Our father [Anba Mattheus] held out his hands and prayed, and when he finished his prayer and said Amen, the earth opened its mouth and swallowed the wretched girl little by little until she descended under the earth. And a lot of smoke continued to rise from the place until 40 days were completed[13].

These differences in attitude between the Synaxary and the Western legends may help to explain some aspects of the reception of the Western Marian miracles. The changes observed between the Western stories and their early Arabic versions, and between the early Arabic versions and the later ones are aimed to bring the stories of European origin closer to the concepts of Coptic hagiography. Since the lenient treatment of sinners, and especially sinning priests, appears to have been unacceptable by the standards of Coptic hagiography, every effort was made to tone down this aspect. Consequently, the sinners are presented as less sinful, and their repentance is idealized.

---

[13]   Synaxary, 7 Kihak, PO III:398-399.

Furthermore, it seems to me that the difference is not limited to the fact that the Coptic literature I examined presents a more severe moral standard; it is wider than that. The Coptic texts present a rejection of any type of moral ambiguity, while this ambiguity has a central role in the Western Marian legends. The role of the miracle and its performer in the Western stories is precisely to solve the ambiguity of the initial situation of the story. As we have already seen, most often the protagonists are characterized as morally ambiguous - they are either basically virtuous men who erred or sinners who have a redeeming quality[14]. The ambiguity in the Western stories defines Mary's sphere of action, and it is her role to restore order, that is to redefine the character from a moral point of view, either by damning him, or more often by helping him to achieve salvation.

This pattern is particularly evident in stories such as the one already mentioned (no. 52 in the Arabic collection) about the robber who was hanged and buried outside the cemetery. In such stories the ambivalent initial situation is a mistake of judgement originating in a discrepancy between the visible actions of the body and the state of the soul. As no human being could know that these robbers, thieves, and other types of sinners were destined to be judged in the other world as virtuous men, Mary's role in these stories is to solve the ambiguity in this world as well. Thus in many cases the miracle consists of a physical sign - a vision or a transformation of the physical remains of the dead - which testifies to the fate of the protagonist in afterlife.

It is now clear that the Western stories were not adopted uncritically by the Copts, or accorded a higher, liturgical, status. The reception of the Western legends can be characterized by a tendency to "Copticize" the stories on the textual level, which in a broader perspective reflects a rejection of the Western texts and the religious attitudes they represent. An effort was made to adapt the texts to local religious attitudes. But this effort was only partially successful because the problematic feature appears to have been the moral ambiguity of the Western stories. This aspect could be toned down, but because of its central structural function in the Western legends it could not be effaced or eliminated altogether. This probably determined the critical and limited reception of these texts by the Copts.

---

[14]   Sometimes, as in therapeutic miracles, they are morally neutral.

LES ARCHIVES DE JEAN CLEDAT DONNEES AU LOUVRE

Dominique BENAZETH

Cette communication a pour objet de vous présenter une acquisition récente de la section copte du Louvre et son incidence sur notre connaissance du site de Baouit. Cette acquisition n'est pas un objet archéologique ou une oeuvre d'art, mais un important lot d'archives ayant appartenu à Jean Clédat. C'est sa propre fille, madame Jean Mallet, qui les offrit généreusement au musée en 1986.

L'importance de ces papiers fut aussitôt reconnue. Un premier article parut dans la *Revue du Louvre* (1988). De plus, deux manifestations ont rappelé la mémoire du savant en 1991 : une exposition au musée de Périgueux "Dans les pas de Jean Clédat, l'Egypte en Périgord" (avec catalogue) et le quatrième colloque de l'Association Francophone de Coptologie, intitulé "Journées d'études Jean Clédat". Plusieurs d'entre vous, et notre président de l'IACS, étaient présents.

Devant l'enthousiasme de la communauté scientifique et prenant conscience de l'importance de ces documents, madame Mallet vient de consentir une nouvelle donation au Louvre. Il s'agit cette fois de fragments épigraphiques sur papier et papyrus. Une soixantaine d'entre eux, provenant de Baouit, vont pouvoir être publiés avec l'ensemble des documents inédits concernant ce site.

Jean CLEDAT

Il est né en 1871 à Périgueux (France). Vers l'âge de 17 ans, il s'inscrit à l'Ecole des Beaux-Arts à Paris; ses dons pour le dessin lui permettront, plus tard, d'exécuter d'admirables aquarelles et croquis en Egypte. Il se tourne vers les études égyptologiques et les langues anciennes. Il part pour l'Egypte en 1900, comme membre de l'Institut Français d'Archéologie Orientale du Caire. Tout de suite, c'est la découverte du monastère de Baouit, qu'il fouille de 1901 à 1905. Puis il explore toute la région de l'isthme de Suez, en tant que directeur des recherches archéologiques de la Compagnie du Canal de Suez. Il y fait des fouilles et établit cartes et relevés. Il sera nommé directeur du musée créé à Ismaïlia. Entre-temps il collabore aux fouilles de Charles Clermont-Ganneau à Eléphantine (1907-1010). Il regagne la France en 1914. A la suite d'une longue maladie, il s'éteint en 1943, sans avoir pu mener à terme les publications qu'il projetait.

Les archives

Elles se composent de notes, de relevés cartographiques et de photographies, sous forme de plaques de verre et de tirages sur papier.

Les carnets de fouilles concernent toutes les campagnes à Baouit et correspondent d'une part à la publication de Jean Clédat dans les MIFAO (fouilles de 1901 à 1904), d'autre part à la campagne inédite de 1905. Des notes et des planches de photographies déjà numérotées de sa main constituent une étape avancée du travail de publication qu'il projetait.

Un carnet est consacré aux fouilles d'Eléphantine. Douze autres aux fouilles et prospections dans la région de l'isthme de Suez.

Les notes de voyage, observations, relevés épigraphiques, topographiques, occupent plusieurs carnets et dossiers. Cela concerne aussi bien les monuments pharaoniques que ceux d'époque copte. Parmi ces derniers, signalons les notes sur Philae, le couvent de Saint-Siméon à Assouan, les monastères "Blanc" et "Rouge" de Sohag.

Les photographies concernent les mêmes sites.

Pour Baouit, un lot de tirages sur papier et des plaques photographiques correspondent d'une part à des documents déjà publiés, d'autre part à des clichés inédits mais déjà connus de certains chercheurs car ils sont conservés à l'Institut Français du Caire et au Centre Gabriel Millet de l'Ecole Pratique des Hautes Etudes. Enfin un dernier groupe de clichés était jusqu'ici inconnu.

Intérêt de ces archives

L'intérêt que présentent ces archives est triple :

1/ Il est évident pour le musée du Louvre qui les a acquises. En effet, elles ont tout de suite permis d'identifier des objets dont la provenance était perdue. Un grand nombre de pièces d'Eléphantine a pu être reconnu. Un fragment de peinture murale copte a retrouvé son identité grâce à la photographie d'une paroi de Baouit; nettoyé, il a aussitôt été exposé au public. Un lot d'*ostraca*, étudié par Madame A.Boud'hors, qui l'attribuait à un monastère de Moyenne-Egypte, s'est révélé originaire de Baouit.

2/ Mais le contenu de ces archives dépasse le cadre du Louvre. Elles ont déjà été consultées par plusieurs chercheurs (Institut Français du Caire; Ecole Pratique des Hautes Etudes; équipes de fouilles de la région du Canal de Suez).

3/ Le troisième centre d'intérêt est celui des études coptes. La découverte d'importants documents sur le monastère de Baouit a donné naissance au projet de publication des inédits de Baouit. Un volume des MIFAO verra prochainement le jour, complétant la série de Baouit (MIFAO XII, XIII XXXIX et LIX). Il comprendra plusieurs parties : l'archéologie, avec principalement l'exploration de la nécropole proche du monastère et le rapport des fouilles de 1905 (partie préparée par les conservateurs de la section copte du Louvre); l'épigraphie (partie confiée à madame Anne Boud'hors); une partie des *ostraca* est conservée au Louvre, les autres n'ont pas été localisés mais Jean Clédat avait relevé tous les textes. Les *indices*, établis par le professeur R.-G.Coquin, concerneront l'ensemble des MIFAO sur Baouit.

The Coptic Heritage of St. Ephrem the Syrian

Monica J. Blanchard

Various connections with Egypt can be traced both in the development of the cult and in the preservation of the writings of St. Ephrem the Syrian (c.306-373), the great poet-theologian of the early Syriac-speaking Church.[1] Already within the fourth century--and even during Ephrem's lifetime, according to the fifth century church historian Sozomen--Greek works bearing the name of Ephrem made their way into the common literary tradition of the church of the Empire.[2] This Greek literary corpus, which included many ascetical texts different in content and theme from the authentic Syriac works of Ephrem, came to represent the Syrian saint in other language communities. Numerous translations were made into Latin, Arabic, Georgian and other church languages.[3]

Eleven individual Coptic works associated with Ephrem have been identified to date. They address themes of ascetic practice and monasticism, as well as homiletic and moralizing topics of a kind well known in Coptic monastic literature. Briefly they include a Coptic version of the Greek _Sermo asceticus_ in a manuscript (British Library Oriental 6783) copied in A.D. 1003.[4] The same manuscript contains a letter attributed to Ephrem, apparently extant only in Coptic, addressed to a young monk on humility and other virtues.[5] A Coptic letter "of Apa Ephraim the Anchorite on mourning" survives in part in White Monastery fragments in the Borgia collection now in Naples.[6] Two incomplete documents of monastic instruction attributed to Ephrem also appear in these White Monastery fragments.[7] An uncaptioned Coptic treatise addressed to a monastic audience exists in John Rylands Library MS no. 62.[8] A Georgian version of this work in a ninth/tenth century Sinai manuscript lists Ephrem as the author.[9]

The extant Coptic homiletic texts attributed to Ephrem include part of a sermon on the Transfiguration from a Bohairic manuscript of the end of the twelfth century, British Library Oriental 8799.[10] A homily on vainglory and on penitence extant in the Greek corpus of Ephrem appears under the name of John Chrysostom in a ninth century Bohairic manuscript, Vatican Coptic 57.[11] Ephrem's homily on the sinful woman of the Gospels (Lk 7:36, Mt 26:6, Mk 14:3) survives in a tenth century Bohairic manuscript, Vatican Coptic 68.[12] Parts of a Sahidic discourse on the Antichrist attributed to Ephrem are found in the same White Monastery folios that contain the monastic catecheses attributed to him.[13] They include as well a portion of the homily on the Old Testament patriarch Joseph attributed to Ephrem; this Coptic homily also exists in part in folios of a ninth century codex now in the Pierpont Morgan Library.[14]

The Coptic texts associated with St. Ephrem are
consistent with the general treatment of Greek patristic
writers in Coptic translation.[15] Works chosen for
translation seem to have been selected for purposes of moral
edification and spiritual formation. The audience is
largely monastic. There is little apparent concern for
preserving the integrity of an individual work or for
correct attribution of authorship. The fragmentary Coptic
homily on the Transfiguration attributed to Ephrem, for
example, appears in Syriac under the name of John
Chrysostom, and may belong to Isaac of Antioch.[16] Théophile
Lefort included the Coptic treatise in the John Rylands
Library in his edition and translation of the festal and
pastoral letters of Athanasius because part of the text also
appears in a collection of the works of the fifth century
abbot Besa, who identifies it as a work of the patriarch
Athanasius.[17] A paraphrase of the opening lines of Ephrem's
Greek Sermo Asceticus appears in a Coptic catechesis
attributed to Pachomius' disciple Horsiesios.[18]

The Coptic texts associated with Ephrem depend upon the
large Greek corpus of Ephremian texts, and, with the
exception of the Sermo Asceticus, they have little to do
with the authentic Syriac works of St. Ephrem.[19] Given the
heavily monastic content of the Greek corpus, it would not
be surprising to find more of these works in so far
unattributed Coptic texts. In fact, Ephrem Graecus is
fairly well represented among Patristic authors in Coptic
translation.[20] The real interest of these Coptic texts lies
in their clear and consistent identification of Ephrem with
a monastic setting. This is not Mar Afram the Syrian
malpônô of history; but rather Apa Efraim panachoritēs.[21]

Arabic translations of works attributed to Ephrem form
a much larger body of material.[22] Perhaps the most common
place to find these texts is in collections of works loosely
called homilies—including prayers, monastic paraeneses,
homilies, and letters.[23] Collections of various sizes have
survived, the largest and most popular of these being a
collection of 52 homilies of Ephrem extant in some 37
ancient manuscripts. It has been studied most recently by
Fr. Khalil Samir.[24] This collection is characterized by its
standard form in the various manuscripts. Once again texts
attributed to Ephrem in this Arabic collection appear in
other languages under the name of John Chrysostom, or as
unattributed and anonymous works.[25] The collection of 52
homilies was originally translated from Greek into Arabic in
the year 980 by the Melkite writer Ibrāhīm al-Anṭākī.[26] The
Arabic language texts circulated within the various
Arabophone communities—Melkite, Syrian Jacobite, and
Coptic; crossing over confessional boundaries. Many of the
early extant Arabic manuscripts of this collection of 52
homilies come from Egypt, attesting to the popularity of the
collection there.[27] This popularity is confirmed by the

fourteenth century Coptic encyclopedist Abū'l Barakāt Ibn
Kabar, who specifically mentions the collection in his
Misbāḥ al-Zulmah, as this collection of works "of the monk
Saint Ephrem the Syrian which our fathers the monks study
and which has inspired the ascetics who have departed the
world."[28] As Fr. Samir rightly points out, the works of St.
Ephrem in this Arabic format (popularized in medieval Egypt)
have had a lasting impact on the spiritual formation of the
Arabic-speaking descendants of Syriac-speaking Christians.[29]

In 1892 a monk of the Coptic Monastery of al-Baramus in
the Wadi Natrun, Qummuṣ Afrām al-Baramūsī, prepared an
abridged edition of 45 works from this collection.[30] It is
appropriate that this modern edition should come from one of
the monasteries of the Wadi Natrun, because this center of
monastic activity figured prominently both in the
development of the cult of St. Ephrem as well as in the
preservation of a significant part of the Syriac works of
St. Ephrem.

It is to Egypt rather than to the Syriac-speaking
regions of Syria/Mesopotamia that we owe the preservation of
one of the most important extant collections of Syriac
Christian manuscripts. The library of the Monastery of the
Mother of God in the domain of Anba Bishoi, or as it is more
commonly known today, Deir es-Souriani, that is, the
Monastery of the Syrians in the Wadi Natrun, was home to
these manuscripts, many of which are now in the British
Library.[31]

The Monastery of the Syrians originated in the sixth
century as a Coptic monastic foundation.[32] It was sold to a
group of Syrian Jacobites from Tagrit in Iraq probably early
in the eighth century.[33] Tagrit, the metropolitan see and
center of the Jacobite Church in Iraq, maintained a close
relationship with the Monastery of the Syrians, and with a
community of Tagritan merchants resident in Fustat in
Egypt.[34] In the first part of the tenth century the Abbot
Moses of Nisibis (fl. 905-943) made a substantial effort to
increase the library holdings of the Monastery of the
Syrians.[35] In the year 932 at the end of a five year trip
to the Syro-Mesopotamian Syriac communities, Moses returned
with some 250 Syriac books for the library in Egypt,
including a number of valuable works of Ephrem.[36] Among the
Syriac works of Ephrem preserved here one might mention
briefly British Library Add. 14,571 dated to A.D. 519, which
includes Ephrem's Hymns on the Nativity and his Hymns on
Paradise;[37] Vatican Syriac MS 112 dated to A.D. 551/552,
which contains these same hymns;[38] Vatican Syriac MS 113, in
a hand similar to that of 112, contains Ephrem's Hymns on
Faith.[39] Vatican Syriac MS 111 dated to A.D. 522 includes
Ephrem's Hymns on the Church, On Faith, On Paradise, and
also the Hymns against Heresies.[40] The sixth century
Vatican Syriac MS 110 contains the only copy (albeit

incomplete) of Ephrem's commentary on the biblical books of
Genesis and Exodus.[41] A precious copy of Ephrem's Syriac
commentary on the Diatessaron in an estrangelo script of the
late fifth or early sixth century, Chester Beatty Library
no. 709, also may have belonged to the Monastery of the
Syrians.[42] These manuscripts provide the earliest and in
some cases the unique texts of Ephrem's Syriac works. It
should be noted that these collections of Ephrem's authentic
Syriac works almost fell out of the tradition of the Syriac-
speaking churches, except for selected hymns surviving
anonymously or in abbreviated form in breviaries and other
liturgical works.[43] Meanwhile, the Greek literary corpus
attributed to Ephrem, but now circulating in Arabic, came in
fact to define the intellectual heritage of the Syrian saint
in the Christian Near East.[44]

Much information about the veneration of St. Ephrem
comes to us through the agency of the Monastery of the
Syrians in the Wadi Natrun, a center of Syriac-speaking
Christianity in post-Chalcedonian Egypt. The monastery
professed a special regard for St. Ephrem, and over time a
number of Coptic elements made their way into the saint's
hagiographical dossier.[45]

A twelfth century manuscript from Deir Souriani
contains the oldest extant recension of the Syriac Life of
Ephrem (Vatican Syriac MS 117).[46] It tells of Ephrem's
visit to Egypt and of his meeting with a certain Apa Bishoi,
who turns out upon investigation to be representative of a
number of Egyptian desert fathers.[47] A somewhat similar
story is told in the Syriac Life of Apa Bishoi (Paris Syriac
MS 236, ff. 21-33) in a manuscript dated to A.D. 1193/1194.
Other sources for the Life of Ephrem do not mention Bishoi
in this connection, nor do the surviving Greek, Arabic and
Ethiopic sources for the Life of Bishoi identify Ephrem as
one of Bishoi's visitors. According to the Life of Ephrem,
the Syrian saint miraculously learned Coptic in order to
converse with Apa Bishoi. After staying a week with Bishoi
in his cave at the site of the future Monastery of Anba
Bishoi in the Wadi Natrun, Ephrem spent an additional eight
years in Egypt combatting Arians and writing learned books
in the Coptic language. Regarding Ephrem's alleged Coptic
literary compositions, the Syriac scholar Rubens Duval
suggested a possible confusion of Ephrem Syrus with an
Egyptian Ephrem or, as he is better known, Abraham of
Farshut.[48] According to the Copto-Arabic Synaxary for 24
Tubeh (19 January) this Ephrem or Abraham fled the religious
advances of the 'unorthodox' emperor Justin (emp.518-d.527),
and went to the Monastery of Apa Shenoute in Atripe.[49]
There he transcribed the writings of Shenoute, putting the
finished copies in sealed jars and sending them to the
Monastery of Abou Masis for safekeeping. The monks ran out
of food, and they broke open the jars. Finding the writings
of Shenoute, they read them and were greatly edified. The

name of Ephrem is spelled variously in the Coptic texts as
ⲉⲫⲣⲁⲓⲙ, ⲉⲫⲣⲉⲛ, ⲫⲣⲉⲛ, ⲉⲩⲫⲣⲓⲙ, ⲉⲩⲫⲣⲉⲉⲛ.[50]   The Syriac ܐܦܪܝܡ and
Arabic افرام bear some resemblance to the Graeco-Coptic ⲁⲃⲣⲁⲙ,
ⲁⲃⲣⲁⲙ.[51]

The Syriac _Life_ of Bishoi belongs to a group of
individual _Lives_ of the founders of the four great
monasteries of the Wadi Natrun.   These are the _Life_ of
Macarius of Egypt attributed to Serapion, Bishop of Thmuis;
the _Life_ of John the Little by Zacharias, Bishop of Sakka;
the _Lives_ of Maximus and Dometius, the Romaioi in whose
honor the Monastery of al-Baramus was founded, written by
Pshoi of Constantinople; and the _Life_ of Abba Bishoi,
composed by John the Little.[52]

These _Lives_, which in fact are panegyrics honoring the
saints, appear together in a small group of Syriac
manuscripts mostly from the twelfth and thirteenth
centuries, with connections to the Wadi Natrun
monasteries.[53]   Along with them are _Lives_ of Egyptian desert
fathers and monks, including the _Life_ of Shenoute, whose
fame was limited to Coptic Egypt.[54]   These _Lives_ testify to
an authentic meeting of the Syriac and Coptic traditions
through the medium of translation activity from Arabic into
Syriac of Coptic originals.[55]   We know that such work was
already in progress at the Monastery of the Syrians in the
tenth century from a manuscript note that the _Life_ of John
the Little was translated from Arabic into Syriac at this
monastery in 936.[56]   These Syriac manuscripts testify as
well to a keen Syrian interest in the Egyptian desert
fathers.   Interspersed among the Egyptian _Lives_ are a number
of texts on ascetic and monastic themes attributed to
Ephrem, such as the homilies On the end of the world and the
last judgment, On repentance, On doctrine, a prayer of
Ephrem for use by a monk "when retiring to rest", the
History of Abraham Kidunaya by Ephrem, as well as the _Life_
of Ephrem himself.[57]

St. Ephrem the Syrian is commemorated in the Coptic
calendar on 15 Abib (9 July).   Sometime between the year
1088, when Mawhūb ibn Mansūr ibn Mufarrij al-Iskandarānī
(c.1025-1100) described the relics he saw in the monasteries
of the Wadi Natrun,[58] and the late thirteenth or early
fourteenth century--the proposed date of a Coptic Difnar,
perhaps from the Monastery of John the Little, which
includes a celebration of the translation of the bodily
remains of St. Ephrem to the Monastery of Abba Bishoi--
Ephrem's relics arrived at this site of his legendary
meeting with Apa Bishoi, and were placed with those of
Bishoi and his friend the Coptic hermit Paul of Tamma.[59]   H.
J. Polotsky has suggested that the arrival of the relics of
Ephrem may have provided the incentive for the story of
Ephrem's visit to Bishoi.[60]   At any rate, it seems likely
that it was at the Monastery of the Syrians that this

element in the Life of Ephrem originated. Once established,
the legend of St. Ephrem's visit to Egypt continued to grow.
An oral tradition first attested to in the seventeenth
century by European travellers to Egypt tells of a tamarind
tree which flourishes miraculously on the spot where Ephrem
dropped his staff near the cave of Bishoi.[61] Even today
visitors to the Wadi Natrun can admire the tree, and take
home from Egypt a remembrance of St. Ephrem the Syrian.

Monica J. Blanchard
Institute of Christian Oriental Research
The Catholic University of America
Washington, D.C.   20064 U.S.A.

Notes

[1]For overviews of the life and works of St. Ephrem the
Syrian see E. Beck, "Éphrem le Syrien (saint)," Dictionnaire
de spiritualité 4 (1960), cols. 788-800; E. Beck, "Ephraem
Syrus," Reallexikon für Antike und Christentum 5 (1962),
cols. 520-531; Robert Murray, "Ephraem Syrus (ca. 306-373),"
Theologische Realenzyklopädie 9 (1982) 755-762.

[2]Sozomen, Historia ecclesiastica III:16 [PG 67:1086-
1094]. Chapter 115 of Jerome's De viris illustribus [PL
23:707-708], written some 20 years after the death of
Ephrem, records Jerome's access to a Greek translation of
one of Ephrem's works. For more information about Greek
works attributed to Ephrem see D. Hemmerdinger-Iliadou,
"Vers une nouvelle édition de l'Éphrem grec," in F. L. Cross
(ed.), Studia Patristica (Vol. III, part I; TU, 78; Berlin:
Akademie-Verlag, 1961) 72-80; idem, "Éphrem grec,"
Dictionnaire de spiritualité 4 (1960) 800-815; M. Geerard,
Clavis Patrum Graecorum II. Ab Athanasio ad Chrysostomum
(Corpus Christianorum; Turnhout: Brepols, 1974) 366-468
[hereafter cited as CPG II].

[3]CPG II.3905-4175; J. Kirchmeyer, "Autres versions
d'Éphrem," Dictionnaire de spiritualité 4 (1960) 819-822.
For Latin versions see also D. Hemmerdinger-Iliadou, "Ephrem
Latin," Dictionnaire de spiritualité 4 (1960) 815-819; T. S.
Pattie, "Ephraem the Syrian and the Latin Manuscripts of "De
Paenitentia," The British Library Journal 13 (1987) 1-24.
Armenian translations are listed in L. Ter-Petrossian & B.
Outtier, Textes arméniens relatifs à S. Ephrem (CSCO v. 473-
474. scriptores Armeniaci t. 15-16; Louvain: Peeters,
1985). For information about Georgian and Arabic versions
see n. 9 and 23 below. On the authentic Syriac works of
Ephrem see n. 19 below.

[4]B.L. Or. 6783, a Sahidic Coptic miscellany, is described in Bentley Layton, <u>Catalogue of Coptic Literary Manuscripts in the British Library Acquired Since the Year 1906</u> (London: The British Library, 1987) 177-179. The MS was completed in 16 August A.D. 1003 according to its colophon, which also records that it was a donation to the Monastery of St. Mercurius in Edfu. The text, titled ⲡⲁⲥⲕⲏⲧⲕⲟⲛ ⲛⲁⲡⲁ ⲉⲫⲣⲁⲓⲙ, is found on ff. 45ᵛ-63ʳ. It is edited and translated in E. A. Wallis Budge, <u>Coptic Martyrdoms etc. in the Dialect of Upper Egypt. Edited with English Translations</u> (London: Printed by Order of the Trustees [of the British Museum], 1914) 157-178 (Coptic text), 409-430 (English translation).

[5]ⲛⲧⲟϥ ⲟⲛ ⲁⲡⲁ ⲉⲫⲣⲁⲓⲙ ⲉϥⲥⲕⲁⲓ ⲉⲣⲁⲧϥ ⲛⲟⲩⲏⲉⲣⲓⲧ ⲛⲧⲁϥ ⲉϥⲭⲓ ⲥⲃⲱ ⲛⲧⲟⲟⲧϥ, ff. 63ᵛ-67ᵛ. It too is edited and translated in Budge, <u>Coptic Martyrdoms etc.</u> 179-183 (Coptic text), 431-435 (English translation).

[6]See Georgio Zoega, <u>Catalogus codicum Copticorum manu scriptorum qui in Museo Borgiano velitris adservantur</u> (Romae: Typis Sacrae Congregationis De Propaganda Fide, 1810; reprinted, Leipzig: J. C. Hinrichs, 1903) 608, Num. CCLIV = Naples B.N. I.B. 12/431. There are 6 folios numbered p. 171 [ⲣⲟⲁ], again p. 171 [ⲣⲟⲁ]-p. 181 [ⲣⲡⲁ]. The text, p. 178 [ⲣⲟⲏ]-p. 181 [ⲣⲡⲁ], is titled: ⲟⲩⲉⲡⲓⲥⲧⲟⲗⲏ ⲛⲧⲉ ⲁⲡⲁ ⲉⲫⲣⲁⲓⲙ ⲡⲁⲛⲁⲭⲱⲣ ⲓⲧⲏⲥ ⲉⲧⲃⲉ ⲛ2ⲏⲃⲉ. Zoega places these folios in his paleographical class vi, of which the exemplars in his <u>Tabula</u> V--Num. CLXIX and CLXXI--may belong to the eleventh century. See Henri Hyvernat, <u>Album de paléographie copte pour servir a l'introduction paléographique des Actes des martyrs de l'Égypte</u> (Paris: E. Leroux; Rome: Librairie Spithoever, 1888) 13; Gérard Garitte (ed.), <u>Lettres de S. Antoine: version géorgienne et fragments coptes</u> (CSCO v. 148. Scriptores Iberici t. 5; Louvain: L. Durbecq, 1955) iv. Tito Orlandi cites Num. CCLIV and CCLIII as White Monastery folios containing Coptic texts attributed to Ephrem in his <u>Elementi di lingua e letteratura copta. Corso di lezioni universitarie</u> (Milano: La Goliardica, 1970) 117-118. For more information about the Borgia Coptic MSS now in Naples see J.-M. Sauget, "Introduction historique et notes bibliographiques au Catalogue de Zoega," <u>Le Muséon</u> 85 (1972) 25-63, esp. 60; A. van Lantschoot, "Cotation du fonds copte de Naples," <u>Le Muséon</u> 41 (1928) 217-224, esp. 223. Regarding the reconstruction of the ancient White Monastery library see Tito Orlandi, "Un projet Milanais concernant les manuscrits coptes du Monastere Blanc," <u>Le Muséon</u> 85 (1972) 403-413.

[7]See Zoega, <u>Catalogus</u> 608 Num. CCLIII = Naples B.N. I.B. 11/430. Collected here are 27 paginated folios, which include at least four incomplete texts attributed to Ephrem

44

(See notes 13 and 14 below). Titles of the two texts of
monastic instruction are found on p. 151 [ⲣⲙⲁ]: ⲍⲟⲙⲁ ⲕⲱⲥ
ⲍⲉⲛⲥⲃⲟⲟⲩⲉ ⲛⲧⲉ ⲁⲡⲁ ⲉ⳿ⲫⲣⲁ ⲓⲙ ⳾ⲁ ⲍⲉⲛⲥⲛⲏⲩ, and on p. 171 [ⲣⲟⲁ]:
ⲍⲟⲙⲁ ⲓⲟⲥ ⲁⲡⲁ ⲉ⳿ⲫⲣⲁ ⲓⲙ ⲉ⳿ⲧⲥⲃⲱ ⲝⲉ ⲉⲩⲡⲉ ⲉ⳿ⲧⲣ ⲉ ⲛⲙⲟⲛⲁⲭⲟⲥ ⲁⲩⲡⲉ ⲛⲧⲉⲗⲓⲟⲥ.
Zoega describes them as "Characteres classis v, sed
obtusiores," perhaps of the tenth century. On the problems
of Coptic palaeography see Bentley Layton, "Towards a New
Coptic Palaeography," in Tito Orlandi & Frederik Wisse
(eds.), Acts of the Second International Congress of Coptic
Study, Roma, 22-26 September 1980 (Roma: C.I.M., 1985) 149-
158.

    [8]Rylands Coptic 62, ff. 2, 5, 6. See W. E. Crum,
Catalogue of the Coptic Manuscripts in the Collection of the
John Rylands Library, Manchester (Manchester: At the
University Press, 1909) 24-27. Crum compares the script to
two dated eleventh century MSS: B.L. Or. 5420 and B.L. Or.
1320. See note 17 below on the attribution of this Coptic
text to Athanasius.

    [9]Sinai Georgian MS 97, ff. 74[V]-85[V]. See Gérard
Garitte, Catalogue des manuscrits géorgiens littéraires du
Mont Sinai (CSCO v. 165. Subsidia t. 9; Louvain: L.
Durbecq, 1956) 284; I. Imnaišvili, Sakitchavi cigni jvel
kartcul enasi (2 vols.; Tiflis, 1963-1966) II.48-49. For
Georgian versions of works attributed to Ephrem see Bernard
Outtier, "Les Recueils géorgiens d'oeuvres attribuées à S.
Éphrem le Syrien," Bedi Kartlisa 32 (1974) 118-125; idem,
"Les enseignements des Pères, un recueil géorgien traduit de
l'arabe," Bedi Kartlisa 31 (1974) 118-125; idem, "Une
Homélie sur le jeûne et la pénitence attribuée à S. Éphrem
en géorgien," Bedi Kartlisa 32 (1974) 109-117; G. Garitte,
"Homélie d'Ephrem "sur la Mort et le Diable", version
géorgienne et version arabe," Le Muséon 82 (1969) 123-163..

    [10]For a description of B.L. Or. 8799, a Bohairic
miscellany, see Layton, Catalogue 398-400. The MS colophon
provides a date of 29 August AD 1198/28 August 1199, and
information that the codex was donated by a monk of the
Monastery of Pehoout in the Wadi Natrun to the local Church
of St. Elias the Prophet. The homily, ff. 44[Γ]-54[Γ], is
titled: ⲟⲩⲗⲟⲅⲟⲥ ⲛⲧⲉ ⲡⲓⲁⲅⲓⲟⲥ ⲫⲣⲉⲙ ⲉⲫⲉⲉ ⳿ⲧⲙⲉⲧⲁⲙⲟⲣ⳿ⲫⲱⲥⲓ ⲥ ⲛⲧⲉ ⲛⲉⲛⲟ̅ⲥ̅ ⲓⲏ̅ⲥ̅ ⲡⲭ̅ⲥ̅.
The text is edited and translated by E. A. Wallis Budge, "On
a Fragment of a Coptic Version of Saint Ephraim's Discourse
on the Transfiguration of Our Lord," Proceedings of the
Society of Biblical Archaeology 9 (1886) 317-329.

    [11]Vatican Coptic MS 57, ff. 66[V]-74. See A. Hebbelynck
& A. van Lantschoot, Codices Coptici Vaticani,
Barberianiani, Borgiani, Rossiani (Vol. I; Bibliothecae
Apostolicae Vaticanae codices manu scripti recensiti; [Citta
del Vaticano]: Bibliotheca Vaticana, 1937) 368-384, esp.
371-372. This text is attributed to Ephrem in the Greek
corpus. See CPG II.4031.

12For a description of Vatican Coptic 68, ff. 105-117ᵛ
see Hebbelynck & van Lantschoot, Codices Coptici Vaticani
I.499-515, esp. 506-507. The title is: ογλογος ητε πενιωτ εθογλβ
εττλιηογτ κλτλ сηοτ ηιβεη λββλ εφρεη εηβε †cτιηι πρεφερηοβι ετⲑεη
πιεγλⲅⲅελιон. The MS is dated to the tenth century on
palaeographical grounds. The Bohairic text is edited by I.
Guidi, "La Traduzione copta di un' omelia di S. Efrem,"
Bessarione 7 (1903) 1-21.

13Zoega Num. CCLIII p. 114 [ⲣⲓⲁ]: ⲍⲟⲙⲁⲓⲟⲥ ⲁⲡⲁ ⲉⲫⲣⲁⲓⲙ ⲉϥϫⲁⲝⲉ
ⲉⲧⲃⲉ ⲡⲁⲛⲧⲓⲭⲣⲏⲥⲧⲟⲥ.

14Zoega Num. CCLIII p. 252 [ⲥⲛⲃ]; also Morgan Codex
M578, f. 69ʳ-97ᵛ, classified separately as M601 in Henri
Hyvernat, A Check List of Coptic Manuscripts in the Pierpont
Morgan Library (New York, Privately printed, 1919) 18, no.
XLVII. For the traditional association of this work with
Ephrem, see Paul-Hubert Poirier, "Le sermon pseudo-éphrémien
In pulcherrimum Ioseph: typologie et midrash," Cahiers de
Biblia Patristica 2 (1989) 107-122; Michael Hollerich, "The
Tashitha dhe-Yauseph and Exegesis in Edessa: Antecedents
and Influence of a Christian Midrash," to appear in vol. 1
of Journal for Middle Eastern Christian Studies. The name
of Ephrem is spelled variously in the Morgan codex ⲉⲩⲫⲣⲓⲙ, ⲉⲩⲫⲣⲉⲉⲙ.

15On this subject see most recently the introductory
remarks of Rowan A. Greer in Leo Depuydt (gen. ed.),
Homiletica from the Pierpont Morgan Library: Seven Coptic
Homilies Attributed to Basil the Great, John Chrysostom, and
Euodius of Rome (CSCO v. 525. Scriptores Coptici t. 44;
Lovanii: E. Peeters, 1991) v-xxiii, esp. viii-x. See too
Tito Orlandi, "Coptic Literature," in B. A. Pearson & J. E.
Goehring (eds.), The Roots of Egyptian Christianity (Studies
in Antiquity & Christianity; Philadelphia: Fortress Press,
1986) 51-81, esp. 70-73; idem, "The Future of Studies in
Coptic Biblical and Ecclesiastical Literature," in R. McL.
Wilson (ed.), The Future of Coptic Studies (Coptic Studies,
1; Leiden: Brill, 1978) 143-163, esp. 151-155.

16CPG II.3939. It appears in a Georgian version under
the name of Theodore of Harran, i.e. Theodore Abū Qurrah.

17See L.-Th. Lefort (ed. & trans.), S. Athanase,
Lettres festales et pastorales en copte (CSCO v. 150-151.
Scriptores Coptici, t. 19-20; Louvain: L. Durbecq, 1955)
150.xxxi-xxxiii; K. H. Kuhn (ed. & trans.), Letters and
Sermons of Besa (CSCO v. 157-158. Scriptores Coptici t. 21-
22; Louvain: L. Durbecq, 1956) 158.79 n. 35.

18See L. Th. Lefort (ed. & trans.), Oeuvres de S.
Pachôme et de ses disciples (CSCO v. 159-160. Scriptores
Coptici t. 23-24; Louvain: L. Durbecq, 1956) 159.75-76
(text); 160.75 (trans.).

46

[19] For information about the authentic Syriac works of Ephrem see J. Melki, "Saint Éphrem le Syrien, un bilan de l'édition critique," Parole de l'Orient 11 (1983) 44-88; also Sebastian Brock, "A Brief Guide to the Main Editions and Translations of the Works of St. Ephrem," The Harp 3 (1990) 7-25.

[20] See the lists of "Autori Egiziani" and "Autori non Egiziani" in Tito Orlandi, Elementi di lingua e letteratura copta 69-124. For more information about Coptic translations of Greek patristic writers see Tito Orlandi, "Patristica copta e patristica greca," Vigiliae Christianae 10 (1973) 327-341; idem, "Traduzioni dal greco al copto: quali e perche," G. Fiaccadori (ed.), Autori classici in lingue del vicino e medio oriente. Atti del III, IV e V Seminario sul tema: "Recupero di testi classici attraverso recezioni in lingue del Vicino e Medio Oriente" (Brescia, 21 Novembre 1984; Roma, 22-27 Marzo 1985; Padova-Venezia, 15-16 Aprile 1986) (Roma: Istituto Poligrafico e Zecca dello Stato, 1990) 93-104.

[21] These differing perspectives have been addressed by Sidney H. Griffith, "Images of Ephraem: the Syrian Holy Man and his Church," Traditio 45 (1989-1990) 7-33; Bernard Outtier, "Saint Éphrem d'après ses biographies et ses oeuvres," Parole de l'Orient 4 (1973) 11-33; Edward G. Mathews, "The Vita Tradition of Ephrem the Syrian, the Deacon of Edessa," Diakonia 22 (1988-1989) 15-42; and most recently Joseph P. Amar, "Byzantine Ascetic Monachism and Greek Bias in the Vita Tradition of Ephrem the Syrian," Orientalia Christiana Periodica 58 (1992) 123-156.

[22] CPG II.4160-4164; Georg Graf, Geschichte der christlichen arabischen Literatur (5 vols.; Studi e Testi, 118, 133, 146, 147, 172; Citta del Vaticano: Biblioteca Apostolica Vaticana, 1944-1953) I.421-433; Khalil Samir, "L'Éphrem arabe, état des travaux," Symposium Syriacum 1976 celebre au Centre Culturel "Les Fontaines" de Chantilly (France) (Orientalia Christiana Analecta, 205; Roma: Pontificium Institutum Studiorum, 1978) 229-240; also W. Heffening, "Die griechische Ephraem-Paraenesis gegen das Lachen in arabischer Übersetzung: Ein Beitrag zum Problem der arabischen Ephraemübersetzungen und ihrer Bedeutung fur eine kritische Ausgabe des griechischen Ephraem," Oriens Christianus 3. ser. v. 2 (1927) 94-119; Sebastian P. Brock & Simon Hopkins, "A Verse Homily on Abraham and Sarah in Egypt: Syriac Original with Early Arabic Translation," Le Muséon 105 (1992) 87-146.

[23] Joseph Nasrallah, Histoire du mouvement littéraire dans l'église melchite du Ve au XXe siècle. Contribution a l'étude de la littérature arabe chrétienne (multi-vol. set in progress; Louvain: Peeters, 1979+) II,2.168-182; and Gérard Troupeau, "La littérature arabe chrétienne du Xe au

XIIe siècle," Cahiers de Civilisation Médiévale, X^e-XIIe siècles 14 (1971) 1-20, esp. 14-15. In addition to the collections of homilies cited in note 24 below, individual works of Ephrem appear in Arabic homiliaries intended for specific liturgical use. See, e.g., Joseph-Marie Sauget, "Une ébauche d'homéliaire copte pour la semaine sainte: le manuscrit Borgia arabe 99," Parole de l'Orient 14 (1987) 167-202; idem, "Un homéliaire copte en arabe pour le carême et la semaine sainte: le Vatican arabe 75," in Antidoron: Hulde aan Dr. Maurits Geerard bij de voltooiing van de Clavis Patrum Graecorum (2 vols.; Wetteren: Cultura, 1984) I.201-240; idem, "L'Homéliaire arabe de la Bibliothèque Ambrosienne (X. 198 Sup.) et ses Membra Disiecta," Analecta Bollandiana 88 (1970) 391-475.

[24]Khalil Samir, "Le recueil Éphrememien arabe des 52 Homélies," Orientalia Christiana Periodica 39 (1973) 307-332; idem, "Le recueil Éphremien arabe des 30 homélies (Sinai arabe 311)," Parole de l'Orient 4 (1973) 265-315; idem, "Eine Homilien-Sammlung Ephrams der Syrers, Codex sinaiticus arabicus Nr. 311," Oriens Christianus 58 (1974) 51-75. See too J.-M. Sauget, "Le dossier Éphremien du manuscrit arabe Strasbourg 4226 et ses membra disiecta," Orientalia Christiana Periodica 42 (1976) 426-458.

[25]CPG II.4160 (5).

[26]See Graf, Geschichte der christlichen arabischen Literatur II.45-48; Nasrallah, Histoire du mouvement litteraire III,1.289-305.

[27]K. Samir, "Le recueil Éphremien arabe des 52 homélies," 309.

[28]Aziz S. Atiya, "Ibn Kabar," The Coptic Encyclopedia 4 (1992) 1266-1268; K. Samir, (ed.), Abū l-Barakāt Ibn Kabar, Misbāh az-Zulmah fi idah al-khidmah (Cairo: Maktabat al-Karuz, 1971) 293; idem, "Le Recueil Éphremien arabe des 52 homélies," 330-332.

[29]See K. Samir, "Le Recueil Éphremien arabe des 52 homélies," 332.

[30]Afrām al-Baramūsī, Kitāb maqālat Mar Afrām (Cairo, 1892). Afrām ^{c}Adad, whose floruit comprised the last two decades of the nineteenth century, was a Syrian monk who joined the Coptic Monastery of al-Baramus in the Wadi Natrun. He took the name al-Baramūsī, often simply calling himself ar-rāhib al-Baramūsī. See Graf, GCAL IV.115, 145-148.

[31]For brief histories of the dispersal of these manuscripts from the monastery and their deposition in the British Museum see the preface in William Cureton (ed.), The

Festal Letters of Athanasius Discovered in an Ancient Syriac
Version (London: Printed for the Society for the
Publication of Oriental Texts, 1848) i-lxii; also the
preface in W. Wright, Catalogue of the Syriac Manuscripts in
the British Museum, Acquired since the Year 1838 (3 vols.;
London: British Museum, 1870-1872) 3.i-xxxiv. Much of our
knowledge about the Monastery of the Syrians comes from the
work of two individuals: Hugh Evelyn White and Jules Leroy.
Evelyn White's classic study of the Wadi Natrun monasteries
remains the most comprehensive overview: H. G. Evelyn
White, The Monasteries of the Wadi 'n Natrûn (3 vols.;
Publications of the Metropolitan Museum of Art Egyptian
Expedition, 2, 7, 8; New York, 1926-1933). The many studies
of Jules Leroy are collected in the bibliography of his 1982
monograph: Jules Leroy, Les peintures des couvents du Ouadi
Natroun (Memoires publiés par les membres de l'Institut
Français d'Archéologie Orientale du Caire, t. CI; Le Caire,
1982).

[32]In the sixth century in the Wadi Natrun divisions
between monks holding the opposing Christological doctrines
of Julian of Halicarnassus and of Severus of Antioch led to
the construction of duplicate monasteries to house the
latter group of monks. The duplicate monasteries were
dedicated to the Theotokos, thus underlining the doctrinal
differences between those monks and the Julianists who
controlled the original monasteries. See Evelyn-White,
Monasteries of the Wadi 'n Natrûn 2.228-235. At some point
after the resolution of the situation in 710, the duplicate
monastery of Abba Bishoi was sold to Syrians.

[33]See W. Wright, Notulae Syriacae (printed for private
circulation, Christmas 1887) 14-15; Evelyn-White,
Monasteries of the Wadi 'n Natrun 2.plate VI.

[34]See J. M. Fiey, "Tagrit; esquisse d'histoire
chrétienne," L'Orient Syrien 8 (1963) 289-342; reprinted in
his Communautes syriaques en Iran et Irak des origines à
1552 (London: Variorum Reprints, 1979) no. X; idem,
"Coptes et Syriaques, contacts et echanges," Studia
Orientalia Christiana, Collectanea 15 (1972-1973) 295-365.

[35]The known facts about Moses of Nisibis are presented
in Jules Leroy, "Moïse de Nisibe," Symposium Syriacum 1972
(Orientalia Christiana Analecta, 197; Rome, 1974) 457-470.
For information about the library, see "Excursus: the
Library of the Syrian Monastery," in Evelyn White,
Monasteries of the Wadi 'n Natrûn 2.439-458.

[36]Leroy, "Moïse de Nisibe," 464-465.

[37]Wright, Catalogue of Syriac Manuscripts 2.410-413.

[38]For Vatican Syriac MS 112 see Stephen Evodius Assemani & Joseph Simon Assemani, *Bibliothecae Apostolicae Vaticanae codicum manuscriptorum catalogus, in tres partes distributus* (Pt. I, tom. 1-3; Romae: Ex Typographia Linguarum Orientalium, 1756-1759; reprinted Paris: Maisonneuve, 1926) I,3.79-87.

[39]For Vatican Syriac MS 113 see S. E. Assemani & J. S. Assemani, *BAVC* I,3.81.

[40]For Vatican Syriac MS 111 see S. E. Assemani & J. S. Assemani, *BAVC* I,3.77-79.

[41]For Vatican Syriac MS 110 see S. E. Assemani & J. S. Assemani, *BAVC* I,3.76-77; T. Jansma, "The Provenance of the Last Sections in the Roman Edition of Ephraem's Commentary of Exodus," *Le Muséon* 85 (1972) 155-169; P. Feghali, "Notes sur l'exégèse de Saint Ephrem. Commentaire sur le déluge (Gn 6,1-9,17)," *Parole de l'Orient* 8 (1977-78) 68.

[42]See Louis Leloir, "Le Commentaire d'Ephrem sur le Diatessaron: Quarante et un folios retrouvés," *Parole de l'Orient* 15 (1988-1989) 41-63, esp. 41-46; *idem, Saint Ephrem, Commentaire de l'Évangile Concordant. Texte syriaque (Manuscrit Chester Beatty 709): folios additionnels édités et traduits* (Chester Beatty Monographs, No. 8; Leuven: Peeters, 1990) v-x.

[43]See, e.g., Joseph Melki, "Saint Éphrem le Syrien, un bilan de l'edition critique," 3-5; Sebastian Brock, *Saint Ephrem, Hymns on Paradise: Introduction and Translation* (Crestwood, New York: St. Vladimir's Seminary Press, 1990) 33-36.

[44]K. Samir, "L'Éphrem arabe," 238.

[45]See Monica J. Blanchard, "Apa Bishoi and Mar Ephrem," to appear in v. 1 of *Journal of Middle Eastern Christian Studies*.

[46]The manuscript tradition of the Syriac *Life* of Ephrem has been studied by Joseph P. Amar, "The Syriac *Vita* Tradition of Ephrem the Syrian" (Unpublished Ph.D. dissertation, The Catholic University of America, Washington, D.C., 1988).

[47]Blanchard, "Apa Bishoi and Mar Ephrem."

[48]Rubens Duval, *La Littérature syriaque des origines jusqu'à la fin de cette littérature après la conquete par les arabes au XIIIe siècle* (Amsterdam: Philo Press, 1970), p. 332. For this Egyptian Ephrem or as he is better known, Abraham of Farshut, see Réné-Georges Coquin, "Abraham of Farshut," *The Coptic Encyclopedia* 1 (1992) 11-12.

[49]His story is told in the Copto-Arabic Synaxary. See René Basset, Le Synaxaire Arabe Jacobite (Mois de Toubeh et d'Amchir (Patrologia Orientalis, 11; Paris: Firmin-Didot, 1915), pp. 684-685.

[50]For another appearance in Egypt of the name Εὐφρημ see Carl Wessely, Griechische Texte zur Topographie Agyptens (Studien zur Palaeographie und Papyruskunde, X; Leipzig: E. Avenarius, 1910) 297 [p. 157, line 16]. One finds this form of the name of Ephrem still current in Egypt in the seventeenth century. See the letter dated 30 October 1646 from a Greek priest, Fr. Athanasius to the French chancellor Seguier: "Mes consortz, les marchands d'Egipte, qui sont à Paris, m'ont adverti que Vostre Grandeur a désir d'avoir les oeuvres de S. Ufrene [St. Ephrem], et estat des manuscriptz du convant de S. Macaire et d'autres qui ce treuveront en Egipte." Henri Omont, Missions Archéologiques Françaises en Orient aux XVII et XVIII siècles. Documents publiés (2 vols.; Paris: Imprimerie Nationale, 1902) I.11.

[51]In the Copto-Arabic synaxary the name Ephrem appears as افرام. René Basset, Le Synaxaire arabe jacobite (Les mois de Baounah, Abib, Mesore et jours complémentaires) (Patrologia Orientalis, 17; Paris: Firmin-Didot, 1923) 655-657. The name of Abraham of Farshut appears as افرامام in this same Synaxary. See note 49 above.

[52]Anton Baumstark, Geschichte der syrischen Literatur mit Ausschluss der christlich-palastinensischen Texte (Bonn: A. Marcus & E. Webers, 1922; reprinted Berlin: Walter de Gruyter, 1968) 283-284; Blanchard, "Apa Bishoi and Mar Ephrem "

[53]B. L. Add. MS 14728, B. L. Add. MS 14732, B.L. Add. MS 14735, Cambridge Add. MS 2016, Paris B. N. MS 234, Paris B. N. MS 235, Paris B.N. MS 236.

[54]B.L. Add. MS 14732, Cambridge Add. MS 2016, and Paris B.N. MS 236 all contain the Syriac Life of Shenoute, as well as the Syriac Life of Bishoi.

[55]See Ignazio Guidi, "Le Traduzione dal Copto," Nachrichten von der Königlichen Gesellschaft der Wissenschaften und der Georg-Augusts-Universität zu Göttingen no. 3 (6. Februar 1889) 45-56; Baumstark, Geschichte der syrischen Literatur 283-284; F. Nau, Histoire de Jean le Petit. Hégoumène de Scété, au IVe siècle: version syriaque editée et traduite (Paris: Picard, 1914) i-iv.

[56]B.L. Add. MS 14645. See W. Wright, Catalogue of the Syriac Manuscripts in the British Museum. Acquired Since the Year 1838 (3 vols.; London: British Museum, 1870-1872) 3.1111-1116.

[57]The homily On the end of the world and the last
judgment is found in B.L. Add. 14735, ff. 134a-136a,
followed by another extract of the same or a similar work,
ff. 136a-136b; On repentance is found in Cambridge Add. MS
2016, ff. 233b-238; On doctrine appears in B.L. Add. 14735,
ff. 83a-89a; Ephrem's prayer is in B.L. Add. 14,728, ff.
42a-42b; the history of Abraham Kidunaya by Mar Ephrem is
told in Paris B.N. MS 234, ff. 172-186 and Paris B.N. MS
235, ff. 3-12; the Life of Ephrem is found in Paris B.N. MS
235, ff. 125-142.

[58]Evelyn-White, Monasteries of the Wadi 'n Natrûn
2.363-365; Johannes den Heijer, "Mawhūb Ibn Manṣūr ibn
Mufarrij al-Iskandarānī," The Coptic Encyclopedia 5 (1991)
1573-1574.

[59]Evelyn-White, Monasteries of the Wadi 'n Natrûn
1.143, 215-216. See too O. H. E. Burmester, "The
Translation of St. Iskhiron of Ḳillin," Le Muséon 47 (1934)
1-11; idem, "The Translation of St. Iskhiron of Ḳillin
(Additional Note)," Le Muséon 48 (1935) 81-85.

[60]H. J. Polotsky, "Ephraem's Reise nach Aegypten,"
Orientalia n.s. 2 (1933) 269-274.

[61]Evelyn-White, Monasteries of the Wadi 'n Natrûn
2.114, 316. See, e.g., the description in Gabriel de
Bremond, Viaggi fatti nell'Egitto superiore, et inferiore:
nel Monte Sinay, e lvoghi piv' cospicivi di qvella regione:
in Gerusalemme, Giudea, Galilea, Sammaria, Palestina,
Fenicia, Monte Libano, & altre Prouincie di siria...Opera
del Signor Gabrielle Bfremond, Marsiliese, da lui scritta in
Francese, e fatta traderre in Italiano, da Giuseppe Corvo
(Bologna, per Gio. Recaldini, 1680) 136-137.

L'EVANGILE DE MARC EN COPTE-SAHIDIQUE:
ESSAI DE CLARIFICATION

ANNE BOUD'HORS

En 1973, dans un lumineux compte-rendu de la remarquable édition donnée par H. Quecke (1), T. Orlandi faisait l'hypothèse d'une division de la tradition textuelle de l'*évangile de Marc* en deux branches: l'une avait pour témoin le manuscrit PPalau 182, objet de l'édition, l'autre était représentée par le manuscrit M569 de la collection Pierpont Morgan, et par les manuscrits répertoriés dans l'édition critique de Horner (2). Les différences entre ces deux branches étaient d'ordre stylistique (emploi de ⲁⲩⲱ ou de ⲁⲉ, emploi de l'état direct ou absolu d'un verbe, différences dans le choix d'un temps), lexical, syntaxique, ou encore textuel (c'est à dire renvoyant à deux modèles grecs différents); elles permettaient de voir dans le manuscrit PPalau 182 un témoin d'une rédaction plus brève, et sans doute plus ancienne, de l'évangile. T. Orlandi repérait aussi, parmi les manuscrits de l'édition de Horner, un autre témoin possible de cette rédaction: le manuscrit n°72, dont quelques versets seulement sont conservés, et qui est plus tardif que PPalau 182. Il en venait à conclure que les deux branches avaient probablement cohabité, la plus longue prenant cependant le dessus dans l'usage.

Sans connaître l'article de T. Orlandi -ignorance difficilement excusable-, je découvris de mon côté, au hasard du catalogage des fragments bibliques de la Bibliothèque nationale de Paris, un autre manuscrit de Horner apparenté à PPalau 182: le manuscrit n°18, également très fragmentaire. L'examen des variantes textuelles contenues dans ce manuscrit conduisait aussi à supposer l'existence de deux branches, l'une (PPalau 182 et Horner n°18) représentant un type de texte égyptien, tandis que les variantes attestées par la majorité des autres manuscrits renvoyaient à un type palestinien. Seul le manuscrit M569 résistait à un classement net dans l'une ou l'autre branche(3).

Deux publications récentes ont permis d'approfondir cette recherche: d'une part l'édition critique du manuscrit M569(4), de l'autre le catalogue de tous les manuscrits sahidiques des évangiles, établi par l'Institut für Neutestamentliche Textforschung de München(5). Grâce à ces instruments de travail, j'ai pu commencer à satisfaire ma curiosité sur trois points: I) Existe-t-il d'autres témoins de la rédaction "ancienne"? II) Quelle(s) relation(s) peut-on établir entre les deux branches? III) Comment rendre compte de l'existence de ces deux branches pour cet évangile, et pour lui seulement? Je livre ici les premiers résultats de ces investigations, qui sont loin d'être achevées.

I) MANUSCRITS TEMOINS DE LA BRANCHE "ANCIENNE"

Horner	*Liste*	date	texte Mc	cote
---	sa 1	5°s.	1:1-16:8	Barcelone, PPalau 182
n° 18	sa 143	7°-8°s.	2:12-28, 3:4-10	Paris BN 129[7] f.28
			7:30-8:26	Leyde, Copte 51
			9:17-20,24-26 32-34,39-42	Paris BN 132[4] f.312 +133[1]f.3
			15:15-16,42-43	Paris BN 133[1] f.35c
n° 70	sa 109	10°s.	7:24-8:9	Vienne, K9042
			9:18-20,24-25 29-31,34-36	Paris, Louvre E10021 (6)
			10:15,20,25,30	Paris BN 132[2] f.122
n° 72 +n°77	sa 162	10°s.	2:27/28-3:5, 19-24	Paris BN 129[5] f.89
			3:30-4:4,5-12, 16-19	Paris BN 129[6] f.4
n°103 +n°108	sa 134	11°s.	7:4-32	Paris BN 161[3] f.26f
			8:23-9:13	Paris BN 161[4] f.26g
			11:18-12:12	Oxford Bodl. Copt. b.11 f.6
			13:25-14:15	Oxford, Bodl. Copt. b.11 f.2 +Paris BN 161[4]

f.26n
+Paris BN 161[4]
f.26o
+Paris Académie
193.28

N.B. - Dans la suite de cet article, j'utiliserai exclusivement les sigles de la *Liste*.

- Ces manuscrits sont des évangéliaires dont on a des fragments pour les quatre évangiles, sauf sa 1 (*Luc-Jean-Marc*) et sa 162 (fragments conservés de *Mc* et *Jean*). Le cas des lectionnaires sera abordé en fin d'article.

- A l'exception de sa 1 **(7)**, ces manuscrits proviennent du Monastère Blanc, et leurs dates s'échelonnent entre le 5° et le 11° siècle, c'est à dire une grande partie de la période sahidique.

- Les principaux manuscrits de Horner attestant les mêmes passages sont les suivants: sa 102 (Horner 8), sa 112 (Horner 114 + 134), sa 113 (Horner 38 + 86), sa 120 (Horner 9), sa 123 (Horner 73), sa 127 (Horner 110), sa 133 + sa 113D/3 + sa 121Q/1 (Horner 50), sa 144 (Horner 15), sa 147 (Horner 74), sa 183 (Horner 64), sa 198 (Horner 113).

II)DIFFERENCES ENTRE LES DEUX BRANCHES

L'étude a porté principalement sur le premier chapitre, puis sur les passages les plus abondamment attestés par l'une et l'autre branche: chap.2-4 et 7-9. Les différences ont été classées en trois catégories, qui permettaient une description précise, en particulier pour la situation flottante du manuscrit sa 9: différences lexicales (A), morpho-syntaxiques (B), variantes textuelles (C). Ne sont pas prises en compte les variations orthographiques, celles surtout qui caractérisent le manuscrit sa 1 par rapport au reste de la tradition sahidique, et ne sont pas pertinentes dans le classement envisagé ici. Afin d'alléger la description qui suit, j'appelle T1 la tradition représentée par sa 1 et ses témoins, T2 celle qu'attestent les autres manuscrits de Horner. Quelques exemples sont donnés pour chaque catégorie.
N.B. Le texte grec de base est celui de Nestle-Aland: *Novum Testamentum graece*, Stuttgart 1898, 1979 (26°éd.).

A- Différences lexicales
1) T1 emploie un mot grec/T2 un mot égyptien

Exemples:
- 1:4 T1: ⲔⲎⲢⲒⲤⲤⲈ/T2: ⲦⲀϢⲈⲞⲈⲒϢ (grec: ϰηρύσσω)
- 1:7 T1: 2ⲒⲔⲀⲚⲞⲤ/T2: ⲘⲠⲰⲖ (grec: ἱϰανός)
- 8:23, 26, 27 T1: ⲔⲰⲘⲎ/T2: ϯⲘⲈ (grec ϰώμη)

2) T1 et T2 emploient deux mots égyptiens différents: il semble alors que le choix de T2 corresponde à un usage plus courant, à un souci de précision ou d'unification de la traduction.

Exemples:
- 3:22, 8:11,12, etc. T1: ⲔⲰⲦⲈ (ⲚⲤⲀ)/T2: ϢⲒⲚⲈ (ⲚⲤⲀ) (grec: ζητεῖν)
- 8:23 T1: ⲦⲞⲞⲦ(ϥ)/T2: ϬⲒⲜ (grec: χείρ)
- 7:21 T1: ⲘⲈⲈⲨⲈ/T2: ⲘⲞⲔⲘⲈⲔ (grec: διαλογισμός)
- 7:22 T1: ⲘⲚⲦⲢⲈϥⲬⲰ2Ⲙ/T2: ⲤⲰⲰϥ (grec: ἀσέλγεια) (N.B.: ⲬⲰ2Ⲙ traduit plus fréquemment ϰοινεῖν dans l'évangile de Marc).
- 8:20 T1: 2ⲘⲈ ⲚϢⲈ (40 x 100)/T2: ϥⲦⲞⲞⲨ ⲚϢⲞ (4 x 1000) (grec: τετραϰισχιλίους = 4 x 1000)
- 7:30 T1: ⲈⲀ(ⲠⲆⲀⲒⲘⲞⲚⲒⲞⲚ) ⲖⲞ 2ⲒⲰⲰⲤ/T2: ⲈⲒ ⲈⲂⲞⲖ Ⲛ2ⲎⲦⲤ (grec: ἐξεληλυϑός); le souci d'unification de la traduction en T2 semble net ici: le même verbe grec, un verset plus haut, est traduit par ⲈⲒ ⲈⲂⲞⲖ 2Ⲛ dans toute la tradition sahidique; le manuscrit sa 143 présente pour 7:30 une intéressante solution moyenne, qui n'a pas été notée par les éditeurs: ⲈⲒ ⲈⲂⲞⲖ 2ⲒⲰⲰⲤ.

En examinant de plus près ces variations, on s'aperçoit que T1 paraît présenter un état lexical différent -et probablement plus ancien-, non seulement de celui de T2, mais aussi de celui des autres évangiles, et même de celui de la langue du Nouveau Testament en général. Voici en effet les résultats de quelques sondages effectués dans la concordance du Nouveau Testament sahidique (8):
- Le mot ⲔⲰⲘⲎ (grec ϰώμη) n'est jamais employé dans la version sahidique, sauf dans les trois passages cités ci-dessus.
- Le verbe ⲔⲰⲦⲈ (ⲚⲤⲀ) ne traduit jamais le grec ζητεῖν sauf dans neuf passages qui appartiennent tous à T1 (deux d'entre eux ont été conservés dans T2); en revanche, ce sens est fréquent dans la version sahidique des Psaumes et dans la langue de Chenouté.
- Le mot 2ⲢⲞⲞⲨ n'est employé régulièrement et sûrement pour traduire φωνή que dans T1 (T2 est souvent mal attesté pour les cinq passages concernés) et dans l'Apoca-

lypse, alors que ϹⲘⲎ se trouve dans tous les autres textes.

- Pour traduire σώζειν, T1 (T2 aussi, mais certains passages sont mal attestés)utilise de préférence ⲚⲞⲨⳏⲘ: sept
occurrences contre une seule attestation de ⲦⲞⲨⲬⲞ; la
proportion est à peu près inverse dans les évangiles de
Matthieu et de Luc; la version des Psaumes paraît faire un
emploi à peu équilibré des deux mots.

- Des vingt-sept cas du Nouveau Testament où ⲦⲞⲞⲦ-
traduit réellement χείρ, et non un préverbe grec, quinze se
trouvent dans T1, et le plus souvent aussi dans T2, le
passage le plus intéressant étant 8:23 (cité ci-dessus:
ⲚⲦⲈⲢⲈϤⲀⲘⲀⳘⲦⲈ ⲚⲦⲞⲞⲦϤ), où ⲦⲞⲞⲦ- n'est pas adjoint à
une forme directe du verbe (ⲔⲀ-, ⲦⲀⲖⲈ-, ⳘⲒ-, etc.), mais
employé comme complément d'objet d'un verbe à la forme
absolue; (mais ⲀϤⲀⲘⲀⳘⲦⲈ ⲚⲦⲈϹϬⲒⳘ en 1:31 dans T1 et T2)).

Par rapport à T1 dont elle conserve d'ailleurs certains
traits, T2 représenterait donc sur le plan lexical une sorte
de révision, effectuée dans un sens de précision et d'unification interne, et vraisemblablement aussi, influencée
par les passages parallèles de l'évangile de Matthieu .
Exemples:
- 1:7 T1: ⲠⲀⲒ ⲈⲀⲚⲄⲞⲨⳘⲒⲔⲀⲚⲞϹ ⲀⲚ ⲈⲦⲢⲀⲠⲀⳘⲦ.../T2: ⲠⲀⲒ
ⲈⲚⳠⲘⲠϢⲀ... Mt 3:11: ⲠⲀⲒ ⲈⲚⳠⲘⲠϢⲀ ⲚϤⳘ...
- 7:21 T1: ⲈⲨⲚⲎⲨ ⲄⲀⲢ ⲈⲂⲞⲖ ⳘⲒⳘⲞⲨⲚ ⳘⲘⳘⳘⲎⲦ ⲚⲚⲢⲰⲘⲈ ⲚϬⲒ
ⳘⲘⲈⲈⲨⲈ ⲈⲐⲞⲞⲨ/T2: ... ⲚϬⲒ ⳘⲘⲞⲔⲘⲈⲔ ⲈⲐⲞⲞⲨ Mt 15:19:
ⲈⲨⲚⲎⲨ ⲄⲀⲢ ⲈⲂⲞⲖ ⳘⲘⳘⳘⲎⲦ ⲚϬⲒ ⳘⲘⲞⲔⲘⲈⲔ ⲈⲐⲞⲞⲨ

Dernier point à préciser pour cette catégorie: sa 9 se
range de façon nette du côté de T1; quelques exceptions
sont à relever cependant: T1 ⲐⲈⲢⲀⲠⲞⲨ/T2 et sa 9 ⲢⳠⲀⳘⲢⲈ
(3:2, grec: θεραπεύειν); T1 ⲚϹⲈⳠⲘⲚⲀⲨ/T2 et sa 9 ⲚϹⲈⳠ-
ⲘⲈⲒⲰⲢⳘ (4:12, grec: καὶ μὴ ἴδωσιν).

B- Différences morpho-syntaxiques
1)Dans le choix de la forme verbale .
Exemples:
- 1:2 T1 ⲚϤϹⲞϤⲦⲈ/T2 ⲠⲀⲒ ⲈⲦⲚⲀϹⲞⲂⲦⲈ (grec: ὃς παρασκευά
σει) .
- 1:5 T1 ⲀϹⲂⲰⲔ ⲈⲂⲞⲖ/T2 ⲚⲈϹⲚⲎⲨ ⲈⲂⲞⲖ (grec: ἐξεπορεύε-
το).
- 7:27 T1 ⲔⲀⲚϢⲎⲢⲈ ⲈⲦⲢⲈⲨϹⲈⲒ ⲚϢⲞⲢⲠ/T2 ...ⲚϹⲈⲒ ⲚϢⲞⲢⲠ
(grec: ἄφες πρῶτον χορτασθῆναι τὰ τέκνα).
2) Dans l'emploi des prépositions, préverbes, particules.

Exemples:
- 1:5 T1 N̄TOOT4/T2 EBOλ 2ITOOT4 (grec: ὑπ' αὐτοῦ).
- 1:9 T1 N̄TN̄IⲰ2ANNHC/T2 EBOλ 2ITN̄IⲰ2ANNHC (grec: ὑπὸ Ἰωάννου).
- 1:11 T1 AYⲰ OYCMH/T2 AYⲰ EIC OYCMH (grec: καὶ φωνή).
- 7:6 T1 EBOλ M̄MOI/T2 N̄CABOλ M̄MOI (grec: ἀπ'ἐμοῦ).
- 8:29 T1 N̄TⲰTN̄ ΔE/T2 EIE N̄TⲰTN̄ (grec: ὑμεῖς δέ).
3) Dans la tournure de la phrase.
Exemples:
- 3:5 T1 ΠTⲰM N̄2HT M̄ΠEY2HT/T2 ΠEYTⲰM N̄2HT
(grec: τῇ πωρώσει τῆς καρδίας αὐτῶν).
- 8:7 T1 N̄TEPE4CMOY ΔE EPOOY A4OY·A2CA2NE EKANEI-
KOOYE 2APⲰOY/T2 AYⲰ NEIKOOYE A4CMOY A4OYE2
CA2NE EKAAY 2APⲰOY (grec: καὶ εὐλόγησας αὐτὰ εἶπεν
καὶ ταῦτα παρατίθεναι).
4) Dans la coordination des phrases: le partage est net
entre T1 et T2 pour la traduction de καί en début de phrase: j'ai relevé 29 occurrences où T1 donne AYⲰ, tandis que
T2 donne ΔE, et le contraire ne se rencontre quasiment
pas.
   Les différences qui viennent d'être décrites semblent
reposer sur les mêmes principes que celles de la catégorie
précédente:
- D'une part il y a eu en T2 élimination d'un certain nombre d'imprécisions de la traduction qui existaient en T1,
imprécisions qui renvoient à un état de langue ancien, si-
non archaïque. Deux traits morphologiques sont à relever
à l'appui de cette affirmation: l'emploi de THNOY comme
pronom de la deuxième personne du pluriel (classique:
THYTN̄), déjà relevé par H.Quecke (*op.cit.* p.39), et dont le
manuscrit sa 143 conserve une attestation (9:41); l'emploi
de EPE- comme relatif (classique: ETEPE-), que l'on
trouve dans sa 1, et une fois dans sa 162 (3:3 sa 1 = AYⲰ
ΠEXA4 M̄ΠPⲰME EPETE46IX MOOYT/sa 162 =...EPETE46IX
ⲰOYⲰOY/T2 et sa 9 = ΠEXA4 ΔE M̄ΠPⲰME ETEPETE46IX
ⲰOYⲰOY; l'apparat critique de sa 9 est erroné dans l'édition de G. Aranda pour ce passage).
- D'autre part on constate, et de façon encore plus nette,
l'influence des passages parallèles de l'évangile de Matthieu. Exemples:
* 1:5 T1 AYⲰ ACBⲰK NA4 EBOλ N̄6I TEXⲰPA THPC N̄ŤOY-
ΔAIA MN̄NA⊖IEPOCOλYMA THPOY AYXIBAΠTICMA N̄TOOT4
       T2 AYⲰ NECNHY EBOλ EPAT4 N̄6I ΠΠEPIXⲰPOC THPC

ⲚϮⲞⲨⲆⲀⲒⲀ ⲘⲚ̄ⲚⲀⲐⲒⲈⲢⲞⲤⲞⲀⲨⲘⲀ ⲀⲨⲱ ⲚⲈⲨⲬⲒⲂⲀⲠⲦⲒⲤⲘⲀ ⲈⲂⲞⲀ
ϨⲒⲦⲞⲞⲦϤ

Mt 3:5-6 ⲦⲞⲦⲈ ⲚⲈⲤⲚⲎⲨ ⲈⲂⲞⲀ ⲈⲢⲀⲦϤ Ⲛ̄ϬⲒ ⲐⲒⲈⲢⲞⲤⲞ-
ⲀⲨⲘⲀ (ⲦⲎⲢⲤ) ⲘⲚ̄ϮⲞⲨⲆⲀⲒⲀ (ⲦⲎⲢⲤ) ⲘⲚ̄ⲦⲠⲈⲢⲒⲬⲱⲢⲞⲤ ⲦⲎⲢⲤ
Ⲙ̄ⲠⲈⲒⲞⲢⲆⲀⲚⲎⲤ ⲈⲨⲬⲒⲂⲀⲠⲦⲒⲤⲘⲀ ⲈⲂⲞⲀ ϨⲒⲦⲞⲞⲦϤ.

* 1:11 T1 ⲀⲨⲱ ⲞⲨⲤⲘⲎ/T2 ⲀⲨⲱ ⲈⲒⲤ ⲞⲨⲤⲘⲎ/ Mt 3:17 ⲀⲨⲱ
ⲈⲒⲤ ϨⲎⲎⲦⲈ ⲈⲒⲤ ⲞⲨⲤⲘⲎ.

* Cette contamination a joué également pour le remplace-
ment de ⲀⲨⲱ par ⲆⲈ: la fréquence de καί en début de
phrase dans le texte grec est caractéristique de l'évangile
de Marc, alors que les autres emploient de préférence δέ;
ⲀⲨⲱ était donc la traduction la plus logique de καί, et ⲆⲈ
n'est pas une correction de cette traduction, mais plutôt
le résultat d'un alignement sur les passages parallèles
(cf. Mc 2:14/Mt 9:9, Mc 2:17/Mt 9:12, Mc 3:7/Mt 12:15, Mc
3:22/Mt 12:24, etc.).

Si donc toutes les différences ne sont pas réductibles à
une influence de l'évangile de Matthieu (et, dans une
moindre mesure, de l'évangile de Luc), elle semble bien
prépondérante pour la catégorie décrite ici.

La position de sa 9 n'est pas aussi claire que sur le plan
du lexique: il est tantôt du côté de T1, tantôt du côté de
T2. Cependant cette hésitation n'est pas totalement arbi-
traire, elle semble plutôt refléter une situation différente
selon les péricopes. Exemples:
- 1:1-12 (baptême de Jésus): sa 9 est du côté de T1.
- 2:1-12 (guérison du paralytique): sa 9 est plus proche de
T2.
- 3:1-7 (l'homme à la main sèche): *id.*
- 7:14-fin (le pur et l'impur): sa 9 est du côté de T1.
- 8:1-14(multiplication des pains): sa 9 est proche de T2.
N.B.: un autre manuscrit, sa 123 (anciennement Horner 73),
qui est beaucoup plus fragmentaire, présente également
un certain flottement entre T1 et T2, sans pour autant
être toujours du même côté que sa 9, et mériterait un
examen détaillé.

C- Variantes textuelles
Sont abordées ici les variations entre T1 et T2 qui renvoient à deux textes grecs différents (9). On peut encore
en distinguer deux sortes:
1) Celles où T1 a la leçon commune en grec, tandis que T2
a une leçon différente; celle-ci consiste généralement en

un ajout, et elle est souvent attestée par un groupe de manuscrits grecs rattachés au type dit "palestinien"; dans certains cas, elle est plus difficile à interpréter. Exemples:

- 1:2 T1: ϯⲚⲀϪⲞⲞⲨ ⲘⲠⲀⲀⲄⲄⲈⲖⲞⲤ ϨⲒϨⲎ ⲘⲘⲞⲔ ⲚϤⲤⲞϤⲦⲈ ⲚⲦⲈⲔϨⲒⲎ

T2: " " ϨⲀⲦⲈⲔϨⲎ ⲠⲀⲒ ⲈⲦⲚⲀⲤⲞⲂⲦⲈ ⲚⲦⲈⲔϨⲒⲎ ϨⲒϨⲎ ⲘⲘⲞⲔ/ var. ⲘⲠⲈⲔⲘⲦⲞ **(10)**.

Les deux premières différences entre T1 et T2 appartiennent à la catégorie B. Quant à l'addition en fin de phrase, elle correspond à une variante attestée en grec (+ ἐμπρόσθεν σου), mais non caractéristique d'un type de texte. En revanche, la comparaison avec le passage parallèle de l'évangile de Matthieu est éclairante:

Mt 11:10 ϯⲚⲀⲦⲚⲚⲞⲞⲨ ⲘⲠⲀⲀⲄⲄⲈⲖⲞⲤ ϨⲀⲦⲈⲔϨⲎ ⲠⲀⲒ ⲈⲦⲚⲀⲤⲞⲂⲦⲈ ⲚⲦⲈⲔϨⲒⲎ ⲘⲠⲈⲔⲘⲦⲞ ⲈⲂⲞⲖ.

Cela signifie que, pour la variante copte, le passage par le texte grec est possible, mais pas obligatoire.

- 2:16 T1: ⲈⲦⲂⲈⲞⲨ ϤⲞⲨⲰⲘ (T1 est attesté ici par sa 1 et sa 143; l'apparat critique de l'édition de G. Aranda est erroné).

T2: ⲈⲦⲂⲈⲞⲨ ⲠⲈⲦⲚⲤⲀϨ ⲞⲨⲰⲘ.

La variante de T2 consiste en l'addition de ὁ διδάσκαλος ὑμῶν, variante attestée en grec, qui divise le type égyptien. Mais il est tentant de faire l'économie de cette explication en faisant appel au parallèle:

Mt 9:11 ⲈⲦⲂⲈⲞⲨ ⲠⲈⲦⲚⲤⲀϨ ⲞⲨⲰⲘ

- 8:9 T1: ⲚⲈⲨⲚⲀⲢϨⲘⲈ ⲚϢⲈ

T2: ⲚⲈⲦⲞⲨⲰⲘ ⲆⲈ ⲚⲈⲨⲚⲀⲢϨⲘⲈ ⲚϢⲈ.

Cette variante grecque (+ οἱ φαγόντες) est caractéristique du type palestinien. Ici encore cependant, il faut citer le texte parallèle :

Mt 14:21 ⲚⲈⲦⲞⲨⲰⲘ ⲆⲈ ⲚⲈⲨⲚⲀⲢⲀϯⲞⲨ ⲚϢⲞ.

On pourrait multiplier les exemples : pour presque toutes les variantes de ce genre, il est possible d'éviter la remontée aux textes grecs, ou tout au moins d'invoquer aussi la contamination par les textes parallèles.

2) Les variantes où T1 a un texte différent (généralement plus bref) de la leçon commune du grec attestée par T2. On peut supposer alors que T1 a une leçon ancienne, souvent de type égyptien, et que T2 a utilisé un autre modèle grec. Exemples:

- 1:1 T1: ⲦⲀⲢⲬⲎ ⲘⲠⲈⲨⲀⲄⲄⲈⲖⲒⲞⲚ Ⲛ Ⲓ̅Ⲥ̅ ⲠⲈⲬ̅Ⲥ̅ (sa 1 est ici le seul témoin de T1)/ T2 ajoute Ⲡ(ⲱ)ⲎⲢⲈ ⲘⲠⲚⲞⲨⲦⲈ, comme le grec υἱοῦ θεοῦ.
- 7:4 T1: Ⲛⲙ̅�2ⲈⲚ3ⲈⲤⲦⲎⲤ Ⲛⲙ̅2ⲈⲚⲬⲀⲖⲔⲒⲚ (sa 1 est encore le seul témoin de cette leçon)/ T2 ajoute ⲘⲚ̅2ⲈⲚⲘⲀ Ⲛ̅ⲚⲔⲞⲦⲔ, comme le grec καὶ κλινῶν.
- 7:26 T1: ⲦⲈⲤ2ⲒⲘⲈ ⲆⲈ ⲚⲈⲨ2ⲈⲖⲖⲎⲚ ⲦⲈ Ⲛ̅Ⲣⲙ̅ⲦⲈⲪⲞⲒⲚⲒⲔⲎ Ⲛ̅ⲦⲤⲨⲢⲒⲀ (T1 est attesté ici par sa 1 et sa 109)/ T2 ajoute 2ⲘⲠⲈⲤⲄⲈⲚⲞⲤ, comme le grec τῷ γένει.
- 8:3 T1: ⲈⲨⲚ2ⲞⲒⲚⲈ Ⲛ̅2ⲎⲦⲞⲨ ⲈⲨ(ⲱ)ⲞⲞⲠ 2Ⲙ̅ⲠⲞⲨⲈ (T1 est attesté par sa 1 et sa 143).

    T2: ⲚⲈⲨⲚ2ⲞⲒⲚⲈ ⲄⲀⲢ Ⲛ̅2ⲎⲦⲞⲨ ⲈⲀⲨⲈⲒ ⲬⲒⲚⲙ̅ⲠⲞⲨⲈ.

La leçon de T2 est la plus commune en grec: καί τινες αὐτῶν ἀπὸ μακρόθεν ἥκασιν; celle de T1, avec εἰσιν, est attestée par le manuscrit B de la tradition grecque (type égyptien).

3) Certaines variantes de l'une ou l'autre tradition résistent à l'interprétation, en l'absence de témoins grecs et de parallèles dans les autres évangiles. Exemples:
- 1:22 T1: Ⲛ̅ⲐⲈ ⲀⲚ ⲈⲦⲞⲨ†ⲤⲂ(ⲱ) Ⲛ̅ϬⲒ ⲚⲈⲄⲢⲀⲘⲘⲀⲦⲈⲨⲤ ⲀⲖⲖⲀ 2(ⲱ)Ⲥ ⲈⲨⲚⲦϤ ⲦⲈ3ⲞⲨⲤⲒⲀ Ⲙ̅ⲘⲀⲨ.

    T2: 2(ⲱ)Ⲥ ⲈⲨⲚⲦϤ Ⲉ3ⲞⲨⲤⲒⲀ Ⲙ̅ⲘⲀⲨ ⲀⲨ(ⲱ) Ⲛ̅ⲐⲈ ⲀⲚ Ⲛ̅ⲚⲈⲨⲄⲢⲀⲘⲘⲀⲦⲈⲨⲤ.

    grec: ὡς ἐξουσίαν ἔχων καὶ οὐχ ὡς οἱ γραμματεῖς.
- 7:28: T1: (ⲱ)ⲀⲨⲞⲨ(ⲱ)Ⲙ ⲈⲂⲞⲖ 2Ⲛ̅ⲚⲈⲤⲢⲈϤⲢⲒϤⲈ (ⲈⲦ)2ⲀⲦⲈⲦⲢⲀⲠⲈ3Ⲁ Ⲛ̅Ⲛ(ⲱ)ⲎⲢⲈ.

    T2: (ⲱ)ⲀⲨⲞⲨ(ⲱ)Ⲙ 2ⲀⲢⲀⲦⲤ Ⲛ̅ⲦⲈⲦⲢⲀⲠⲈ3Ⲁ Ⲛ̅ⲚⲢⲈⲤⲢⲒϤⲈ ⲈⲦ2ⲎⲨ Ⲛ̅ⲦⲞⲞⲦⲞⲨ.

    grec: ὑποκάτω τῆς τραπέζης ἐσθίουσιν ἀπὸ τῶν ψιχιῶν τῶν παιδίων.

On aura remarqué que dans cette catégorie de variations (surtout en C 2)), T1 n'est pas aussi homogène que dans les deux premières: sa 1 est souvent le seul manuscrit à présenter les "variantes brèves", comme si les autres témoins de T1 avaient été influencés par les leçons communes de T2.

Quant au manuscrit sa 9, sa position reste flottante: il n'atteste pas les "variantes brèves"; pour les autres variantes, la division en péricopes esquissée ci-dessus pour la catégorie B semble s'appliquer assez bien ici.

III) POURQUOI DEUX TRADITIONS ?

Etant donné d'une part la proximité de T1 et T2 de manière générale, d'autre part la relative facilité avec laquelle on peut repérer et classer les variations, compte-tenu enfin du caractère de ces variations, on peut conclure que T2 est une révision de T1.

Soit donc une traduction ancienne, dont le premier témoin conservé est sa 1 (5° siècle). Elle est désormais bien établie, puisqu'elle est attestée par quatre autres manuscrits, qui ne sont pas cependant des copies exactes de sa 1. Cette traduction ancienne, révisée, donne naissance à une tradition T2, représentée par la majorité des manuscrits sahidiques connus.

Le manuscrit sa 9 occupe une position intermédiaire, tout en ayant aussi des traits originaux (relevés par son éditeur; cf. note 4). Représente-t-il une étape de la révision, sur un modèle qui ne serait pas sa 1 ? Ou le résultat d'un mélange des deux traditions ? Certains manuscrits de l'édition de Horner témoignent quant à eux très probablement d'influences réciproques entre T1 et T2.

Le schéma suivant tente de représenter la situation envisagée:

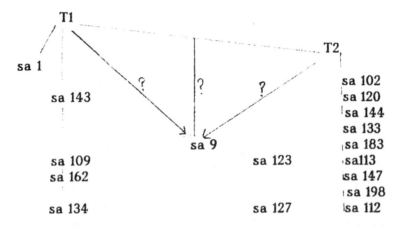

Si la révision semble répondre à un souci d'actualisation, elle paraît être aussi un alignement sur les passages parallèles de l'évangile de Matthieu. Cela n'est pas très étonnant, étant donné la proximité des deux évangiles, et le succès de l'évangile de Matthieu. Par ailleurs, le comportement du manuscrit sa 9, qui diffère selon les péricopes, amène à se demander si cette révision n'a pas été faite précisément par péricopes, plutôt que systématiquement par catégories de langage, comme je l'ai présentée.

Pourquoi existe-t-il pour l'évangile de Marc une tradition manifestement plus ancienne que pour les autres évangiles ? Je n'ai pas de réponse à cette question.

Pourquoi avoir effectué cette actualisation ? L'hypothèse qui vient à l'esprit, quand on a fait celle du traitement par péricopes, est liée à l'usage liturgique: dans sa version T1, le texte de Marc était trop discordant, donc inapte à entrer avec les autres dans un calendrier liturgique. Voici encore un exemple:

8:31 T1: ⲘⲚⲚⲤⲀϢⲞⲘⲚⲦ Ⲛ2ⲞⲞⲨ ("après trois jours").

     T2: 2ⲘⲠⲘⲈ2ϢⲞⲘⲚⲦ Ⲛ2ⲞⲞⲨ ("le troisième jour")

= Mt 16:21.

La différence n'était certainement pas anodine pour les théologiens.

Une fois harmonisé avec le texte de l'évangile de Matthieu, l'évangile de Marc était donc utilisable dans la liturgie, ce qui aurait pu se justifier par l'importance de la légende entourant le personnage de Saint Marc.

Mais rien ne permet pour le moment d'étayer cette hypothèse: d'une part l'évangile de Marc est resté, et de loin, le moins utilisé dans les lectionnaires, le moins cité en général dans la littérature copte; d'autre part, pour autant que je puisse en juger après un rapide sondage, les lectionnaires ne se rangent pas tous du côté de T2, comme on l'attendrait. Soient en effet les trois manuscrits 14L (= M615), sa 15L (= M573), et sa 338L (= B.L.Or.6801): pour les passages du premier chapitre de l'évangile, sa 15L est nettement dépendant de T1, sa 14L de T2, tandis que sa 338L occupe une position intermédiaire.

La tradition T1 est donc restée vivante, puisque non seulement elle a été recopiée au fil des siècles, mais encore elle a été utilisée dans des lectionnaires. La question posée reste alors entière. Mais avant d'éliminer l'hypothèse liturgique, il faudra procéder à un recensement complet et à une analyse précise des passages de lectionnaires et des citations.

La question de la date de T2 est également préoccupante. Mais là encore, les indices sont maigres. Aucun témoin n'est assignable avec certitude à une date plus haute que le 6° siècle, pourtant elle a très probablement été faite avant. Est-elle à mettre en relation avec un événement historique? A-t-elle été le fait d'une initiative régionale? L'enquête est bien loin d'être terminée.

NOTES

(1) H.Quecke: *Das Markusevangelium saïdisch. Text der Handschrift PPalau Rib. Inv.-Nr.182 mit den Varianten der Hanschrift M569.* Barcelone (*Papyrologica Castroctaviana*), 1972.
Compte-rendu de T. Orlandi dans *Studia Papirologica* XII, 1973, p.107-109.
(2) G.Horner: *The coptic version of the New Testament in the southern dialect.* 7 vol., Oxford, 1911-1924, réimpr. Osnabrück, 1969. L'évangile de Marc est contenu dans le volume I, tandis que le répertoire des manuscrits se trouve à la fin du volume III.
(3) A.Boud'hors: "Fragments coptes-sahidiques du Nouveau Testament à la Bibliothèque nationale de Paris", *Actes du colloque "Bible et Informatique: le texte"* (Louvain-la-Neuve, 2-4 sept. 1985), p.389-398. Cette étude avait été menée grâce à l'aide de C. Amphoux, spécialiste de critique textuelle du Nouveau Testament; les variantes de l'évangile de Marc étaient relevées dans l'édition de C.E.Legg: *Novum Testamentum graece [...]. Evangelium secundum Marcum*, Oxford, 1935. Les principaux témoins grecs du type égyptien sont les manuscrits ,B; L et Δ quand ils sont cités en même temps qu'un des deux précédents. Ceux du type palestinien sont ϑ, f1, f13, 28, 565, 700, 0188, 1071, 1424. La conclusion de l'article de 1985 est erronée sur un point: le texte de Horner ne représente pas le type le plus ancien, mais le plus récent des deux, comme on le verra ici.
(4) G.Aranda Pérez: *El evangelio de San Marcos en copto sahidico (Texto de M569 y aparato critico).* Madrid (*Textos y estudios "Cardenal Cisneros"*), 1988.
(5) F.-J.Schmitz, G.Mink: *Liste der koptischen Handschriften des Neuen Testaments. I Die sahidischen Handschriften der Evangelien.* Berlin, 1986 (1. Teil), 1989 (2. Teil, 1. Halfband), 1991 (2. Teil, 2. Halfband) = *Arbeiten zur Neutestamentlichen Textforschung* 8, 13, 15. Dans la suite de l'article, cet ouvrage sera désigné par l'abréviation:

Liste.
(6) Ce fragment n'est pas inclus dans la *Liste*. Plusieurs autres fragments d'évangiles de la collection du Louvre sont dans le même cas, comme j'ai pu m'en rendre en commençant le catalogage de ce fonds.
(7) Sur l'appartenance possible de sa 1 à la bibliothèque du monastère de Pachôme, cf. J.M.Robinson, Introduction à: *The Chester Beatty Codex AC. 1390[...]* , Leuven (Peeters), 1990 (part. p.1-8).
(8) *Concordance du Nouveau Testament sahidique. I Les mots d'origine grecque* par L.-Th.Lefort, Louvain, 1950 (*CSCO* 124 = *Subsidia* 1). *II Les mots autochtones* par M. Wilmet, Louvain, 1957-1959 (*CSCO* 173, 183, 185 = *Subsidia* 11, 13, 15).
(9) Pour le détail des variantes grecques, cf. l'édition de Legg citée à la note 3.
(10) Cette variante est attestée dans un manuscrit publié par H. Munier: "Mélanges de littérature copte II: Manuscrits coptes de Cheikh Abadéh", *Annales du Service des Antiquités de l'Egypte* 21, 1921, p.81. Il porte le sigle K3 dans l'édition de G.Aranda, mais je n'ai pas réussi à le trouver dans la *Liste*. En se reportant à la publication, on s'aperçoit que ⲘⲠⲈⲔⲘⲦ[Ⲟ .] est en fin de ligne, et qu'il y a assez de place pour restituer le texte de la lacune ainsi: ⲘⲠⲈⲔⲘⲦ[Ⲟ ⲈⲂⲞⲗ].

INFORMATISATION DES OBJETS COPTES DU LOUVRE

Jean Luc Bovot

Depuis quelques années l'informatique, surtout la micro-informatique, a transformé le travail des chercheurs en sciences humaines : aucun domaine n'échappe a cet outil puissant et commode. Les prodigieux progrès de la technologie des machines (*hardware*) comme ceux de la conception des programmes (*software*) offrent à tous les moyens de réaliser de plus en plus d'activités qui jusqu'alors auraient rebuté plus d'un savant! Une des applications classiques de l'informatique correspond à la gestion documentaire et, dès les années 1970, le ministère des Affaires Culturelles lançait une grande opération d'enregistrement des collections conservées dans les musées de France. Parmi ces bases pionniers, PHARAON[1], devait intéresser les objets du département des antiquités égyptiennes du musée du Louvre , c'est à dire 50000 environ documents intégrant les quelques 5000 monuments de la collection copte. A la fin de cette année la moitié des objets coptes auront été informatisés ; il était intéressant de signaler à l'attention des scientifiques l'existence de cette base de données, bien connue des égyptologues, dont le but final est l'enregistrement exhaustif de la collection du Louvre.

Pour comprendre le fonctionnement de cette base de données des explications techniques élémentaires seront nécessaires avant d'examiner les principes de la saisie et d'illustrer son contenu par quelques exemples récemment enregistrés.

Le matériel et le logiciel Mistral

Si la saisie des objets est réalisée au Louvre, c'est une grosse machine, un ordinateur BULL DPS 8 avec les systèmes d'exploitations GECOS et UNIX qui gère les 25 bases de données du ministère et fonctionne comme centre serveur. Du centre de calcul, où il est logé, un réseau de terminaux relie le DPS 8 aux diverses bases : des micro-ordinateurs pourvus de carte modem dialoguent avec lui par l'intermédiaire du réseau téléphonique TRANSPAC.

Le département égyptien du Louvre dispose à cet effet d'un micro-ordinateur PC compatible avec processeur INTEL 386 et carte KORTEX et d'un terminal WYSE 80 avec modem. Naturellement toutes les recherches

---

[1] Voir Sylvie Guichard "Catalogue informatisé des Antiquités Egyptiennes du Musée du Louvre", *GM* 51, 1981 ,p 63 à 73; "Informatisation des collections égyptiennes du Musée du Louvre", *Informatique et Egyptologie*, 1985, n°1, p 71 à 76; idem 1990, n°7, p 51 à 63.

peuvent être imprimées soit sur des imprimantes de bureau type DESKJET, soit sur l'imprimante du centre de calcul. Dès l'origine le choix du logiciel documentaire fût fixé : il s'agit du logiciel MISTRAL[2] qui , comme tous les programmes, a connu de nombreuses améliorations au fil des années. La version actuelle est la cinquième développée par la société CII HONEYWELL BULL!

L'écriture de la grille de saisie était réalisée sur feuille de papier (bordereau de saisie) qui était informatisé à l'extérieur. Avec le développement du logiciel MICRO-DOCUM cette étape est effectuée directement au département su Louvre sous un traitement de texte tel que WORD5 de Microsoft ou TEXTO de Logotel.

MISTRAL assure plusieurs fonctions : il sélectionne les documents correspondant à une question qui lui est posée, il trie ces documents selon les critères qu'on lui impose et il doit répondre de manière pertinente. La saisie des objets doit être réalisée sous la forme d'un découpage en champs du document dont la quantité et le contenu dépend de la nature de l'objet. Dans le cadre de la civilisation égyptienne cette nature est très contrastée mélangeant matériels funéraire et domestique, morceaux d'architecture et humbles amulettes, tissus, peintures ou statues, etc. C'est donc une cinquantaine de champs, constituant la fiche informatique de l'objet, qui furent définis afin d'englober la diversité de l'Egypte pharaonique, copte et romaine.

Ces champs peuvent être alphanumérique, numérique ou date; leur contenu peut faire l'objet d'un index. Lorsque cet index existe (il s'agit en fait d'un lexique contenant tous les termes du champ ou mots-clé et regroupés dans un thesaurus) l'interrogation de la base est directe; on parle de recherche primaire.

La grille de saisie des objets

Sur la grille l'indicatif des champs soumis à la stricte utilisation de lexiques fermés est **en gras**; les autres champs fonctionnent en langage libre mais ne peuvent être directement interrogés; ils contiennent des compléments d'informations.

REF	**Référence informatique**
INV	numéro(s) d'inventaire de l'objet
DENO	**catégorie de l'objet**
PDEN	précision sur la catégorie
TITR	titre d'usage de l'oeuvre
DESC	**description de l'objet (3 dimensions)**

---

[2] "Mistral et histoire de l'art au Ministère de la Culture", Recherche d'information, encart n°6 dans *Supplément au Communicateur*, Paris, 1984.

PDES	précision sur cette description
REPR	**description du décor des objets (2 dimensions)**
PREP	précision sur ce décor
TYPO	**typologie**
PTYP	précision sur la typologie
FORME	forme hors typologie
ETAT	**état de conservation de l'objet**
PETA	précision sur l'état de conservation
INSC	**langue ou écriture**
PINS	précision sur la langue ou l'écriture
TEXT	**contenu du texte**
PTEX	précision sur le contenu du texte
NOM	**noms propres, titres, liens de parenté**
PONO	précision sur l'onomastique
DECV	**lieu de découverte**
PDEC	précision sur la provenance géographique
EXEC	**lieu de fabrication**
PEXE	précision sur le lieu de fabrication
FNCT	**fonction de l'objet**
ASSO	objets associés
EPOQ	**datation**
SCLE	**datation en siècles**
PDAT	critère de datation
MATR	**matière principale**
PMAT	précision sur la matière
MAT2	**matières secondaires**
PMAT2	précision sur les matières secondaires
TECH	**technique principale**
PTEC	précision sur la technique
TECH2	**techniques secondaires**
PTEC2	précision sur les techniques secondaires
COUL	couleurs
DIMS	**dimensions**
PDIM	précision sur les dimensions
DACQ	**date d'acquisition**
MACQ	**mode d'acquisition**
APTN	**dernières appartenances**
LOCA	**localisation géographique de conservation de l'objet**
EDIF	**nom de l'édifice conservant l'objet**
PROP	**musée propriétaire de l'objet**
DDPT	**date des dépôts**
PADM	**commentaires administratifs**
BIB	**bibliographie**
PHOTO	**numéros des négatifs**
LABO	analyses de laboratoire

PHOTO	numéros des négatifs
LABO	analyses de laboratoire
VIDEO	indexage de l'image sur le vidéodisque ou le serveur

Examinons rapidement le contenu de la grille de saisie appliquée aux objets coptes : elle regroupe plusieurs types d'informations :

* **des données administratives** : le(s) numéro(s) d'inventaire de l'objet(INV), ses date et mode d'acquisition(MACQ & DACQ), son appartenance à diverses collections antérieures (APTN) , le lieu où il est conservé (LOCA, EDIF), sa bibliographie (BIB);

* **des données archéologiques** : sa description (DENO,DESC,REPR,TYPO), sa provenance géographique (DECV), sa datation (EPOQ,SCLE);

* **des données techniques** : son état de conservation (ETAT), sa matière (MAT), ses dimensions, techniques, couleurs (DIMS,TECH,COUL);

* **des données philologiques** : l'écriture de son inscription (INSC), le contenu du texte (TEXT) et l'onomastique (ONOM).

Nous verrons plus bas à l'aide d'exemples comment dans la pratique une fiche est remplie. Il faut cependant savoir que toute la puissance du logiciel MISTRAL , et donc de la subtilité de la recherche, réside dans sa faculté à gérer les relations sémantiques liant un ou plusieurs termes d'un ou plusieurs champs. En effet MISTRAL est capable, sur 255 niveaux, de relier des termes selon leur **synonymie** et leur **hiérarchie**.

La synonymie est une relation d'équivalence entre plusieurs termes différents mais ayant tous le même sens . Par exemple dans le camps DECV, *Akhmim = Panopolis* ou l'inverse. On peut donc poser indifféremment la question avec l'un ou l'autre terme pour que MISTRAL fasse l'équivalence dans les réponses.

La hiérarchie est une relation de niveaux liant un terme générique à ses termes spécifiques. Quinze niveaux hiérarchiques sont autorisés. Par exemple dans le champ DESC on aura,

Equipement de la tombe

- Equipement du cadavre

-- Linceul

--- Linceul peint

et à toute question sur le terme générique MISTRAL répondra en tenant compte de toutes les fiches remplies avec les termes spécifiques.

La recherche

Les recherches dans la base PHARAON se font de manière classique à l'aide des opérateurs booléens (*et, ou, sauf*) qui permettent d'affiner la question. Par exemple :

Decor architectural et *Baouit* = sélection de tous les documents qui sont des fragments architecturaux provenant de Baouît

Decor architectural ou *Element d'architecture* = sélection de tous les documents qui ont l'un ou l'autre terme ou les deux ensemble

Decor architectural sauf *Peinture murale* = sélection de tous les décors (relief mural, etc) qui ne sont pas des peintures murales

Tous ces opérateurs peuvent être combinés; par exemple :

(*Decor architectural* et *Baouit*) sauf *Peinture murale* = sélection des décors de Baouît qui ne sont pas des peintures murales.

Toutes ces questions se font au niveau primaire mais une fois la sélection obtenue il est possible de rechercher une chaîne de caractères au niveau secondaire dans cette sélection. Ainsi à la dernière question on pourrait ajouter la recherche sur PDEC (champ précision découverte) des *fouilles Cledat* pour sélectionner les objets provenant uniquement de cette campagne.

De nombreuses autres commandes, que l'on ne détaillera pas, sont encore disponibles pour permettre une recherche aussi aisée que possible. Retenons le masque, qui permet de cacher un caractère (recherche sur des noms propres à l'orthographe incertaine) et la troncature (recherche sur le début d'un terme).

Toute la qualité de la base documentaire tient dans sa disponibilité immédiate aux utilisateurs (conservateurs, chercheurs, étudiants avancés) interdisant une fiche de saisie trop complexe nécessitant de longues recherches érudites. Mais l'importance de la constitution des *thesaurii* ne saurait être négligé. Voyons comment le Louvre résout ce problème.

Les *thesaurii*

PHARAON, fondé sur un vocabulaire égyptologique dont Jean Louis de Cenival actuel chef du département égyptien est l'initiateur, possède un ensemble de lexiques largement constitué. Le principe de l'informatisation des objets coptes a été d'adopter ces lexiques en les enrichissant de termes indispensables mais en refusant de les alourdir par un trop grand nombre de termes d'usage restreint. Ce choix empêche l'inflation indéfinie des *thesaurii* !

Reprenons rapidement les divers lexiques et examinons les solutions adoptées pour chacun.

DENO (mination) : ce lexique de presque 700 termes a pour but de définir la catégorie de l'objet de manière générique

DESC(ription) & REPR (ésentation) : un même lexique de 1800 termes pour décrire les objets en volume (desc) et leur décor (repr); avec l'informatisation du catalogue des bois coptes de Marie-Hélène Rutschowscaya(RMN,Paris, 1986) ce lexique est actuellement enrichi de termes spécifiques tel que *croix pattee*, *croix latine, frette, etc.* Cependant les termes appropriés à la description d'un seul objet sont rejetés en champ commentaire (pdes et prep).

TYPO(logie) : le parti adopté dans ce lexique de 800 termes est celui de descripteur correspondant à un groupe bien défini d'objet par leur caractéristiques formelles comme dans une certaine mesure par leur datation. Par exemple : pour les lampes à huile nous pouvons avoir
les descripteurs : a^3 *la grenouille, a la grenouille stylisée, aux palmes, etc.*.
Tous les autres cas appartiennent au champ commentaire FORM(e) .

ETAT(de conservation) : environ 340 termes tel que *entier, fragment, fragments, sans partie sup, sans pied, etc* décrivent l'état actuel de l'objet précisé ensuite dans le champ PETA; par exemple : *brise, recolle, corrode,etc.*

INSC(ription), TEXT(e) & ONOM(astique) : ces trois champs et leur lexique respectif intéressent particulièrement les chercheurs! La nature documentaire de la base PHARAON et la technique informatique utilisée interdisaient l'introduction sur la fiche de tout caractère non latin. L'information donnée par ces trois lexiques est cependant suffisante pour autoriser le chercheur à déterminer un ensemble pertinent d'objets.

Le lexique INSC décrit la langue ou l'écriture utilisée; par exemple *copte* que nous pouvons préciser : *copte oncial, copte cursif...*

Le lexique TEXT définit le contenu du texte : *titre, nom, souhait, sentence,lettre,etc.* La traduction intégrale, en français, du texte est donnée dans le champ commentaire PTEX[4].

Le lexique ONOM regroupe les noms propres, les titres éventuels, les relations familiales. C'est un lexique ouvert qui grandit avec chaque nouveau texte; il compte actuellement 7200 termes surtout pharaoniques; pour le domaine copte il ne pourra s'enrichir qu'avec l'informatisation des papyri, des ostraca, etc.

DECV : un lexique de 1112 termes décrit l'Egypte du nord au sud dans le détail, et le Proche-Orient. Le champ commentaire PDEC donne obligatoirement les précisions sur la découverte, par exemple *Edfou (DECV)* implique *Fouilles IFAO (PDEC).*
Le champ EXEC renseigne sur le lieu de fabrication de l'objet si il est connu.

EPOQ(ue) & SCLE : ces deux lexiques précisent la datation de l'objet : *epoque copte (EPOQ), VIE S ap JC(SCLE)*; le critère de datation est obligatoirement donné dans le champ commentaire PDAT : *D'apres contexte fouille, D'apres style...*

MATR, MAT2, TECH,TEC2, COUL, DIMS : le matériau principal dans lequel est fabriqué l'objet est mentionné dans le champ MATR, les autres matériaux sont donnés dans le champ MAT2; la définition précise du matériau (*tamaris* pour un bois) n'est donnée que par analyse.

---

[3] Les termes ne portent aucun accent ou ponctuation dans les lexiques.
[4] Voir exemples ci-dessous.

Même principe pour les techniques de fabrication (TECH,TEC2). Le champ COUL(eur) n'a pas de thesaurus; il est purement indicatif car trop soumis à la subjectivité de l'observateur. Les dimensions (DIMS) sont toujours données en centimètres.

APTN : ce lexique résume l'histoire de l'objet avant son arrivée au Louvre; il n'est pas rempli pour les récentes acquisitions ou si le vendeur ou le donateur désire garder l'anonymat.

BIB(liographie) : il donne la bibliographie intégrale de l'objet et fonctionne en recherche primaire. A tout moment les nouvelles références peuvent être introduites dans ce champ.

Examinons quelques exemples tirés du dernier lot d'objets coptes informatisés à partir du catalogue *Bois de l'Egypte Copte* déjà cité et qui regroupe environ 550 objets.

L'AVENIR

Dés l'origine l'idée d'associer des images aux fiches documentaires a conduit le ministère à développer des projets basés sur le vidéodisque[5]. Ce support capable de fournir 54000 images de manière sûre et rapide pouvait être lié par une interface à la base PHARAON. A cet effet un champ VIDEO contient le numéro de la photographie de l'objet sur le disque; lorsqu'on appelle la fiche, l'interface va chercher la photographie. Deux expériences ont montré les limites du système : la nécessité d'avoir une couverture photographique intégrale de la collection et la difficulté de modifier le contenu du vidéodisque.

Actuellement le Louvre a adopté, expérimentalement, un autre système : les photographies sont numérisées, puis stockées sur des CD Kodak enregistrables qui alimenteront un serveur central. Autrement dit à l'appel de la fiche le serveur fournira la photographie correspondante (et inversement) par un réseau interne de fibres optiques...

L'accessibilité de la base PHARAON au grand public pourrait dans l'avenir passer par le système de communication TELETEL à la norme française fonctionnant sur le terminal MINITEL : une des bases du ministère est déjà opérationnelle et chaque usager peut si il le désire dialoguer avec l'ordinateur.

L'avenir de la base PHARAON passera par la mico-informatique : sans abandonner le système central, et compte tenu des *copyright* existant sur ce travail, une base légère dérivée peut être développée sur machines de bureau. C'est en ce sens qu'une équipe internationale organisée autour du professeur Van der Plas[6] de l'Université d'Utrecht a décidée de traduire les *thesaurii* du

---

[5] Vidéodisque de Thomson-CSF en 1982; vidéodisque *Vidéo Catalogue* du Ministère de la Culture en 1989.

[6] Dirk Van der Plas "IEDS - ein Integriertes Ägyptologisches Datenbanksystem IED - eine Internationale Ägyptologische Datenbank", *ZÄS* 119 (1992), p 38 à 43.

MISTRAL peuvent y être reversées! Mistral conserve quand même l'avantage de la hiérarchisation et de la synonymie mais ISIS, lié à un logiciel comme WINGLYPH, pourra donner les textes dans la fonte copte...

Quoiqu'il en soit PHARAON est actuellement consultée au Louvre presque quotidiennement ce qui prouve, si il fallait une preuve, la nécessité d'une base documentaire pour une collection aussi importante que celle du département égyptien du Louvre.

VOIR EXEMPLES PAGES SUIVANTES

Document n°1 : étui à kohol AF 1347

```
REF     : AE036447
INV     : AF 1347
DENO    : ETUI A KOHOL
PDES    : TUBE A 5 CAVITES CYLINDRIQUE
REPR    : BANDE (ENTRE) -LIGNE (2)
PETA    : EBRECHE
DECV    : EDFOU
PDEC    : FOUILLES IFAO 1921 1922
EPOQ    : EPOQUE COPTE
PDAT    : D'APRES STYLE-AVANT LE XE S AP JC
MATR    : BOIS
PMAT    : CORDIA
MAT2    : PLOMB
PMAT2   : SULFURE DE PLOMB DANS LA CAVITE
TECH    : TOURNAGE-INCISION
DIMS    : 9.78 H-3.8 LA-0.05 EP
MACQ    : DON FOUILLES
LOCA    : PARIS
EDIF    : PARIS MUSEE DU LOUVRE AE
PROP    : PARIS MUSEE DU LOUVRE AE
BIB     : RUTSCHOWSCAYA (CATALOGUE DES BOIS DE L'EGYPTE COPTE,1986,NO 44)
LABO    : ANALYSE
```

44

Document n°2 : étui à kohol E 17211

```
REF    : AE036445
INV    : E 17211
DENO   : ETUI A KOHOL
DESC   : AU RECTO-AMPHORE (SUR) -SUPPORT DE VASE (PIED, 4, CONTRE) -
         SOCLE (?, REGISTRE, 3) #AU VERSO-TYCHE (DEBOUT, CALATHOS, ROBE
         PLISSEE, TENANT, CORNE D'ABONDANCE, VOILE, ENTRE, COLONNE, CHAPITEAU, 2)
REPR   : FEUILLE-CHEVRONS
PETA   : CASSURES
EPOQ   : EPOQUE COPTE
SCLE   : VE S AP JC
PDAT   : D'APRES STYLE
MATR   : TAMARIS
MAT2   : PLOMB
PMAT2  : SULFURE DE PLOMB DANS LA CAVITE
TECH   : INCISION
DIMS   : 21.1 H-7 LA-5.6 EP
DACQ   : 1945
MACQ   : ACHAT
LOCA   : PARIS
EDIF   : PARIS MUSEE DU LOUVRE AE
PROP   : PARIS MUSEE DU LOUVRE AE
BIB    : L'EGYPTE EN PERIGORD (CAT., PERIGUEUX, 1991, NO 71) -RUTSCHOWSCAYA (THE
         COPTIC ENCYCLOPEDIA, T. 7, 1991, P. 2338, 2339) -RUTSCHOWSCAYA (CATALOGUE DES
         BOIS DE L'EGYPTE COPTE, 1986, NO 42) -RUTSCHOWSCAYA (LA SCULPTURE
         COPTE, 1981, P. 11) -3000 ANS DE PARFUMERIE (CAT, GRASSE, 1980, NO 29) -
         RUTSCHOVSCAYA (REVUE DU LOUVRE, 1976, 1, P. 1, 5) -? (BULLETIN DES MUSEES DE
         FRANCE, XI, 1946, I, FIG. 2)
LABO   : ANALYSE
```

42

Document n°3 : boîte à poids AF 900/AF 5153

```
REF     : AE036650
INV     : AF 900-AF 5159
DENO    : INSTRUMENT DE MESURE-BOITE A POIDS
DESC    : BOITE(ALVEOLE,10,BALANCE,POIDS)-SERRURE-
          PLATEAU(ALVEOLE,10,BALANCE,POIDS)-COUVERCLE DE BOITE-ANNEAU
PDES    : COUVERCLE COULISSANT-PLATEAU MOBILE CONSTITUANT UN SECOND NIVEAU
REPR    : BOITE-A L'EXTERIEUR#DECOR GEOMETRIQUE(LIGNE,CERCLES POINTES)#FACE SUP-
          ENTRELAC-VOLUTES(EAU)#FACE AVANT-
          PUTTO(2,AILE,TENANT,COURONNE,PORTANT,AIGLE,AILES DEPLOYEES,DANS)-
          ACANTHE(SERIE)#FACE ARRIERE-CROIX-SUR LE COUVERCLE#FACE SUP-ENTRELAC-
          CANNELURES#FACE INF-CROIX(A
          L'INTERIEUR,CHAPELLE,FRONTON,COLONNE,2,CERCLES POINTES)
FORME   : RECTANGULAIRE-FOND ARRONDI
PETA    : INCRUSTATIONS MANQUANTES
INSC    : GREC
TEXT    : TEXTE RELIGIEUX
PTEX    : A LA GRACE DE DIEU-SUR LE COUVERCLE
DECV    : ANTINOE
PDEC    : FOUILLES GAYET
EPOQ    : EPOQUE COPTE
SCLE    : VIE S AP JC-VIIE S AP JC
PDAT    : D'APRES STYLE
MATR    : BUIS
MAT2    : CUIVRE-SAULE(?)
PMAT2   : LANGUETTE EN CUIVRE SUR LE COUVERCLE-PLATEAU MOBILE EN SAULE(?)
TECH    : INCISION-INCRUSTATION
DIMS    : 27.8 LO-12.5 LA-4.36 EP
MACQ    : DON FOUILLES
APTN    : EGYPTE
LOCA    : PARIS
EDIF    : PARIS MUSEE DU LOUVRE AE
PROP    : PARIS MUSEE DU LOUVRE AE
BIB     : RUTSCHOWSCAYA(CATALOGUE DES BOIS DE L'EGYPTE COPTE,1986,NO 271)-
          RUTSCHOWSCAYA(LA SCULPTURE COPTE,PARIS,1981,P. 11)-UN SIECLE DE
          FOUILLES FRANCAISES EN EGYPTE,1880 1980(CAT,PARIS,1981,P. 301,NO 8,9)-
          RUTSCHOWSCAYA(REVUE DU LOUVRE,1979,1,P. 1,6,NO 358)
LABO    : ANALYSE
```

Document n° 4 : linteau E 16497

```
REF      : AE036937
INV      : E 16947
DENO     : LINTEAU
REPR     : PERSONNAGE (2, DEBOUT, 1, ASSIS, ENTRE) -
           DECOR (QUADRILLAGE, DANS, ENCADREMENT, FLEUR, FACE SUP) -MEANDRE (FLEUR, A
           L'INTERIEUR, FACE INF) -PERSONNAGE (?, MARCHANT, SUR LA TRANCHE DROITE) -
           SAINT MENAS (DEBOUT, ADORANT, ENTRE, DROMADAIRE, 2, ENTRE, TENTURE, 2, SUR LA
           TRANCHE GAUCHE)
PREP     : SUR LA FACE SUP LE DECOR SEPARE DEUX INSCRIPTIONS-LA FACE EXTERIEURE
           DES RETOUR D'ANGLE EST DECOREE-SUR LA TRANCHE DROITE LE PERSONNAGE EST
           PEUT ETRE MOISE RECEVANT LES TABLES   .
FORME    : POUTRE AUX EXTREMITES A ENCASTRER-DEUX ELEMENTS ANGULAIRE A TENON
PETA     : ABRASURES-ENDOMMAGE-BRISURES
INSC     : GREC
TEXT     : TEXTE DEDICATOIRE
PTEX     : APA ANOUP APA PRAWE LE PERE DE DIEU (A GAUCHE) -NOTRE BIEN AIME PERE APA
           APOLLO APA PHIB APA JEREMIE L'ECONOME (A DROITE) -LETTRES
           GRECQUES (INCRUSTATIONS EN PLOMB)
DECV     : BAQUIT
PDEC     : FOUILLES CHASSINAT CLEDAT-EGLISE SUD
EPOQ     : EPOQUE COPTE
SCLE     : VIE S AP JC
PDAT     : D'APRES CONTEXTE FOUILLES
MATR     : ACACIA
MAT2     : TAMARIS-PLOMB
PMAT2    : RETOURS D'ANGLE EN TAMARIS-INSCRIPTIONS EN PLOMB
TECH2    : ASSEMBLAGE PAR TENON ET MORTAISE-PLAQUAGE-GRAVURE-INCRUSTATION
DIMS     : 285 LO-30 LA-20 EP
DACQ     : 1902
MACQ     : DON FOUILLES
APTN     : EGYPTE
LOCA     : PARIS
EDIF     : PARIS MUSEE DU LOUVRE AE
PROP     : PARIS MUSEE DU LOUVRE AE
BIB      : RUTSCHOWSCAYA (CATALOGUE DES BOIS DE L'EGYPTE COPTE, PARIS, 1986, NO 530) -
           RUTSCHOWSCAYA (REVUE ARCHEOLOGIQUE, 1978, 2, P. 305, FIG. 10) -
           RUTSCHOWSCAYA (BIFAO, T. LXXVII, 1977, P. 185, 186, PL. XXIX, 5, PL.
           XXX, 6, 7, PL. XXXI, 8, 9)
LABO     : ANALYSE
```

IC XC
ΑΠΑ ᵨ ΑΝΟΥΠ
ΑΠΑ ᶺ ΠΡΑϢ
ΠΙϢΤΥΤ ᴨ ᴏ ᴨ ᵉ
             ОC

ΠΕ ΝϢΗΡΙΤ
ΝΙϢΤ ⲱ ΑΠΑΑ
              ΠΟΛΛ
ΑΠΑ ΦΙΒ Ϣ
ΑΠΑ ΙΕΡΕϢΙΕ
ΠΕΚΟΝΟϢΟC ᶜ

À gauche : *Apa Anoup/Apa Pra-*
we/le Père du lieu.

À droite : *Notre Bien-aimé/Père*
Apa Apollo/Apa Phib/Apa Jérémie-
/l'économe.

AN EASTER CALENDAR ON LIMESTONE

S. KENT BROWN

Introduction

When one speaks of the measurement of time among the ancients, the celestial body that predictably went through visible change on a regular basis was the moon. On the other hand, the seasons of planting and harvesting also came regularly and were tied to the sun, whose seasonal movements in the sky were less perceptible. Thus, there were two time sequences being measured by the sun and the moon; but the time measurements seemed to have nothing to do with one another. Herein lies the dilemma of ancient calendars and herein lies the dilemma facing early Christians when they attempted to determine when to celebrate their annual Easter.

Easter is the oldest Christian commemoration. In its earliest form, it was celebrated weekly on the first day of the week in honor of the resurrection of Jesus. It was the attempt to determine the appropriate annual interval for commemorating the resurrection that led to difficulties among early Christians. Differences of opinion about the timing of the annual celebration of Easter, which at times have led to serious divisions among Christians, persist to this day.

Why do I mention this predicament? It is because among the ostraca of the Coptic Museum there exists a small, inscribed limestone piece from Deir el-Bahri that apparently attempts to set out the dates that affected the celebration of Easter. I have concluded that the dates specified on this ostracon have to do with Easter because, first, they fall within the time frame during which Easter is celebrated — in the spring of the year — and, second, one finds a succession of dates that are eleven days apart, a feature that one expects to find in a calculation of annual dates that are tied to a lunar calendar whose dates are also moving against the backdrop of a solar calendar.[1] A review of the difficulties associated

---

[1] See Richard A. Parker, *The Calendars of Ancient Egypt*, Studies in Ancient Oriental Civilization No. 26 (Chicago: University of Chicago Press, 1950), pp. 1-7.

with determining the date of Easter will help us to understand some of my conclusions about the significance of the dates noted on the ostracon.

A Brief Review of the Dispute over Easter

Because Jesus was crucified and resurrected at the time of Passover, Christians who tried to determine the date for the annual celebration of Easter looked to the time of that feast. The Jewish calendar is governed by the moon. Passover was tied to the full moon of the month Nisan, with the celebration itself beginning on the fifteenth day of the month, which usually fell after the spring equinox. In this connection, it is worth noting that the Jewish calculation of Passover was rather random until the fourth-century reform of Hillel II.[2] It is also important to note that the Jewish calendar is linked to certain requirements that have nothing to do with Passover, but have to do with the beginning of the new year and with the celebration of Yom Kippur nine days later. Because of the Jewish preoccupation with the beginning of the year, rather than with a holiday that fell midway during the year, as Passover does, Christians could never be sure more than a few months in advance precisely when the Jewish Passover would occur.[3] Thus, because of possible frustrations at not knowing when Passover, and therefore Easter, were to be celebrated, it is understandable that Christians tried to base their calculations on a date tied to a regular solar manifestation, that of the spring equinox.

---

[2] There is no firm evidence that the Jewish calendar was regularized before the fourth century reform of Hillel II. From that point on, the Jewish lunar calendar became a nineteen-year cycle. See Noële M. Denis-Boulet, *The Christian Calendar* (New York: Hawthorn, 1960), p. 19, and Uta C. Merzbach, article "Calendars," in Joseph R. Strayer, editor, *Dictionary of the Middle Ages*, 13 volumes (New York: Scribner's, 1985), 3:24-25.

[3] For instance, even if the phases of the moon dictated otherwise, the day of preparation for the high holy day of the New Year was not allowed to fall on a Sabbath. The same applies to Yom Kippur, the Day of Atonement. Because it too was a high holy day, its day of preparation was not to fall on a Sabbath. To avoid the day of preparation for either of these days occurring on a Sabbath, Jewish calendar experts would delay the beginning of the new year by one day, thus adding a day to the old year, and then they would subtract one day from the following year by shortening the third month, Kislev, by one day, leaving twenty-nine instead of thirty days in that month. See Merzbach, "Calendars," *Dictionary of the Middle Ages*, 3:25-26.

Among Christians, the first serious dispute about the annual celebration of Easter occurred about 155 A.D. The persons involved were two important bishops, Polycarp of Smyrna and Anicetus of Rome. It is Eusebius who has preserved an account of this difference of opinion, a difference that persisted thereafter, even though Polycarp and Anicetus parted company with good will. Polycarp represented the view that the date of Easter was to be celebrated according to the Jewish calendar, on Nisan 14, the day of the full moon after the spring equinox. This date agreed with the date of Jesus' crucifixion as it is recorded in the gospel of John. In Polycarp's view, and in the view of Christians in Asia Minor, the annual celebration of Easter was to fall on the yearly anniversary of Jesus' death, not his resurrection. As a result, it could fall on any day of the week. As authority for his means of calculating Easter, Polycarp appealed to the memory of the apostle John who had spent his last years in Ephesus (Eusebius, *Hist. Eccl.* 5.23-24). Those Christians who followed this Easter custom came to be known as Quartodecimans, because they adhered to the fourteenth day of the lunar month Nisan.[4] In subsequent generations, Quartodecimans were regularly numbered among the heretics of the church.

For Anicetus, and for most other Christians in the second century, including those in Egypt,[5] the case was very different. In conformity with the custom in Asia Minor, Easter was to be celebrated after the spring equinox. But in contrast, Easter was to be celebrated on a Sunday, underscoring its connection with Jesus' resurrection rather than his crucifixion. Further, the Sunday of the Easter festival was to follow the first full moon after the spring equinox. For this custom, Anicetus had also apparently appealed to the authority of the apostles ("the elders") who had visited Rome, the city where he served as bishop.

The respectful difference of opinion that had characterized the discussion between Polycarp and Anicetus over this issue turned into acrimony about forty years later when Victor was bishop of Rome and Polycrates was bishop of Ephesus. Eusebius has preserved the reply of Polycrates to a letter from Victor, now lost, in which Victor had

---

[4] For a discussion of the character of the Easter dispute in the second century, see C.W. Dugmore, "A Note on the Quartodecimans," in F.L. Cross, editor, *Studia Patristica*, vol. 4, Texte und Untersuchungen 79 (Berlin: Akademie-Verlag, 1961), 411-21.

[5] Eusebius specifically mentions Alexandria (*Hist. Eccl.* 5:25).

threatened to excommunicate all those Christians in Asia Minor, and elsewhere, who would not adhere to the dating of Easter as practiced in the church at Rome. Although Eusebius does not inform us whether Victor carried out his menacing promise, we do learn that it was Irenaeus, bishop in Lyons, who tried to settle the matter amicably by urging Polycrates to adopt the Roman method of dating and by asking Victor to withdraw his threat.

Even after this unpleasant difference of opinion, regional variations among Christians persisted for centuries, variations that depended on the local calendar in use. The first attempt at a general solution to the differences in calculating the date of Easter came at the Council of Nicea. Constantine was eager to establish a basis for a uniform calculation of Easter that was independent of the Jewish calendar. However, even though the council agreed to adopt the method of reckoning used by the Alexandrians, within the next forty years the annual date of Easter differed no fewer than six times between Alexandria and Rome.

One reason for local deviations was because of differences in the accepted date of the spring equinox. In Rome the equinox had been fixed on March 18 by Hippolytus early in the third century.[6] In Alexandria at this period, the spring equinox was tied to March 21. Over the years, of course, this three-day difference in the equinox date led to serious divergences in dates for celebrating Easter. If, for instance, the full moon appeared on March 20 of a certain year, coming between these two dates established for the equinox, Easter in Rome would fall approximately one month earlier than it did in Alexandria.

In 525, two centuries after the failed Easter decision at Nicea, Dionysius Exiguus was commissioned by John I of Rome to work out a system whereby future Easters could be computed in a manner agreeable to other Christians. Dionysius' work, known as a *computus*,[7] succeeded in replacing other systems then in use, and thereafter became the norm for establishing the dates of Easter throughout the West in the Medieval

---

[6] Charles W. Jones, editor, *Bedai Opera de Temporibus* (Cambridge, MA: Medieval Academy of America, 1943), p. 12.

[7] "By ecclesiastic computus we mean the science of reckoning time by the course of the moon and the sun in order to fix the dates of Easter." Vincenzo Loi, article "Computus, Ecclesiastical," in Angelo Di Berardino, editor, *Encyclopedia of the Early Church*, 2 vols. (New York: Oxford, 1992), 1:188.

period. In his calculations he accepted the date of March 21 as the spring equinox and, on the basis of the nineteen-year lunar cycle,[8] long employed at Alexandria for such calculations, produced a ninety-six year calendar (4 X 19) that set the extremes of Easter celebration between March 22 and April 25.[9] Because of certain imprecisions between Dionysius' calculation of future equinoxes and their actual occurrence, the calendar had to be reformed several centuries later, a task performed under the direction of Pope Gregory XIII in 1582.

Ostracon no. 4554 in the Coptic Museum

With this background in mind, we move to a discussion of the ostracon in the Coptic Museum. Although the text of the ostracon is rather fragmentary, particularly on the verso where the successive annual dates are noted, one can make out the author's interest in the fourteenth day of the moon's cycle on the recto, and the series of dates on the verso that are annually to be observed. A translation of the text follows, with the equivalent Julian calendar dates set off in brackets following the dates noted on the verso as well as the years in which an extra month of thirty days was added:

Recto:

1. _____
2. fourteenth (day) of the moon makes ___
3. __ fourteenth (day) of the moon __
4. ____ it is the fourteenth (day) __
5. fourteenth (day) of the moon in order that __
6. _____ those who did not ____

---

[8] The nineteen-year lunar cycle seems to have come into Greco-Roman society from two independent sources, the Jewish reckoning of the year and the old Babylonian calendar. According to legend, the Greek savant Meton discovered the lunar cycle of nineteen years, or "golden number," in 432 B.C. See Denis-Boulet, *The Christian Calendar*, pp. 19-21.

[9] "As extreme limits of the new moons of Easter, Dionysius fixed 8 March and 18 April, so that the extreme limits of Easter became 22 March and 25 April, since Dionysius allowed Easter to be celebrated from the 15th day of the moon." Loi, "Computus, Ecclesiastical," *Encyclopedia of the Early Church*, p. 189. (Loi's second date, 18 April, is incorrect; it has to be 4 April.)

7.   _____ those who will ___

8.   _____ it is the fourteenth (day) __

Verso:

1.   _____ the house, in fact, of those who ..[

2.   [Pharmouth]i 10 is the fourteenth   { =April 5}

3.   [Pha]menōth 29   { = March 25, 11 days advance}

        — Intercalation —

4.   [Pha]rmouthi 18   { = April 13, 19 days retreat}

5.   [Pharmou]thi 7   { = April 2, 11 days advance}

        — Intercalation —

6.   [Pharmouthi] 26   { = April 21, 19 days retreat}

7.   [Pharmou]thi 15   { = April 10, 11 days advance}

8.   [Pharmou]thi 4   { = March 30, 11 days advance}

        — Intercalation —

9.   [Pharmou]thi [23]   { = April 18, 19 days retreat}

10.   [Pharmo]uthi [12]   { = April 7, 11 days advance}

11.   [Pharmou]thi [1]   { = March 27, 11 days advance}

At this point it is important to indicate what can be learned from the ostracon. On the recto the phrase "fourteenth day of the moon" appears at least five times: in the first four lines and in the last line. In addition, near the end of the recto, the scribe has written about "those who did not" and "those who will." One wonders whether the scribe had opponents in mind in the first instance and fellow believers in mind in the second instance, believers who shared his views about the proper application of the fourteenth day of the moon, that is, the full moon. In any event, obviously the scribe was chiefly preoccupied with establishing the importance of the fourteenth day of the lunar month.

On the verso one can make out a few very faint letters at the top which refer to "the house" of someone. It is not clear whether the house is associated with those who share the scribe's views or whether its inhabitants represent a different point of view. One may argue with me, of course, that I am making too much of a few partially legible phrases by seeing theological friends and opponents of the scribe. Perhaps I am creating too much from fragmentary readings. But the few phrases that can be deciphered lead me to suggest — however tentatively — that the scribe, in establishing future dates for the fourteen day of the lunar month, is doing so for a reason. And that reason can involve a couple of possibilities: first, he was facing opposition to his views or, second, he was deeply fascinated by astronomical calculations concerning the celebration of Easter. I am inclined to believe that the scribe is responding to a difference of opinion that has arisen among fellow Christians concerning the proper calculation of the full moon after the spring equinox.

On the verso, there is a series of ten dates. The first date is the tenth of the month Pharmouthi, equivalent to April 5th in the Julian calendar. Actually, this date is arrived at by making two observations. First, the last letter of the word Pharmouthi is visible, followed by the number ten. Second, one notes that the following date is clearly the 29th of Phamen-ōth, a date which is followed by a year in which there is an intercalation — or the addition of a lunar month — because the next, or third date, retreats nineteen days in the year rather than advancing eleven days. Hence, because it is the nature of lunar calendar dates to advance when compared to solar dates, one deduces that the visible number 10 that appears in the second line must belong in the month of Pharmouthi and is separated from the date that follows on line 3 by eleven days. In the Julian calendar, the first two dates represent April 5 and March 25. The third date, following the intercalation that usually occurs every three years, retreats or backs up to April 13th.[10] The dates in lines 4 and 5, Pharmouthi 18 and Pharmouthi 7, show the expected eleven-day gap. But then after a mere two years we find another intercalation which manifests itself in line 6, the 26th of Pharmouthi, representing a retreat of nineteen days.

So far, it is clear that the lunar calendar dates are being adjusted to those of a solar calendar. But it is not clear whether these dates represent Quartodeciman calculations of the exact dates on which Easter is to fall, no matter what day of the week, or whether these dates simply establish the dates of the full moon so that Orthodox Christians could plan their Easter celebrations for the Sundays that followed each date. After examining the matter closely, I have not been able to reach a definitive conclusion. However, some intriguing possibilities have

---

[10] In the Jewish calendar, after the reform of Hillel II, the intercalations took place in the 3rd, 6th, 8th, 11th, 14th, 17th and 19th years; see Merzbach, "Calendars," *Dictionary of the Middle Ages*, 3:25. For a summary of how the 19-year cycle worked, see C.W. Jones, *Bedae Opera* 31-33.

presented themselves. Before I review the evidence, I should draw attention to further specific features in the text.

It is worth observing that all of the dates fall between March 25 and April 21, conforming to the requirement that Easter follow the spring equinox. This view, of course, was common to most Christians. Furthermore, these dates fit within the time frame fixed in many regions for celebrating Easter. In Egypt, from the late third century to late in the fourth, the determination of the date of Easter followed a rule established by Anatolius of Laodicea to the effect that the equinox was calculated to be March 22nd of every year of the Julian calendar.[11] Moreover, in conformity with a tradition that went back to an earlier date than this decision, as we have seen, Easter was to fall on the first Sunday following the first full moon after the equinox (Eusebius *Hist. Eccl.* 5.23-25). The effect of these two customs was that Easter would not occur any earlier than March 23 and would not fall on a date later than April 25 or 26. Apparently, our text conforms to this requirement since no date later than April 21 appears. Moreover, the earliest date is Phamenoth 29, in line 3, the equivalent of March 25.[12]

I first attempted to place the dates within the nineteen-year lunar cycle adopted by Dionysius in the early sixth century. If one follows this approach, one reaches the conclusion that the dates written on the ostracon represent either the fourth through the thirteenth years of one cycle, or the fifteenth year of one cycle through the fifth year of the following cycle of nineteen years.[13] In these sequences of years, the intercalation or addition of an extra lunar month of thirty days[14] occurs

---

[11] Denis-Boulet, *The Christian Calendar*, pp. 44-45; Loi, "Computus, Ecclesiastical," *Encyclopedia of the Early Church*, 1:189.

[12] From the time of Theophilus of Alexandria (385-412), the equinox was set on March 21 (Jones, *Bedae Opera*, 29). The dates noted in the ostracon fall well after both dates set for the equinox.

[13] See the Easter table of Dionysian dates for Easter in James J. Bond, *Handy-Book of Rules and Tables for Verifying Dates with the Christian Era* (New York: Russell & Russell, 1966 [reprint]), p. 134.

[14] The added month is always thirty days long. See Merzbach, "Calendars," *Dictionary of the Middle Ages*, 3:22; and Jones, *Bedae Opera*, 32-33.

precisely as we see it in the ostracon and precisely as we expect in the customary nineteen-year cycle.[15]

Another characteristic of these dates is that they represent dates of the full moon. They cannot be a series of Sundays, and therefore they are not the dates of Orthodox Easter. A simple calculation illustrates this point. The first date is Pharmouthi 10, or April 5. If this day were a Sunday, and if the list of dates represented a series of Easter Sundays, then the next date, Phamenoth 29 or March 25, should also be a Sunday. But it cannot be. It would be a Thursday in a normal year, and a Friday in a leap year. If we carry this process to the next date, Pharmouthi 18 or April 13, assuming April 5 to be a Sunday, this third date would be a Wednesday in a normal year and a Thursday in a leap year. Hence, on the limestone piece we are looking at dates for the full moon, not dates for the Easter celebration itself.

There is a further characteristic worth noting. It is evident from the listing of dates on the ostracon that the author's assumed date for the spring equinox is March 22, or a day later. Further, he may not have celebrated Easter on Sundays. The key date for both of these observations is the date in line 6, Pharmouthi 26 or April 21. Let me first examine the matter of the equinox.

By the fourth century, the Jewish calendar and the generally accepted nineteen-year cycle added an extra month in their leap years during the spring of the year. This extra month was thirty days long. In the Jewish calendar, the extra month was inserted between the month of Adar, which consisted of 29 days, and the month of Nisan, which was 30 days long. Its name was Second Adar (Hebrew: *weadar*). The date noted in line 6 follows an intercalation or inserted month, which would have been added just a few weeks before. This means that both the month that was recently added and the very next lunar month, the equivalent of Nisan, in which the full moon appeared on April 21 or Pharmouthi 26, consisted of thirty days. Why is this important? It is because the full moon prior to April 21 would have been calculated to appear on March 22, thirty days earlier rather than 29, the length of the shorter lunar months. And because the equinox was also calculated to fall on March 22, that date could not be used for Easter. For Easter follows the spring equinox and

---

[15] The usual sequence of intercalations within the nineteen-year cycle is set out in Merzbach, "Calendars," *Dictionary of the Middle Ages*, 3:25; and Jones, *Bedae Opera*, 32.

is not to fall on that date. Let me offer a hypothetical example. If, for instance, the equinox date accepted by our author were March 21, then April 21 would represent the second full moon since the equinox, the first having fallen on March 22. In this hypothetical case, Easter would therefore have occurred on March 22 and not on April 21. But it did not. Hence, the date accepted by the author of the ostracon for the spring equinox was no earlier than March 22.

We should now set out the issues involved in a Sunday celebration. From the time of the Easter calendar reform by Anatolius of Laodicea in the third century, the last possible day to celebrate Easter was set at April 25. This date was held in Alexandria and was also adopted by Dionysius Exiguus in his reform almost three hundred years later. From a consideration of the dates on the ostracon, specifically that of Pharmouthi 26 or April 21 in line 6, it is possible that the author did not celebrate Easter on Sunday. Let us consider a further hypothetical case. If April 21 fell on a Monday, then Orthodox Easter could not be commemorated until the following Sunday, the 27th. On the other hand, if April 21 were to occur between Wednesday and Saturday, then Easter would fall on or before April 25, dates clearly within the limits accepted by Orthodox Christians. However, because one cannot establish which day of the week April 21 fell on, the question remains open whether the author of the ostracon was a follower of the Orthodox calendar, or whether he subscribed to that of the Quartodecimans who celebrated Easter at the full moon, no matter which day of the week.

Concerning the matter of placing the dates on the ostracon within a larger framework of time, two observations point in promising directions. First, the hand of the scribe appears to come from the fourth or fifth century, early by comparison with most other ostraca in the Coptic Museum. If in fact the scribe wrote as early as the fourth century, some of his dates match a series of full moons known from the annual Easter letters that Athanasius wrote when he was Bishop of Alexandria (A.D. 326-373). The letters in question were the four written from 329 to 332.[16] Because the date of Easter celebrated in Alexandria is also

---

[16] The source is *Patrologia Graeca*, 26:4360-76; the editors have allowed occasional mistakes to remain in the published dates. It is clear that the Julian dates are accurate when the Egyptian dates are not. A partial control is found in H. Burgess, "Letters of Athanasius," in *Select Writings and Letters of Athanasius, Bishop of Alexandria*, Archibald Robertson, editor, Nicene and Post-Nicene Fathers, series II, 14 volumes (Grand Rapids,

known for 328,[17] we have a series of five dates to compare to those listed in the ostracon. The dates of the full moons after equinox in the years 328-332 are April 10, March 30,[18] April 18, April 7, and March 27. These dates match precisely the last five recorded on the limestone piece. It is tempting to say, therefore, that the years represented on the ostracon are A.D. 323-332, both because of the correlation of dates and because paleographically the hand of the scribe may well belong to the fourth century. However, for at least two reasons such a view must be considered tentative. First, it is not clear that the basis for computing the full moon is the same for the limestone text and for Athanasius' letters.[19] Second, even if the basis for the computations could be shown to be the same, the corresponding five dates may be too few to demonstrate that the years in question are identical.

* * * * * *

In conclusion, one can say that the dates written on the ostracon are certainly tied to the celebration of Easter. Moreover, one can ascertain that the sequence of dates moves according to the annual lunar cycle,

---

MI.: Eerdmans, 1952), 4:502, 506-17 (reprint). Coptic fragments of Athanasius' letters one and two were published by L.-Th. Lefort (S. Athanase: Lettres festales et pastorales en Copte, Corpus Scriptorum Christianorum Orientalium 150 [Louvaine: L. Durbecq, 1965), pp. 1-11), but the extant remnants do not contain the segments in which Athanasius deals with the Easter dates.

[17] The date for the full moon in 328 was April 10 and the date for Easter was April 14. See H. Burgess, "Letters of Athanasius," 502; and PG 26:1351. The Egyptian dates in the published discussions, Pharmouthi 18 (PG 26:1351), or Pharmouthi 19 (Burgess, 502), would yield dates for Easter of April 11 and April 12, respectively. But these cannot be correct. The Roman date of xviii Kal. Maii (April 14) must be correct because of the dates of the full moons in following years.

[18] The published date of Pharmouthi 11 (March 31) has to be a miscalculation on the part of Athanasius' associates (PG 26:1351, 1360). The advance of the lunar calendar of eleven days from one year to the next requires a date of March 30, a fact seen by A. Robertson in his table in Burgess, "Letters of Athanasius," 502.

[19] For the same years (328-332) the Easter table of the Codex Remensis has a very different set of dates for the full moon; see Bruno Krusch, Studien zur christlich-mittelalterlichen Chronologie: Der 84Järige Ostercyclus und seine Quellen (Leipzig: Verlag von Veit & Comp., 1880), pp. 189-91.

against the backdrop of the dates of the solar calendar that are written on the piece. This aspect is illustrated not only by the eleven-day advancement of successive dates on the verso but also by the evidence of three intercalations within a period of ten years. Further, because of the appearance of Pharmouthi 26, or April 21, one concludes that the date accepted by the author for the spring equinox must have been March 22, or perhaps a day later. In addition, paleographic indicators and the correlation of dates with the Easter letters of Athanasius point to a possible composition in the first half of the fourth century. Such an early date would raise the possibility that the author shared views at home among Quartodecimans, a sect that died out not long afterwards in the early Christian church.

DIE IDENTIFIZIERUNG DES APA BANE, DES ÄLTESTEN AUTHENTISCHEN HEILIGEN ÄGYPTENS

HELMUT BUSCHHAUSEN / WOLFGANG PAHL / THOMAS PERTLWIESER

Seit 1987 ergräbt ein internationales Team aus sieben europäischen Universitäten und Institutionen unter Leitung von Helmut Buschhausen vom Institut für Byzantinistik und Neogräzistik der Universität Wien südlich der Provinzhauptstadt Minya in Mittelägypten inmitten der libyschen Wüste eines der ältesten Klöster im christlichen Ägypten namens „Abu Fano" mit der ungeheuren Ausdehnung von ca. 3 ha. Noch um 1400 berichtet der arabische Historiker al-Maqrizi (ed. F. Wüstenfeld, vol. 1, 1845, S. 41 und 101; vol. 2, 1853, S. 505), einst hätten in Abu Fano 1000 Mönche gelebt, zu seiner Zeit aber nur noch zwei. Das Kloster erlangte im späten 4. Jh. die Ausdehnung einer antiken Stadt, als die monastische Bewegung ganz Ägypten ergriff. Der Einfluß des ägyptischen Mönchtums auf das abendländische bis hin zu den Jugendjahren eines hl. Benedikt von Nursia und auf den abendländischen Bildungsstand ist ja hinlänglich bekannt.

Das Projekt Abu Fano wird getragen vom Fonds zur Förderung der Wissenschaftlichen Forschung und vom Bundesministerium für Wissenschaft und Forschung in Österreich.

An historischen Nachrichten über das Leben des Apa Bane geben uns aus der Spätantike der Anhang mit fünfzehn vita-artigen Stücken über die fünf Väter Symeon den Syrer, Bane, Daniel, Niram und Dioskoros zu der sa'idischen Version der Apophthegmata Patrum Auskunft (M. Chaine, Les manuscrit de la version copte en dialecte sahidique des Apophthegmata Patrum. Bibliothèque d'Etudes Coptes VI. Kairo 1960, Nr. 243–249, 75–77, Übersetzung 146–148). Die Stücke stammen aller Wahrscheinlichkeit nach aus einer verlorengegangenen Handschrift der Vitae et Narrationes oder Historia Monachorum in Aegypto aus dem 5. Jh., die im sa'idischen, also dem für Oberägypten maßgeblichen Dialekt verfaßt war, und unbekanntes Material von lokalen Heiligen erhalten hat und daher nicht aus den griechischen Apophthegmata Patrum übersetzt worden ist. Danach lebte Apa Bane achtzehn Jahre lang in einer völlig finsteren Zelle auf dem Berg al-Howr; er stand stets auf seinen Füßen, aß keine von Menschenhand gefertigte Speise, war fromm und von asketischer Lebensweise. Die Hochgestellten der Gegend begegneten ihm mit Ehrfurcht und Respekt; sie drangen in ihn, ihren Anteil vom Geld unter die Armen zu verteilen. Der Aufgabe unterzog sich Apa Bane so gewissenhaft, daß er durch die Städte und Dörfer Ägyptens zog und bis zu zehn Tage vom Kloster fern blieb. Er nutzte die Zeit zu strengem Fasten

durch Verweigerung von Speise und Trank. — Er befahl seinen Schülern, drei
kleine Steine aus dem Gebirge herbeizuholen, damit Gott das Eisenwunder
des Elisäus (2 Reg. 6, 5–6) an einem der Steine wiederhole (Du Chaine, Nr.
244, S. 75, Übersetzung S. 147). — Auf Befragen der Alten gibt Abraham
die Auskunft, Apa Bane könne vierzig weniger drei Tage
(Bescheidenheitstopos zu Mt. 4, 2) lang fasten und sei den Heiligen gleich-
zustellen (Nr. 245, S. 76, S. 147). — Bane meint auf Befragung des Abraham, man solle den Rat anderer einholen (Nr. 146, S. 76, S. 147). — Er sagt
einem Priester, der den Kirchendienst versah, den Tod Kaiser Theodosius
(wohl des I., † 395, weil dieser auch die Vaticinia des Johannes von Lykopolis eingeholt hatte) voraus (Nr. 247, S. 76f., S. 148). In der syrischen Version ist der Tod des Kaisers auch der bekannten Prophezeiung des Einsiedlers
in der Thebais, des sel. Johannes aus Lykopolis, angeschlossen, den Theodo-
sios I. vor den siegreichen Schlachten 388 bei Siscia und Poetovio gegen
Maximus bzw. 394 am Frigidus gegen Eugenius über den Ausgang befragt
hatte (Rufinus 11, 19 und 32. Theodoret, h. e. 5, 24, PG 82, 1251 A. —
Sozomenos, h. e. 7, 22, 3, Bidez-Hansen, GCS 50, 336, 3). — Während des
Essens stand er immer auf seinen Füßen; zum Schlaf legte er sich mit der
Brust auf eine eigens dafür errichtete, sicher sehr unbequeme Mauer (Nr. 248,
S. 77, S. 178). — Im Gespräch mit den Ältesten wertete Apa Bane die As-
kese in der finsteren Zelle höher als die Werke der Barmherzigkeit, die er in
seiner Wanderzeit vollbracht hatte (Nr. 249, S. 77, S. 148). — Eines Tages
befragten die Alten den Abraham nach dem Grund für Nr. 248. Dieser gab als
Rechtfertigung, Apa Bane könne jetzt (offensichtlich im Alter vom Geben der
Almosen befreit) mit seinen erhobenen Händen für den ganzen Erdkreis seiner
Generation den Segen Gottes herabflehen (Nr. 249, S. 77, S. 148). Aus dem
17. und 18. Jahrhundert stammen vier vitae in arabischer Sprache: 1. Paris,
Bibl. Nat., cod. arab. 153, fol. 216r–225r (G. Troupeau, Bibliothèque Nationale. Catalogue des manuscrits arabes I: Manuscrits chrétiens, Bd. 1, Nos. 1–
323, Paris 1972, 125. — G. Graf, Geschichte der christlichen arabischen Literatur. 1: Die Übersetzung (Studi e Testi 118), Città del Vaticano 1944,
533) aus dem 17. Jahrhundert, 2. eine Sammelhandschrift im koptischen Pa-
triarchat zu Kairo, Nr. 641 (= Hist. 81 [4], fol. 191r–210r (M. Simaika
Pasha, Catalogue of the Coptic and Arabic Manuscripts in the Coptic Museum, the Patriarchate, the Principal Churches of Cairo and Alexandria and
the Monasteries of Egypt II, Kairo 1942, 292), die seit längerer Zeit als ver-
loren gilt, von der aber Kamil Salih Nakhlah dankenswerterweise zuvor ein
Resumé veröffentlicht hat (Kamil Salih Nakhlah, Summary of the Life of
Saint Abu Fanah, Risalat nahdat al Kana'is 3 [1942], 16–18 und 52–54), 3.
eine Sammelhandschrift in der Kirche der Jungfrau Maria in Haret al-Rum zu

Kairo, Nr. 79, Hist. 8, fol. 61r–75r aus dem 17. bis 18. Jahrhundert und 4. aus dem Antonius-Kloster am Roten Meer die Sammelhandschrift Nr. Hist. 95 (= alte Nummer Hist. 91), fol. 18r–36v aus dem Jahr 1751 vom Schreiber Priester Hassab Alla. In Anbetracht der Grabungen in Abu Fana hat Dr. Gabra Gawdat, Direktor des Koptischen Museums in Alt-Kairo, die beiden letzten Vitae ediert (Gawdat Gabra, Zur Vita des Bane [Abu Fana], eines Heiligen des 4./5. Jahrhunderts, BSAC 29 [1990], 26–42). Die Übereinstimmungen zwischen den Apophthegmata Patrum und den Vitae sind trotz des zeitlichen Abstandes so evident, daß eine gemeinsame Vorlage aus dem 4. bis 5. Jahrhundert, also unmittelbar nach dem Tod des Apa Bane, anzunehmen ist, die nicht aus den griechischen Apophthegmata stammt. Wir müssen also annehmen, daß der koptische Urtext über Bane in jenem Gebiet entstand, wo er sein Leben als berühmter Mönch verbrachte, nämlich in Oberägypten. Der Umfang des Urtextes läßt sich nicht rekonstruieren; um die Vita enkomiastisch zu steigern, wurden Begebenheiten aus dem Leben anderer Wüstenväter auf Apa Bane übertragen. Die beiden Vitae paraphrasieren die fraglichen Texte in den Apophthegmata Patrum. Es seien daher nur wenige Punkte aus den späten Viten ausgewählt. Demnach stammt Apa Bane aus sehr begütertem Haus in Memphis und ist dann in das Kloster in der Nähe der antiken Stadt Busiris im Hermopolites eingetreten. Man möchte annehmen, daß er sein reiches Erbe in das Kloster eingebracht hat. — Die Gebete unter ausgebreiteter Hand bezogen sich auf Wasser. Altorientalische Vorstellungen vom Gebet des Heiligen um Wasser mögen hier hereingespielt haben. Nach dem Tod am 25. Emschir um 6 Uhr morgens wurde der Heilige in kostbares Linnen gehüllt und aufgebahrt. An seinem Grab ereigneten sich Wunder. Das Datum des Todes findet sich nicht in den Apophthegmata Patrum und dürfte auch nicht mit der spätantiken Tradition übereinstimmen; denn in einem Papyrus unbekannter Herkunft zu Gießen aus dem 6. bis 7. Jahrhundert, P.Iand. Inv.-Nr. 318, wird als Festtag des Heiligen der 10./11. Dezember angegeben. Das Fragment zu Gießen ist ein Kalender für die Angabe des Todesdatums, an dem die Agape gefeiert werden soll (P. J. Sijpesteijn, K. A. Worp, Einige Papyri aus den Giessener Papyrussammlungen VI, Aegyptus 67 [1987], 69f., Nr. 61, Z. 1, Taf. 12. — J. Gascou, Un nouveau Calendrier de Saints Egyptien (P.Iand. Inv. 318), Analecta Bollandiana 107 [1989], 384–391, dort 389). Das Datum stimmt nicht mit dem Todesdatum des Apa Bane in dessen arabischen Vitae überein. Darüberhinaus wird Abu Fana in zahlreichen, vornehmlich hagiographischen Quellen genannt. Herr Dr. Hermann Harrauer, Wien, macht auf den Papyrus graecus Nr. 26252 vom 11. Oktober 553 n. Chr. der Österreichischen Nationalbibliothek aufmerksam, in welchem bereits ein „Banos" gut bezeugt wird (H. Gerstinger, Byzantinische Urkunden in

Briefen, in: Symbolae Raphaeli Taubenschlag dedicatae, Vratislawa –
Varscava 1965 = Eos 48 [1956], 206ff.), das offensichtlich zum Kloster Abu
Fana gehört hat. Der Ort wird 716 erneut genannt im Papyrus London 4419,
697.

Aus der Spätantike erhaltengeblieben ist die mächtige Memorialkirche
aus der Zeit um 500 von der Größe der Katherinenkirche im Sinaikloster: drei
Schiffe, ein zusätzliches Westschiff, sechs Joche, geschlossene Westwand mit
Kreuzdarstellungen, Satteldach, unregelmäßiger Trikonchos über einer Kuppel
im Osten. Der Bau wurde 1706 durch P. Sicard (Nouveaux Mémoires des
Missions de la Compagnie de Jésus dans le Levant II, Paris 1717, 256–260
(wir verdanken eine Kopie des Textes Herrn Professor Dr. Dr. Martin Krause,
Münster, der sie nach der Handschrift Tq 800 der Herzog Anton Bibliothek
Wolfenbüttel für uns hergestellt hat) erstmals beschrieben. Vor 1721 aber ist
er eingestürzt und wurde von E. F. Jomard in dem veränderten Zustand beschrieben und in Skizzen festgehalten (Description de l'Egypte ou recueil des
observations et des recherches qui été faites en Egypte pendant l'expedition de
l'Armées Francaise, 2. ed. publiée par C. L. F. Panckoucke, Paris 1821,
Kap. IX, 327–329, Antiquités-Description, Taf. 67. — U. Monneret de
Villard, Les Couvents près de Sohag [Deyr el-Abiad et Deyr el Ahmar] I,
Mailand 1925, 62, Nr. 2 und Abb. 95). Man hatte die sechs Joche durch eine
mächtige Querwand in eine Kirche im Osten und einen Vorhof für die Brun-
nenanlage im Westen des ehemaligen Langhauses unterteilt. Die Kirche
wurde im 12. Jh. mit bedeutenden Wandmalereien ausgestattet: ein monu-
mentales Kreuz in der Hauptapsis und, 1992 freigelegt, eine Hetoimasia in
der Südapsis, welche auf Wandmalereien in einer spätantiken Einsiedelei im
Osten des Klosterbereichs zurückgreift; die Wiederbelebung der Antike hat
sich also in Abu Fano selbst orientiert. Im Norden schließt sich an den Hügel
mit der Memorialkirche die mächtige Klosteranlage an; sie besteht aus zwei
Teilen: im Süden sind in dem rektangulären System des Klosters in Bawit
Baulichkeiten des liturgischen Bereichs und Wohnteile aneinandergereiht,
während im Norden ein Netz aus horizontalen und vertikalen Straßenzügen
mit Innenhof, Zeilen von Einsiedeleien die Anlage in insulae aufgliedert. Im
Osten stehen zahlreiche isolierte Einsiedeleien, von denen die meisten vollständig ausgemalt sind.

Im Nordteil wurden die wichtigsten Bauten bereits ergraben. Die Grabeskirche des Apa Bane (Abb. 1) von 12,80 × 28m an Ausdehnung mit drei
Schiffen, zusätzlichem Westschiff, sechs Jochen, von Annexräumen einge-
schlossener Westapsis und einem dreiteiligen Narthex mit zentralem Treppen-
aufgang zum flach gedeckten Westschiff zur Betätigung des Semantron (H.
Buschhausen, J. Albani, M. Schwarz, Die Ausgrabungen in Abu Fana in

Ägypten im Jahr 1988, JÖB 39 [1989], 258). Nach einem Umbau schloß sich im Süden an die Grabeskirche ein gewaltiger Saal von 10,50 × 29m an mit zentralem Brunnen und ungewöhnlich vielen Bänken, die offensichtlich den Agapefeiern dienten; Kirche und größter Agaperaum der Antike sind einheitlich mit Wandmalereien geschmückt. Weiter östlich liegt die Trapeza der Mönche und weiter westlich eine der ältesten Anlagen Ägyptens zur Gewinnung von Zucker aus Zuckerrohr. Ungewöhnlich viele Münzen als Streufunde aus der Zeit zwischen 340 und 425 datieren die Klosteranlage in die spätkonstantinische und theodosianische Zeit. Die Bearbeitung der Münzen hat G. Demsky vorgenommen. Der frühchristliche Gräberbezirk erstreckte sich im Westen der Klosteranlage bis weit in die Wüste hinein: er ist bis heute mit Gräbern der Kopten belegt, deren Grabesruhe aber nicht gestört werden darf. Das Kloster erstreckte sich einst unter die heutige Friedhofsanlage, jedoch können die Mauerzüge nicht weiter verfolgt werden.

Der nördliche Teil der Klosteranlage wird von einer etwa 20m hohen Sanddüne bedeckt, welche sich wohl nur mit großem Aufwand entfernen läßt; jenseits der Sanddüne finden sich Siedlungsspuren, so daß anzunehmen ist, daß die Anlage bis hierher gereicht hat (Ausgrabungen 1989, S. 259).

Die genannte Grabeskirche (Abb. 1) des Apa Bane und der Mönche ist über einem wesentlich kleineren, wahrscheinlich einschiffigen Vorgängerbau mit halbrunder Apsis errichtet worden, auf dessen Fundamenten der Außenmauern die Basen für den zweiten, sogenannten Pavimentbau errichtet wurden. Der westliche Abschluß des Vorgängerbaus ist noch nicht ergraben worden. Die Kirche stand nicht mit dem Agaperaum in Verbindung (H. Buschhausen, J. Albani, A. Dostal, H. Harrauer, U. Horak, M. Khorshid, B. Mencarelli, H. Plach, Die Ausgrabungen von Dair Abu Fana in Oberägypten im Jahr 1989, Ägypten und die Levante 2 [1991], 132ff., Taf. 1–4). Im Bereich des Pavimentbaus wurden 15 Gräber gefunden, von denen vier pagane waren und in nordsüdlicher Richtung ausgerichtet sind (1/91, 2/92, 6/92 und 11/92). Auch für die Anlage des Grabes des hl. Kafka (1/90 = A/9) hat man ein paganes Frauenskelett durchstoßen (Ausgrabungen 1989, Abb. 8–9). Offensichtlich war die Grabeskirche des Apa Bane über einem antiken Friedhof errichtet, und es stellt sich die Frage, ob der nördliche Teil der Anlage jene antike Stadt Busiris = Abusir gewesen ist, an dessen Südrand in einem solchen Fall die Klosteranlage errichtet worden ist. Nach Beisetzung des Apa Bane ist der Vorgängerbau sicherlich infolge der Wunder am Grab des Heiligen durch den wesentlich größeren Pavimentbau ersetzt worden, welcher unmittelbar darauf zusammen mit dem Agapesaal (Ausgrabungen 1989, Taf. 1–3, 8–9) vollständig ausgemalt worden ist. Von den Malereien haben sich erhebliche Teile erhalten (Ausgrabungen 1988, Abb. 7–9). Das Paviment ist in zwei Phasen verlegt worden, einen älteren westlichen Teil bis zum Ende des 4. Jochs und einen neueren westlichen Teil im 5. und 6. Joch. Im Paviment fanden sich die ältesten koptischen Votivtafeln mit den Namen Apa Kafka (1/1990 = A/3), Apa Herakleides (2/1990) und Apa Schontz (A/2) (Ausgrabungen 1988, Abb. 10–12). Die beiden Gräber unter den Tafeln des Apa Kafka und des Apa Schontz sind nach Verlegung des Pavimentes angelegt worden: Nach Hebung einiger Pavimentplatten wurde ein schmaler Schacht angelegt, in dessen schuhförmige Erweiterung am Ende die Mumie hineingeschoben worden ist.

Im Paviment des neueren Teils fand sich auf der Rückseite einer Platte die Vorzeichnung zur verworfenen Votivtafel des Apa Schontz; das Grab dürfte also vor Errichtung des Paviments bereits bestanden haben. Gleiches gilt auch für das Grab des Apa Herakleides (2/1990), dessen Votivtafel eigenartig weit vom Grab entfernt liegt. Insgesamt wurden 12 neue Gräber gefunden, 8/92 und 7/92 sind mit einer Erstreckung von nur 1m aber für eine Grablege eigentlich zu kurz. Einige der Gräber waren ausgeraubt. Im Grab A/1 fand sich ein theodosianisches Kugelgefäß aus Glas mit geschliffenen Bildern; es ist wesentlich älter als die einzigen Vergleiche aus Gerasa, heute Amman und in Washington/Dumbarton Oaks Collection. Als einer der wesentlichsten Funde der ganzen Grabung wurde 1992 das Grab des Apa Bane gehoben, der 1,70m groß war (Abb. 2) (3/1992).

Es lag genau in der Mitte des Schiffes der Grabeskirche und war von einem Grabmonument aus Ziegeln im Mörtel (Abb. 3) überbaut, welches anläßlich der Verlegung des Pavimentes bis auf das Fundament entfernt worden ist. Die unter dem Fundament gefundene Münze läßt sich leider nur allgemein ins 4.–5. Jh. datieren. Apa Bane ist in einem einfachen Schachtgrab beigesetzt, welches sich von den späteren Grablegen insofern unterscheidet, als es auf ein bereits bestehendes Paviment keine Rücksicht zu nehmen hatte. Der Heilige war gleich einer Mumie mit kostbarem Linnen bandagiert, das jedoch stärkerer Konsistenz war als die Bandagierungen der übrigen Mumien. Zudem war ein Teil des Gewandes purpurn gefärbt, womit das kostbare Linnen gemeint sein dürfte, von dem die Viten anläßlich der Aufbahrung berichten. Der Heilige war mit ungewöhnlich großen Mengen an Weihrauch vornehmlich auf Höhe der Beine ausgestattet (Abb. 4). Die Bandagierung hatte im Bereich des Kopfes die Gestalt einer Haube, ähnlich denen der heutigen koptischen Würdenträger. Die Untersuchungen des Skeletts haben aber schließlich eine Identifizierung des Heiligen ermöglicht.

Der Fund der balsamierten Mumie, die leider nicht mehr mit pharaonischen Einbalsamierungstechniken präpariert worden war und daher bei Luftzutritt sofort verfiel, konnte nicht gerettet werden. Nach anthropologischer und paläomedizinischer Untersuchung des Skeletts konnten an der Wirbelsäule krankhafte Veränderungen im Sinne der Bechterev'schen Krankheit festgestellt werden, die ein Schwinden der Bandscheiben und ein Aneinanderwachsen der Wirbel bezeichnet (Abb. 5–6).

Deutlich erkennbar im Mumienfund von Abu Fano ist die Spangenbildung, welche die separaten Wirbelknochen miteinander verbindet und dadurch die Beweglichkeit des erkrankten Menschen stark beeinträchtigt bis hin zur völligen Versteifung des Rückgrates. Außerdem konnte ein außergewöhnlich stark entwickelter Muskelapparat wie der von einem Athleten nachgewiesen werden, der sicher die fehlende Beweglichkeit der Wirbelsäule auszugleichen hatte.

Deutlich zu erkennen war das dorsalwärts arthritisch veränderte Hinterhauptloch. Die Versteifung des Rückgrats von Apa Bane war so weit vorgeschritten, daß er sich, einmal zu Fall gekommen, nicht mehr aus eigener Kraft hätte erheben können. Hierdurch lassen sich Eigentümlichkeiten aus der Lebensbeschreibung des Heiligen erklären, welche bereits im 5. Jh. kurz nach dessen Tod verfaßt worden ist und daher authentisch berichtet.

Apa Bane verbrachte 18 Jahre seines Lebens bis zu seinem Tod in einer völlig finsteren Höhle beständig auf seinen Füßen stehend; er nahm auch die Mahlzeiten stehend zu sich und lehnte sich zum Schlaf über eine eigens dazu errichtete Mauer. Arabischsprachige Lebensbeschreibungen aus späterer Zeit malen diesen Zustand realistisch aus; die Füße des Heiligen seien infolge des Stehens ledern wie die von einem Elephanten geworden.

Die Bechterev'sche Krankheit hat im Volksmund den Namen Palmenkrankheit, weil neben der gekrümmt steifen Verwachsung der Wirbelsäule auch ein Versteifen der Wirbelsäule in gerader und unbeweglicher Haltung des Kranken erfolgen kann, der sich dann aufrecht halten muß wie ein Palmstamm, wobei die so miteinander verwachsenen Wirbel an den Nahtstellen Ringe bilden wie der Stamm mancher Palmen.

Es ist möglich, daß der Heilige erst in der Gegend aufgrund seines äußeren Erscheinungsbildes den Namen „Palme" — im oberägyptischen Dialekt der Gegend heißt Palme „Bane" — als Beinamen erhalten hat.

Ergebnisse der paläopathologischen Untersuchung der Mumie: Keine Auffälligkeiten am Integument. Keine Knochenfrakturen. Hingegen zeigen sich neben einem desolaten Zahnbefund gravierende Veränderungen am postkranialen Skelett, vereinzelt auch am Schädel. Zu ihnen zählen sklerotischer Umbau im Bereich des Foramen occipitale magnum, ein kyphotische Fehlstellung der BWS, eine fortgeschrittene Ankylosierung der Wirbelsäule dorsolumbal, massive Rückenzackenbildung, d. h. flächenhafte osteophytäre Brückenbildung an den Vorder- und Seitenkanten (bevorzugt ventrolateral rechts), unregelmäßig verteilt über die gesamte Wirbelsäule. Eine Ankylosierung der Iliosakralfugen fehlt, geringgradige Deckplatteneinbrüche an den Wirbelkörpern der BWS, Befall der kleinen Wirbelgelenke (Knochenproduktion/partielle Versteifung). Angedeutet ist ein Wachstum der Syndesmophyten entlang der Wirbelsäulen-Längsachse. Keine Keilwirbel, keine Sinterung.

Differentialdiagnostisch infrage kommen:

a. eine ankylosierende **Spondylosis deformans**

b. eine chronische Entzündung im Sinne einer Spondylitis ankylopetica (Spondylitis ankylosans), sog. **Morbus Bechterew.**

Erste ist vor allem eine Erkrankung des höheren Lebensalters, die mit Bewegungseinschränkungen und Schmerzzuständen einhergeht.

Der **Morbus Bechterew** zeigt seinen Beginn gewöhnlich im ausgehenden 2. Lebensjahrzehnt, wobei Männer im Verhältnis 10:1 signifikant häufiger befallen sind als Frauen. Im jahrelangen Prodromalstadium werden rezidivierende Rücken- und Kreuzschmerzen angegeben. Gelegentlich wird über eine Periostreizung im Sternalbereich, am Fersenbein, am Sitzbein, der Tuberositas tibiae etc. geklagt. Im späteren Stadium kommen periostale Knochenauswüchse an den Darmbeinstacheln, den Sitzbeinästen sowie an anderen Stellen des Skeletts vor. Nach und nach entwickelt sich eine Kyphosierung der Wirbelsäule. Als Endstadium gilt die Verschmelzung der Wirbelkörper in der Art eines Bambusstabes („**Bambusstab-WS**") (Abb. 5–6).

Diagnose: Anhand der eruierten Daten läßt sich eine definitive Diagnose nicht stellen, doch weisen u. E. die Mehrzahl der erhobenen Befunde eher auf die Bechterewsche Erkrankung als auf eine altersbedingte Spondylosis deformans hin. Tuberkulöse Ätiologie des Geschehens ist auszuschließen.

Interpretation: Der paläopathologische Befund am Einbalsamierten aus Abu Fana und Aussagen der Pariser Vita des Apa Bane zeigen einige auffällige Parallelen. Sie betreffen im wesentlichen die „Stehposition" sowie die „Ruhelage" des Bane. Möglicherweise war damit eine spürbare Entlastung des Bewegungsapparates verbunden. Beachtet man dazu noch die Dauer dieser Positionierung (die letzten 18 Lebensjahre), so muß davon ausgegangen werden, daß initiale Symptome der möglichen Krankheit bereits — ausgehend vom berechneten Sterbealter — zu Beginn des 2. Lebensjahrzehnts aufgetreten sind. Bemerkenswert sind im Zusammenhang mit der Erkrankung auch die ausgeprägten Knochensporne und extrem ausgebildete Muskelmarken, bevorzugt im Bereich der Extremitäten.

Hier könnte man beinahe auf eine hochleistungstrainierte Muskulatur schließen. Da eine entsprechende Betätigung eher ausgeschlossen werden kann, bliebe hier neben der Ausdeutung als anatomisch-anthropologische

Normvariante am ehesten der Schluß, daß die jahrelange verkrampfte Stehhaltung des Apa Bane entsprechende Veränderungen am Skelett ausgelöst haben könnte. Im übrigen stellen Knochenauswüchse auch einen Begleitbefund des Morbus Bechterew dar.

Die Chronologie des Klosters läßt sich somit außerordentlich genau bestimmen. Aufgrund des Skelettbefundes ist der Heilige 40 Jahre alt geworden, 18 Jahre lang hat er in der stockfinsteren Zelle gelebt. Der Vorgängerbau ist aufgrund der Münzen gegen 375 bis 380 errichtet worden, möglicherweise als Grablege des Heiligen. Dieser hatte 395 das Vaticinium auf den Tod des Kaisers Theodosius I. und dürfte kurz darauf ebenfalls verstorben sein. Er ist demnach kurz nach 355 geboren worden und dürfte gegen 376 im Alter von 22 Jahren von der Bechterev'schen Krankheit befallen worden sein.

Seine anfänglichen monastischen Bemühungen, das Verteilen von Almosen, möglicherweise und ganz im christlichen Sinne aus dem elterlichen Erbe, dürften ihn aber nicht zu jenem besonderen Heiligen mit einem Leib, welcher dem der Engel glich, gemacht haben. Hierzu bedurfte es des Außerordentlichen, eben seiner spezifischen Erscheinung. Diese war im Grunde bedingt durch seine Erkrankung, wurde aber im asketischen Sinne umgedeutet.

Um den pneumatischen Leib zu erhalten, mußte er besondere christliche Askese üben und besondere Momente haben, die ihm durch seine Erkrankung vorgegeben waren, die er aber rein christlich gedeutet hat. Seine stocksteife Erscheinung dürfte ihm den Beinamen „Palme" eingebracht haben, und zwar immerhin einige Jahrzehnte vor dem ältesten überlieferten Styliten Symeon d. Ä.. Es stellt sich daher die Frage, ob wirklich die paganen Phallusbesteiger von Hierapolis das einzige Vorbild für die Styliten waren und nicht eher der ebenfalls gleich einer Säule oder einer Palme stocksteif erscheinende Apa Bane.

Die Möglichkeit, einen Heiligen durch Übereinstimmung des Knochenbefundes nach anthropologischer und paläomedizinischer Untersuchung mit der ältesten Lebensbeschreibung identifizieren zu können, hat es bisher in Ägypten nicht gegeben. Erstaunlich ist der außerordentlich frühe Zeitansatz in die 2. Hälfte des 4. Jh. Somit dürfen die Kopten in diesen Gebeinen mit Recht den ältesten völlig erhaltenen, in seinem Grab geborgenen und authentisch identifizierten Heiligen Ägyptens verehren. Es versteht sich von selbst, daß seine Auffindung als einer wichtigsten Funde des spätantiken Ägyptens gewertet werden muß.

Das Kloster dürfte noch vor der islamischen Eroberung Ägyptens zugrundegegangen sein, vielleicht aufgrund klimatischer Veränderungen, oder näherliegend aufgrund einer Seuche, die eine nachweisbare Dezimierung der Mönche zur Folge hatte. Hierfür käme die große Pest von 540 infrage zusammen mit den darauf folgenden verschiedenen Schüben der Seuche.

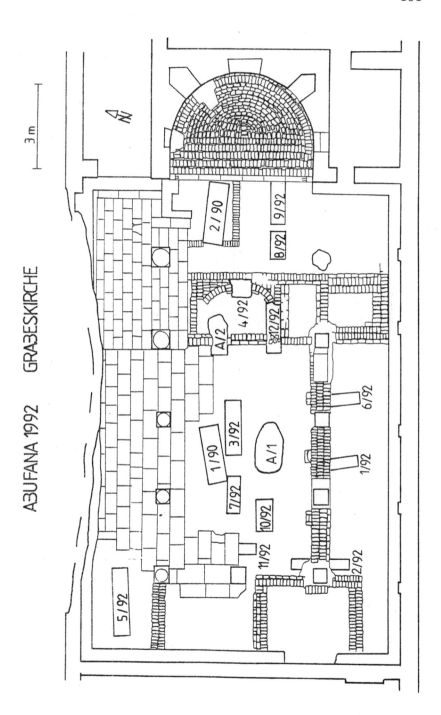

ABUFANA 1992   GRABESKIRCHE

Abb. 2

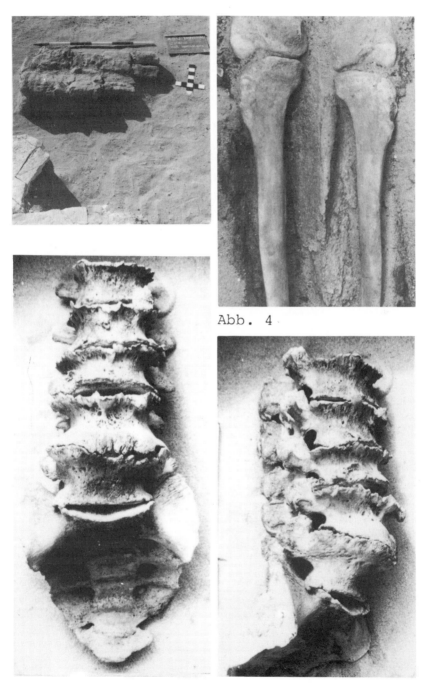

Abb. 4

Abb. 5   Abb. 6

SULL'ORIGINE DELLA QUARESIMA IN EGITTO[*]

ALBERTO CAMPLANI

1. *Introduzione alla questione delle origini della Quaresima*

Lo studio dell'istituto quaresimale in Egitto investe la storia più generale di questa prassi liturgica nell'intero mondo cristiano. Dal momento che le due uniche menzioni del termine *Quadragesima / Tessarakostê* fino al concilio di Nicea, occorrenti rispettivamente nell'*Omelia sul Levitico* X, 2 di Origene, che conosciamo nella traduzione latina di Rufino, e nel quinto canone di Nicea, risultano sospette, la prima potendosi spiegare come un'aggiunta rufiniana, la seconda essendo riferibile all'Ascensione, celebrata quaranta giorni dopo la Pasqua (SALAVILLE 1910; PERI 1960; 1961), le sue prime attestazioni sicure, immediatamente dopo il Concilio, occorrono nel *De sollemnitate paschali 4-5* di Eusebio di Cesarea (PG 24, 697) e nella lettera festale che Atanasio invia per la Pasqua del 334, durante il sesto anno di episcopato (CURETON 1848 p. 6 [cifra in siriaco]). Di conseguenza, la Palestina e l'Egitto sembrano aver giuocato un ruolo non indifferente nella storia della Quaresima.

Ritengo di aver dimostrato che la cronologia reale delle lettere festali atanasiane, diversa da quella presupposta dalle raccolte siriaca e copta che le trasmettono, non permette di affermare che la Quaresima sia stata importata in Egitto da Roma, secondo una vecchia convinzione (DUCHESNE 1920 p. 255 ss.), né che sia stata introdotta gradualmente (LEFORT 1953, seguìto da COQUIN 1967a; cfr. CAMPLANI 1989 pp. 159-189). Le lettere dal 329 al 333 non contengono l'annuncio della data di inizio della Quaresima, anche se possibilmente vi è qualche velata allusione ad essa, mentre dal 334 in poi l'annuncio è presente in maniera continuativa. Tale dato è corroborato dal fatto che esso è assente nella lettera festale che Pietro di Alessandria redige per la Pasqua del 309 (RICHARD 1973 p. 267; RICHARD 1974.).

[*] Il testo del presente contributo è la rielaborazione di quello letto al Congresso. Ringrazio H. Brakmann per i suoi utili suggerimenti e T. Orlandi per aver ancora una volta guidato il mio accesso all'archivio fotografico del CMCL. L'interesse per la Quaresima in Egitto è nato in relazione al progetto di edizione delle versioni siriaca e copta delle lettere festali atanasiane e di alcune lettere festali del V-VI secolo, cui sto attualmente lavorando. I riferimenti bibliografici sono abbreviati: si rimanda il lettore alla lista bibliografica posta alla fine del contributo.

Dunque il 334 segna l'anno di svolta che lo storico può interpretare in due modi completamente diversi: Atanasio introduce in quell'anno un costume fino ad allora sconosciuto in Egitto; oppure un costume preesistente riceve la sua ufficializzazione. Quest'ultima ipotesi sembra la più fruttuosa, in quanto non mancano testimonianze, la cui validità deve essere vagliata criticamente, circa la preistoria della Quaresima in Egitto. Al di là di queste, sembra in ogni caso lecito supporre che il Concilio di Nicea abbia costituito un momento di confronto per diverse tradizioni liturgiche. Se la questione della data pasquale è stata al centro degli interessi del Concilio (DAUNOY 1925), lo stesso non può dirsi per la Quaresima, a stare alle notizie dei contemporanei, le modalità della cui pratica risultano estremamente differenziate nelle diverse regioni per tutto il quarto e il quinto secolo (è nota la testimonianza di Socrate in *Historia Ecclesiastica* V, 22, PG 67, 632-633), cosa inspiegabile se il Concilio avesse emanato disposizioni in merito (come proposto in maniera dubitativa da COQUIN 1967b): tuttavia l'incontro di tanti responsabili della vita comunitaria può aver favorito il diffondersi del costume quaresimale nelle regioni in cui non era conosciuto, il suo rafforzarsi laddove esisteva, divenendo oggetto dell'azione pastorale dei vescovi. Il moltiplicarsi improvviso delle testimonianze circa la sua esistenza a partire dagli anni '30 del IV secolo, poco dopo il Concilio, e la loro quasi totale assenza prima di questo, sono dati in armonia con tale ipotesi.

2. *Una Quaresima prima di Nicea ?*

L'unica caratteristica ritenuta dalla maggioranza delle fonti che parlano della Quaresima consiste nel fatto che essa è concepita come periodo di digiuno prepasquale, come tempo della purificazione e dell'ascesi in vista della Pasqua.

E' merito di R.-G. Coquin quello di aver raccolto una serie di notizie offerte da autori tardi, dal IX al XIV secolo, in particolare Pseudo-Giorgio di Arbela (COQUIN 1967b p. 180), Eutiche, patriarca melchita di Alessandria nel X secolo, Girgis b. 'Amid al-Makin, Abu al-Barakat (COQUIN 1967a pp. 140-144; TALLEY 1991 p. 229 n. 71), nelle quali si disegna l'assetto, supposto come originario, del tempo liturgico a partire dall'Epifania, festa del battesimo di Gesù: anticamente la Quaresima sarebbe stata osservata a partire dal giorno successivo all'Epifania, in cosciente imitazione di Cristo, mentre la settimana di Pasqua sarebbe stata celebrata separatamente, in una data che non coincidesse con quella della Pasqua giudaica; solo in un secondo momento sarebbe avvenuta la sua congiunzione con la settimana di Pasqua. Coquin ha ipotizzato, in base a qualche riscontro più antico, che tale notizia possa avere qualche fondamento.

Quella che era una teoria formulata con una certa prudenza è diventata affermazione corrente anche a livello manualistico (VIAUD 1978 p. 43; DU BOURGUET 1988 p. 45; BRADSHOW 1988 pp. 5-6; cfr. invece AUF DER MAUR 1983). Recentemente essa ha subìto una rielaborazione affascinante per opera di Talley, che con il suo volume *The Origins of the Liturgical Year* ha voluto dimostrare come questo assetto dell'anno liturgico, giudicato originario, abbia non solo avuto un ruolo determinante sulla tradizione alessandrina più tarda, ma si sia riflesso anche in alcuni aspetti della liturgia di Costantinopoli e di Gerusalemme (TALLEY 1991 pp. 163-223). Di fronte a questa ricostruzione storica la domanda che si deve porre il coptologo o lo studioso di liturgia è, a mio vedere, la seguente: tale ricostruzione è basata su un insieme di dati sufficientemente ampio e di qualità non sospetta? esiste la possibilità di proporre un'alternativa?

Le seguenti note hanno lo scopo di presentare alcune riflessioni preliminari sui dati della questione e non pretendono di prospettare soluzioni definitive. Ciò in parte è dovuto alla contraddittorietà delle fonti, in parte al fatto, non certo secondario, che un consistente numero di documenti deve ancora essere indagato a fondo: le lettere festali emanate dai patriarchi fino in epoca araba inoltrata; i testi letterarii che in molti casi alludono ai costumi liturgici in corso; i papiri documentari; i manoscritti liturgici. Se ho potuto prendere visione delle lettere festali oggi conosciute, edite o inedite, sui testi letterari restano da compiere approfondite letture; la documentazione papirologica e i manoscritti liturgici sono stati oggetto soltanto di qualche sondaggio, i cui risultati sono tuttavia incoraggianti (su questi ultimi cfr. ZANETTI 1985 pp. 14-21). Confessati i limiti della documentazione consultata, non resta che passare all'esposizione della teoria di Talley (che, è necessario ricordarlo, è stata preceduta dagli studi più parziali di VILLECOURT 1922; 1923b; 1923; 1924; 1925; e di COQUIN 1967a; 1967b), e alla sua valutazione critica.

3. *Base documentaria della teoria della Quaresima postepifanica*

L'ipotesi si basa sostanzialmente sulle seguenti testimonianze:

1) Gli autori sopra menzionati che, a partire dal X secolo, concordemente parlano di una Quaresima di quaranta giorni iniziante il giorno successivo all'Epifania. Particolare importanza assumono le osservazioni di Abu 'l-Barakat contenute in quella sezione della sua enciclopedia che tratta delle feste di Cristo nella liturgia del suo tempo. Parlando della festa delle Palme, VII Domenica del digiuno, afferma che quando la Quaresima iniziava il 7 gennaio, questa domenica era la Pasqua (= la fine) del digiuno quaresimale e non la Pasqua di Resurrezione. Poco prima lo stesso autore osserva che la VI Domenica è la Domenica del battesimo, nella quale in passato si cuoceva il crisma e

che si dice fosse il giorno nel quale era stato conferito il battesimo agli apostoli (VILLECOURT 1925 pp 314-315; p. 269).

2) La lettera del vescovo Macario di Memfi (X secolo), citata in un'epistola che un anonimo prete copto invia al mafriano di Mossul tra il 1189 e il 1199 (VILLECOURT 1923b). Macario di Memfi critica il costume di consacrare il crisma il Giovedì santo invece che il giorno tipico nella tradizione copta, il venerdì della VI settimana di digiuno (si tratta probabilmente di quello della VII settimana, immediatamente prima della festa delle Palme), che era una volta la fine del digiuno e «si dice che è il giorno nel quale Cristo Signore battezzò i suoi discepoli» (si noti che per Abu 'l-Barakat tale battesimo è avvenuto la Domenica precedente): questo era anche il giorno in cui il patriarca di Alessandria conferiva il battesimo alla gente di ogni paese. Macario descrive a lungo l'antico battesimo del venerdì, preceduto dallo scrutinio (*fishishin*) del mercoledì e da un digiuno che comprendeva il mercoledì e il giovedì. Dal momento del battesimo era lecita la gioia e l'allegria, che durava il Sabato e la Domenica successivi. In seguito a sconvolgimenti politico-religiosi, che possiamo identificare con l'instaurazione del patriarca calcedonense ad Alessandria e il trasferimento del rito nel monastero di Abu Macario, tale battesimo sarebbe stato abolito, e sarebbe rimasta soltanto la consacrazione del crisma, ritardata in seguito al Giovedì santo, nuovo costume contro cui Macario polemizza.

3) Un testo copto di ambiente pacomiano pubblicato da W.E. Crum, cui possiamo riferirci come *Historia Horsiesi* (CRUM 1915; recentemente T. ORLANDI 1990 ha identificato tra i reperti della Missione archeologica dell'Università di Pisa e pubblicato un parallelo faiumico all'ultima sezione del testo; il tipo di scrittura è presumibilmente del VII-VIII sec.), nel quale si narra dell'incontro tra Orsiesi e Teofilo di Alessandria nel suo primo anno di episcopato, come chiariscono non solo alcune espressioni del testo ma anche la *Storia dei Patriarchi di Alessandria* (PO I p. 427) che riporta l'episodio in forma abbreviata. L'incontro avviene in seguito alla fallita consacrazione del fonte battesimale nella notte di un sabato non altrimenti specificato, ma certamente anteriore al Sabato santo. Tale insuccesso consiste nel fatto che a Teofilo non appare, come accadeva ai suoi predecessori, un bastone di luce che segnava le acque battesimali. Una voce gli comunica che il miracolo non può realizzarsi senza la presenza di Orsiesi. Teofilo invia due diaconi a cercarlo e questi, trovatolo, tornano con lui dal sud ad Alessandria in sei giorni. Giungono nella notte tra il Venerdì e il Sabato santo. In presenza di Orsiesi naturalmente il miracolo ha luogo e Teofilo può procedere al battesimo, il Sabato santo (forse la notte), davanti al popolo. Dopo aver menzionato la celebrazione della domenica di Pasqua il testo presenta un'asserzione di fondamentale importanza: «e in questo modo la festa fu raddoppiata: la Resurrezione e il

battesimo; e così si fa fino ad oggi». A stare alla lettera del passo, il battesimo sarebbe stato trasferito alla notte paquale per opera di Teofilo.

4) I *Canoni* dello Ps. Ippolito, conservati in traduzione araba edita da Coquin (PO 31, 2), il cui testo originario lo studioso data alla prima metà del IV secolo. In essi si nota una distinzione tra Quaresima e Settimana santa. Per quanto riguarda il battesimo vi si afferma che esso è preceduto da quaranta giorni di preparazione (canone 12). Nella settimana finale è fatta concessione ai catecumeni di mangiare il V giorno (giovedì) e imposto di digiunare il venerdì; il battesimo viene conferito la notte del sabato (canone 19). Il testo non specifica in quale momento dell'anno liturgico esso abbia luogo.

5) I *Canoni* dello Ps. Atanasio (RIEDEL - CRUM 1904), probabilmente del IV o V secolo. Nel XVI canone si afferma che l'Epifania è la festa del battesimo di Gesù e dell'inizio dell'anno. Ma Epifanio riporta in *Panarion* 51.29.7 che il 6 gennaio viene celebrata in Egitto l'incarnazione, ed Epifanio è testimone oculare delle cose egiziane. Cassiano in *Conlationes* X 2 afferma che l'Epifania egiziana è festa del battesimo e della natività (TALLEY 1991 pp. 121-129).

6) Le lettere festali di Atanasio (cfr. CAMPLANI 1986 pp. 24-30 per le edizioni). In esse non è ravvisabile alcuna menzione del battesimo. Nella sezione dedicata all'annuncio delle date vi si nota una distinzione netta tra la Quaresima e l'inizio della Settimana santa.

7) Il frammento di Mar Saba attribuito (SMITH 1973) a Clemente di Alessandria, attestato soltanto da una sequenza di due pagine e mezzo in scrittura corsiva del XVIII secolo. Contiene notizie su un testo espanso del Vangelo di Marco usato ad Alessandria in connessione con i riti dell'iniziazione battesimale. L'aggiunta, secondo l'autore (Clemente ?) dello scritto, era posta dopo Mc 10, 34 e raccontava della resurrezione di un giovane da parte di Gesù. In seguito al miracolo Gesù rimaneva nella casa del risorto. Dopo sei giorni gli diceva cosa fare e il giovane si presentava a lui rivestito soltanto di lino. Gesù rimaneva tutta la notte con lui e gli insegnava i misteri del regno di Dio. La pericope di questo vangelo segreto e il contesto in cui è inserita sono chiaramente ricalcati sull'episodio della resurrezione di Lazzaro in Gv. 11. Secondo Talley potrebbe trattarsi dell'origine della tradizione copta circa il battesimo conferito da Gesù ai suoi discepoli: come in Macario di Memfi, il battesimo è conferito il sesto giorno (TALLEY 1991 pp 205-214).

Dagli storici e liturgisti arabi, dalla lettera di Macario di Memfi, dai *Canoni* dello Ps. Ippolito e dello Ps. Atanasio, dalla narrazione pacomiana e dal silenzio delle lettere festali atanasiane circa il battesimo, Talley ricava una tradizione copta riguardante la Quaresima e il battesimo che potrebbe corrispondere allo stato di cose originario. Anticamente, prima del Concilio di Nicea, dopo il giorno dell'Epifania, festa del battesimo di Gesù e festa dell'inizio dell'anno, cominciava la Quaresima, concepita come imitazione del digiuno di Gesù nel deserto, al termine della quale veniva conferito il battesimo, in quanto è alla fine della Quaresima che Macario pone la cerimonia antica del battesimo, nonché il ricordo del giorno in cui si raccontava che Gesù avesse conferito il battesimo (TALLEY 1991 pp. 202-203).

In seguito, due avvenimenti segnerebbero un mutamento progressivo dell'antico costume liturgico: 1) in una certa epoca, e probabilmente sotto l'episcopato atanasiano, la Quaresima sarebbe stata trasferita dall'Epifania al tempo pasquale, divenendo un digiuno di preparazione alla Pasqua; 2) sotto Teofilo (*Historia Horsiesi*) anche il battesimo sarebbe stato spostato alla notte pasquale (TALLEY 1986 pp. 214-215).

L'intera ricostruzione sarebbe confermata dal frammento di Mar Saba. In effetti se il giorno dell'Epifania era la festa del battesimo di Gesù e dell'inizio dell'anno, come afferma il XVI canone ps. atanasiano, allora si iniziava a leggere il Vangelo di Marco, singolarmente silenzioso circa la nascita di Gesù (come il XVI canone ps. atanasiano), dall'inizio fino all'episodio del battesimo. Quindi nella prima settimana del digiuno postepifanico si leggeva il brano delle tentazioni nel deserto (in Mc. molto succinto) e nelle settimane seguenti si proseguiva nella lettura del Vangelo così familiare alla tradizione liturgica egiziana. Nella settimana finale, in relazione con il battesimo, si leggeva la pericope segreta posta dopo Mc. 10, 34. Ciò poteva accadere il venerdì, in accordo con la testimonianza di Macario di Memfi: il sabato e la domenica erano dedicati alla lettura della parte restante di Mc. 10 e di Mc. 11, l'entrata trionfale di Gesù in Gerusalemme. Qualcosa del genere Talley riscontra nella tradizione liturgica costantinopolitana: lettura pressoché continuativa di Marco per le prime cinque settimane; al sabato della sesta settimana, lettura di Gv. 11, 1-45 (la resurrezione di Lazzaro), corrispondente ai versetti aggiunti in Mc.; la domenica successiva lettura di Gv. 12, 1-18. La sostituzione di Gv. 11, 1-45 alla pericope interpolata sarebbe già avvenuta nel corso dell'evoluzione della liturgia alessandrina, la quale a sua volta avrebbe fortemente influenzato quella costantinopolitana (TALLEY 1991 pp. 210-211).

4. *Alcuni dati utili all'interpretazione delle testimonianze*

Ricordo che la revisione critica di questa ricostruzione deve basarsi sulla verifica dei seguenti elementi: 1) la qualità delle testimonianze suffraganti l'ipotesi generale; 2) la loro corretta interpretazione; 3) la coerenza dei dati che se ne desumono; 4) l'ampiezza della documentazione usata per il delineamento del quadro in cui si inseriscono i diversi momenti dell'evoluzione liturgica. Tuttavia, prima di passare all'analisi diretta dei testi, sembra utile soffermarsi brevemente su alcuni dati che conosciamo circa i tempi del digiuno, le modalità della sua pratica, e altri elementi che possano rendere più agevole l'interpretazione dei diversi documenti sopra menzionati.

4.1 *L'evoluzione della Quaresima e la data del battesimo.* Preliminarmente si ricorderanno due fatti che hanno segnato profondamente la liturgia egiziana. Il primo è il passaggio da una Quaresima di sei settimane a una di otto. Esso si è verificato tra il 596 e il 646 nella chiesa copta anticalcedonense (CAMPLANI 1992), forse per opera di Beniamino; per opera del predecessore Andronico secondo Abu 'l-Barakat (VILLECOURT 1925), che dà una spiegazione del mutamento incoerente dal punto di vista cronologico, influenzata probabilmente dagli *Annali* di Eutiche, laddove lo storico spiega l'origine del digiuno di Eraclio, prima settimana, o settimana di introduzione, della Quaresima (CSCO 472 p. 109).

L'altro fatto importante è l'uso, attestato da fonti letterarie, dalla letteratura canonica, da manoscritti liturgici, di conferire il battesimo in una settimana diversa da quella pasquale, probabilmente quella precedente la Domenica delle Palme.

Due fra i più importanti manoscritti liturgici in saidico, della Collezione Pierpont-Morgan di New York, M 573 (VII-VIII sec.) e M 615 (IX secolo), testimoni della Quaresima di otto settimane, chiamano il sesto sabato e la sesta domenica, quella che precede la Domenica delle Palme, rispettivamente come ⲡⲥⲁⲃⲃⲁⲧⲟⲛ ⲙ̄ⲡⲃⲁⲡ̄ⲧⲓⲥⲙⲁ e ⲧⲕⲩⲣⲓⲁⲕⲏ ⲙ̄ⲡⲃⲁⲡ̄ⲧⲓⲥⲙⲁ. Non sappiamo in quale momento si sia affermata l'usanza di chiamare in questo modo la terzultima domenica di Quaresima e il sabato precedente, se già quando era in vigore la Quaresima di sei settimane (si tratterebbe dunque della domenica della quarta settimana), oppure solo in concomitanza o posteriormente all'estensione del digiuno. I manoscritti testimoni di una Quaresima di sei settimane non sono espliciti su questo punto: il quarto sabato e la quarta domenica sono designati come tali, ad esempio nel mss. copto Leide 75, che non fa menzione del battesimo (PLEYTE-BOESER 1897; su questo tipo di mss. liturgici cfr. QUECKE 1978 pp. 189-190 e nota 113).

Mentre le fonti liturgiche sopra accennate parlano di un sabato e di una domenica del battesimo, alcune fonti letterarie alludono a una settimana del battesimo. Un testo monastico copto, molto probabilmente anteriore al VII secolo, accenna alla visita del vescovo Psulusia di File presso Teofilo avvenuta, secondo la corretta interpretazione del testo, «il sabato della settimana in cui si facevano i battesimi» (e non «the seventh day after the Sabbath» come in BUDGE 1915, traduzione p. 985, testo copto p. 470; cfr. ORLANDI 1984 pp. 71-125, in particolare il f. 36v e ss.): il fatto che questa settimana non sia chiamata settimana di Pasqua induce a pensare che il battesimo, al momento in cui scriveva il redattore della storia monastica, era conferito in un momento diverso dalla notte di Pasqua. Il medesimo procedimento di raccontare gli episodi del passato, veri o leggendari, inserendoli nello schema dell'anno liturgico contemporaneo al redattore, oppure di ricreare artificiosamente lo schema antico sotto l'influenza della prassi liturgica contemporanea, risulta particolarmente evidente nella *Storia dei Patriarchi* laddove si racconta di una donna di Antiochia che vuole far battezzare i due suoi bambini ad Alessandria al tempo dell'arcivescovo Pietro. Tralasciando i particolari di questa leggenda, rileviamo soltanto che nel testo si dice che la donna arriva ad Alessandria un giorno «nella settimana del battesimo, che è la sesta settimana del digiuno, quando si usa battezzare i bambini» (PO I p. 387). Dopo l'incontro con l'arcivescovo, questi l'accoglie in casa fino alla «Festa della santa Pasqua» (PO I p. 389-390). Sono evidenti gli anacronismi: il battesimo dei bambini al tempo di Pietro; un digiuno che dura più di sei settimane (dunque otto). Il redattore, o una sua fonte, allude alla settimana del battesimo come sesta settimana della Quaresima, anche se non è chiaro il conteggio presupposto (probabilmente è seguito lo schema: settimana di introduzione + sei settimane di Quaresima + settimana pasquale, su cui ritorneremo). Il legame tra Quaresima e Pasqua mi sembra evidente nel testo, contro quanto pensa BRADSHOW, (1988, p. 6). Infine, J. den Heijer mi comunica che la recensione primitiva della *Storia dei Patriarchi* colloca l'usuale verificarsi del miracolo di cui parla l'*Historia Horsiesi* non la notte di sabato, ma il mercoledì della settimana del battesimo, quella, secondo quanto specifica il testo, che precede la settimana pasquale. Anche in questo caso la leggenda attestata dal testo copto è stata rielaborata dal redattore della storia patriarcale in accordo a come pensava che si svolgesse il tempo liturgico quaresimale in passato.

4.2 *I tempi del digiuno*. La sesta lettera festale di Atanasio chiarisce in maniera particolarmente perspicua i tempi del digiuno. Come ogni lettera festale, essa apre la sua sezione finale con la data di inizio della Quaresima, cui segue la data di inizio della settimana santa e la data della chiusura del digiuno, il sabato sera. La data della Pasqua può anche essere omessa. E' da rilevare che è l'unica lettera festale oggi conosciuta che indica il momento di chiusura della Quaresima, la Domenica precedente la Pasqua. Il lunedì si riprende la disciplina ascetica dei «sei giorni della Pasqua».

Notiamo alcuni elementi apparentemente contradditorii. Il periodo complessivo fino al Sabato santo è di quarantuno giorni: dunque, a rigore, la Quaresima, concepita come periodo di quaranta giorni, termina il venerdì sera; il giorno di inizio della Quaresima è sempre un lunedì; i giorni di reale digiuno non sono quaranta, ma trenta, in quanto, come chiarisce questa lettera, il sabato e la domenica non sono giorni di digiuno. Se la Quaresima è periodo di ascesi di quaranta giorni, essa si sovrappone parzialmente alla Settimana santa. Tuttavia quest'ultima è distinta dalla prima: da una parte si sottolinea terminologicamente l'unitarietà del periodo di digiuno, dall'altra si mette in rilievo il diverso significato dei due costumi parzialmente sovrapposti, il primo concepito come periodo di ascesi e preparazione, il secondo come la memoria della passione di Cristo. E' chiaro da tutto ciò che si tratta di due periodi liturgici aventi diversa origine e che dunque è errato vedere nella Quaresima l'esito finale di quel processo di estensione progressiva dei giorni che precedono la festa della Resurrezione in atto nel corso dei secoli II e III. Nello stesso tempo, la distinzione qualitativa delle due prassi non implica necessariamente la loro originaria distinzione cronologica.

Le cose non cambiano quando, dopo il 596, nella chiesa anticalcedonense si passa al digiuno di otto settimane. Contrariamente a quanto pensa Talley, la distinzione tra Quaresima e Settimana santa non si accentua, anzi in un certo senso si attenua. In effetti, nei finali delle lettere di Beniamino, se da una parte vengono annunciate la data di inizio della Quaresima e quella della Settimana santa, dall'altra si sottolinea che la *Tessarakostê* è di otto settimane, dunque comprendente anche la settimana pasquale. Poco sappiamo di ciò che accade nella chiesa melchita, anche per il fatto che non conosciamo lettere festali posteriori a quella di Eulogio del 583 o del 588 (CAMPLANI 1992 p. 424 n. 6). Dagli *Annali* del patriarca melchita Eutiche si potrebbe dedurre che il conteggio delle settimane avvenisse come nella chiesa bizantina: sei settimane di Quaresima + settimana pasquale, l'insieme preceduto da una settimana equivalente a quella della tirofagia, ma che, per un voto fatto dai Cristiani al tempo di Eraclio, si era trasformata in settimana di digiuno vero e proprio, potendosi scorgere in questa strana leggenda il tentativo della chiesa melchita di adattarsi al rigore di quella anticalcedonense.

Un'ultima osservazione concerne il modo di calcolare le settimane di Quaresima: per unanime consenso dei manoscritti liturgici di vario tipo, la prima settimana è quella che va dal lunedì di inizio della Quaresima alla domenica; i singoli giorni della settimana sono espressi secondo il numero d'ordine della settimana cui appartengono, per cui il sesto venerdì di Quaresima sarà il venerdì della sesta settimana, la prima domenica sarà quella posta alla fine della prima settimana, ecc. Esiste tuttavia la possibilità di calcolare anche in modo diverso: se vi è una settimana di introduzione, la prima settimana di Quaresima corrisponderà alla seconda del primo sistema di calcolo, e, nello stesso modo, il sesto venerdì corrisponderà al settimo. E' questo il sistema seguito da Eutiche, e forse anche dal redattore della *Storia dei Patriarchi* e da Macario di Memfi.

4.3 *Modalità del digiuno*. Le lettere festali, in forza della loro circolazione capillare e del loro carattere di espressione dell'autorità patriarcale, hanno avuto un ruolo determinante nel diffondere nuovi costumi liturgici, per cui è difficile credere che alcune regioni dell'Egitto vi abbiano aderito in ritardo o li abbiano rifiutati. Quando, all'inizio del VII secolo, si allunga il periodo quaresimale, attestazioni epigrafiche del Sud riflettono immediatamente tale mutamento (CAMPLANI 1992). Lo stesso è lecito pensare in relazione all'introduzione vera e propria della Quaresima prepasquale: le difficoltà sono subito segnalate ad Atanasio, il quale nel biglietto a Serapione e nella lettera per la Pasqua del 347 insiste nell'imporre questo costume liturgico.

Per il V e VI secolo segnalo soltanto alcuni testi significativi per l'argomento di cui stiamo trattando. Un discorso quaresimale di Shenute (KUHN 1983 pp. 190-193) allude alla tendenza a digiunare una o più settimane prima dell'inizio del digiuno quaresimale di sei settimane. Alcuni però, denuncia l'archimandrita, sottraggono i giorni di digiuno aggiuntivi a quelli della Quaresima. Shenute esorta di conseguenza ad attenersi alle indicazioni della santa proclamazione, che notifica quale giorno di quale mese iniziare il digiuno (ⲛⲥⲟⲩⲏⲡ ⲛⲁ ⲩ ⲛ ⲉ ⲃⲟⲧ) e in quale giorno di quale mese interromperlo la sera del Sabato. La tendenza ad allungare il digiuno quaresimale, come abbiamo visto, sarà ufficializzata due secoli dopo. Il ruolo determinante delle lettere festali appare anche nella più tarda *Vita di Pisenzio di Keft* (BUDGE 1913 pp. 105-106). Un passo di Besa, il successore di Shenute, ci dà altre utili indicazioni sulle modalità del digiuno (n. 27, XIV,1-4, CSCO 157 pp. 89-90). L'archimandrita denuncia che durante la Quaresima molti dei suoi monaci mangiano ogni sera, ciò che suona tanto più vergognoso per il fatto che alcuni laici fanno digiuno continuato per periodi ripetuti di due giorni consecutivi, di quattro, o anche di una settimana intera. Naturalmente l'interpretazione del passo deve tener conto del carattere parenetico di questo sermone. Se ne evince l'uso comune di astenersi dal cibo durante il giorno fino a tarda sera e la tendenza a praticare il digiuno continuato per più giorni di seguito.

Se torniamo al IV secolo, la prassi concreta del digiuno in Quaresima appare meno ascetica. Certamente il digiuno della Settimana santa doveva essere più esigente di quello quaresimale, ma uno strano testo, segnalatomi da R.-G. Coquin (*Bibliotheca Orientalis* 48 p. 549-550), fa pensare che anche durante la settimana pasquale il digiuno non fosse assoluto. In effetti, nella *Vita Pachomii* (Bo 35, CSCO 89 pp. 105-106), si racconta che Teodoro, *durante la Quaresima*, chiede a Pacomio perché mai nel corso della settimana di Pasqua si digiuni soltano due giorni e non anche i primi quattro. Pacomio risponde richiamandosi ai canoni della chiesa che così prescrivono. L'insieme del testo va probabilmente interpretato nel senso che per Pacomio il venerdì e il sabato della settimana pasquale sono giorni di digiuno assoluto e continuato, mentre per i primi quattro giorni è ammesso mangiare la sera quel che basti per affrontare i doveri della vita monastica (VEILLEUX 1968 pp. 253-254). La menzione della Quaresima nella *Vita Pachomii* non permette di pensare che qui sia riflesso un uso più antico e prequaresimale (VEILLEUX 1968 pp. 250-252).

4.4 *La formazione di un lessico quaresimale copto*. Ben presto assistiamo alla formazione di un lessico propriamente copto che tende a distinguersi da quello greco corrispondente per indicare i momenti del tempo pasquale. Accanto a ⲧⲧⲉⲥⲥⲁⲣⲁⲕⲟⲥⲧⲏ compare ⲡⲉⲍⲙⲉ ⲛ̄ⲍ̄ⲟⲟⲩ: Shenute li usa indifferentemente (in CHASSINAT 1911 f. 49r compaiono ambedue). Per indicare lo scioglimento del digiuno tra il sabato e la domenica viene usato ⲠⲂⲰⲗ ⲈⲂⲟⲗ, che a un certo punto finisce per precedere o anche sostituire l'espressione ⲠⲁⲤⲬⲁ o ⲀⲚⲁⲤⲧⲁⲤⲒⲤ: ⲠⲤⲁⲂⲂⲁⲧⲟⲚ ⲘⲠⲂⲰⲗ ⲈⲂⲟⲗ (ad es. Leide 75) e ⲠⲒⲂⲰⲗ ⲈⲂⲟⲗ ⲚⲧⲈ ⲠⲒⲠⲁⲤⲬⲁ (*Vita Pachomii* CSCO 89 p. 205) indicano il sabato santo. Per la domenica di Pasqua troviamo oltre al più comune ⲦⲔⲨⲣⲒⲁⲔⲏ ⲚⲦⲁⲚⲁⲤⲧⲁⲤⲒⲤ anche ⲦⲔⲨⲣⲒⲁⲔⲏ ⲘⲠⲂⲰⲗ ⲈⲂⲟⲗ (M 573 f. 61v) o ⲦⲔⲨⲣⲒⲁⲔⲏ ⲚⲦⲁⲚⲁⲤⲧⲁⲤⲒⲤ ⲘⲠⲂⲰⲗ ⲈⲂⲟⲗ (Leide 82.4) o ⲠⲰⲁ ⲘⲠⲂⲰⲗ ⲈⲂⲟⲗ (BUDGE 1913 p. 90).

La domenica che precede il lunedì di inizio della Quaresima, da distinguersi dalla I domenica di Quaresima posta alla fine della I settimana, è chiamata fin dal tempo di Shenute ⲦⲔⲨⲣⲒⲁⲔⲏ ⲘⲠⲘⲟⲨⲣ ⲈⲌⲟⲨⲚ (KUHN 1983 p. 190 e Leida 75 che testimonia la Quaresima di sei settimane); nei manoscritti liturgici troviamo così designato anche il sabato che la precede: ⲠⲤⲁⲂⲂⲁ-ⲧⲟⲚ ⲘⲠⲘⲟⲨⲣ ⲈⲌⲟⲨⲚ (M 573 e M 615).

La quinta domenica, quella delle Palme, nei mss. che attestano la Quaresima di sei settimane è qualificata con termini connessi a ⲤⲦⲁⲨⲣⲰⲤⲒⲤ: ⲦⲔⲨ-ⲣⲒⲁⲔⲏ ⲚⲚⲈⲤⲢⲟⲨ in Leida 75; ⲦⲔⲨⲣⲒⲁⲔⲏ ⲚⲚⲈⲤⲢⲈ in Leida 82. Nei manoscritti che descrivono una Quaresima di otto settimane, essa diventa la settima ed è chiamata ⲦⲔⲨⲣⲒⲁⲔⲏ ⲚⲈⲨⲗⲟⲅⲏⲘⲈⲚⲟⲨ (M 573 e M 615, con lettura di Gv. 12, 12-28).

Segnalo poi una domenica che in un manoscritto (Leida 75) porta un nome particolare: ⲦⲔⲨⲣⲒⲁⲔⲏ ⲘⲠⲬⲁⲒⲈ che richiama immediatamente l'espressione ⲠⲰⲁ ⲘⲠⲬⲁⲈⲒⲈ ⲚⲁⲠⲁ ⲰⲈⲚⲟⲨⲧⲈ ⲠⲈⲌⲟⲟⲨ ⲘⲠⲤⲚⲁⲨ ⲌⲚⲦⲘⲈⲌⲤⲚⲦⲈ ⲚⲌⲈⲂⲆⲰⲘⲁⲤ ⲌⲘⲠⲈⲌⲘⲈ ⲚⲌⲟⲟⲨ ⲈⲧⲟⲨⲁⲂ del famoso ms. Paris Nationale 68 (f. 4r) studiato da QUECKE (1970 pp. 488-505). Il ms. che attesta la prima espressione descrive chiaramente una Quaresima di sei settimane, il secondo di otto. La domenica ⲘⲠⲬⲁⲒⲈ è quella che precede quella ⲘⲠⲘⲟⲨⲣ ⲈⲌⲟⲨⲚ. Non mi riconosco la competenza per entrare nel merito della festa di Shenute e della possibile identificazione tra la festa di questa domenica e quella del lunedì della seconda settimana di Quaresima indicata come la data della festa nel ms. Paris Nationale 68. Si potrebbe ipotizzare che tale domenica desse il nome a tutta la settimana seguente. Ma se si tratta della medesima celebrazione, essa può esser stata spostata per ragioni liturgiche al lunedì quando la domenica ⲘⲠⲬⲁⲒⲈ è diventata, dopo l'espansione del digiuno a otto settimane, la prima domenica di Quaresima, cioè quella posta alla fine della prima settimana e seguita dal lunedì della seconda settimana.

5. *Valutazione critica della teoria della Quaresima postepifanica*

A questo punto non resta che passare all'analisi critica delle testimonianze a favore di una Quaresima originariamente postepifanica. Alla teoria di Talley vanno mosse tre critiche di carattere metodologico: 1) essa fa affidamento a testimonianze estremamente tarde; 2) tende a rendere coerente un insieme di dati che in alcuni casi si contraddicono; 3) fa un uso improprio dei testi più antichi, quelli del quarto e quinto secolo, per suffragare le affermazioni dei testi scritti a partire dal X secolo: infatti, se andiamo a verificare i singoli passi, questi non mostrano l'insieme delle caratteristiche di una Quaresima postepifanica, ma solo singoli elementi che possono essere contestualizzati in altra maniera. In altri termini: si disegna il quadro della Quaresima originaria a partire da testi molto tardi, cercando di attenuare le loro contraddizioni; a partire da questo quadro interpretativo si leggono le testimonianze più antiche reperendovi i singoli elementi costituenti e usandoli come conferma del quadro ipotetico delineato in antecedenza. Rileggiamo dunque le singole testimonianze.

5.1 *Le lettere festali.* Nelle lettere festali, sia quelle che annunciano la Quaresima di sei settimane, sia quelle che ne annunciano una di otto settimane, non si riscontra una netta suddivisione tra Quaresima e Settimana santa. Per quanto concerne le lettere di Atanasio, possiamo affermare con certezza che esse non sono da confondere con omelie di carattere mistagogico. L'assenza di allusioni al battesimo può dunque spiegarsi con questa loro caratteristica, di essere scritti indirizzati a tutte le categorie di cristiani, quelli già battezzati, i catecumeni veri e propri, coloro che non sono ancora catecumeni. Del resto la menzione del battesimo è rarissima anche nelle lettere di Teofilo e in quelle di Cirillo, scritte in un momento in cui il battesimo, secondo Talley, era stato trasferito alla Settimana santa; e quando compare essa non è mai rapportata alla settimana pasquale ma inserita in contesti estremamente generici. Di conseguenza sembra inopportuno evincere da questa assenza la convinzione che al tempo di Atanasio il battesimo non fosse praticato la notte di Pasqua.

5.2 *Canoni dello Ps. Ippolito.* Il fatto che la Quaresima e la Settimana santa siano oggetto di due canoni diversi può essere interpretato nel senso che esse vengono avvertite come due usanze liturgiche diverse. Ma questo diverso significato non implica necessariamente che i due costumi fossero originariamente distinti anche dal punto di vista cronologico. Più problematica è la prescrizione contenuta nel canone XIX di bagnarsi e mangiare il V giorno della settimana del battesimo e di digiunare il venerdì; il sabato i battezzandi vengono riuniti e vegliano tutta la notte fino al momento del battesimo. Dal momento che durante la Settimana santa non si può mangiare, sarebbe con ciò escluso che il battesimo sia conferito durante il suo corso. Propongo tre interpretazioni possibili del canone, sottolineando che comunque i *Canoni*, come ha dimostrato BRAKMANN (1978), sembrano fare riferimento a tradizioni liturgiche piuttosto particolari proprie di ambienti circoscritti: 1) che si tratti, nonostante tutto, della Settimana santa: il canone prescrive di mangiare dopo la cerimonia, ciò che potrebbe indicare la sera; la testimonianza della *Vita Pachomii* sopra menzionata, nella quale Pacomio dichiara come assolutamente obbligatorio solo il digiuno del venerdì e del sabato della Settimana santa, mentre nei giorni precedenti è lecito mangiare di sera lo stretto necessario, potrebbe essere una conferma di questa interpretazione; 2) che si tratti della terzultima settimana della Quaresima, durante la quale il digiuno imposto sembra essere meno severo di quello della Settimana santa: in questo caso saremmo in presenza di una delle prime testimonianze circa il conferimento del battesimo in un momento diverso dalla Pasqua; 3) che si tratti di una settimana qualsiasi del tempo liturgico ordinario. In ogni caso la prescrizione sembra in contraddizione con le testimonianze più tarde in quanto fa riferimento a un corso settimanale in cui la preparazione finale al battesimo ha luogo: invece, se stiamo alla notizia di Abu 'l-Barakat, la fine del digiuno della Quaresima originaria, cadendo in data fissa, poteva capitare in qualsiasi giorno della settimana. Rispetto alla notizia di Macario di Memfi vanno segnalate due differenze: 1) che, secondo il canone XIX, il battesimo è conferito la notte del sabato, mentre per Macario ciò avveniva il venerdì; 2) che, secondo Macario, il mercoledì e il giovedì si doveva digiunare, mentre lo Ps. Ippolito ammette la possibilità di mangiare il giovedì.

5.3 *Testi pacomiani.* Uno dei fondamenti della teoria della Quaresima postepifanica è il fatto che solo con Teofilo si è cominciato a battezzare la notte del sabato pasquale, secondo la testimonianza della *Historia Horsiesi*, mentre precedentemente il battesimo sarebbe stato conferito nella stagione postepifanica, in accordo alla tradizione più antica, di cui Atanasio sarebbe testimone. P.F. Bradshow, che pure è influenzato da tale teoria, ha recentemente richiamato l'attenzione su due passi della *Vita Pachomii* che attestano l'uso di conferire il battesimo ai catecumeni durante i giorni di Pasqua anche prima di Teofilo (BRADSHOW 1988 p. 8). Naturalmente si potrebbe sospettare che si tratti di due note redazionali posteriori al supposto trasferimento del battesimo, se non venisse a conferma dell'usanza una lettera di Teodoro stesso scritta in occasione della Pasqua di un anno a noi sconosciuto. In essa Teodoro invita i confratelli a partecipare alla riunione pasquale, cui non si deve mancare se non per gravi necessità. Quindi afferma riguardo ai catecumeni: «Quanto ai catecumeni nei monasteri, che aspettano la temibile remissione dei peccati e la grazia del *mistero spirituale*, si sentano dire da voi che devono piangere e versare lacrime sui peccati passati e prepararsi alla santificazione dell'anima e del corpo per poter ricevere il sangue e il corpo del Signore e Salvatore» (BO-

ON 1932 p. 106). E' difficile immaginare espressioni più esplicite circa il battesimo pasquale.

5.4 *Index delle lettere festali di Atanasio e Historia Acephala*. A partire dal numero dei giorni che il redattore dell'*Historia Acephala* attribuisce al secondo esilio atanasiano (339-346) e dall'analisi del metodo del tutto particolare usato per calcolarli, A. MARTIN (SCh 317 p. 81-83) ha potuto stabilire che la partenza di Atanasio per Roma è avvenuta il 16 aprile del 339, il giorno successivo alla Pasqua. L'*Index* delle lettere festali aggiunge un particolare molto significativo ai fini del nostro discorso: che Atanasio fugge «dopo aver battezzato molti» (SCh 317 pp. 236-237). Se ne ricava che il vescovo ha aspettato la Pasqua e il conferimento del battesimo, prima di fuggire per il secondo esilio. Il battesimo a Pasqua non sembra dunque soltanto una particolarità della liturgia pacomiana. A questo punto è lecito domandarsi se sia mai esistito un battesimo staccato dalla Pasqua nell'Egitto preniceno.

5.5 *Historia Horsiesi*. Secondo il redattore della storia, il battesimo sarebbe stato conferito a Pasqua in seguito all'incontro di Horsiesi e Teofilo, mentre in precedenza ciò avveniva il sabato di una settimana indeterminata, prima di Pasqua. Il testo ha uno scopo evidente, come ha dimostrato ORLANDI (1990): quello di presentare il cenobitismo pacomiano come indispensabile all'autorità patriarcale. Si ha l'impressione che il redattore viva ormai abbastanza lontano nel tempo, tanto da aver perso la nozione del battesimo pasquale come costume normale nel IV secolo. Si potrebbe di conseguenza proporre la seguente interpretazione del curioso passo in questione. Esso è la spia di un atteggiamento difensivo nei confronti del diffondersi dell'usanza del battesimo non pasquale, usanza che è giunta e si è affermata anche ad Alessandria, alla quale però i monasteri pacomiani non hanno aderito: l'autore reagisce ideando una leggenda con scopo apologetico (la difesa del rito pacomiano) e etiologico (l'origine ormai sconosciuta del conferimento pasquale del battesimo). Sia l'orientamento ideologico specifico del testo, sia l'ignoranza del suo autore circa le usanze battesimali pacomiane del IV secolo, rendono la sua testimonianza inutilizzabile per la storia della Quaresima egiziana.

5.6 *Macario di Memfi*. L'asserzione che il battesimo era anticamente conferito il venerdì della VI (= VII) settimana di Quaresima ed era seguito dall'interruzione del digiuno il venerdì sera, il sabato e la domenica, rende impossibile pensare che Macario si riferisca alla Settimana santa, nella quale il venerdì e il sabato sono giorni di digiuno continuato. Il quadro che l'autore ricostruisce per il passato è compatibile con i dati a nostra disposizione per il periodo successivo al 596: digiuno di otto settimane e battesimo praticato in un settimana diversa da quella pasquale. La cerimonia dello scrutinio celebrata il mercoledì è un dato in armonia con quanto il redattore della storia patriarcale (o una delle sue fonti) ritiene accadesse al tempo di Teofilo (cfr. sezione 4.1). Dunque, l'autore cerca di ricostruire il quadro liturgico del passato, ma, tentando di far ciò, si lascia influenzare dalla liturgia dei suoi tempi e dalle notizie, più o meno verosimili, che si avevano sulla liturgia antica. Quella relativa al battesimo celebrato il venerdì non mi sembra che abbia riscontri. Si noti inoltre che il venerdì è il giorno in cui, secondo il vescovo, si dice che Gesù abbia battezzato i suoi discepoli, mentre per Abu 'l-Barakat è la domenica precedente. Ciò che comunque Macario non dice è che sia esistita una Quaresima postepifanica.

5.7 *Eutiche / Abu 'l-Barakat*. L'esistenza di una Quaresima postepifanica, attestata a partire da Eutiche, ha tutte le sembianze di una notizia artefatta nata da un semplicissimo ragionamento: dato che il battesimo di Gesù veniva celebrato il 6 gennaio, da ciò poteva essere facilmente dedotta la supposizione che la Quaresima, concepita come imitazione e ricordo del digiuno di Gesù nel deserto, iniziato il giorno seguente il suo battesimo, dovesse essere praticata anticamente a partire dal 7 gennaio. Le incoerenze di tale fittizia ricostruzione, che pure ha avuto una fortuna notevole in chiese di diverso orientamento dogmatico, sono molteplici. Essa presuppone una Quaresima che non ha un vero e proprio ritmo settimanale, legata com'è alla fissità della data dell'Epifania, che può cadere in qualsiasi giorno della settimana: e ciò in contraddizione con tutte le notizie che, compresa quella piuttosto isolata di Macario, attribuiscono grande importanza a tale ritmo e al fatto che la fine della Quaresima deve cadere il venerdì. In secondo luogo, la notizia viene resa sospetta non solo dal fatto che è molto tarda rispetto al periodo di cui vuole essere testimonianza, ma anche dalla collocazione della riforma liturgica, consistente nell'unione della Quaresima alla Settimana santa, in tre momenti diversi: Demetrio, Agrippino, il Concilio di Nicea. In terzo luogo essa è fortemente influenzata dalla prassi di una Quaresima di otto settimane, periodo che può ben essere concepito come somma del periodo quaresimale di quaranta giorni e della settimana santa, mentre è del tutto inverosimile se rapportata a una Quaresima di sei settimane, di cui l'ultima è la settimana santa.

Conclusioni

L'esistenza di una Quaresima originariamente postepifanica in Egitto non sembra provata da fonti sufficientemente attendibili, in quanto tarde e contraddittorie. I testi più antichi usati dagli studiosi per suffragarla possono essere interpretati in modo completamente diverso, più coerente, ai miei occhi, con il contesto liturgico in cui sono stati redatti. Rimangono molti punti oscuri nella storia della Quaresima egiziana non solo per le difficoltà interpretative offerte dalle fonti studiate, ma anche perché un gran numero di manoscritti sia letterarii che liturgici aspetta di essere ricostruito e indagato in modo sistematico. Tale indagine potrebbe permettere di affrontare alcune questioni oggi an-

120

cora aperte, come quella relativa ai mutamenti liturgici provocati dall'estensione del digiuno quaresimale.

Per ora ritengo di poter proporre questo quadro provvisorio: I) nel 334 la Quaresima viene per la prima volta menzionata ufficialmente; la sua introduzione nell'intero territorio egiziano incontra notevoli resistenze; nel contempo, per tutto il IV secolo, il battesimo viene conferito durante la notte pasquale; II) le modalità del digiuno quaresimale e di quello della settimana santa variano nel tempo: ad un periodo in cui vi è una certa libertà di interpretazione succede un periodo, quello di Shenute e di Besa, in cui il digiuno diventa più severo; III) in un'epoca che non è facile da determinare, compresa tra l'inizio del V secolo e il VII secolo, il battesimo non è più celebrato durante la notte pasquale, ma durante la V / VII settimana di digiuno secondo alcuni autori, oppure, secondo quanto si potrebbe dedurre dai manoscritti liturgici, nella notte del IV / VI sabato (a seconda che si tratti di una Quaresima di sei o di otto settimane); IV) il digiuno quaresimale passa dalle sei alle otto settimane nel primo terzo del VII secolo.

RIFERIMENTI BIBLIOGRAFICI

AUF DER MAUR 1983 = AUF DER MAUR, *Feiern im Rhythmus der Zeit I: Herrenfeste in Woche una Jahr. Gottesdients der Kirche. Handbuch der Liturgiewissenschaft*, Teil 5, Regensburg 1983.

BOON 1932 = A. BOON, *Pachomiana latina. Règles et epîtres de s.Pachôme, epître de s.Théodore et «Liber» de s.Orsiesius*, Louvain 1932.

BRADSHOW 1988 = P.F. BRADSHOW, *Baptismal Practice in the Alexandrian Tradition, Eastern or Western?*, in *Essays in Early Eastern Initiation*, Bramcote 1988, 5-17.

BRAKMANN 1979 = H. BRAKMANN, *Alexandreia und Kanones des Hippolyt*, in *Jahrbuch für Antike und Christentum* 22 (1979) 139-149.

BUDGE 1913 = E.A.T. WALLIS BUDGE, *Coptic Apocrypha in the Dialect of Upper Egypt*, British Museum 1913.

BUDGE 1915 = E.A.T. WALLIS BUDGE, *Miscellaneous Coptic Texts in the Dialect of Upper Egypt*, British Museum 1915.

CAMPLANI 1989 = A. CAMPLANI, *Le lettere festali di Atanasio di Alessandria. Studio storico-critico*, Roma 1989.

CAMPLANI 1992 = A. CAMPLANI, *La Quaresima egiziana nel VII secolo: note di cronologia su Mon. Epiph. 77, Manchester Ryland Suppl. 47-48, P. Grenf. II 112, P. Berol. 10677., P. Köln 215 e un'omelia copta*, in *Augustinianum* 32 (1992) 423-432.

CHASSINAT 1911 = E. CHASSINAT, *Le quatrième livre des entretiens et epîtres de Schenouti*, in *Mémoires publiés par les membres de l'Institut Français d'Archéologie Orientale* 23, Cairo 1911.

COQUIN 1967a = R.-G. COQUIN, *Les origines de l'Épiphanie en Égypte*, in *Noël, Épiphanie, retour du Christ* (= Lex Orandi 40), Paris 1967, 139-170.

COQUIN 1967b = R.-G. COQUIN, *Une réforme liturgique du Concile de Nicée (325)?*, in *Académie des Inscriptions & Belles-lettres. Comptes Rendus*, Paris 1967, 178-192.

CRUM 1915 = W.E. CRUM, *Der Papyruscodex Saec. VI-VII der Phillipps-Bibliothek in Cheltenham* (=Schriften der wiss. Gesellsch. in Strassburg 18), Strassburg 1915.

CSCO = *Corpus Scriptorum Christianorum Orientalium*, Louvain.

CURETON 1848 = W. CURETON, *The Festal Letters of Athanasius*, London 1948.

DAUNOY 1925 = F. DAUNOY, *La question pascale au concile de Nicée*, in *Échos d'Orient* 24 (1925) 424-445.

DU BOURGUET 1988 = P. DU BOURGUET, *Les Coptes* (= Que sais-je 2398), Paris 1988.

DUCHESNE 1920 = L. DUCHESNE, *Origines du culte chrétien*, Paris 1920 (V ed.).

KUHN 1983 = K.H. KUHN, *Two Shenute Texts* in *Fetschrift Papyrussammlung Erzherzog Rainer*, Wien 1983, pp. 187-193.

LEFORT 1953 = L.T. LEFORT, *Les lettres festales de saint Athanase*, in *Bulletin de l'Académie Royale de Belgique*, S. 5, 30 (1953) 643-656.

ORLANDI 1984 = T. ORLANDI, *Vite di monaci copti*, Roma 1984.

ORLANDI 1990 = T. ORLANDI, *Due fogli papiracei da Medinet Madi (Fayum): l'*Historia Horsiesi, in *Egitto e Vicino Oriente* (1990) 109-126.

PERI 1960 = V. PERI, *Lo stato degli studi intorno all'origine della Quaresima*, in *Aevum* 34 (1960) 525-555.

PERI 1961 = V. PERI, *La cronologia delle lettere festali di sant'Atanasio e la Quaresima*, in *Aevum* (1961) 28-86.

PEYTE-BOESER 1897 = W. PEYTE- P.A.A. BOESER, *Manuscrits coptes du Musée d'Antiquités des Pays-Bas à Leide*, Leiden 1897.

PG = *Patrologia Graeca*, ed. J.-P. Migne, Paris.

PO = *Patrologia Orientalis*, Paris.

QUECKE 1970 = H. QUECKE, *Untersuchungen zum koptischen Studengebet* (= Publications de l'Institut Orientaliste de Louvain 3), Louvain 1970.

QUECKE 1978 = H. QUECKE, *Zukunftschancen bei der Erforschung der koptischen Liturgie*, in *The Future of Coptic Studies*, ed R.McL. Wilson, Leiden 1978, 164-196.

RICHARD 1973 = M. RICHARD, *Le florilège du cod. Vatopédi 236 sur le corruptible et l'incorruptible*, in *Le Muséon* 86 (1973) 249-273.

RICHARD 1973 = M. RICHARD, *Le comput pascal par octaétéris*, in *Le Muséon* 87 (1974) 307-339.

RIEDEL-CRUM 1904, W. RIEDEL- W.E. CRUM, *The Canons of Athanasius of Alexandria, the Arabic and Coptic Versions*, London 1904.

SALAVILLE 1910 = S. SALAVILLE, *La Tessarakosté du V canon de Nicée (325)*, in *Échos d'Orient* 13 (1910) 65-72.

SCh = Sources Chrétiennes, Cerf, Paris.

SMITH 1973 = M. SMITH, *Clement of Alexandria and a Secret Gospel of Mark*, Cambridge, Mass., 1973.

TALLEY 1991 = T.J. TALLEY, *The Origins of the Liturgical Year*, Collegeville, Minnesota, 1991 (II ed.).

VEILLEUX 1968 = VEILLEUX A., *La liturgie dans le cénobitisme pachômien au quatrième siècle* (Studia Anselmiana 57), Roma 1968.

VIAUD 1978 = G. VIAUD, *La liturgie des Coptes d'Égypte*, Paris 1978.

VILLECOURT 1922 = L. VILLECOURT, *Un manuscrit arabe sur le saint chrême dans l'Église copte*, in *Revue d'Histoire Ecclésiastique* 18 (22) 5-19.

VILLECOURT 1923b = L. VILLECOURT, *La lettre de Macaire, évêque de Memphis, sur la liturgie antique du chrême et du baptême à Alexandrie*, in *Le Muséon* 36 (1923) 33-46.

VILLECOURT 1923; 1924; 1925; = L. VILLECOURT, *Les observances liturgiques et la discipline du jeûne* in *Le Muséon* 36 (1923) 249-292; 37 (1924) 201-280; 38 (1925) 125-320.

ZANETTI 1985 = U. ZANETTI, *Les lectionnaires coptes annuels. Basse-Égypte* (= Publications de l'Institut Orientalist de Louvain), Louvain-la-Neuve 1985.

THE MICHAELIDES COPTIC MANUSCRIPT COLLECTION IN THE CAMBRIDGE UNIVERSITY LIBRARY AND BRITISH LIBRARY WITH EXCURSUSES ON THE MONASTERIES OF APA APOLLO AND TWO UNCOMMON EPISTOLARY FORMULAE.

SARAH CLACKSON

§1 Introduction

This paper provides an introduction to the Coptic manuscripts from the oriental manuscript collection of the late George Michaelides, which are now in the Cambridge University Library and the British Library (in this article abbreviated to CUL and BL respectively). I am currently preparing a catalogue raisonné of all of these manuscripts together with an edition of selected texts, and I am grateful to both libraries for granting me permission to study and publish them.[1]

§2 Acquisition details

George Michaelides, the Greek collector who died in 1973,[2] possessed a fine collection of manuscripts in addition to his collection of Egyptian artefacts. CUL acquired part of this manuscript collection in May and October 1977, comprising texts written in Hieratic, Demotic and Coptic; Greek and Latin; and Arabic, Persian and Turkish. In 1976 and 1979 the BL acquired Demotic and Coptic, Armenian, Greek and Latin, and Arabic and Hebrew manuscripts.

---

[1] I am grateful to James Clackson and John Tait for their helpful comments on this paper, and to Professor K.H. Kuhn for help with the literary manuscripts and in particular for identifying some of the biblical pieces. I also wish to thank the Spalding Trust, the Divinity Faculty of Cambridge University, and the Egypt Exploration Society, for funding my research into this collection; the latter two also funded my attendance at this conference.

[2] See the entry for him in the forthcoming third edition of *Who was who in Egyptology* ed. M. Bierbrier. I am grateful to Peter A. Clayton for providing me with information about Mr Michaelides.

124

§3 Number and material of manuscripts

CUL possesses about three quarters of the two hundred and forty or so Coptic manuscripts acquired by the two libraries:[3] one hundred and sixty-one are on papyrus, fifty on parchment, and twenty-eight on paper. One linen fragment is very fragile and has not yet been studied. None of these texts has been published previously, as far as I know.

§4 Content

Most of the texts are incomplete and carry less than fifteen lines of writing. About thirty texts are too fragmentary to be worth studying, and some of the others need to be conserved before they can be fully interpreted. There appears to be only one forgery.

The non-literary material (see §§7-15, Excursuses 1-3) is primarily monastic and consists of about ninety private letters, over thirty lists and accounts, and twenty legal texts. In the semi-literary category (see §16) there are six magical and medical texts. Finally there are over fifty literary pieces (see §17), including biblical (see §17.1) and liturgical items.

§5 Dates

There is only one securely dated document among all of these texts: CUL Michael. 807, a trilingual πιττάκιον (order for payment document), composed chiefly in Arabic and Coptic with only a few lines of Greek. The Arabic portion bears a date of Jumada 2nd A.H. 136 (December 753 A.D.).[4]

Another text, BL Or. 13886.22, bears an oath which can be restored to mention the emperor Heraclius and his co-emperor son, Heraclius the New Constantine, which would date the text to between 613 and 641 A.D.

Other texts with dates from this collection include at most only the indiction date.

Generally speaking two distinct palaeographical categories are evident in the manuscripts: the

---

[3] All of the CUL inventory numbers included in this article are temporary and represent the original Michaelides Collection numbers, with the exception of those beginning with the letter "Q".

[4] I am grateful to Dr Geoffrey Khan for reading this Arabic date for me.

predominant grouping is of 6th-9th Century papyri in pure Sahidic dialect, or Sahidic with characteristics found in texts from the Hermopolite nome; there is a smaller number of 10th-11th Century paper texts in Faiyumic dialect.

The earliest text in the collection may be that of some papyrus fragments of *I Samuel*, CUL Michael. 1112, which could be dated on palaeographical grounds to the 5th Century. CUL Michael. 1114, a liturgical paper text with Arabic rubrics, appears to be the latest manuscript, having a very similar hand to a Coptic text in the Vatican Collection (P. Vatican copt. 18) which is dated to 1531 A.D.[5] I shall include detailed comment on the palaeography of the texts in the catalogue.

§6 Provenance

As a whole the texts are not related to one another, although some connections can be made. None are securely provenanced nor is there any information on where they were acquired, apart from an article written by George Michaelides in 1952 which refers to fellahin bringing him Greek and Coptic papyri from the Faiyum.[6]

§6.1 Dialects

A rough idea of provenance is provided by the dialects found in the texts, which are, in descending order of prevalence: Sahidic, including Sahidic with features characteristic of texts from the Hermopolite nome; Faiyumic; and Bohairic.

§7 Placenames in the texts

The placenames found in the texts indicate that a number of documents come from Middle Egypt, and in particular the Hermopolite nome, for which see §7.1 below. Three texts might possibly derive from Aphrodito, for which see §9 below. Other placenames in the texts include: ⲡⲁⲃⲓⲗⲱⲛ, ⲃⲁⲃⲧⲗⲱⲛ Babylon (CUL Michael. 1101(A) l. 2, (B) l. 13 and 1235(A) l. 1 respectively); ⲡⲥⲧⲉϩ Pishtheh

---

[5]See M. Cramer, *Koptische Paläographie* (Wiesbaden, 1964), no. 53 pl. 90.

[6]See G. Michailides, "Papyrus contenant un dessin du dieu Seth à tête d'âne", *Aegyptus* 32 (1952), 45.

(CUL Michael. 827 l. 17);[7] and cϩⲱⲟⲩ Saha (CUL Michael. 1047/1(A) l. 14).[8]

§7.1 Hermopolite nome placenames

The following Hermopolite nome placenames are mentioned: ⲡⲁⲩⲏⲧ Bawit (CUL Michael. 815/2(A) l. 9);[9] ⲡⲓⲁϩ ⲡⲉϩⲙⲟⲙ Piah Pehmom (BL Or. 13886.13(A) ll. 3, 4-5, 9);[10] ⲡⲱⲣϥ Poref (CUL Michael. 833(B) ll. 3,7);[11] ⲧⲁⲡⲁⲣⲟⲩ Taparoou (CUL Michael. 822/4 l. 3);[12] ⲧⲁⲡⲟⲥⲓ Taposi (CUL Michael. 1047/2 l. 5); ⲧⲃⲁⲕⲉ Tbake (CUL Michael. 960(A) l. 15);[13] ⲧⲃⲉⲣϣⲏ Tbershe (CUL Michael. 1047/1(B) l. 6 and 1233 l. 2);[14] ⲧⲉⲣⲱⲧ Derut (CUL Michael. 809/1(A) l. 1);[15] ⲧⲓⲧⲕⲟⲁϩ, ⲧⲓⲧⲕⲟⲟϩⲉ Titkooh (CUL Michael. 815/2(A).ll. 4,5

---

[7]See Timm 1944 "Pišteh".

[8]See Timm 2231-7 "Sahā".

[9]See Drew-Bear 197 "Παυητ"; this placename also occurs in P.CtYBR 1827, 1845, and 2334, which I hope to publish in the near future.

[10]See Timm 2064 "[P]ṭi[me] n-Piah-Pe[.]mom", and 1942-3 "Piōh Pemom"; in both entries read W.E. Crum, *Catalogue of the Coptic manuscripts in the Collection of the John Rylands Library* (Manchester, 1909), no. 285:2 as ⲡⲓⲁϩ ⲡⲉ.ⲙⲟⲙ.

[11]See Timm 1999-2000 "Pōrf", adding L.S.B. MacCoull, "Coptic documentary papyri in the Hyvernat Collection", *BSAC* 27 (1985), 58 no. 45 l. 2 to the list of occurrences of this placename.

[12]See Drew-Bear 266 "ⲧⲁⲡⲁⲣⲟⲟⲩⲉ" and Timm 2076-7 "Ptoou n-Taparoooue", 1846 n.1 "Paroou". This placename also occurs in BL Or. 6201 A179 and B52, both of which I am editing; and, as ⲧⲉⲡⲁⲣⲟⲟⲩ, in O. Michigan inv. no. 25292 which was edited in W.H. Worrell et al., *Coptic texts in the University of Michigan Collection* (*University of Michigan Studies, Humanistic Series* 46; Ann Arbor, 1942), 244 no. 18.

[13]See Drew-Bear 270 "Τβακε", adding P.Vindob. K 3200, edited in M. Hasitzka, *Koptische Texte* (*Corpus Papyrorum Raineri* 12; Vienna, 1987), no. 18 l.4, to the list of occurrences of this placename.

[14]See Timm 692-6 "Dēr al-Barša".

[15]See Timm 562-5 "Darūṭ Sarab'am<(m)ūn>".

and 1201(A) l. 2 respectively);[16] ⲧⲁⲕⲉ Dalga (CUL Michael. 1176/1(B) l. 2); and ϣⲙⲟⲩⲛ Ashmunein (CUL Michael. Q102(A) l. 2).[17] ⲧⲁⲡⲟⲥⲓ is only previously attested in P.Würzburg 43,[18] and ⲧⲃⲉⲣϣⲏ, which appears to be the original Coptic form of El-Bersha, does not occur in any previously published manuscripts.

§8 Religious institutions

Monasteries mentioned in the texts include: ⲡⲙⲁ ⲛⲁⲡⲁ ⲁⲛⲟⲩⲡ, "the place, cell, or monastery of Apa Anoup" (CUL Michael. 815/2(A) ll. 3-4);[19] "the monastery of Apa Apollo", on which see Excursus 1 below, is described variously as ⲡⲙⲟⲛ(ⲁⲥⲧⲏⲣⲓⲟⲛ) ⲛⲁⲡⲁ ⲁⲡⲟⲗⲗⲱ ⲡⲣⲏⲥ ϣⲙⲟⲩⲛ "to the south of Ashmunein" (CUL Michael. Q102 l. 2);[20] ⲡⲧⲟⲡⲟⲥ ⲛⲁⲡⲁ ⲁⲡⲟⲗⲗⲱ (CUL Michael. 856/5 ll. 1-2); and

---

[16] See Timm 2077-80 "Ptoou n-Titkooh"; L.S.B. MacCoull, "A reattribution of *P.Vat. Aphrod.* 13", *ZPE* 88 (1991), 209-10. This placename also occurs as ⲇⲓⲇⲕⲟⲟϩⲉ in a damaged inscription at Bawit, read by Jean Clédat as ⲇⲓⲁⲕⲟⲟϩⲉ, in *Le monastère et la nécropole de Baouit* (*MIFAO* 12; Cairo 1904-6), 154, pl. 92.1; this word is transcribed as "Diakobe" in *Dans les pas de Jean Clédat* (Paris-Louvain, 1991), 52. I am currently editing two BL texts which mention ⲧⲓⲧⲕⲟⲟϩⲉ.

[17] See Timm 198-220 "al-Ašmūnēn".

[18] Edited and re-edited in W. Brunsch, "P. Würzburg Inv. Nr. 43 - eine koptische Verzichterklärung", *ZÄS* 108 (1981), 93-105, pll. 2-3; M. Krause, "Zur Edition koptischer nichtliterarischer Texte. P.Würzburg 43 neu bearbeitet", *ZÄS* 112 (1985), 143-53; Brunsch, "'Ὑποβαλλόμενοι κλέπτουσι μύθους' (Soph., *Ajax* 188): noch einmal zu P. Würzburg Inv. Nr. 43", *ZÄS* 114 (1987), 113-7.

[19] Timm 1968-9 "Pma n-Apa-Anoup" n. 2 refers to a Michaelides Collection text which does not appear to be among the texts now in the BL or CUL; it is not dated to the 11th Century in J. Drescher, "A new Coptic month", *JEA* 46 (1960), 111. Note that, despite the cross-reference, there is no entry as yet for "Kloster des Apa Anoup" in Timm.

[20] A parallel for two BL papyri thought to relate to the Bawit monastery: BL Or. 6201 l. 16 & 6203 ll. 16-7, edited in M. Krause, *Das Apa-Apollon-Kloster zu Bawit. Untersuchungen unveröffentlichter Urkunden als Beitrag zur Geschichte des ägyptischen Mönchtums* (Theological Dissertation, Leipzig, 1958).

πτοπος ⲛ̄ϥⲁⲅⲓⲟⲥ ⲁⲡⲁ ⲁⲡⲟⲗⲗⲱ (BL Or. 13886.35(A) ll. 2-3).[21]
Also mentioned is ⲡⲧⲟⲟⲩ ⲛ̄ⲧⲓⲧⲕⲟⲟⲅⲉ "the mount of Titkooh"
(CUL Michael. 1201(A) l. 2), which may be preceded by a
monastery name, possibly that of Apa Apollo, now lost;
and ⲡⲙⲁ ⲛⲁⲁⲩⲣⲓⲛⲉ "the place, cell, or monastery of
Taurinus" (CUL Michael. 1233 l. 7) which may be
identified with monasteries of this name at Aphrodito or
in the Hermopolite nome.[22] Another monastery from
Aphrodito, that of Philasterion,[23] may also occur in CUL
Michael. 833(A) l. 5 (ϕⲩⲗⲁⲥⲧⲏⲣⲛ̄), and CUL Michael. 1089
l.2 (ϕⲓⲗⲁⲥⲧⲏⲣⲓⲟⲛ), although in both contexts this could be
a personal name.[24] CUL Michael. 833(A) l. 7 mentions
ⲧⲉⲕⲕⲗⲏⲥⲓⲁ ⲛ̄ⲡⲱⲣϥ "the church of Poref".

§9 Links with known manuscripts from Aphrodito

Two Michaelides non-literary texts possibly
relating to the Aphrodito monastery of Philasterion have
already been discussed above in §8. Men of ⲡⲙⲁ ⲛⲁⲁⲩⲣⲓⲛⲉ
"the place, cell, or monastery of Taurinus", an Aphrodito
monastery already discussed above in §8, are mentioned
in CUL Michael. 1233 l. 7 along with a ⲙⲱⲩⲥⲏⲥ of ⲧⲃⲉⲣϣⲏ.
This man is also listed in a register of names, CUL
Michael. 1047/1, which include ⲕⲁⲥⲟⲩⲗⲉ and ⲡⲟⲩⲥ; the
former is an uncommon name, and both are included in
the index of *P.Lond.* IV, one of the major publications of
8th Century Aphrodito texts.[25] CUL Michael. 1047/1 also
mentions ⲕⲩⲣⲓⲁⲕⲟⲥ ϕⲁⲙϣⲉ, son of ⲓⲥⲁⲕ, and ⲡⲃⲉⲗⲉ, son of
ⲑⲉⲟⲁⲟⲥⲉ, who both occur in Pierpont Morgan inv. M 662 B

---

[21]The name of this monastery also occurs in CUL Michael.
1048/2(B), a fragment of the end of a Greek or Coptic document.

[22]For the Aphrodito monastery, see Timm 1446 "Kōm Išqāw" no.
19; for the Hermopolite, see Drew-Bear 268 "Ταυρίνου".

[23]Φιλαστρε and Φιλάστηρ respectively in *P.Lond.* IV.1420 ll. 182,
and 219.

[24]For Φιλαστέριον as a personal name see D. Foraboschi,
*Onomasticon alterum papyrologicum: supplemento al Namenbuch
di F. Preisigke* (*Testi e documenti per lo studio dell'antichità* 16;
Milan, 1967-71) s.v.; BL Or. 6201 A31e (unpublished) may also
bear this name.

[25]ⲡⲟⲩⲥ is usually associated with the Arsinoite nome, see B.C.
McGing, "Melitian monks at Labla", *Tyche* 5 (1990), 78 n. to l. 3.

6a (A) text 1, a Coptic papyrus which is unfortunately without provenance.[26]

A ⲙⲱⲧⲥⲏⲥ of ⲧⲃⲉⲣϣⲏ, son of ⲡⲁⲙⲟⲩⲛ and brother of ⲓⲉⲣⲏⲙⲓⲁⲥ, also turns up in a Coptic poll-tax document from the Frank W. Green Collection in the Museum of Archaeology and Anthropology, Cambridge, now only available from the transcriptions made by Paul Kahle Jr.[27] This text bears the distinctive ⲡⲉⲛⲉⲓⲱⲧ ⲡⲉⲧⲥϩⲁⲓ epistolary formula, for which see Excursus 3 below, and is connected with P. Michigan nos. 578, 1300 and 1524,[28] which have been assigned the provenance of Wadi Sarga; Aphrodito is another possibility.

CUL Michael. 827 mentions the personal names ⲯⲁⲭⲟ and ⲯⲓⲙⲁⲛⲱⲃⲉⲧ, and the toponym ⲡⲁⲡⲅⲟⲧⲅ, all of which occur in *P.Lond.* IV.[29]

<u>§10 Epistolary formulae</u>

Most of the epistolary formulae exhibited in the letters belong to well-represented groups from which little idea of the provenance or date can be gathered, but two uncommon formulae stand out: ⲁⲛⲟⲕ ⲡⲁⲥⲟⲛ (name) ⲉⲓⲥϩⲁⲓ and ⲡⲉⲛⲉⲓⲱⲧ ⲡⲉⲧⲥϩⲁⲓ. These will be dealt with in Excursuses 2 and 3 below.

<u>§11 Personal names</u>

Noteworthy personal names of interest in the texts include:[30] ⲁⲡⲁⲗⲗⲓⲧⲓ (CUL Michael. 1022(A) l. 22, (B) l. 13),

---

[26]See editio princeps in MacCoull, "*P. Morgan copt.*: documentary texts from the Pierpont Morgan Library", *BSAC* 24 (1979-1982), 4 no. 3 (↑); and my forthcoming re-edition of this text along with other texts from this collection.

[27]See notebook 24 of Paul Kahle Jr's papers in the Griffith Institute, Oxford.

[28]All three texts are edited in E.M. Husselman, "Some Coptic documents dealing with the poll-tax", *Aegyptus* 31 (1951), 332-8.

[29]See *P.Lond.* IV indices, where ⲯⲓⲙⲁⲛⲱⲃⲉⲧ occurs as Ψιβανωβετ, and ⲡⲁⲡⲅⲟⲧⲅ as Παπκουκ.

[30]Some are not found in G. Heuser, *Die Personennamen der Kopten* (*Studien zur Epigraphik und Papyruskunde* 1.2: Leipzig, 1929); see W. Brunsch, "Index zu Heusers *Personennamen der Kopten*", *Enchoria* 12 (1984), 119-53, for an index to this work.

ⲕⲁⲥⲟⲩⲗⲉ (CUL Michael. 1047/1(A) l. 9, see above §9), ⲡⲁⲡⲟⲥⲧⲟⲗⲟⲥ (CUL Michael. 823/1 l. 5), ⲡⲉⲥⲁⲩ (CUL Michael. 1102(B) l. 13), ⲡⲓⲗⲑⲉⲉⲧⲥ (CUL Michael. Charta c.37(B) l. 9), ⲡⲓϩⲁⲣⲟⲩⲁⲃ (CUL Michael. 828/1 l. 15), ⲡⲟⲧⲥ (CUL Michael. 1047/1(B) l. 5, see above §9), ⲥⲁⲣⲙⲁⲧⲁ (CUL Michael. 836/1(A) l. 7), ⲥⲓⲙⲟⲑⲉ/ⲥⲓⲙⲟⲑⲓ (CUL Michael. 818/3 l. 2; 832/1 ll. 12, 15; and 1159 l. 1), ⲫⲁⲛⲧⲁⲩ (CUL Michael. 828/1 ll. 11, 12),[31] ⲯⲁⲭⲟ (CUL Michael. 827 l. 16, see above §9), ⲯⲓⲙⲁⲛⲱⲃⲉⲧ (CUL Michael. 827 l. 21, see above §9), and ϩⲏⲅⲉⲁ (CUL Michael. 1224 l. 4). CUL Michael. 1047/1, already mentioned in §9, is a register full of interesting personal names or nicknames, such as ⲡⲥⲁⲗⲉⲡϣⲁⲁⲛⲧϥ "the broken-nosed", ⲧⲉϩⲗⲟ ⲕⲁⲥⲣⲟ "the old jawbone", ⲡⲉϣⲟⲩⲉ "the persea tree", and ⲃⲁⲡⲁⲧ "collarbone".

§12 Titles and trades

Apart from the usual monastic and ecclesiastical titles found in the texts, there are some less-common trades such as: ⲕⲁⲗⲉⲫⲁⲧⲏⲥ "caulker", in a monastic letter about a delivery of pitch (CUL Michael. 1036(A) l. 5); and ⲕⲟⲩⲙⲁⲣⲓⲧⲏⲥ (CUL Michael. 1048/3 l. 2) "gardener, vine-dresser".[32] A trade which could be restored as ⲥⲁⲕϩⲁⲗⲱⲙ occurs in a letter (CUL Michael. 856/5 l. 4) from a monk of the monastery of Apa Apollo and possibly applies to a man who deals in cheese; I base my restoration on the fact that this trade occurs in a papyrus letter from a monastery of the same name transcribed by James Drescher in a letter to Paul Kahle Jr.[33]

§13 Accounts and lists

The most substantial item in the collection is an 11th Century monastic account book in Faiyumic dialect,

---

[31] I include ⲫⲁⲛⲧⲁⲩ here, although it is attested as a toponym (see Timm 1917-21 "Phantoou n-Sōpehes") and not as a personal name, because in context it appears to be a personal name.

[32] For an examination of this word, see O. von Lemm, *Koptische Studien* I-LVIII (*Subsidia byzantina* 10; Leipzig, 1972), no. XXV, pp. 303-5.

[33] See P.E. Kahle, *Bala'izah* (London, 1954), vol. II p.657 n. 1. The full text of the papyrus can be found in a letter from Drescher in item 17 of Paul Kahle Jr's papers in the Griffith Institute, Oxford.

comprising thirty-four paper leaves detailing various items of expenditure.[34] It features many Arabic words written in Coptic.

There are a few wine accounts (CUL Michael. 824/5, 834/5+7; 960(B), 1089, 1217, Q109/2), including one which mentions ηρπ ναλ2α "boiled wine" (CUL Michael. 1217 l. 1), much encountered in *P.Lond.* IV as ἕψημα. Other accounts involve payments made to sailors of the κοτρεα κοῦρσα (CUL Michael. 1047/2), general foodstuffs (CUL Michael. 960(A)), and clothing (CUL Michael. 1068).

Apart from lists involving names and corresponding amounts in solidi, there is one documentary list, CUL Michael. 1121, which includes identifiable Arabic words written in Coptic such as αλκαс "raw silk", αλχεβωρ "camphor", αλ2αρεερ "silk", and αссαβραν, which can be interpreted either as *al-aṣfar* "yellow, or saffron", or as *aṣ-ṣabra* "myrrh, or aloe extract"; and 2ντ which can be interpreted as "Indian", possibly standing for one of the products of this country, for example aloe wood, or iron.[35]

§14 Legal texts

These are mostly fragmentary and deal with financial agreements but there is one λογος απνοττε document, assuring a safe return to the monastery for a fugitive (BL Or. 13886.26); and one Arabic, Coptic and Greek πιττατεν πιττάκιον (order for payment document), CUL Michael. 807, already mentioned above in §5.

§15 Taxes

The Michaelides texts mention the following taxes: ἀνδρισμός "poll-tax" (CUL Michael. 829/1), ἐμβολή "corn-tax" (CUL Michael. 1218), and δημόσιον (CUL Michael. 824/1, 828/3, and Q102), which can refer to the public money-tax or specifically the land tax.

§16 Semi-literary texts

In this category there are a few magical texts, one of which, CUL Michael. 1186, bears a drawing of πααχε

---

[34]Parts of this account book were cited by Drescher in loc. cit. (see n. 19 above), and "The Coptic dictionary: additions & corrections", *BSAC* 16 (1961-1962), 288.

[35]See the entry in E.W. Lane, *An Arabic-English Lexicon* (London, 1863-1893), 2904.

"the enemy", i.e. the devil, a winged, long-nosed, long-eared creature with a tail. CUL Michael. 918 has a drawing of a winged man encircled by what could be seven angels bearing crowns, palimpsested over a biblical text containing part of *Matthew* 5 (see §17.1 below). Besides a fever amulet, BL Or. 13886.10, there are two medical texts, CUL Michael. 819/2 and 1073, involving preparations for ophthalmic disorders, the latter for psorophthalmia.

§17 Literary texts

Four literary manuscripts now belonging to the BL have been described in Bentley Layton's catalogue.[36]

§17.1 Biblical texts

The fifteen biblical items identified so far are: papyrus fragments of *I Samuel* 14, 15, 17 and 28-30 (CUL Michael. 1112); a paper fragment of *Psalm* 2 (CUL Michael. 1166); parchment fragments of *Psalms* 7 (CUL Michael. 1259), 105 (CUL Michael. Q123) and 148 (CUL Michael. 1132); *Susanna* 5-10 of the Theodotion version (CUL Michael. 1235); *Matthew* 5 (CUL Michael. 918, see §16 above), 6 (CUL Michael. Q130), 12 (CUL Michael. Q127), 13 (CUL Michael. Q129), and 28 (CUL Michael. Q122); *Mark* 5 (CUL Michael. Q121); *John* 2 (CUL Michael. 1282/1+7-8); *Romans* 3 and 4 (CUL Michael. Q125); and *II Corinthians* 3 (CUL Michael. 37/7). Some texts also contain biblical paraphrases: parchment fragments of *Isaiah* 6.3 (CUL Michael. 37/6), a collation of *Matthew* 26.26-8 and *I Corinthians* 11.23-5 (CUL Michael. 37/4+37/6), and paper fragments of *Matthew* 23.37/*Luke* 13.34 (CUL Michael. 1114) and *Luke* 18.10-14 (CUL Michael. 1154(A)).

§17.2 Other literary texts

CUL Michael. 834/6 contains the introduction to the Panegyric on Macarius, Bishop of Antaeopolis, attributed to Dioscorus, Archbishop of Alexandria, written in Faiyumic dialect.[37] There is also a parchment

---

[36]B. Layton, *Catalogue of Coptic literary manuscripts.in the British Library acquired since 1906* (London, 1987), nos. 31, 38, 79, and 113.

[37]See the edition of this text by D.W. Johnson, *A Panegyric on Macarius, Bishop of Tkôw, attributed to Dioscorus of Alexandria* (*Corpus Scriptorum Christianorum Orientalium* 415-416, *Scriptores Coptici* 41-42; Louvain, 1980).

fragment, CUL Michael. Q120, which refers to "Our lord and father Apa Apollo, he who is one with God and equal to the angels". The latter epithet is only partially preserved but, if correct, would apply to Apollo of Titkooh and founder of Bawit, who is commemorated on the 25th of Paope in the *Synaxarium Alexandrinum*.[38] This may be connected with the non-literary material, mentioned above in §8 above and Excursus 1 below, which possibly relates to the Monastery of Apollo at Bawit or Titkooh.

Excursuses

In the course of preparing my edition of Coptic texts from the Michaelides Collection I have examined texts relating to monasteries of Apa Apollo and epistolary formulae which are potentially related to these texts.[39] I present the following brief excursuses, with minimal bibliography, as an introduction to my findings.

Excursus 1 Monasteries of Apa Apollo

When considering the Michaelides texts relating to a monastery of Apa Apollo (see §8 above) one must ascertain which of at least six sites of monasteries of this name is in question:[40] Aphrodito,[41] Bala'izah,[42] Bawit,[43]

---

[38]See R.-G. Coquin, "Apollon de Titkooḥ ou/et Apollon de Bawīṭ?",*Orientalia* N.S. 46 (1977),436-7; and H. Torp, "La date de la fondation du Monastère d'Apa Apollô de Baouît et de son abandon", *Mélanges d'archéologie et d'histoire* 77 (1965), 156-62.

[39] I am currently preparing a doctoral dissertation at University College London on the monasteries of Apa Apollo.

[40]For the most recent discussion of this question and much of the relevant bibliography, see Krause: "Die Inschriften auf den Türsturzbalken des Apa-Apollon-Klosters von Bawit", *Mélanges Antoine Guillaumont: contributions à l'étude des christianismes orientaux* (*Cahiers d'Orientalisme* 20; Geneva, 1988), 113-20; "Die ägyptischen Klöster. Bemerkungen zu den Phoibammon-Klöstern in Theben-West und den Apollon-Klöstern", in W. Godlewski ed., *Coptic Studies. Acts of the Third International Congress of Coptic Studies. Warsaw 20-25 August 1984* (Warsaw, 1990), 205-7; see also his remarks in "Publikationen koptischer nichtliterarischer Texte der Jahre 1984-1988", to appear in the forthcoming *Actes du IVe Congrès International des Études Coptes, Louvain-la-Neuve*.

Djeme,[44] Oxyrhyncus,[45] and Titkooh,[46] are all possible locations.[47]

BL Or. 13886.35 is a document concerning a loan written by a monk of "the monastery of the holy [Apa Apol]lo" whose name may be restored as Enoch (ενωχ): if this is correct, he may be identified with Apa Enoch, a monk of the Titkooh monastery of Apollo who occurs in P. Med. copto inv. 76.21,[48] although Enoch is a common Coptic name. He may also be identified with the Enoch of a monastery of Apa Apollo who occurs in P.Michigan 6860,[49] and a papyrus in the Hermitage Museum.[50] The editor of the latter text assigned it a Bawit provenance

---

[41]Timm 1444 "Kŏm Išqāw" no. 2, and 1331-3 "Kloster des Apa Apollōs".

[42]Timm 686-91 "Dēr al-Balā'iza".

[43]Timm 643-53 "Dēr Anbā Abullū' (Kloster des Apa Apollo bei Bawit)". See Krause, "Die ägyptischen Klöster ..." (cited in n. 40 above), 207 for other manuscripts from this monastery; I am grateful to Mme A. Boud'hors for giving me details of the Louvre Museum's Coptic ostraca from Jean Clédat's excavations at Bawit which she is currently studying along with other scholars.

[44]See Coptic Museum, Cairo, letters nos. 3431 and 3091 cited by G. Robinson, "International photographic archive of Greek papyri, 1987. Photography of the papyrus collections of the Coptic Museum, Cairo", *Enchoria* 15 (1987), 50.

[45]Timm 290 "al-Bahnasā".

[46]See Timm 2077-80 "Ptoou n-Titkooh", correcting p. 2078 "Pap. Amhurst" references to "P. Amsterdam". See also the forthcoming publication of the Greek Papyrological Society's collection of Greek manuscripts from this monastery dating to the 6th Century. Many thanks to Prof. B. Mandilaras for sending me details of these texts.

[47]For a less specific monastery of Apa Apollo reference, see Timm 1969 "Pma n-Apa-<A>pollo".

[48]Edited in S. Pernigotti, "I papiri copti dell'Università Cattolica di Milano. I", *Aegyptus* 65 (1985), 101-5.

[49]Edited in Worrell et al., op. cit. (n. 12 above) 210-12 no. 20.

[50]Edited in P.V. Jernstedt, *Koptskije teksty Gosudarstvennogo Ermitagea* (Moscow-Leningrad, 1959), no. 3.

but Leslie MacCoull has suggested Aphrodito.[51] I do not think that the man in BL Or. 13886.35 can be compared with the 6th Century Enoch of the Monastery of Apa Apollo at Aphrodito.[52]

There do not seem to be obvious connections between the other Michaelides texts and texts from monasteries of Apollo at Aphrodito, Bala'izah, and Oxyrhyncus. I have not seen the two letters in the Coptic Museum, Old Cairo, which are apparently from the Monastery of Apollo at Djeme,[53] but the dialect of the Michaelides texts is more suggestive of a provenance in Middle Egypt.

The occurrence of the placenames Bawit and Titkooh, see §7.1 above, in some of the Michaelides texts strongly suggests that one or both of these is the most likely provenance for the Michaelides Monastery of Apa Apollo texts. CUL Michael. Q120, a literary fragment already mentioned in §17.2 above, reinforces the connection with these two places by mentioning Apa Apollo ϩⲧⲥⲟⲥ ⲛⲛⲁⲅⲅⲉⲗⲟⲥ "equal of the angels", who is usually connected with them. CUL Michael. 815/2, an elliptical letter concerning an agreement, refers to ⲡⲙⲁ ⲛⲁⲡⲁ ⲁⲛⲟⲧⲡ, ⲧⲓⲧⲕⲟⲁϩ, and ⲡⲁϯⲏⲧ in such a way that all of these places appear to have been situated close to one another. This text is unique, as far as I know, for mentioning both the placenames Titkooh and Bawit,

---

[51] See MacCoull reference cited in n. 16 above, p. 210 n. 3: the Enoch who is cited here as occuring in l. 6 of J. Maspero, *Papyrus grecs d'époque byzantin* vol. II. *Catalogue général des antiquités égyptiennes du Musée du Caire* (Cairo, 1913), no. 67234 is in fact interpreted by J. Maspero as possibly referring to the monastery of the holy Abba Enoch; l. 3 does not contain the name Enoch at all.

[52] For this man, see Maspero, *Papyrus grecs d'époque byzantin* vol. I. *Catalogue général des antiquités égyptiennes du Musée du Caire* (Cairo, 1911), nos. 67094.11,19,20, and 67096.6,17 (thanks to Leslie MacCoull for providing me with the latter reference). P. Barison, "Ricerche sui monasteri dell'Egitto bizantino ed arabo secondo i documenti dei papiri greci", *Aegyptus* 18 (1938), 101 erroneously connects him with a non-existent Enoch in Maspero op. cit. no. 67067 l. 11.

[53] See note 44 above.

which at one time were considered to be names for one place used at different periods.[54]

Excursus 2 The ⲁⲛⲟⲕ ⲡⲁⲥⲟⲛ (name) ⲉⲓⲥϩⲁⲓ formula

This formula has a strong connection with at least one of the monasteries of Apa Apollo. Four of the sixteen instances of this formula known to me from papyrological texts are in the BL and CUL Michaelides collection: BL Or. 13886.35, and CUL Michael. 856/5, 968, and Q102.[55] Of the other twelve texts, only one, P.Würzburg 43, has been published;[56] the other eleven texts derive from various sources and are being edited by me. Twelve of the sixteen texts mention an unspecified monastery of Apa Apollo and, indeed, this formula also occurs in epigraphic texts from Bawit. It is also found in inscriptions from the Monastery of Jeremias at Saqqara, which had close contacts with the Bawit monastery in antiquity.

Similar formulae, such as ⲁⲛⲟⲕ ⲡⲁⲥⲟⲛ (name) ⲁⲓⲥϩⲁⲓ, and ⲁⲛⲟⲛ ⲡⲁⲥⲟⲛ (name) ⲙⲛ ⲡⲁⲥⲟⲛ (name) ⲉⲛⲥϩⲁⲓ, also occur, but again usually in texts mentioning a monastery of Apa Apollo.

The word ⲡⲁⲥⲟⲛ, without personal concord in the context, meaning "brother", not "my brother",[57] is a title often encountered in papyri which mention a monastery of Apa Apollo and in inscriptions from Bawit, although it also occurs in texts and inscriptions from other places in Egypt.

Excursus 3 The ⲡⲉⲛⲉⲓⲱⲧ ⲡⲉⲧⲥϩⲁⲓ formula

Unlike ⲁⲛⲟⲕ ⲡⲁⲥⲟⲛ (name) ⲉⲓⲥϩⲁⲓ, this formula does not have obvious links with a particular monastery, but analysis of related texts in which it occurs may provide a specific provenance. It is found in at least eleven

---

[54] For a résumé of this discussion, see Drew-Bear 300-1 "Τιτκῶις".

[55] Possibly include here CUL Michael. 1201, a letter from a monk of the monastery of Titkooh, the site of a monastery of Apa Apollo.

[56] See n. 18 above for publication details.

[57] See W.E. Crum, *A Coptic Dictionary* (Oxford, 1939), 343a ⲥⲟⲛ; and J.E. Quibell, *Excavations at Saqqara (1907-8)* (Cairo, 1909), 28 n.1.

published texts,[58] and a further twenty unpublished
examples are known to me. Five of these are in the BL
and CUL Michaelides collections: BL Or. 13886.37, and CUL
Michael. 818/3, 830, 1120, and 1232.[59] A provenance of
Wadi Sarga has been assigned to four of the published
texts bearing this formula, but analysis of the
unpublished examples may provide a new insight into
their date and origin; for a possible provenance of
Aphrodito see §9 above. One of the unpublished texts
bearing this formula, P.CtYBR inv. no. 2103 qua (B) text 2,
occurs on a papyrus which also mentions a monastery of
Apa Apollo.

Appeal for information:

I would be most grateful for any information on
the current whereabouts of manuscripts originally from
the collection of George Michaelides which are not now
in the British Library or Cambridge University Library.
I am aware that at least one Coptic papyrus and thirty-
one Greek papyri are not now in the above-mentioned
collections.

---

[58]These are: 1) P. Berlin 22 123 edited in H. Satzinger, *Koptische
Urkunden* vol. 3 (Berlin, 1967-8), no. 367; 2) P.CtYBR inv. no.
1853 edited in MacCoull, *Coptic documentary papyri from the
Beinecke Library (Yale University)* (*Publications de la Société
d'archéologie copte. Textes et documents* 17; Cairo 1986), no. 17;
3) P.CtYBR inv. 1861 edited in id. ib. no. 21; 4) P.CtYBR inv. 2037
edited in id. ib. no. 28; 5) P.Meyer inv. 13 edited in G.M. Browne,
"Coptic papyri from Peoria", *Studia Papyrologica* 19 (1980), 102;
6-8) P.Michigan 578, 1300, and 1524, see n. 28 above for
publication details; 9) A. Vogliano, *Papiri della R. Università di
Milano* vol. 3 (Milan, 1965), Testi copti no. 3; 10) P.Palau Ribes
inv. 41 edited in B.E. Klakowicz, "Coptic papyri in the Palau-
Ribes Collection (inv. 39-41; 44; 51-2; 59; 84)", *Studia
Papyrologica* 20 (1981), 46-7; and 11) W.E. Crum, H.I. Bell, *Wadi
Sarga. Coptic and Greek texts from the excavations undertaken by
the Byzantine Research Account* (*Coptica* 3; Copenhagen, 1922),
no. 175.

[59]The other fifteen texts are in various British and American
collections, and are being edited by me.

Abbreviations used in
SARAH CLACKSON

THE MICHAELIDES COPTIC MANUSCRIPT COLLECTION IN THE CAMBRIDGE UNIVERSITY LIBRARY AND BRITISH LIBRARY
WITH EXCURSUSES ON THE MONASTERIES OF APA APOLLO AND TWO UNCOMMON EPISTOLARY FORMULAE

BSAC = *Bulletin de Société d'archéologie copte.*
Drew-Bear = M. Drew-Bear, *Le Nome hermopolite* (*American Studies in Papyrology* 21; Missoula, Montana, 1979)
JEA = *Journal of Egyptian Archaeology.*
MIFAO = *Mémoires publiés par les membres de l'Institut français d'Archéologie Orientale du Caire.*
P.Lond. IV = H.I. Bell, W.E. Crum, *Greek papyri in the British Museum* vol. IV (London, 1910)
Timm = S. Timm, *Das christlich-koptische Ägypten in arabischer Zeit. Eine Sammlung christlicher Stätten in Ägypten in arabischer Zeit unter Ausschluß von Alexandria, Kairo, des Apa-Mena-Klosters (Der Abu Mina), der Sketis (Wadi n-Natrun) und der Sinai-Region.* vols 1-5 (Wiesbaden, 1984-91)
ZÄS = *Zeitschrift für ägyptische Sprache und Altertumskunde.*
ZPE = *Zeitschrift für Papyrologie und Epigraphik.*

THE "CRUCIFIXION WITH THE TWELVE APOSTLES" AT THE BENAKI MUSEUM

Lila de Chaves

The "Crucifixion with the twelve Apostles" (fig.1), a unique embroidered panel (283cm X 48cm), was purchased in May, 1929 by Anthony Benaki, the founder of the Museum, from Nahman, an antique dealer, for the price of 100 sterling pounds. It appears listed for the first time in the 1935 Catalogue of the Benaki Museum, with the simple description "The Crucifixion with the Twelve Apostles".
The same description is used, by the director of the Museum Prof. A. Delivorrias in "The guide to the Benaki Museum" Athens 1980, with only addition "Tentatively assigned to the 7th century" and by Otto Meinardus in "The Collection of Coptica in the QAṢR of the Monastery of St Antony" who describes it as an embroidery of "the Crucifixion on silk with six Apostles on each side, one of whom slightly elevated" (1).
From the Early Christian period, the theological interpretation of the death of Christ found expression through the Crucifixion (2) in works of minor art (manuscript illustration, weaving, metalwork, engraving) such as the Crucifixion on the Monza ampula and that on a 5th century ivory relief from North Italy, (British Museum).
It became common from the 9th century and after the Iconoclastic Controversy, in the East, Syria, Armenia, Egypt and the West, especially during the late Carolingian and Ottonian periods, in a great number of iconographic variations; in some instances, it might be accompanied by the Virgin, St. John, the thieves, or other figures associated with the Passion. The representation of the "Crucifixion" in question, with Christ in the center and six Apostles on either side, standing next to each other in frontal poses is quite a rare one. The earliest similar type occurs, on a Greek sealstone, 3d century, in the British Museum, but this type as attested by Gertrud Schiller most probably comes from heretical circles (3).
Usually, in the various christian iconographic depictions of the Crucifixion, the twelve Apostles are never presented all together, since Judas had already died. If this occurs, in a rare case, then Matthew B is selected as the 12th Apostle, in the place of Judas. From (Chapter B, of the Acts of the Apostles), it is derived that the depiction with the

twelve Apostles is established iconographically with the Pentecost. That is, when the number of the twelve Apostles is complete, and all of them together receive The Holy Spirit, after which, they start preaching in the different languages. This is also mentioned in the First Epistle (16,8) of Apostle Paul to the Corinthians.
The Crucifixion with the twelve Apostles, although rendered stylistically in a primitive and non-naturalistic way, with a total absence of any decorative elements, has undoubtetly a monumental nature. The Christ, nailed on the cross, occupies the center of the panel dividing the scene in two symmetrical parts in an unusual compositional configuration. On either side, stand six Apostles, one next to each other, in frontal poses, all of equal size except for the one far right who is smaller. Only the Crusifix is larger thus the scene aquires importance and becomes centrobaric. Neither the Apostles, or the figure of Christ seem to be supported firmly on any pictorial ground. They all look rather suspended in the narrow space of the textile in an endless arrangement; thus being in accordance with the aesthetic expression, of the two dimentional surface, on which everything is suspended in a world that is transcendental and symbolic, so deer to the Copts. Christ his eyes closed in death (4), depiction which was first traced on an icon from Mount Sinai of the 8th century as presented by K. Weitzmann and M. Chatzidakis, is nailed to a T - shape cross (Crux Comissa patibulata), or cross of St. Antony of Egypt (5). The cross is embroidered in purplish brown with some details in black, which evidently, although rendered in a naive way, play the role of the Chiaroscuro around Christ's figure. His arms are outstretched and nailed, blood is also traced in salmon pink (6).
Both his legs, the right one on the top of the left, are nailed to the upright of the cross, with only one nail and are not supported on a suppedaneum. This type of Crucifixion with only three nails, has its roots in the North and it first appeared in the 12th century. This representation shows a new outlook on the Passion, Arma Christi (7), frequently appearing in many regions. Eventually it travelled to the East with the Crusades, during the 12th - 13th centuries (8). Christ has a dark beard embroidered in black and lighter hair embroidered in brown. According to G.A. Sotiriou, these iconographic features are of a Jewish type (9).
His body is portrayed frontally rendered in a primitive style, with obvious disproportion, his legs being much shorter than his torso. His posture

is heavy and stiff without any realistic leaning
either to the right (Byzantine type), or to the
left, contraposto, (western type).
He is wearing a perizoma (loin-cloth) which replaced
the colobium or sleevelen Chiton (Tunic) from the
9th century onwards. Though, an interesting scene
with the Christ wearing a colobium in later time
(10), can be noticed on a fresco from the Episcopi
church in Eurytania, first layer, middle 12th
century in the Byzantine Museum in Athens.
In either of the two lateral compositions flanking
the Crucifix the massive figures of the Apostles,
are portrayed They all have bell-shaped
conventionally rendered bodies, a style which is
properly Coptic, as evidence is found in various
iconographic sources, on works of minor arts, on
icons and frescoes as presented in detailed articles
and works of Maggy Rassart-Debergh, Piotr O. Scholz,
P.P. du Bourguet, M.- H. Rutschowskaya, L.A. Hunt,
to mention only a few of the many experts. Some of
the Apostles are wearing colobia, others Chitons,
with a small cross on the breast and himatia
(ΒΙΚΟΥΚΛΙΟΝ in Coptic that is, the Byzantine
Phelonion, or the Catholic Chasuble) (11).
Their heads are larger in proportion to the rest of
the bodies. Their eyes are rendered with just a
black line, the same goes for the eyebrows and the
nose which is rendered in an oblong V shape. Their
mouths are marked with only a small, either red or
salmon pink line or dot. Their hair are embroidered
in black and only one Apostle has a brown
embroidered hair line on top of the black one.
Most probably the embroiderer meant to portray a
figure of a fair complexion. It is worthwhile to
note, that none of the Apostles in this case is
portrayed with white hair, that is, in an elderly
age. Usually in the Eastern iconographical
prototypes, in codices, gospel illustrations etc.
the Apostles are represented threw out the Byzantine
era with naturalistic features that follow specific
iconographic rules, as presented in the most
important work of the 17th century by Denys de
Fourna, representing an iconographic variety of ages
(12). Though at first sight, the Apostles, all look
alike, one will soon notice that each one has its
own particular features and thus personality. Two of
the twelve look younger, with oval faces traced in
black, three wear a beard and the rest have fat
almost round faces with no apparent neck.
Their feet are bare portrayed in the traditional
Coptic style. A custom still preserved in Coptic
ritual, where the priest is barefooted through the
liturgy, sympolizing God's command to Moses to
approach barefooted (exodus 3,5). This can also be

traced in many icons and fresco depictions of
Saints, as seen for instance in the icon of St.
Antony and St. Paul in the Coptic Museum, or as
well, as in the icon and the fresco of St. Thomas
the Hermit.
Inspite of the fact, that the Apostles seem to be in
a static state, their feet show moovement only five
of them been staying still. Three on the right side
of the Crucufix, seem to walk towards Christ. The
same goes for one Apostle in the other lateral
composition, who also walks towards Christ only in
the opposite direction.
The three of the Apostles who wear a beard (perhaps
ment to be older and wiser) two on the left and one
on the right side of the scene, have their right
hands raised in a gesture of testimony. Each one is
holding an orb with an inscribed red cross, in their
left hand. They are believed to represent the
Apostles Peter, James and John (John XVII, 23), who
are rendered in this same pose to symbolize the
transfiguration (St. Catherine, Sinai) and the
Ascension (The Rabbula Gospels) (13).
Both these iconographic scenes belong to the cycle
of the Theophany, that is of God's devine nature. At
this point, we must turn our attention to the figure
on the far right of the iconographic Crucifixion
scene. As Otto Meinardus has already noticed, this
Apostle is not on the same level with the others,
but is elevated and seems some how detached from the
rest (fig.2). He is smaller in size, differently
dressed and seems to be mooving away from the main
dominant image, thus playing a second part in the
scene.
As I have already pointed out the iconographic
represen- tation of all twelve Apostles is referring
either to the Ascension or to the Pentcost.
Consequently, at this point, a question rises. Does
this elevated figure represent Matthew (Chapter B of
the Acts of the Apostles) thus replacing Juda in a
symbolic depiction reminiscent of Juda's death,
hunged by the tree, therefore being elevated and not
touching the ground?, as shown, for instance, in the
depiction on an ivory carved casket in the British
Museum (14).
In any case, we believe, that this unique
representation of the Crucifixion with the Twelve
Apostles which involves also the Ascension is not
only an unusual and unique composi-tional formula,
but allows us to assume that it represents Christ's
Death as a triumph over Death emphasizing along with
the other factors the non-Chalcedonic origin of the
embroidered panel.
The scene of the Crucifixion is enframed by a row of
small embroidered crosses on top, alternatively

displayed in black and white. The two vertical sides
left and right, have respectively twelve crosses in
white. On top of the scene lenghtwise there is a row
of seventy crosses. We believe that the embroiderer
has not embroidered the crosses merely by chance,
but he or she must have chosen these respective
numbers on purpose, trying to emphasize their
symbolic meaning.
If we are on the right track, the twelve crosses on
the vertical sides are referring to the twelve
Apostles (Number twelve being the symbolic
representation of the twelve tribes of Israel
(Matthew XVIII, 28) and (Luke VI, 13).
As for the seventy crosses all along the top of the
crucifixion scene, they must represent the Seventy
Apostles; disciples which were named by Christ
himself during his liftime to spred his Word all
over the World (Luke X, 1).
On the other hand, little crosses which surround an
icon, or decorate a haical door, a haical curtain or
an iconostassis or even the ecclesiastical vestments
on the ΠΙΒΑΛΛΙΝ as found in the extensive works of
A.J. Butler, Evelyn White, L.A. Hunt and others are
of typically Coptic style, used for the exorcism of
Satan, as pointed out by Reverend Pola Amba Bishoi,
of the Coptic Church in Athens.

Inscription

Last but not least is the issue of the inscription
which is embroidered in black lengthwise, in one
line, exactly under the scene. It is separated in
intervals by a Chrisme embroidered also in black
(fig.3).
I am far from being an expert in the field of
inscriptions. Nevertheless, being Greek I am
familiar with the letters of the Greek alphabet and
I believe, can recognise certain abbreviations
common to my field of knowledge. In that respect and
only, I permitted myself to present the inscription
on the Crucifix, pointing out certain remarks,
though I am well aware of the fact that to an expert
these might be of trivial value.
The embroidered inscription is written in Greek and
Coptic characters while in some parts there is a
variation of other letters, as is pointed out by
Reverend Pola Amba Bishoi of being Syriak
Tentatively, I recognized myself a galgolitic one (Q)
Some other letters are unidentifiable such as
is it Arabic?
Nevertheless the first three abbreviations at the
beginning of the inscription give us a clue that
they are of Greek meaning. The first abbreviation,
even though, misspelled is referring to the Monogram
of Christ IHIΣ. The second one adding (Σ) could

be read as (ΕΛΕΗΣΕ /have mercy) and the third (X̄Ē)
is deciphered with a great certitude as ΧΡΙΣΤΕ (Oh!
Christ) (15). Thus we are led to the conclusion that,
this inscription is a Δοξαστικον of either the holy
Friday (ΔΟΞΑΣΤΙΚΟΝ of the Crucifixion) or a
ΔΟΞΑΣΤΙΚΟΝ of the twelve Apostles, (30th of June). A
coptic inscription with same chrisme, lozenge
shaped, at intervals, is also traced on a late
coptic tapestry fragment in the Louvre, that P.P. du
Bourguet has described, as curtain or an altar
hunging, from the Fayoum, 12th century (16).
In conclusion, the iconographic scene of the
Crucifix with the twelve Apostles in the Benaki
Museum, is a most particular, mysterious and unique
representation of the Crucifixion. It is a hybrid,
which has no similar. Iconographically it has
elements from both the East, the West and the North
as prooved, stylistically in many details which are
not apparent at first sight, one can trace Armenian
connotations as for instance in the protuberant knot
of Christ's loin-cloth (perizoma). In addition one
can notice a Syrian influence especially in the
rendering of the Apostles faces. The inscription in
itself is a synthesis of letters from different
Alphabets. However its obvious cyncretism, the
particular personality of Coptic Art prevales, with
its abstract, conventional forms and its pronounced
mysticism and symbolisme, that nonetheless remains
deeply Christian (17). As for its place of origin
only by instinct I would assign it to the Low Egypt
region of Fayoum. Having no iconographic or
stylistic parallels of the Crucifixion here
examined, it is practically impossible to gain any
insight in its earlier history and in its origin.
Dated at the 13th - 14th century.

TECHNICAL CONTEXT

Both the fibers of the textile and those of the
embroidered figures, have been examined by
Microtonic section, at the (Institut Textile de
France) ITF Paris laboratories, in 1992. The results
were as follows.
Textile: purplish brown and orange fibers - Silk
Embroidery: Crucifix, Apostles undyed white fibers -
Cotton
- Inscription, crosses, black dyed fibers Cotton
(of particularely good quality).
Technique of textile
Despite the damage to parts of the Textile (263cm x
48cm), the crucifixion is a rare complete example of
late coptic monastic embroidery. The narrative scene
is embroidered on a purplish brown silk field in
plain weave, which is decorated with three

perpendicular to the embroidery woven bands (263cm x
7,5cm) of unspan orange silk threads in samit (2Z1).
The third orange samit band, under the iconographic
scene on which an inscription is embroidered
lengthwise, is cut in the middle. This attests that
the textile was wider. The upper larger band of the
embroidered panel is decorated with an inlay-
brocated pattern with the same orange unspun silk
threads. It consists of a repetition of geometric
designs, such as the diaper scheme and a motif
reminiscent of the candelabra tree ending to a
smaller "head" upperelement, an important motif of
the Umayyad period and soon adopted by the Coptic
weavers of the time (18). Something which has
persisted throughout the Mamluk period. By a happy
chance, the salvedge at the top of the embroidered
scene, (that is, at the right side of the textile,
on which the embroidery was made), has been
preserved and shows along with the weaving, the
close fitted dents of a proper reed. This enables us
to assume, taking into consideration the technical
evolution of the draw-loom, that the textile must
have not been weaved before the late 12th - 13th
centuries. Therefore we are dealing with a silk
textile, excellently woven, but nevertheless,
associated with a draw-loom mainstream production,
which limits us to date it, between the 13th - 14th
centuries.

TECHNIQUE OF EMBROIDERY

The scene is embroidered on part of the textile,
occupying the space between the orange bands in the
self-couched and knotted stem stiches, which were
not only characteristic of the late Coptic period,
but also used commonly in Meddieval Eastern and
Western Monasteries (19). The embroidered version of
the "Crucifixion and the twelve Apostles", shows a
primitive and inferior technique. In spite of that,
the effort of the embroiderer is obvious, which is,
the portrayal of various iconographical details.
This can be seen on the garments of the Apostles,
the details of which have been rendered only by
means of using a different direction of the stitch.
This is a consequence of the fact that the
embroidery mainly embroidered with white threads,
except for some details which were rendered in red,
brown, blue, salmon pink (cotton dyed threads). Some
of these colors have faded with time. The textile at
the places of the embroidered figures, has shrunk
and unsightly folds appear, which were created by
the reaction of the cotton threads possibly, due to
the fact, that the embroidery remained for a long
time in a humid environment. The wears and holes on

part of the textile are due to oxidation the origin
of which has not been, yet   chemically determined.

NOTES

1. Otto Meinardus, The collection of Coptica in the
QAṢR of the Monastery of St. Antony, <u>Bulletin de la
Societe d' Archeologie Copte</u>, vol. XVIII,p.272; A.
Delivorrias, <u>Guide to the Benaki Museum</u>, Athens
1980, p.34.
2. For the evolution of the iconography of the
Crucifixion see G. Millet, <u>Recherches sur
l'iconographie de l'evangile</u>, Paris 1916, and
Gertrud Schiller, <u>Iconography of Christian art</u>,
vol.2, New York 1972, figs. 323-324.
3. Gertrud Schiller, op.cit., fig.321. A similar
arrangement of the Apostles is to be found in a
scene of the Ascension. Fresco in the Baouit
Monastery VII. R.P. Pierre du Bourguet, <u>L'art copte</u>,
Paris 1968, p.42.
4. In the East the iconography of the dead Christ
first appeared after the iconoclast controversy in
843 AD, as it did in the West (School of Reims); see
Radbertus, <u>De corpore et Sanguine Domini</u> 831-3, p.9.
5. It is also used as the head of Pastoral staffs
for the actual or symbolic support of ecclesiastics
in the Orthodox and Coptic church. Heather Child and
Dorothy Colles, <u>Christian symbols - ancient and
modern</u>, Bell and Hyman, London 1960, p.18.
6. G.A. and M. Soteriou, <u>Eikones tes Mones Sina -
Icones du Mont Sinai</u>, 2 vols., Athens 1956-8, figs.
24-27. K. Weitzmann in <u>Icons from South Eastern
Europe and Sinai</u>, London 1968.
7. For Arma Christi see Gertrud Schiller,
<u>Iconography of Christian Art</u>, vol. 2, The Passion of
Jesus Christ, New York 1971-1972, p.146.
8. G. Millet, op.cit., p.412.
9. G.A. Soteriou, <u>Ὁ Χριστός ἐν τῇ τέχνῃ</u>, 1914,
p.109.
10. Gertrud Schiller, op.cit., p.100.
11. For an extensive description of Coptic
ecclesiastical vestments, see A;fred J. Butler, <u>The
Ancient Coptic Churches of Egypt</u>, vol.II, Oxford
1884.
12. For the Apostles representations see Διονυσίου
τοῦ ἐκ Φουρνά "<u>Ἑρμηνεία ζωγραφικῆς τέχνης</u>" ἐν
Πετρουπόλει 1909, p.298-299. French translation
Denys de Fourna, <u>Manuel d'iconographie Chretienne</u>
par A. Papadopoulos-Kerameus, St. Petersbourg 1909.
13. Icon in the Benaki Museum. Ascension. 17th
century. <u>Guide to the Benaki Museum</u>, Athens 1980,
p.77; manuscript illustration in the Bibliotheque
Laurentienne, Florence; cf. A. Grabar, <u>La peinture
Byzantine</u>, Genève 1953, p.164.

14. Rowena Loverance, Byzantium British Museum, London 1988, fig. 15, p.15.
15. On a unique icon of the Cretoitalian School, in the Byzantine Museum of Athens (T.2638) 15th century is depicted a most rare representation of both the crucifixion and the resurection in the East (Εἰς Ἀδου Κάθοδος) and west prototypes. The icon underneath has a two row inscription of a supplicatory troparion and has been eventually a donation.
16. Pierre du Bourguet, Catalogues des etoffes Coptes I, Musée National du Louvre, Paris 1964, L1 AC827, p.647.
17. Evelyn White, The History of the Monasteries of Nitria and the Scetis, New York 1931 and Publications of the Metropolitan Museum of Art, Egyptian Expedition, vol.VIII, New York 1973.
18. Carl Johan Lamm, Cotton in medieval textiles in the Near East, Paris 1937, p.10,12,53,55,145. For a most extensive information on Textiles see Deborah Thomson in Bulletin de Liaison du C.I.E.T.A. Nos 61-62, Lyon 1985, 1-2 vol. fig.8, p.35-49.
19. P.P. du Bourguet, Les etoffes Coptes du Musée du Louvre, 13,15p.646. Also in Bildkataloge des Kestner-Museums Hannover Textilien I. Weberein und Stikerein des Mittelalters, 1964 (Medieval stitches in Western monasteries).

I would like to extend warm thanks to:
M. Rassart-Debergh, Prof.D. Johnson, Prof.A. Delivorrias, Prof. Maria Theoharis, Marie-Hélène Rutschowskaya, R. Pola Amba Bishoi,

In memory of   Lascarina Bouras
               Doula Mouriki

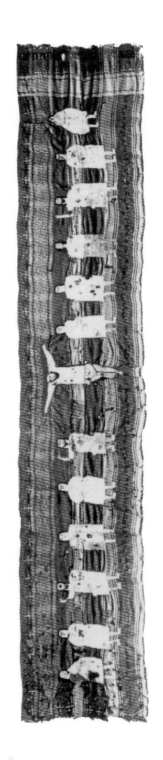

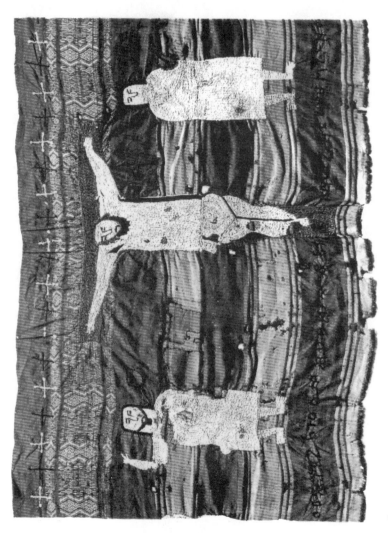

1 a

1 b

SHENOUTE'S LITERARY CORPUS:
A CODICOLOGICAL RECONSTRUCTION

Stephen Emmel

The surviving works of Shenoute are known almost exclusively from the deteriorated and now dismembered remains of the library of his own monastery, the so-called White Monastery, near Sohag in Upper Egypt, where thousands of pages of his writings were once housed. In contrast to this treasure house of Shenoute manuscripts, the sources of relevant information that have been found outside the White Monastery are few: copies of only two or three undoubted works; a few dozen brief excerpts surviving on ostraca, or in the standard Coptic holy week lectionary, or as quotations in works of other authors; and three book lists with vague references to works of Shenoute. It is clear from this meager evidence that Shenoute was known and read well beyond the confines of his own community, but the fact remains that only the library of the White Monastery has given us the possibility of recovering Shenoute's literary corpus to any appreciable extent. Thus the reconstruction of Shenoute's corpus depends on reconstructing the White Monastery library, whose extensive but nonetheless very incomplete remnants are now scattered piecemeal through several dozen libraries and museums, from Cairo across Europe to North America.

I want to report briefly here on my effort to reconstruct the White Monastery codexes containing works of Shenoute. In some respects, this effort has been more successful than I dared hope at the outset almost a decade ago,[1] because it has led not only to the partial reconstruction of almost one hundred codexes containing Shenoute's works, but also to the recovery of the bibliographical structure of his literary corpus as it has been transmitted to us, a structure that was previously thought to be unrecoverable.

Basing my work on empirical evidence and an explicit methodology, I have endeavored to achieve a codicological reconstruction of the core of

---

NOTE: Collections of Coptic manuscripts are referred to below according to the abbreviations established in Emmel, *Directory*.

[1] See Emmel, "Report." Although preliminary work for this project was conducted during 1983 and the subsequent years, most of the codicological research was accomplished during 1989–1991.

Shenoute's corpus, a core whose components can be accepted as established with a high degree of probability. Just as the codex reconstructions are based on a conservative empirical method, involving simultaneous consideration of script, page format, codex structure, and textual continuity, so also have I used conservative criteria for attributing works to Shenoute, relying primarily on explicit internal and external attributions, and excluding reliance on features of literary style or grammatical usage. My goal at this stage of research is to identify by noncontroversial criteria the corpus that was *transmitted under Shenoute's name*, without yet broaching the questions of whether or not this corpus includes false attributions, and whether or not genuine works of Shenoute have been transmitted outside this corpus. It is likely that some works that were in fact transmitted under Shenoute's name have been excluded from my reconstruction for lack of decisive evidence, and I hope that future research will provide grounds for admitting such works to the core corpus.

Such a reconstruction as I have achieved has necessarily required consideration of a large number of manuscript fragments. Every fragment that has been attributed to Shenoute by modern scholars, on whatever grounds, has been considered, as well as many others besides. All in all, mostly on the basis of microfilms and photographs, some six thousand White Monastery leaves and fragments were examined. This number was systematically reduced so as to include only the fragments that can be assigned to Shenoute's corpus in accordance with the criteria for fragment placement and attribution that were established for this project.

The resulting reconstruction entails about 1,900 leaves and fragments surviving from about 90 parchment codexes. Probably the extant fragments are at best only one tenth of the total number of leaves that these codexes originally contained, and thus Shenoute's corpus remains fragmentary to a lamentable degree. Nevertheless, there is in the fragmentary corpus a coherent bibliographical structure that can now be used in the service of further reconstruction, and the discernible structure also makes it possible to know in some detail what the corpus as a whole comprises.

In his foundational study of Shenoute published in 1903, Johannes Leipoldt drew attention to evidence that the works of Shenoute were transmitted, at least in part, in an arrangement that was fixed by a systematic numeration of various components of the corpus.[2] The most obvious piece of evidence for such a system is a codex leaf in Vienna that

---

[2] Leipoldt, *Schenute*, 10 (referring to the "Wiener Bücherverzeichnis"; cf. n. 3 below), 102–3, and 189 n. 1.

contains the last fifty-seven items in a numbered list of ninety-one incipits that are attributed to Shenoute.[3] But Leipoldt pointed out also that the manuscripts themselves show traces of a similar numbering system having been applied to works, or groups of works, called "canons": Leipoldt cited occurrences of the titles "second canon," "third canon," "eighth canon," and, in a reference in the Arabic *Life of Shenoute*, "ninth canon." But he despaired of being able to recover fully the systematization of the corpus to which this scanty evidence attests, remarking only that it shows "wie lückenhaft unsere bisherige Kenntnis der Werke Schenutes ist."[4]

As a working hypothesis, I assumed that the Vienna incipit list and the occurrence of numbered "canons" both pointed to a single organizing principle underlying Shenoute's corpus. But the gradual accumulation of facts eventually disproved this hypothesis and indicated a more complex bibliographical structure. I am now convinced that the corpus comprises two main components: two numbered multi-volume sets of collected works, copied in a fixed order. One of these two sets of volumes is the *Canons*, called ⲔⲀⲚⲰⲚ in the manuscript tradition. The other set of volumes I call the *Discourses*, echoing the term Ⲗⲟⲅⲟⲥ, which is often used with reference to works in this second set of volumes. For the most part, both these multi-volume sets—the *Canons* and the *Discourses*—survive in multiple copies. If the extant Shenoute codexes had survived intact, the bibliographical structure of these volumes would be plainly evident. But as it is, this structure must be recovered by rearranging scattered pieces of scant surviving evidence into a coherent pattern. Because the evidence for the arrangement of the *Canons* is more complete than is the evidence for the *Discourses*, I will describe the *Canons* first.

The key to reconstructing the *Canons* turns out to be the unique codex of excerpts from works of Shenoute that Leipoldt dubbed "florilegium Sinuthianum,"[5] a codex of two hundred leaves, forty-eight of which survive at least in part—a high survival rate as these things go. What is true of nearly all Shenoute codexes is particularly true of the florilegium:

[3] AT-NB K 9634 (*Stud.Pal.* IX 50a-b; this is the text that Leipoldt called the "Wiener Bücherverzeichnis").

[4] Leipoldt, *Schenute*, 103. Leipoldt's examples showing that "man hat die Predigten... Schenutes ebenso fortlaufend numeriert, wie seine 'Kanones'" (p. 189 n. 1) must be used only with caution.

[5] Leipoldt, *Sinuthii Opera* 3:2 (no. 6) etc.; cf. Leipoldt, *Schenute*, 10–11 ("Blütenlese"; the suggestion made here that two other copies of the florilegium might be identifiable was mistaken). In the system of two-letter sigla for White Monastery ("MONB") codexes that has been established by Tito Orlandi for the "Corpus dei Manoscritti Copti Letterari," the Shenoute florilegium will be known as codex XL.

from the published editions of Shenoute texts, it is almost impossible to gain a clear idea of how this codex is organized *as a book*. It is well known that the florilegium is a collection of excerpts from longer works, many of them works of Shenoute that are known from other codexes. But it has not yet been clearly recognized that these excerpts are grouped under higher-level headings that present the excerpts as a series of sequentially numbered "canons." Four such headings survive, introducing "canons" 5, 7, 8, and 9.[6] When one maps the parallels to the florilegium in other codexes—and there are more parallels than have yet been noted in print—it becomes clear that the parallels to each canonical section are restricted to a discrete group of codexes. It is also clear that the codexes within each of these groups are parallel to one another throughout, that is, all the codexes in a given group are copies of a single volume. Furthermore, the excerpts from these volumes occur in the florilegium in precisely the same order in which the excerpted passages occur in the source volumes themselves. And finally, the surviving volume titles that explicitly identify some of the codexes as complete copies of *Canons* 2, 3, 6, 8, and 9 are in perfect accord with the canonical arrangement of the florilegium. On the basis of these firm data for most of Shenoute's *Canons*, it is possible to identify copies of all the volumes in the set. In sum, we have copies of nine volumes of *Canons*—accounting for about forty of the surviving Shenoute codexes—plus the florilegium that is a series of excerpts extracted in sequence from all nine volumes.

Each volume of the *Canons* contains a group of Shenoute's works, some of them attributed to him explicitly in headings in the codexes. The works in these volumes are concerned generally with matters of governance and discipline in Shenoute's communities. They are the sources of most of the fragments that Leipoldt published as *De vita monachorum*.[7] But the *Canons* also include works that are more strictly homiletic, such as the famous sermon *De gladio prophetico*,[8] which occurs in *Canon* 7. Thus the principle of selection that underlies the compilation of these volumes, including the florilegium, is not obvious. It is an interesting question, however, because there is internal evidence suggesting that the codification of these works might go back to Shenoute himself.[9]

---

[6] XL 107 (AT-NB K 9597[A]), 261 (EG-CF Copte 189[B]), 294 (FR-BN Copte 130[4] f. 148[R]), and the verso of an unplaced leaf (FR-BN Copte 130[4] f. 132[V] + 132[4] f. 303[V]; see below with n. 10). The relevant texts are all unpublished.

[7] Leipoldt, *Sinuthii Opera* 4:41–173 (nos. 54–75, 77, and 80).

[8] Leipoldt, *Sinuthii Opera* 4:11–21 (no. 49).

[9] See esp. Leipoldt, *Schenute*, 10 and 182, Amélineau, *Oeuvres de Schenoudi* 1:xxi and 2:533–35 (this text [FR-BN Copte 130[4] f. 131 (not 130[1] f. 136, as Amélineau reported),

Although there is explicit evidence for attributing many of the individual works in the *Canons* to Shenoute, it is reasonable to ask if there is evidence for attributing these *Canons* to Shenoute in their entirety. Doubt on this point might be raised by the fact that the excerpts in the florilegium are not explicitly attributed to anyone, being headed simply ⲦⲞⲨ ⲀⲨⲦⲞⲨ, "by the same person." Presumably all these laconic references depend on an explicit statement of authorship at the very beginning of the volume, which is not known to survive. Even the major headings in the volume do not name any author—with one fortunate exception. The last major heading, which occurs on a leaf that must be reconstructed out of two fragments, torn right through the heading, reads: "Likewise *Canon* 9 of holy Apa Shenoute, prophet and archimandrite."[10] Altogether, the evidence strongly favors accepting the entire florilegium, as well as the forty or so codexes to which it provides a kind of index, as one major component of Shenoute's corpus.

The hypothesis that a second major component of Shenoute's corpus consists of another set of numbered volumes of works, distinct from the *Canons*, is based primarily on the following observation: the order of Shenoute's works that is given in the list of ninety-one incipits partly surviving in Vienna is reflected in several of the extant Shenoute codexes, two of which bear volume numbers 4 and 8,[11] and these two volumes are not copies of *Canons* 4 and 8. The works in the volume numbered 4 are listed at the beginning of the extant part of the Vienna list, those in vol. 8 are listed near the end, and thus the list as a whole can be divided among a total of eight (or nine?) volumes, which I call the *Discourses*. Due to the fragmentary state of the surviving codexes, and the complete loss of the first thirty-four incipits of the Vienna list, it is impossible at present to reconstruct this component of Shenoute's corpus in as much

with a parallel in GB-OB Clarendon Press.b. 4 f. 25] is the introduction not to the florilegium, as Leipoldt supposed, but to *Canon* 9); Munier, *Manuscrits coptes*, 115 – 18 and 189 (no. 9270), with an unpublished parallel in FR-BN Copte 130² f. 117$^{V/R}$ (the end of *Canon* 1).

[10] FR-BN Copte 130⁴ f. 132^V + 132⁴ f. 303^V:ii.25 – 28 (unpublished).

[11] Codex XH 375, "4(th volume), ten epistles," and a statement in the colophon (XH 376) that the manuscript was copied from "the fourth old book of discourses" of Shenoute (EG-CF Copte 1 f. 101, ed. Chassinat, *Quatrième livre*, 209 – 10; cf. van Lantschoot, *Colophons* 1.1:153 – 55 and 1.2:60 – 61); codex HD 1, "Discourses of Shenoute, 8(th volume)" (FR-BN Copte 130⁵ f. 79^R, ed. Leipoldt, *Sinuthii Opera* 3:218, Amélineau, *Oeuvres de Schenoudi* 1:180 n. 2; I disagree with both Leipoldt's and Amélineau's interpretations of the numeral here as meaning either "8th sermon" or "8 sermons" (Leipoldt, *Schenute*, 8 [no. e.25], 189 n. 1; Amélineau, *Oeuvres de Schenoudi* 1:xcvii and 180 n. 2; Leipoldt, *Sinuthii Opera* 3:218 n. 7; Amélineau, review of Leipoldt, *Sinuthii Opera*, 368 – 69).

detail as is possible in the case of the *Canons*. With some help from ten liturgical typikon fragments containing references to works of Shenoute, it is possible to identify copies of vols. 4, 5, 7, and 8 of the *Discourses*, accounting for twelve of the surviving Shenoute codexes. The hypothesis that the *Discourses* are a distinct component of the corpus finds confirmation in an interesting fact, one that also suggests the motive for the organized transmission of this body of works: the well-attested liturgical usage of Shenoute's writings is limited to works that occur in what I call the *Discourses*, to the exclusion of the works in the *Canons*.

In contrast to the *Canons*, the *Discourses* are the main body of Shenoute's sermons and tracts. For example, vol. 4 is the great Shenoute codex in the Institut français in Cairo, published by Chassinat in 1911,[12] while vol. 8 includes the long series of sermons published by Guérin a decade earlier.[13] Of the fifty-five extant incipits in the Vienna list, many survive or can be reconstructed in the identifiable copies of Shenoute's *Discourses*, and I am hopeful that with further work on all the Shenoute codexes—including preparation of much-needed editions and especially indexes—it will become possible to reconstruct this set of volumes in still more detail.

Apart from the copies of Shenoute's *Canons* and *Discourses* that are identifiable, there are about two dozen codexes that contain different groupings of works from these two main components of the corpus (but with the *Discourses* heavily favored), and they also include works that do not occur in either the *Canons* or the *Discourses* so far as we know them at present. However, some of the works in this latter category are represented in the liturgical typika, and so they might well belong in vols. 1, 2, or 3 of the *Discourses*, the contents of which are obscured for us by the loss of the beginning of the Vienna list. At present, in fact, the combined evidence of the Vienna list, the typika, and these composite codexes, warrants the hypothesis that the *Canons* and the *Discourses* together account for nearly all the works of Shenoute that have been transmitted to us.[14]

I say "nearly" all, because there is a third component of Shenoute's corpus, unfortunately now badly mutilated: Shenoute's correspondence, actual letters to and from a variety of persons, including government

---

[12] Chassinat, *Quatrième livre*. Pp. 173/174 of this codex (XH) have been identified by Bentley Layton in the British Library (Layton, "Shenute Fragments").

[13] Guérin, "Sermons inédits" (FR-PL E. 10612, from codex GP).

[14] In addition to these composite codexes and the copies of the *Canons* and *Discourses*, the Shenoute codexes include about half a dozen lectionaries with sections excerpted for liturgical reading from his works (but not from works in the *Canons*).

officials, local citizens, and members of the ascetic communities under Shenoute's care. Some of these letters are found in the *Canons* and *Discourses*, but others were copied, perhaps not in a fixed order, at the ends of some volumes of the *Discourses*—perhaps even just some copies of some volumes of the *Discourses*—without their incipits having been included in the Vienna list, at least as we know it at present. Given the especially fragmentary state of this part of the corpus, and the lack of any external guide to its contents, it is impossible at present to gauge the full extent of the transmitted collection of letters.

It is obvious that a primary benefit of reconstructing the codexes of Shenoute's works is to increase the amount and coherence of the recoverable text, both by placing fragments in individual codexes, and also by relating the contents of two or more codexes such that lacunas in one can be filled with text that survives elsewhere. A less obvious but no less important benefit of the reconstruction is to augment the evidence for attributing works to Shenoute, and thereby confirming or even adding to his undoubted corpus. One example will serve to illustrate the kind of progress that can be made in this regard.

In 1985, Tito Orlandi published a substantial part of a polemical work that he entitled "Shenute contra Origenistas."[15] The beginning of this work is missing, and although the end survives in one codex, there is no accompanying statement of attribution there.[16] To justify attributing this work to Shenoute, Orlandi cited the author's style, his apparent historical context, and the concurring opinions of several knowledgeable Coptologists.[17] But, as Orlandi noted, an objection to this attribution had been raised by Enzo Lucchesi, who identified the author as the Alexandrian bishop Dioscorus.[18] To my knowledge, Lucchesi has not published a detailed argument in favor of this attribution, but his claim that the text published by Orlandi is a part of Dioscorus's "Hypomnesticon contra Origenistas" suggests that he relates it to a work whose beginning survives in White Monastery codex XZ, which is codicologically similar to one of the codexes containing the work published by Orlandi.[19] I myself

---

[15] Orlandi, *Shenute contra Origenistas.*

[16] Codex DS 221/222 (FR-BN Copte 131[5] f. 46), not included in Orlandi's edition, where the text was purposely concluded before the long quotation from Theophilus's paschal letter of 401 (see Orlandi, *Shenute contra Origenistas*, 12).

[17] Orlandi, *Shenute contra Origenistas*, 11–12.

[18] Lucchesi, "Pères de Nicée," 396 n. 9; see also Lucchesi, "Chénouté a-t-il écrit en grec?" 206–7 n. 10.

[19] The beginning of the work survives on XZ 69–73 (GB-CU Or. 1699B ff. 3–4, ed. Thompson, "Dioscorus and Shenoute," 372–73; EG-C C.G. 9285 f. 1, ed. Munier, *Manuscrits coptes*, 146–49), and codexes XZ and DS are similar. Orlandi's contrary statement

have found no codicological relationships and no textual relationships between XZ and any of the codexes that attest to the work in question, and hence the attribution to Dioscorus cannot be accepted as assured. On the contrary, the attribution to Shenoute can be established, on the following codicological grounds.

Two of the codexes on which Orlandi based his edition are copies of a single volume: codexes DQ and HB, in which "Contra Origenistas" occurs in first position.[20] On the basis of a table of contents at the end of a third codex, XN, and also considering other codicological factors, it can be demonstrated that XN is another copy of the same volume,[21] and hence the contents of all three codexes are indicated by XN's table of contents. This table lists five incipits, but names no author.[22] However, in HB and elsewhere[23] there is evidence for attributing the last three of these incipits to Shenoute. Just the fact that "Contra Origenistas" occurs in a volume alongside three works for which there is explicit attribution to Shenoute argues in favor of attributing this work to Shenoute as well.[24] But the attribution is confirmed by additional evidence as well,

---

notwithstanding (*Shenute contra Origenistas*, 11), also GB-CU Or. 1699B (*sic*) and FR-BN Copte 131[4] f. 160 belong to two different codexes (XZ and XE respectively).

[20] Codex DS has only "Contra Origenistas" in common with DQ and HB. It may be noted here that the table of attestation provided by Orlandi (*Shenute contra Origenistas*, 5) is misleading: the fragments listed there as DS 47–56 belong to a different codex (XY; cf. n. 24 below), and in any case the parallels between DQ and HB indicate that only one to two pages of text are missing between DQ 15 and HB 17. The parallels indicate also that in DS, "Contra Origenistas" does not begin until about p. 60 and thus is preceded by one or more other works (DS 1–60, entirely wanting at present).

[21] A full demonstration of the textual relationships among these and other related codexes will be found in my forthcoming dissertation (see n. 26 below). I hypothesize that this volume belongs to the *Discourses*, but if so it must be either vol. 1, 2, or 3, all of whose incipits are lost from the beginning of the Vienna list.

[22] XN 270 (IT-NB IB4 f. 22[V], ed. Giorgi, *Fragmentum Evangelii S. Iohannis*, clxvii–clxviii; Zoega, *Catalogus*, 452–53; Leipoldt, *Sinuthii Opera* 3:62; Amélineau, *Oeuvres de Schenoudi* 1:363), where the works are attributed laconically to "our father"; the immediately following colophon indicates that the codex was to be donated to the "monastery of Shenoute" at Rifeh (see van Lantschoot, *Colophons* 1.1:112–13, and 1.2:46–47 and 151 [no. 68]; cf. 1.2:33–34 n. 3), and hence attribution of the works in the codex to Shenoute might be implied even though it is not clearly stated.

[23] Codexes DR and XT, and the liturgical typika.

[24] Such an argument for attributing "Contra Origenistas" to Shenoute was already put forward by Crum (*Papyruscodex*, xviii n. 4), but on false grounds because "der Text unserer Rainerhs. [by which Crum referred to the codex that now bears the siglum DS], S. 55, 56 (Wessely Nr. 42b)," which Crum rightly attributed to Shenoute by means of a complex of parallels in codexes XW and DD, belongs to a codex (XY) that does *not* contain "Contra Origenistas" (XY 49/50 and 55/56 [*Stud.Pal.* IX 42a–b] were wrongly associated with DS 110–121 and 160–167 [*Stud.Pal.* IX 42c–m] by Krall and/or Wessely).

for the incipit of this work can be shown to be included in the Vienna incipit list of works of Shenoute.

From XN's table of contents we learn the probable lost incipit of "Contra Origenistas": since this work is in first position in DQ and HB, its incipit is the first item in XN's table of contents, that is, ϯⲣⲙⲟⲓϩⲉ, "I am amazed." This observation correlates with the fact that "Contra Origenistas" occurs also in the one White Monastery codex that is identifiable as a copy of *Discourses* 7,[25] the penultimate work in which is represented by incipit no. 54 in the Vienna list: ϯ<ⲣ̄>ⲙⲟⲉⲓϩⲉ ⲛ̄ⲛⲉⲧ-ⲱⲉⲉⲓ ϩⲛ̄ⲛⲉⲓⲱⲁϫⲉ ϫⲉⲁ, "I am amazed at those who go astray with the words '...'" Thus incipit no. 54 in the Vienna list can be identified with the first item in XN's table of contents. And thus the Vienna list provides explicit evidence that "Contra Origenistas," the work to which incipit no. 54 refers, was transmitted as a work of Shenoute.

The codicological reconstruction that I have tried to establish on a reliable basis is the *sine qua non* of a comprehensive reconstruction of Shenoute's literary work as such. The core of the publication that I am preparing, which is about to materialize first as a doctoral dissertation at Yale University,[26] is a detailed presentation of the reconstructed Shenoute codexes by means of codicological descriptions and tables with annotated bibliographies. On the basis of this reconstruction, and taking into consideration the relevant external testimonia, I will also present a catalog of Shenoute's works, stating the grounds for attributing each work to Shenoute and indicating briefly its contents. These catalogs of codexes and works will be prefaced by a detailed methodological statement and a recapitulation of the history of the White Monastery library that has made such a reconstructive enterprise both so unavoidable and so difficult. I hope that my results will serve as a reliable basis from which further progress can be made toward a complete edition of the works of Shenoute.

[25] Codex XE, from which only one leaf of "Contra Origenistas" survives: FR-BN Copte 131⁴ f. 160 = XE 143/144 (thus Porcher, "Analyse" 1:239; 153/154 and 183/184 might also be possible readings; ed. Orlandi, *Shenute contra Origenistas*, 20 – 22). XE is identifiable as a copy of *Discourses* 7 because the work beginning on XE 21 (IT-NB IB11 f. 3ᴿ, ed. Zoega, *Catalogus*, 589; Amélineau, *Oeuvres de Schenoudi* 2:332) corresponds to incipit no. 51 of the Vienna list, while the work in progress on XE 105/106 (IT-NB IB11 f. 38, ed. Zoega, *Catalogus*, 599; Amélineau, *Oeuvres de Schenoudi* 2:404 – 6) corresponds to incipit no. 53 (cf. *Stud.Pal.* XVIII 262b:7 – 9), and the known contents of *Discourses* 5 (Vienna list nos. 40 – 45) and 8 (beginning with Vienna list no. 56) indicate that *Discourses* 7 is likely to comprise Vienna list nos. 50 – 55.

[26] Emmel, "Shenoute's Literary Corpus" (Ph.D. diss., Yale University, in progress).

162

References

Amélineau, É. *Oeuvres de Schenoudi: Texte copte et traduction française.* 2 vols. Paris 1907–1914.

——. Review of Leipoldt, *Sinuthii Opera,* vol. 2. *Journal asiatique,* 10th ser., 15 (1910): 367–73.

Chassinat, Émile. *Le quatrième livre des entretiens et épîtres de Shenouti.* Mémoires publiés par les membres de l'Institut français d'archéologie orientale du Caire, vol. 23. Cairo 1911.

Crum, W.E. *Der Papyruscodex saec. VI–VII der Phillippsbibliothek in Cheltenham: Koptische theologische Schriften.* Schriften der Wissenschaftlichen Gesellschaft in Straßburg, vol. 18. Strasbourg 1915.

Emmel, Stephen. *An International Directory of Institutions Holding Collections of Coptic Antiquities outside of Egypt.* Rome 1990.

——. "[Report concerning codicological research on the manuscripts of Shenoute]." *Corpus dei Manoscritti Copti Letterari, Bollettino d'informazione,* no. 5 (1984): 16–18.

Giorgi, Agostino Antonio. *Fragmentum Evangelii S. Iohannis Graeco-Copto-Thebaicum Saeculi IV.* Rome 1789.

Guérin, H. "Sermons inédits de Senouti. (Introduction. texte. traduction.) Thèse soutenue a l'École du Louvre." *Revue égyptologique* 10 (1902): 148–64; 11 (1904): 15–34.

Layton, Bentley. "Two Unpublished Shenute Fragments *Against Kronos:* Layton, *Brit. Lib.,* Nos. 90 and 91." *Journal of Coptic Studies* 2 (1992): in press.

Leipoldt, Johannes. *Schenute von Atripe und die Entstehung des national ägyptischen Christentums.* Texte und Untersuchungen, vol. 25.1. Leipzig 1903.

——. *Sinuthii Archimandritae Vita et Opera Omnia.* With the assistance of W.E. Crum. 3 vols. (numbered 1, 3, and 4). Corpus Scriptorum Christianorum Orientalium, vols. 41, 42, 73 (Copt. 1 [= II.2.T], 2 [= II.4.T], 5 [= II.5.T]). Paris 1906–1913.

Lucchesi, Enzo. "Chénouté a-t-il écrit en grec?" In *Mélanges Antoine Guillaumont: Contributions à l'étude des christianismes orienteaux,* edited by René-Georges Coquin, 201–10. Cahiers d'orientalisme, vol. 20. Geneva 1988.

——. "318 ou 319 pères de Nicée?" *Analecta Bollandiana* 102 (1984): 394–96.

Munier, Henri. *Manuscrits coptes.* Catalogue général des antiquités égyptiennes du musée du Caire, nos. 9201–9304. Cairo 1916.

Orlandi, Tito. *Shenute contra Origenistas: Testo con introduzione e traduzione.* Rome 1985.

Porcher, E. "Analyse des manuscrits coptes 131[1–8] de la Bibliothèque nationale, avec indication des textes bibliques." *Revue d'égyptologie* 1 (1933): 105–60, 231–78; 2 (1936): 65–123.

Stud.Pal. IX and XVIII = Wessely, Carl. *Griechische und koptische Texte theologischen Inhalts,* vols. 1 and 5. Studien zur Palaeographie und Papyruskunde, vols. 9 and 18. Leipzig 1909 and 1917.

Thompson, Herbert. "Dioscorus and Shenoute." In *Recueil d'études égyptologiques dédiées à la mémoire de Jean-François Champollion à l'occasion du centenaire de la lettre à M. Dacier relative à l'alphabet des hiéroglyphes phonétiques lue à l'Académie des inscriptions et belles-lettres le 27 septembre 1822,* 367–76. Bibliothèque de l'École pratique des hautes études, IVe section, sciences historiques et philologiques, vol. 234. Paris 1922.

van Lantschoot, Arnold. *Recueil des colophons des manuscrits chrétiens d'Égypte.* Bibliothèque du *Muséon,* vol. 1. Louvain 1929.

Zoega, Georg. *Catalogus Codicum Copticorum Manu Scriptorum Qui in Museo Borgiano Velitris Adservantur.* Rome 1810.

TOWARD A LINGUISTIC CLASSIFICATION
OF THE "SAHIDIC" NAG HAMMADI TEXTS

WOLF-PETER FUNK

In this paper I am talking about the language of what are usually called the "Sahidic" Nag Hammadi texts, that is, the large majority of texts found in the Nag Hammadi library: those texts (or text copies) that were not written or edited to represent what we call dialect *L6* (this excludes all tractates of Codex I, that of Codex X, and the first two of Codex XI). Although these texts are usually labelled "Sahidic" by their modern editors, there has always been a great deal of discussion about precisely in what sense they can or cannot be called "Sahidic", since many of them reveal such a lot of non-Sahidic linguistic and/or spelling features that they can hardly be likened to what we know to be the Sahidic dialect, or Standard Sahidic, the principal variety of Coptic in use all along the Nile valley (i.e., Upper and Middle Egypt) during the ancient period. In a certain way, therefore, what I am talking about here is the meaning of the quotation marks I put around the word "Sahidic" in the title of my paper.

It has been rightly pointed out by several scholars at various occasions that the language of these texts is far from homogeneous. Most of them are, first of all, not homogeneous in themselves, representing rather "dialectologically mixed sources" (Shisha-Halevy 1976: 353, n. 1); but there is also a considerable degree of diversity from one text to another. In fact this diversity is so pervasive that the term "corpus" cannot be properly applied to them as a whole, at least not in a "variation linguistics" sense (implying something like membership in a single linguistic variety) - not even, in most cases, to all the texts found in a single codex. Clearly we have to put up with a multitude of linguistic "corpora" in this collection of books - but just how many? Are there only a few, say, two or three, categories into which all of them may fall, or are there as many varieties (or "blends") as there are texts? Probably, this latter supposition is closer to reality than the former one; but there are also certainly greater or lesser similarities among the texts, which may justify their classification into groups, and the criteria that prove valid and useful for establishing such groups may provide us with new insights that ultimately could help us find an answer to the agonizing question of how all this jumble may have come about historically.

The discussion of the particular non-Sahidic dialect affiliation of these texts has, I believe, hit a dead end several times over the past few years. Serious research had been done earlier only on some texts of Codex II (for which see Nagel 1969), and this, apart from providing important new insights, had also fatal consequences for commonly held opinions. The results of this research were summarized in some newly coined labels for Coptic varieties, ranging from Peter Nagel's "Upper Egyptian Sahidic" (Nagel 1969: 469) to Bentley Layton's very handy "Crypto-subachmimic" (Layton 1977: 66). There is nothing wrong with these labels as long as they are applied to a given text with good reason. But what is true for large parts of Codex II is not necessarily true for other codices.[1] Soon these labels were overly generalized, and their meaning diluted by misuse. Some editors, for the annoying though inevitable remarks on language in their introductory chapters, simply chose the easy way: seeing that some of the texts had been identified previously as "crypto-Subachmimic" (or some equivalent), you just look at the non-Sahidic features of your text and find out which of them can be said to be somehow Subachmimic, and ignore the rest. A legend was born: the legend of most or all of the "Sahidic" Nag Hammadi texts being to a greater or lesser degree influenced by the Subachmimic dialect, or dialects (whatever this may mean). Recently, there were some notable exceptions to this rule;[2] instead of just looking for what may or may not fit the "Subachmimic" Procrustean bed, one should expect an editor to make at least a fair effort to determine from a more neutral point of view which dialect, if any, can be singled out for prominence in a given text. This involves taking into account, as a point of departure, *all* dialects that the particularities found in the text can theoretically be assigned to, and to find out which would fit most frequently. The problem is that this method, even when it is based on correct data for dialectal usage (which is often not the case) leads to definite results only in a few cases. More frequently, in my own experience, the result is an impasse - inconclusive, ambivalent or contradictory (a case in point: my own listing and proportional evaluation for the Dialogue of the Saviour, quoted in Schenke 1986: 179). One reason for this may be that some texts are not long enough, or not well enough preserved, to provide us with a comprehensive picture of their *état de langue*. Another is certainly that we have not learned yet how to distinguish those features that characterize the language of these texts *significantly* from those that do not, or that do only superficially.

It has been my conviction for quite some time that the usual kind of non-Sahidic feature listing we find in those introductory chapters, useful as they may be for the initiation of beginners, will not lead to very much in the way of classifying the texts. Ideally, a classification ought to be based on full-scale

---

[1] This has of course been known for quite some time. Even the fact that there is a marked Bohairic influence in some of the texts was mentioned in publications of the Berliner Arbeitskreis in the mid-seventies (see, e.g., the case of the Three Steles of Seth in Wekel/Schenke, *Theologische Literaturzeitung* 100 [1975] 571: "a number of Bohairic forms") and, with reference to Codex VIII ("striking isoglosses with *B* or *BF*"), by Bentley Layton on the very same page where he coined the term "Crypto-subachmimic" (Layton 1977: 66).

[2] See, e.g., John Turner's summary statement about Allogenes: "written in a Sahidic dialect which betrays many features of a syntax typical of Bohairic" (C. H. Hedrick [ed.], *Nag Hammadi Codices XI, XII, XIII*, 1990, 10). Syntax and morphology also play an important part in what is probably the best linguistic description and characterization of a single Nag Hammadi text to date, viz. Hans-Martin Schenke's introductory chapter of his edition of the Book of Thomas [*Das Thomas-Buch (Nag-Hammadi-Codex II,7)*, 1989, 6-19]; see especially his discussions of general perspective on pp. 9, 15, 18f., which set new standards for this field.

linguistic analysis of all texts involved - which, however, appears to be utopian. Nevertheless, it seems to me that some sort of more principal methodological considerations are required before we can set out for the kind of search that will yield more definitive results. These considerations are by no means new in theory, but they are too often neglected in practice. (I shall briefly outline some of them here, so as to make it clear that I am not pretending to present any definitive solution in this paper.)

(1) If we say, tentatively, that these texts are written in certain "kinds of Sahidic", but not the kind that we know to be "standard Sahidic", then the first question to raise is, obviously, what kinds of Sahidic do they actually represent. In other words, we need a systematic description of the state of their language, in each particular case - which is something profoundly different from the enumeration of non-Sahidic forms and features. Such a description can, for practical purposes, be abbreviated by leaving aside some of the more trivial features in which all texts go along with standard Sahidic; but it has to be at least implicitly systematic: it cannot ignore elements that are connected to the phenomena in question in microsystems, whether these elements are in agreement with standard Sahidic or not.

(2) In order to determine the place that a given text occupies in the entire collection, we can compare these systematic descriptions with one another. This will also give us an indication of how to identify those linguistic items that are of crucial importance for distinguishing the various kinds of quasi-Sahidic encountered in the texts. It is unlikely that there are simply as many different kinds as there are texts. Rather, several definable "types" of quasi-Sahidic are likely to emerge as a result of such a comparison, each represented by a group of texts that share a certain number of features (both Sahidic and non-Sahidic features!). The identification of such groups, which has nothing to do with dialects, should be the primary aim of the comparison. The establishment of "groups" is important: this allows the identification of "most typical members" and "less typical" or "marginal members" within a given group and thus helps further sharpen the focus on its identity in terms of crucial distinct features.

(3) There are several other research operations that can be envisaged on the basis of such well-established groups. It is at this stage, for instance, that we may start asking how the particular kind of quasi-Sahidic as found in a given group may have come about, that is, what kind of explanation - in "historical" terms - we may have for the linguistic peculiarity of a given group. The identification of groups, and of unstable members or features among groups, is more likely to provide us with the valuable information we need for forming an idea about the historical background, than a single text ever can. Particular non-Sahidic dialects will certainly play a part in such explanations, but in addition to identifying the particular dialect(s) that contributed to the liguistic pattern of a group, an "explanation" will also try to define, if possible, *the way* in which they contributed (some well-known options: geographical location or variable capacity of an editor; provenance, habits and capacity of the scribe; dialect of the assumed original Coptic text/translation or "first copy"; provenance and/or habits of persons involved intermediately, etc.).

(4) Finally, such a comparison can be pushed a little further so as to include not only the establishment of groups but also some sort of linear ordering of the individual texts according to their linguistic characteristics. Given the multidimensional nature of the material, there is no a priori guarantee that a stable linear order can be established, but the attempt can be made.

Quite obviously, it cannot be the goal of this paper to do all these things. Full implementation of this programme would probably necessitate substantial contributions from more people than we will ever have in Coptic linguistic research, although a fraction of this is presently under way. What I can communicate at this juncture is only a first, rather preliminary, attempt at a formal comparison of the "Sahidic" Nag Hammadi texts, which presupposes some, but by no means all, of the descriptive analytical work that will be necessary to this end. Its presentation here is meant to be no more than a tool of general orientation, which may provide some insights and at the same time raise some of the inevitable new questions involved.

After some experimenting with calculations using between 18 and 25 linguistic variables (some of which are, unfortunately, rather incompletely attested in the texts), I have chosen an approach involving 21 yes/no variables (which are representative of about 15 multiple-value variables):

LIST OF VARIABLES USED:

The common adverb meaning "down" in connection with verbs such as ЄІ, BⲰK, etc., and/or common adverbials meaning "in the lower part":
(1) ЄⲡЄCHT, (M̄ⲡ)CⲀMⲡЄCHT, etc., respectively.
(2) ЄⲡІ T̄N, (M̄ⲡ)CⲀMⲡ І T̄N, etc., respectively.

The (morpho)phonological representation (+/- i-vowel) of infinitives of the pattern /C(i)Rə/:
(3) ЄІMЄ, ⲡІ PЄ
(4) M̄MЄ, ⲡ̄P PЄ (or ⲡ̄P P І Є)

The (morpho)phonological representation (vowel quality) of the stative of the irregular verbs ЄІ PЄ and ϯ:
(5) $o^{\dagger}$ and $то^{\dagger}$, respectively.
(6) $\epsilon^{\dagger}$ and $тє^{\dagger}$, respectively.

NB: No account is here taken of occurrences of $оЄ і^{\dagger}$ and $тоЄ і^{\dagger}$ because of their extreme rarity. However, these forms tend to co-occur with $o^{\dagger}$ and $то^{\dagger}$, not with $\epsilon^{\dagger}$ and $тє^{\dagger}$.

Purpose clauses: occasional or general usage of the Greek-loaned conjunction ἵνα (with or without ⲭЄ), represented by:
(7) 2 І NⲀ
(8) ⲰІ NⲀ

(9) The preposition {r-}: occasional representation of its prenominal form, expanded by either noun phrases (ⲡⲣⲱⲙⲉ) or infinitives (ⲧⲣⲉ-, ⲥⲱⲧⲙ̄), by ⲁ- instead of Sahidic ⲉ-.

(10) Conjugation: occasional occurrence of /a/-vocalization of base elements such as Imperfect (ⲛⲁϥⲥⲱⲧⲙ̄), Sec. Present (ⲁϥⲥⲱⲧⲙ̄) or Conditional.

(11) Perfect Conjugation: occasional use of forms based on ⲁ2(ⲁ)⸗ (i.e. ⲁ2ⲓ-, ⲁ2ⲁ-, ⲁ2ⲟⲩ-).

   Relative converter preceding Affirm. Perfect conjugation forms, represented by:
(12) ⲉⲛⲧ- or ⲛ̄ⲧ-(ⲁϥⲥⲱⲧⲙ̄).
(13) ⲉⲧ-(ⲁϥⲥⲱⲧⲙ̄).

(14) Perfect Participle: occurrence of the prefix ⲁ2- (usually preceded by a relative converter: ⲉⲧⲁ2-, ⲛ̄ⲧⲁ2-).

(15) Perfect Participle: occurrence of the prefix ⲉⲡ-.

(16) Nominal Sentences with quasi-adverbial predicate: usage of ⲉⲃⲟⲗ as apparent nucleus of the predicate (without ⲟⲩ-, 2ⲉⲛ-).

(17) Definite Determiners: Use of the singular forms of the ⲡⲓ- article (ⲡⲓ-, ϯ-) at a ratio > 0.25 of all singular definite determiners.

(18) Definite Determiners: Use of the plural form of the ⲡⲓ- article (ⲛⲓ-) at a ratio > 0.25 of all plural definite determiners.

   Greek-loaned verbs:
(19) Occurrence of usage as infinitives (non-derived).
(20) Occurrence of usage with nuclear ⲣ̄- .

(Supplementary control variable:)

(21) Sahidic ⲙⲉ "truth": its representation by ⲙⲏⲉ.

NB: All variables except (17) and (18) are valued as event occurrence variables; as a rule, a positive response is registered when the item occurs MORE THAN ONCE in a given text or text group, a negative response when it occurs only once or not at all. A single occurrence exceptionally qualifies for a positive value if it is the sole case of attestation for both sides of what is virtually a two-term variable (i.e., nos. 1+2, 3+4, 5+6). Since only one of the two terms is found to be used in most texts, it is more likely that such a single occurrence (which in that case is all we have) is in fact representative of the normal usage of the text, than the reverse. This exemption from the rule "One doesn't count" considerably enhances the stability of the matrix and thus provides for better results in any treatment of this kind of data.

The variables listed above apply to several levels of linguistic structure: the first two represent variation in the lexicon (citing a case that is common enough to be of some impact on the overall picture; other examples would mostly be too particular to qualify for such a comparison); then there are some that refer to the phonological or morphophonological representation of certain lexeme types and grammatical forms, and finally, there are some syntactic variables (especially nos. 14 to 20). I have added an additional variable (the form MHⲈ) as a control item in order to check the output of several procedures for stability by including or excluding this additional variable. The accounts given here are all based on procedures that included this variable (the results were, however, not essentially different when it was not included). I believe that this approach, while still rather tentative, has already grown to a certain maturity after a lot of experimentation and can be regarded as one of several possible constructs that may be used as a guideline. (Some drawbacks of this particular approach will be mentioned below.)

The results of applying seriation and cluster analysis procedures to this set of variables are displayed in FIGURES 1-5. The first two of these tables display 0,1-matrices providing both input and output of a seriation procedure. To those who are familiar with this kind of approach and with the material involved, it will come as no surprise that a clear-cut and solid seriation (a stable one-dimensional linear ordering) cannot be achieved in this case. The material is so diversified (in reality its variation is definitely not one-dimensional!) that there are several possible solutions to the problem, one hardly much better than the other. But a certain trend may become clear: the most important thing is perhaps that the group of individuals that emerges, later on, in the *hierarchical* ordering (displayed in FIG. 5) as the most distinct single group - i.e., the "northern" group, at the left-hand side of the diagram - is also clearly isolated in any attempt at a *linear* ordering of the material (this is the group near the bottom in the matrices of FIGS. 2-3, starting with ActPt). And another group of relative homogeneity, which I would call the "genuine Sahidic" group, also repeatedly goes together in contiguous arrangement in any such attempts.

In order to demonstrate how "genuine Sahidic" may be identified in this context, I have added another matrix of the same kind (see FIG. 3), based on the same data but with an additional marker row for Standard Sahidic. It is interesting to see that if I had omitted the "control column" (variable no. 21: MHⲈ), I could have done without adding an extra row for Standard Sahidic, since in that case "Eug III" (i.e., the version of Eugnostos preserved in Codex III) would have precisely the same marker as does Standard Sahidic; but there is in fact such a regular "Southernism" as the form MHⲈ in this text, and this, though I do not consider it too important, provides a good chance to distinguish the marker of "Eug III", by a single variable, from Standard Sahidic.[3] The main

---

[3] It is remarkable that this feature (MHⲈ instead of MⲈ) also occurs once in the Pachomian corpus (Letter 11a, line 1; see H. Quecke, *Die Briefe Pachoms*, 1975, 115), which is commonly held to represent pure Standard Sahidic.

purpose of adding this matrix is to demonstrate the precise place where Standard Sahidic will always go when it is asked to look for a nearest neighbour among the texts of the Nag Hammadi library: that is, in the neighbourhood of the first four texts of Codex III (which are often grouped together with the two BG texts included here). Whether it is specifically a position between the Apocryphon of John and the Holy Book, or a slightly different constellation in the same surroundings, depends on the choice of variables and the particular procedure employed. Standard Sahidic also sometimes finds its place just at the borderline between this "genuine Sahidic" Group of Six and the least extreme members of the "northern" group (the group near the bottom of the matrices, starting with ActPt), but it never goes away from that group centered around some Codex III texts. This, in itself, does not necessarily suggest that the most natural linguistic ordering of these texts has much to do with dialect geography. But it indicates that there is in fact a certain "neutral" center, which is roughly identical with Standard Sahidic, and then there is a periphery that is clearly divided between at least two, very different, indeed opposite, extremes.

FIGURE 4 displays the kind of graphic pattern that for me, some years ago, was the first unmistakable suggestion that the linguistic diversity of the Nag Hammadi texts is in fact primarily determined by dialect geography. What I have done here is somewhat unusual. Instead of evaluating a Goldmann, or Petrie, matrix (such as that in FIG. 2) solely for the purpose of serializing the individual items (the Operational Taxonomic Units, or "OTUs"), I have tried to benefit from the fact that such a linear ordering of the OTUs is automatically and (at each stage of the procedure) simultaneously, linked up with a linear ordering of the variables. These variables are written out in the left-hand column of FIG. 4 in the sequential order that was defined by the matrix that rearranges variables *and* individuals so as to find their most natural order. Thus their order mirrors the inherent property pattern of the texts, and nothing else. Now it is interesting to see that this inherent pattern, when it is interpreted in terms of dialect geography (what I did in the right-hand field, by adding serially ordered markers for the better known literary dialects of Coptic), visibly displays a certain "slope" feature, which means a gradual shift from more or less *northern* to more or less *southern* traits.[4] The precise linear order of the variables may of course slightly change with different methods and data being used, but in most cases the result will show up with something that resembles the slope pattern in this diagram. I consider this as a valuable general indicator of the presence of geographical features in the material under examination.

---

[4] There is an apparent "outlier" with regard to this slope feature: variable no. 10 (i.e. /a/-vocalization of Second Present etc.). What the diagram suggests, however, is in fact that this variant, in the specimens under investigation, happens to occur mostly in southern-oriented texts. This implies that it is most likely the *A* part, rather than the *BFWM* part, of the marker that is "activated" in this context. (At the level of Coptic dialect geography, this is obviously one of the discontinuous variables, although *A* is probably not alone in the south: the feature may also be shared by some *I* dialects.)

FIG. 5 displays a tree diagram with the results of a CLUSTER ANALYSIS of the same data. In this particular case I used a "divisive" method based on an information-statistic formula[5] (rather than an "agglomerative" method based on similarity coefficients), which has both advantages and disadvantages. An advantage is that a divisive method proceeds to build up the tree from its trunk: it divides the totality (and, subsequently, each subtotality) along the possible division lines provided by the distribution of the actual properties. Thus one can always identifiy a division with a concrete variable - the one that has emerged from the calculation as the one variable that is most representative of the totality of variation inherent in the material. In the present case, for instance, what delimits the "northern" group from the rest, and identifies its members, is not just an abstract similarity (or dissimilarity) ratio but the extensive use of ΠΙ-/ϯ-/ΝΙ- as a definite determiner.[6] This method also grants a certain stability that may be preferable to the more flexible results of a similarity matrix, which are often rather ambiguous. But this also involves a kind of rigidity that may not always be desirable: it depends on what you are primarily interested in. A case in point, in this diagram, is probably the placement of the Gospel of Thomas (a notorious case of indistinctiveness). Its place, just alongside with the Apocryphon of John of Codex III (!) in the immediate neighbourhood of the "genuine Sahidic" texts is certainly a rather one-sided solution. It has been triggered by the fact that the algorithm of this method found the ΕΠΕϹΗΤ/ΕΠΙΤΝ distinction (or, more preciely, the use or non-use of ΕΠΙΤΝ, i.e. variable no. 2, not 1) to be the most influential of all variables within the non-Northern major group of texts, and Thomas happens to opt for ΕΠΕϹΗΤ, an option usually not found in texts of a more distinctly "Southern" character. This might indicate that Thomas does not belong to them: it rather belongs to the neutral group. In a sense, I think, this is correct, namely, from a purely synchronic point of view, aiming at a characterization of what is to be found in the text as it is extant: Thomas is in fact the most "neutral" of all texts in Codex II. But assuming, for instance, that this feature (ΕΠΕϹΗΤ) is just one of those items in which the person who "Sahidicized" the text of Thomas was successful,

---

[5] This method was originally proposed by G. N. Lance and W. T. Williams in 1968 ("Note on a new information-statistic classificatory program", *Computer Journal* 11: 195) but became accessible to my limited understanding only by Professor Hintze's classes at Humboldt University in 1981. A brief description of Hintze's translation of the procedure for practical purposes can be found in S. Wenig's article in the issue *Die Anwendung numerischer Methoden in der Sudanarchäologie* of the *Wissenschaftl. Zeitschrift der Humboldt-Universität zu Berlin*, Gesellschaftswiss. Reihe, 35 (1986), on pp. 97-8. I am especially grateful to Michael Williams, who provided me with macros based on LOTUS 1-2-3 for both the Goldmann seriation and the Lance-Williams cluster analysis.

[6] To lend further support to the credibility of this result, it may be pointed out that this happens to be the one variable in the present approach whose marker in fact serves to represent several variables at the same time, including, e.g., frequent use of the ΠΗ pronoun as the "determinative" of relative clauses and an excessive, non-Southern, use of the preposition Ν̄ΤΕ-. This circumstance is of course unknown to the algorithm, which chooses the marker for prominence even though it is counted only once.

and there was more care applied to this text than to other ones, this classification cannot tell us much about the original composition, or historical provenance, of the Thomas text (which may be no less "Southern" than, say, that of the Gospel of Philip). In order to come closer to this "diachronic" perspective, we may need to apply one of the "softer" methods of similarity analysis, which will almost certainly place Thomas in a different group.

Apart from the mere aim of arranging the texts into groups whose members share a number of features, this classification of course also provides some very suggestive clues to dialect affiliation. This is no doubt again most evident in the "Northern", left-hand, group. The principal trait that separates these texts from the rest is a syntactic one,[7] for all its "visibility" clearly representing a "deeper level" of linguistic structure, less susceptible to the usual not-too-careful editorial activity. As far as the literary dialects known to date are concerned, this trait points to Bohairic, the northern-most dialect that we know. This does not necessarily mean that *the Bohairic we know* (that is, of course, fourth-century "Early Bohairic": *B4*, by now well attested) is indeed at the source of these texts: there were clearly some other, less known literary dialects in the immediate neighbourhood of Bohairic (for instance, the group of *K* dialects) which are likewise eligible candidates since they seem to share, after all we know, the same syntactic traits. Nor does it mean that such a suggestion of origin tells the whole story: in a number of these texts other dialects are clearly involved as well, and a certain superficial "Southern" flavour, the trade-mark of the final production of the extant manuscripts, is omnipresent. A plain label such as "crypto-Bohairic" could be appropriately applied only to a very small group (made up of, say, Allo, Zost and StelS, which share the striking feature of variable no. 16; maybe also to ActPt, though this would be a very different type). But the general division along the line drawn by variable no. 17 clearly eliminates any known Fayyumic variety from the candidates for dialectal prominence in this group (this would be less evident if any of the other traits tacitly represented by this marker [see note 6] were chosen to name the variable).

However, there are also some fairly convincing affiliations in other parts of the diagram: for instance, the one that emerges at the far southern end of the spectrum (with II 4-6), which is the group that may be labeled "crypto-*L6*", since its distinctive feature, unique in the whole library, is the occurrence of forms

---

[7] There were discussions during the conference session about the validity of a quantitative definition such as the one I proposed for this variable (ⲡ ⲓ -, ⲧ- "at a ratio > 0.25 of all singular definite determiners"). I would like to point out that this notation is not meant to be a quantitative "description" of the material, but rather a tentative short cut for quick dialect comparison (in the absence of a description), based on the observation that across all Coptic literary dialects the quantitative relationship of determiner usage is largely correlated to their functional relationship, notwithstanding the stylistic peculiarities of a given text. Thus proportional shares of more than 25% for ⲡ ⲓ - are to be found only in Bohairic texts (and, of the less known dialects, probably the *K* group) as far as the singular forms are concerned, and in Bohairic and Fayyumic for the plural. Even the southern two-term systems, in which ⲡ ⲓ - assumes all the functions of ⲡⲉ ï -, do not produce such high shares.

modeled on the morphology of the particular *L6* Perfect conjugation paradigm (ⲁϨ Ⲓ - etc.). Then there is a group that could tentatively be labelled "crypto-*A*": "AJ II" plus "AJ IV", together with Noema and Protennoia, but here again we are encountering what may well be a certain bug in the algorithm: instead of DialS, one would expect the Book of Thomas to go straight along with these texts - which it does not, because it does not have the all-decisive ⲈⲦⲀϨ-, whose presence ultimately constitutes the group in this solution.

This has been but a first glimpse at the behaviour of some of the necessary ingredients to an overall linguistic classification of the "quasi-Sahidic" texts in the Nag Hammadi library. A major obstacle to setting up a more comprehensive set of *input data* is the insufficient attestation of some important variables, especially at the syntactic and morphological levels.   A major difficulty in *interpreting* any results in terms of the "historical" and/or "geographical" provenance of the texts lies in the varying degree of editorial care that was applied to each of them by their latest scribes, in a few cases probably with good success. Assuming that the principal source of confusion in most of these texts is in fact their original composition or, more aptly, translation from Greek, in(to) a non-Sahidic dialect of Coptic, from which they were "translated" (or sometimes just superficially transcribed) into a kind of approximative Sahidic - by different people, in different places and with various skills - then, unfortunately, it is only in those cases where these people did a rather poor job that we can easily trace their activities.   To the degree they were really successful, they succeeded in hiding their activities.   To find out in what ways the more obvious cases are related to the more hidden ones may be the greatest challenge to a proper, historically nuanced, linguistic classification of these texts.

BIBLIOGRAPHY

Kasser, R. 1990. "A standard system of sigla for referring to the dialects of Coptic", *Journal of Coptic Studies* 1: 141-151.
Layton, B. 1977. "Editorial Notes on the 'Expository Treatise Concerning the Soul' (Tractate II 6 from Nag Hammadi)", *Bulletin of the American Society of Papyrologists* 14: 65-73.
Nagel, P. 1969. "Grammatische Untersuchungen zu Nag Hammadi Codex II", in: F. Altheim & R. Stiehl (eds), *Die Araber in der Alten Welt*, vol. 5, part II (Berlin: De Gruyter), 393-469.
−. 1972. "Die Bedeutung der Nag Hammadi-Texte für die koptische Dialekt-geschichte", in: P. Nagel (ed.), *Von Nag Hammadi bis Zypern: eine Aufsatzsammlung* (Berlin: Akademie-Verlag), 16-27.
Schenke, H.-M. 1986. Review of: S. Emmel (ed.), *Nag Hammadi Codex III,5: The Dialogue of the Savior*. - *Enchoria* 14: 175-187.
Shisha-Halevy, A. 1976. "Akhmîmoid features in Shenoute's idiolect", *Le Muséon* 89: 353-366.

Var. no.	1	2	3	4	5	6	7	8	9	10	11	12	13	14	15	16	17	18	19	20	21
AJ II	0	1	0	1	1	0	0	0	1	1	0	1	1	1	0	0	0	0	1	1	1
GoTh	1	0	1	0	1	0	0	1	1	0	0	1	1	1	0	0	0	0	1	1	0
GoPh	0	1	1	0	1	0	0	1	1	1	0	1	0	1	0	0	0	0	1	1	0
HA	1	1	1	0	1	0	0	1	1	0	1	1	0	1	0	0	0	0	1	1	0
OW + ES	0	1	1	0	1	0	0	1	1	0	1	1	0	1	0	0	0	0	1	1	0
BoTh	0	1	0	1	1	0	0	0	1	1	0	1	0	0	0	0	0	0	1	1	1
AJ III	1	0	1	0	1	0	0	0	0	0	0	1	0	0	1	0	0	0	1	1	0
HoBo III	1	0	1	0	1	0	0	0	0	0	0	1	1	0	0	0	0	0	1	0	1
Eug III	1	0	1	0	1	0	0	0	0	0	0	1	0	0	0	0	0	0	1	0	1
SJC III	1	0	1	0	1	0	0	0	0	1	0	1	0	0	0	0	0	0	1	1	1
DialS	0	1	1	0	1	0	0	0	0	0	0	1	1	1	0	0	0	0	1	1	1
AJ IV	0	1	1	1	1	0	0	0	0	0	0	1	1	1	0	0	0	0	1	1	0
HoBo IV	1	0	1	0	0	1	1	0	0	0	0	1	1	0	0	0	1	1	0	1	0
Eug V	0	0	1	1	0	1	0	0	0	0	0	0	1	0	0	0	1	1	0	1	0
V 2-4	1	0	1	1	1	1	1	0	0	0	0	1	1	0	0	0	1	1	1	1	0
ApcAd	1	0	1	0	0	1	1	0	0	0	0	0	1	0	0	0	1	1	0	1	0
ActPt	0	0	0	1	1	0	0	0	1	0	0	0	1	0	0	0	1	1	1	1	0
Br + AL	0	1	0	1	1	0	0	0	1	0	0	1	1	0	0	0	0	0	1	1	0
Noema	0	1	0	1	1	0	1	0	1	0	0	1	1	1	0	0	0	0	1	1	0
Og + Pr	0	1	0	0	1	1	0	0	1	0	0	1	0	1	0	0	0	0	1	1	0
Ascl	0	1	0	1	0	1	0	0	1	0	0	1	0	1	0	0	0	0	1	1	0
ParS	0	1	1	0	1	1	0	1	1	0	0	1	0	0	1	0	0	0	1	1	0
2LogS	1	0	1	1	1	1	0	0	0	0	0	1	0	0	0	0	1	1	1	1	0
ApcPt	0	0	1	0	0	1	1	0	0	0	0	1	1	0	0	0	1	1	0	1	0
Silv	0	1	1	1	1	1	0	0	1	0	0	1	0	0	0	0	0	0	1	1	0
StelS	1	0	1	0	0	1	1	0	0	0	0	1	1	0	0	1	1	1	0	0	0
Zost	1	0	1	1	0	1	1	0	0	0	0	0	1	0	0	1	1	1	1	1	0
EpPt	0	0	1	0	0	0	1	0	1	0	0	0	1	0	0	0	1	1	0	1	0
Cod IX	0	1	1	1	1	1	0	0	1	0	0	1	0	1	0	0	0	0	1	1	0
Allo	0	0	1	0	1	1	1	0	0	0	0	1	1	0	0	1	1	1	1	1	0
Sext	0	1	0	1	1	0	0	0	1	0	0	1	0	1	0	0	0	0	0	1	1
Prot	0	1	0	1	1	0	0	0	1	1	0	1	1	1	0	0	0	0	1	1	0
AJ BG	1	0	1	0	1	0	0	0	0	0	0	1	0	0	0	0	0	0	1	1	1
SJC BG	1	0	1	0	1	0	0	0	0	1	0	1	0	0	0	0	0	0	1	1	1

FIG. 1. Basic incidence matrix of variables (input for seriation and cluster analysis; texts arranged according to codices).

Var. no.	11	8	14	2	10	9	21	5	19	4	12	20	15	3	13	1	6	18	7	17	16
OW + ES	1	1	1	1	0	1	0	1	1	0	1	1	0	1	0	0	0	0	0	0	0
GoPh	0	1	1	1	1	1	0	1	1	0	1	1	0	1	0	0	0	0	0	0	0
HA	1	1	1	0	1	0	1	1	0	1	1	0	1	0	1	0	0	0	0	0	0
BoTh	0	0	0	1	1	1	1	1	1	1	1	1	0	0	0	0	0	0	0	0	0
AJ II	0	0	1	1	1	1	1	1	1	1	1	1	0	0	1	0	0	0	0	0	0
Sext	0	0	0	1	0	1	1	1	0	1	1	1	0	0	0	0	0	0	0	0	0
Prot	0	0	1	1	1	1	0	1	1	1	1	0	0	1	0	0	0	0	0	0	0
Ascl	0	0	1	1	0	1	0	0	1	1	1	0	0	0	0	1	0	0	0	0	0
DialS	0	0	1	1	0	0	1	1	1	0	1	1	0	1	1	0	0	0	0	0	0
Br + AL	0	0	0	1	0	1	0	1	1	1	1	1	0	0	1	0	0	0	0	0	0
Cod IX	0	0	1	1	0	1	0	1	1	1	1	1	0	1	0	0	1	0	0	0	0
AJ IV	0	0	1	1	0	0	0	1	1	1	1	1	0	1	1	0	0	0	0	0	0
ParS	0	1	0	1	0	1	0	1	1	0	1	1	1	1	0	0	1	0	0	0	0
GoTh	0	1	1	0	0	1	0	1	1	0	1	1	0	1	1	1	0	0	0	0	0
Noema	0	0	1	1	0	1	0	1	1	1	1	1	0	0	1	0	0	0	1	0	0
Silv	0	0	0	1	0	1	0	1	1	1	1	1	0	1	0	0	1	0	0	0	0
SJC III	0	0	0	0	1	0	1	1	1	0	1	1	0	1	0	1	0	0	0	0	0
Og + Pr	0	0	0	1	0	1	0	1	1	0	1	1	1	0	1	0	1	0	0	0	0
Eug III	0	0	0	0	0	0	1	1	1	0	1	0	0	1	0	1	0	0	0	0	0
SJC BG	0	0	0	0	1	0	1	1	1	0	1	0	0	1	0	1	0	1	0	0	0
AJ BG	0	0	0	0	0	0	1	1	1	0	1	1	0	1	0	1	0	0	0	0	0
HoBo III	0	0	0	0	0	0	1	1	1	0	1	0	0	1	1	1	0	0	0	0	0
AJ III	0	0	0	0	0	0	0	1	1	0	1	1	1	1	0	1	0	0	0	0	0
ActPt	0	0	0	0	0	1	0	1	1	1	0	1	0	0	1	0	0	1	0	1	0
2LogS	0	0	0	0	0	0	0	1	1	1	1	1	0	1	0	1	1	1	0	1	0
V 2-4	0	0	0	0	0	0	0	1	1	1	1	1	0	1	1	1	1	1	1	1	0
EpPt	0	0	0	0	0	1	0	0	0	0	0	1	0	1	1	0	0	1	1	1	0
Allo	0	0	0	0	0	0	0	1	1	0	1	1	0	1	1	0	1	1	1	1	1
Eug V	0	0	0	0	0	0	0	0	0	1	0	1	0	1	1	0	1	1	0	1	0
Zost	0	0	0	0	0	0	0	0	1	1	0	1	0	1	1	1	1	1	1	1	1
ApcPt	0	0	0	0	0	0	0	0	0	0	1	1	0	1	1	0	1	1	1	1	0
HoBo IV	0	0	0	0	0	0	0	0	0	0	1	1	0	1	1	1	1	1	1	1	0
ApcAd	0	0	0	0	0	0	0	0	0	0	0	1	0	1	1	1	1	1	1	1	0
StelS	0	0	0	0	0	0	0	0	0	0	1	0	0	1	1	1	1	1	1	1	1

FIG. 2. Optimal approximation of the matrix of Fig. 1 to a "Petrie matrix" (output of seriation analysis).

Var. no.	11	8	14	10	2	9	21	5	19	4	12	20	15	3	13	1	6	18	7	17	16	
OW + ES	1	1	1	0	1	1	0	1	1	0	1	1	0	1	0	0	0	0	0	0	0	
GoPh	0	1	1	1	1	1	0	1	1	0	1	1	0	1	0	0	0	0	0	0	0	
HA	1	1	1	0	1	1	0	1	1	0	1	1	0	1	0	1	0	0	0	0	0	
BoTh	0	0	0	1	1	1	1	1	1	1	1	1	0	0	0	0	0	0	0	0	0	
AJ II	0	0	1	1	1	1	1	1	1	1	1	1	0	0	1	0	0	0	0	0	0	
Prot	0	0	1	1	1	1	0	1	1	1	1	1	0	0	1	0	0	0	0	0	0	
Sext	0	0	0	0	1	1	1	1	0	1	1	1	0	0	0	0	0	0	0	0	0	
Ascl	0	0	1	0	1	1	0	0	1	1	1	1	0	0	0	0	1	0	0	0	0	
DialS	0	0	1	0	1	0	1	1	1	0	1	1	0	1	1	0	0	0	0	0	0	
Cod IX	0	0	1	0	1	1	0	1	1	1	1	1	0	1	0	0	1	0	0	0	0	
Br + AL	0	0	0	0	1	1	0	1	1	1	1	1	0	0	1	0	0	0	0	0	0	
GoTh	0	1	1	0	0	1	0	1	1	0	1	1	0	1	1	1	0	0	0	0	0	
AJ IV	0	0	1	0	1	0	0	1	1	1	1	1	0	1	1	0	0	0	0	0	0	
ParS	0	1	0	0	1	1	0	1	1	0	1	1	1	1	0	0	1	0	0	0	0	
Noema	0	0	1	0	1	1	0	1	1	1	1	1	0	0	1	0	0	0	1	0	0	
SJC III	0	0	0	1	0	0	1	1	1	0	1	1	0	1	0	1	0	0	0	0	0	
Silv	0	0	0	0	1	1	0	1	1	1	1	1	0	1	0	0	1	0	0	0	0	
Og + Pr	0	0	0	0	1	1	0	1	1	0	1	1	1	0	1	0	1	0	0	0	0	
Eug III	0	0	0	0	0	0	1	1	1	0	1	0	0	1	0	1	0	0	0	0	0	
SJC BG	0	0	0	1	0	0	1	1	1	0	1	0	0	1	0	1	0	1	0	0	0	
AJ BG	0	0	0	0	0	0	1	1	1	0	1	1	0	1	0	1	0	0	0	0	0	
HoBo III	0	0	0	0	0	0	1	1	1	0	1	0	0	1	1	1	0	0	0	0	0	
Std Sah	0	0	0	0	0	0	0	1	1	0	1	0	0	1	0	1	0	0	0	0	0	*
AJ III	0	0	0	0	0	0	0	1	1	0	1	1	1	1	0	1	0	0	0	0	0	
ActPt	0	0	0	0	0	1	0	1	1	1	0	1	0	0	1	0	0	1	0	1	0	
2LogS	0	0	0	0	0	0	0	1	1	1	1	1	0	1	0	1	1	1	0	1	0	
V 2-4	0	0	0	0	0	0	0	1	1	1	1	1	0	1	1	1	1	1	1	1	0	
EpPt	0	0	0	0	0	0	1	0	0	0	0	0	1	0	1	1	0	0	1	1	0	
Allo	0	0	0	0	0	0	0	1	1	0	1	1	0	1	1	0	1	1	1	1	1	
Eug V	0	0	0	0	0	0	0	0	0	1	0	1	0	1	1	0	1	1	0	1	0	
Zost	0	0	0	0	0	0	0	1	1	0	1	0	1	1	1	1	1	1	1	1	1	
ApcPt	0	0	0	0	0	0	0	0	0	0	1	1	0	1	1	0	1	1	1	1	0	
HoBo IV	0	0	0	0	0	0	0	0	0	0	1	1	0	1	1	1	1	1	1	1	0	
ApcAd	0	0	0	0	0	0	0	0	0	0	1	0	1	1	1	1	1	1	1	1	0	
StelS	0	0	0	0	0	0	0	0	0	1	0	0	1	1	1	1	1	1	1	1	1	

FIG. 3. Output of seriation analysis after adding a Standard Sahidic row to the basic incidence matrix.

Variable		B	F	W	M	S	L4	L5	L6	A	P
16	ЄBOλ pred.	B								A	P
17	ПI-, †-	B								A	P
7	2INA	B	F							A	(P)
18	NI-	B	F								
6	Є†, TЄ†		(F?K?)	?							
1	ЄПЄCHT	B	F	?	M	S					
13	ЄT-(λϥCⲰTⲘ)	B	F	W	M		L4			A	P
3	ЄIMЄ, ПIPЄ	(B)	(F)	W	M	S					(P)
15	ЄP- part.	(B)		?	M	(S)					
20	P-(ПICTЄYЄ)	B	F		M			L5	L6	A	
12	(Є)NT-(λϥCⲰTⲘ)						(L4)	L5	L6	A	P
4	Ⲙ̄ⲘЄ, ПP̄P(I)Є	(B)					(L4)	L5	L6	A	(P)
19	Φ-(ПICTЄYЄ)			W	M	S	(L4)	L5	(L6)		P
5	O†, TO†				M	S	L4	L5	L6		P
21	ⲘHЄ						L4	L5	L6	(A)	P
9	λ- prep.						L4	L5	L6	A	P
10	(N)λϥ-(CⲰTⲘ)	B	F	W	M		L4	L5	L6	A	P
2	ЄПITⲚ̄						L4	L5	L6	A	P
14	(ЄT/Ⲛ̄T)λ2- part.							L5	L6	A	P
8	ⲰINA							L5	L6	A	P
11	λ2(λ)= perf.								L6		P

FIG. 4. The serial order of the variables as emerging from the matrix of Fig. 2, with dialect incidences added for each variable (dialect sigla between round brackets stand for occasional usage).

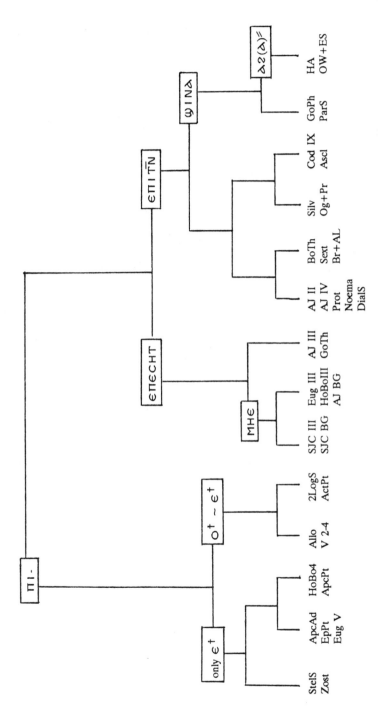

FIG. 5. Cluster diagram for a likely grouping of the "Sahidic" Nag Hammadi texts, on the basis of 21 variables as listed above, using the Lance-Williams divisive clustering method.

THE PROJECT "CATALOGUE GENERAL DU MUSEE
COPTE": PROGRESS OF WORK THROUGH DECEMBER 1991[*]

Gawdat Gabra

During the last six years serious attention has been given
to the reorganization of the Coptic Museum and to making its
monuments available to scholars. In this connection the "Catalogue Général du Musée Copte" was initiated in 1986 as an
ongoing international project to compile an up-to-date catalogue of all the museum's holdings. It goes without saying that
this project is important for Coptology in general and for the
study of Coptic art in particular. The names of the partici-
pants working in cooperation with the curators of the sections
of the Coptic Museum have been known since 1987.[1] A report
on the progress of the work in the various museum departments
through December 1988 is included in the acts of the last
International Congress of Coptic Studies.[2]

It gives me pleasure to state that the project has already
borne its first fruits: two volumes are now ready for publication. One of them, by Prof. Paul van Moorsel, concerns the
icons of the Coptic Museum; the other, which contains the
stelae of Terenuthis (Kom Abu Bellou), has been compiled by
Prof. Henri Riad. Some other scholars have published preliminary reports on their work.[3] I would like to review briefly
the progress made to date in each section.

I. Manuscripts

Mrs. Samiha Abdel-Shaheed is preparing a supplement to
the catalogue of Simaika Pasha concerning the Arabic manuscripts. The first part, which includes thirty-two manuscripts
of the New Testament, is now in press.[4] The second part,
comprising forty-two manuscripts with theological treatises, has
already been prepared for publication. Fifty-three liturgical
manuscripts are under study.

Prof. Siegbart Uhlig has examined the Ethiopian manuscripts. There are four complete manuscripts and three fragmentary texts. He has photographed and described them all.
He plans to come again to Cairo in the near future for final
collation.

Prof. Nur el-Din heads a group of scholars from the
Faculty of Archaeology, Cairo University, who are preparing a
catalogue of thirty-six Coptic texts written on parchment.
These were photographed and examined about a year ago.

II. Ostraca

Prof. Kent Brown has already prepared the first volume on
the ostraca of the Coptic Museum. It includes descriptions and

photographs of the entire collection, with the exception of the Greek ostraca from Abu Mina.[5]

III. Works in stone

Prof. Hans-Georg Severin has finished the fieldwork for his section which comprises more than 2500 pieces. In order to determine the provenance of the objects in the collection, considerable work is continuing in the inventories of both the Egyptian Museum and the Coptic Museum, simultaneous with a thorough review of the many publications of finds from excavations.

IV. Wall paintings

After completing all the fieldwork on the Coptic and Nubian murals in the museum, Prof. Wladzimierz Godlewski is preparing the catalogue. It will include a history of the collection as well as a detailed catalogue of compositions arranged by site. The volume will be supplemented by iconographic and topographic indices.

Many of the wall paintings discovered by the Swiss and French missions at the site of Kellia were transported to the Coptic Museum.[6] Mme Marguerite Rassart-Debergh is preparing a special monograph devoted to them. Fifty percent of this project has been completed. She is hopeful that her monograph will be ready for publication before the end of 1993.

V. Pottery[7]

Dr. Pascale Ballet has studied about 1500 objects from the collection which comprises approximately 2000 items. Four hundred sixty pieces have been photographed and one hundred fifty drawn.

VI. Woodwork, Ivory and Bone[8]

Prof. Helmut Buschhausen had to postpone study of the woodwork because of his excavations at the monastery of Abu Fana. However, the photography of the collection will be continued next autumn. The same is true for objects carved from ivory and bone.

VII. Textiles

Dr. Claudia Nauerth has photographed about 1300 textiles. She has prepared brief descriptions of them and consulted the museum's inventory, especially with a view to establishing the provenance of the pieces. Unfortunately only about twenty percent of the holdings are from a known source. However, those pieces are very important for future studies.[9] Dr. Nauerth will continue her fieldwork in next year.

Dr. Hishmat Messiha and Mr. Girgis Daoud continued their work on the ecclesiastical vestments of the 18th and 19th centuries. Thirty-three sleeves and twenty-two stoles have been examined and described, and the most important ones photographed. Twelve tunics have been examined, but they have not yet been photographed. Many other pieces, such as altar covers, are under study by Messiha and Daoud who hope to have prepared their volume for publication before the end of 1993.

VIII. Metalwork

Mme Dominique Bénazeth[10] examined 1265 objects. With the exception of the jewellery, the entire collection has been photographed. She has completed almost all the fieldwork for her section. Next season she intends to consult the Journal d'Entrée of the Egyptian Museum from which a considerable part of the collection in the Coptic Museum derives.

Regrettably, the enthusiasm shown by some colleagues when they initially applied to participate in the project has not stood the test of time. This is perhaps due to their many obligations and commitments elsewhere, excavations in particular. But there is no doubt that this largest collection of Coptic Art was not generally accessible until the last few years.

In conclusion I would like to take this opportunity to thank all the scholars working on the project for their efforts, as well as the institutions whose financial support made their participation possible.

* I would like to thank the Catholic University of America for enabling me to attend this Congress.

Footnotes:

1 Newsletter: International Association of Coptic Studies (T. Orlandi, ed.) 20, January 1987, p. 3; 21, June 1987, p. 2; see also G. Gabra, "The Project 'Catalogue Général du Musée Copte,'" in: The Greek Presence in Ancient Egypt (Symposium), Delphi, March 17-20, 1988, Lila Marangou, ed., in press; idem, "Nubian Monuments in the Coptic Museum: Exhibition, General Catalogue and Concordance," in: Acts of the 7th International Congress of the Society for Nubian Studies, Ch. Bonnet, ed., in press.

2 G. Gabra, "Das Projekt 'Catalogue Général du Musée Copte': Stand der Arbeiten bis Dezember 1988," in: Actes du IVe Congrès Copte, Louvain-la Neuve, 5-10 septembre 1988, M. Rassart-Debergh - J. Ries, ed., in press.

3 See W. B. Oerter, "Die Leder- und Flechtarbeiten des koptischen Museums Kairo: Ein Arbeitsbericht zum 'Catalogue Général du Musée Copte'," BSAC 29 (1990), 49-54; Dominique Bénazeth, "Catalogue Général du Musée Copte: Les objets de metal," BSAC 30 (1991), 49-51; Hishmat Messiha, "Portable Altars: Luxor Treasure (1983)," BSAC 31 (1992), 130-34.

4 BSAC 32 (1993), in press.

5 See Gabra, note 2, above; P. Grossmann, "Neue Funde in Abu Mena", in: Akten des 12. internationalen Kongresses für christliche Archäologie, Bonn, 22. - 28. September 1991, in press.

6 An important group of wall paintings from Kellia has been exhibited in Geneva: Les Kellia, ermitages coptes en Basse Egypte. Musée d'Art et d'Histoire, Genève 12 octobre 1989 - 7 janvier 1990; for the wall paintings of Kellia, see M. Rassart -

Debergh, "Kellia: paintings," in: The Coptic Encyclopedia, Aziz S. Atiya, ed., vol. 5, New York 1991, p. 1402f.

7 See P. Ballet, in: Actes du IVe Congrès Copte, Lovain-la-Neuve, 5-10 septembre 1988, M. Rassart-Debergh - J. Ries, ed., in press; see also the communication of Fatma Mahmoud in this volume.

8 See H. Buschhausen, in: Actes du IVe Congrès Copte, Lovain-la-Neuve, 5-10 septembre 1988, M. Rassart-Debergh - J. Ries, ed., in press.

9 Cf. e.g., Alexander Badawy, Coptic Art and Archaeology. The Art of the Christian Egyptians from the Late Antique to the Middle Ages, Cambridge, Mass. 1978, p. 283; Diane Lee Carroll, Looms and Textiles of the Copts. First Millennium Egyptian Textiles in the Carl Austin Rietz Collection of the California Academy of Sciences, Seattle and London 1988, p. 3; Marie-Hélène Rutschowscaya, Tissus coptes, Paris 1990, p. 45f.

10 See above, note 3.

NAQLUN 1989-1992

Włodzimierz Godlewski

In the last four years of excavations, the whole area of the monastic complex at Naqlun (Nekloni) has been included in the explorations. The site is located 16 km southeast of Medinet el Fayum in the Fayum oasis.

A survey of the area was concluded in 1989. The objective was to determine the extent of the complex which consists of the erems, the ancient monastery with accompanying architecture, the modern monastery and the cemeteries.

Altogether 89 erems were identified. About 80 of them are scattered in the numerous small valleys, spreading over 1,500 square meters of the Gebel al Naqlun. Although sometimes cut in the rock next to each other, they do not form any recognizable complexes. The remaining erems are built close to a modern canal, at the edge of the rock desert. Since the area has been quarried, the resulting damages make it difficult to tell whether any more erems had exxisted here, particularly since some of them were constructed of stone and brick. So far it has proved impossible to determine either the date or the function of this second group of erems.

Not much yet can be said of the structures on the plateau extending at the foot of the gebel. Dwellings, workareas and church buildings were presumably located here; they were inhabited, to believe the archaeological evidence, from the early 6th to the 14th century. No wall enclosing the monastery has been found, although at some point in time a smaller complex concentrated around the church of Archangel Gabriel was set off by a wall. This complex, with some changes, is still in use today.

In the flat desert west of today's monastic buildings there are the extensive remains of the Nekloni monastery's cemetery; amphorae and textiles from one of the tombs place it in the 7th century.

The erems

Erems 25 and 89, which were excavated in 1989-1991, are both elaborate complexes, hewn in the rock next to each other but presumably operating as separate units throughout their 600 years or so of existence.

Erem 25 consists of a number of units planned around a central courtyard: three cells for monks (A, B, C) and two kitchens (D, E). The evidence would appear to indicate that unit A with kitchen D was added to the erem at a later date, meaning that originally the complex had included two cells for monks (B and C) and a kitchen (E). Each of the monks' cells consisted of two spaces of differing size. The larger of the two was cut rather neatly, with a storage pit near the window and a bench. It also had a number of niches cut in the walls, the most important being the eastern niche, which was usually distinguished by a better finish and by painted decoration. The smaller space was small and dark, very secluded in fact; it was not plastered and presumably served as the sleeping area.

Of the two complexes, B was of definitely higher standard, larger and with a better prepared adjoining space. The kitchen which contained a two-pot oven was located next to the more modest of the units.

The following stages can be distinguished in the development of the complex: the formative stage, a stage of renovation and a final stage when the available space was reduced.

In the formative stage, units B, C and kitchen E were the first to be cut, together with the courtyard closed off from the valley by a wall with one entrance. This presumably occurred in the late 6th or early 7th century at the latest, but a dating even half a century earlier is possible.

In the second stage, storage pits in units B.1 and C.1 were filled, the entrance to kitchen E walled up and the new complex including unit A and kitchen D added. This new unit is clearly smaller and does not have a storage pit; it does have a large niche in the northern wall, presumably for sleeping. Papyri documents, pottery and wooden objects from the filled in pits in B.1 and C.1 date this stage to the mid-7th century.

Units A.1-3 and kitchen D were separated from the rest of the erem, thus reducing the available space in the final stage. Only units B.1-2 provide evidence of longer use. In B.1 there are traces of a primitive hearth and a great deal of broken cooking pots around it, indicating that the space was being used as a kitchen. The fuel, dried reeds in this case, was presumably stored in C.1. At this time the erem was obviously inhabited by just one person.

It is difficult to say how long the erem stayed in use. The pottery discovered inside the complex can be dated to the 8th century, but it is possible that the simple kitchen and storage wares continued basically unchanged for a much longer period. The only more certain evidence are the written texts, in Coptic and Arabic, which do not themselves contain any dates, but which are dated on paleographical grounds to the 11th and 12th centuries, maybe even a little later. These texts are usually written on a thick fleshy paper and are found in the fills deposited on the last floors inside the cells, usually opposite the entrance. This would suggest that they had been blown inside by the winds or were simply thrown away by visitors to the erems.

The total number of texts found inside the erem is quite extensive. They were written on papyrus, parchment and paper, but not one ostracon was recorded. The Greek texts were found almost exclusively in the storage pit fills. With the exception of one document written on a wooden tablet and another one on parchment, all were on papyrus. Altogether there were 21 texts, of which 10 are fully preserved. The texts are almost exclusively psalms copied by the erem's inhabitant onto the backs of used cards. The text on parchment is especially interesting for it is a list of psalms grouped according to their titles and "authors". It could be considered a manifestation of the monk's Biblical erudition. The second part of the text is a kind of horologion for private use.

Of the 58 recorded Coptic texts, 39 are preserved completely or to a large degree. About 20 are part of a papyrus codex containing a text which is most probably a moon calendar. Among the Coptic texts the majority are letters and economic documents.

Arab texts abound — 40 documents in all, written on paper and not yet fully identified; 19 of them are in a better condition that the rest.

The pottery found inside the erem is mainly of a storage and domestic kind, but there is also some tableware. Beside the pottery, there are objects of glass, wood and leather, oil lamps, textiles and two partly preserved book covers. The finds are sufficient to give a picture of the everyday life of the inhabitants of the erems; they also tell a great deal about their religious life.

E r e m   8 9   was cut in the rocky slope just north of erem 25, but differs from it considerably. An ancient rock slide did much to damage it, and the original layout is additionally obscured by a number of constructions of brick, stone and pottery which were set up in the courtyard. Beside a living complex (A.1-2), there were two distinct units, B and D. The former is a typical oratory; the latter's function remains unclear. Unit C is in the courtyard and presumably served as a donkey pen, before being turned into a rubbish dump. No traces of a kitchen were found, but it could have been located either in the part of the courtyard which was later turned into the pen or next to unit D; in the latter case it would have been destroyed by the rock slide.

The evidence suggests that originally the erem consisted of just two units, A.1 and A.2, laid out on a plan typical for Naqlun, with a deep storage pit in A.1 and a courtyard with an entrance located just next to kitchen E belonging to erem 25. A coin of Leon I (457-473), found in the plaster of unit A.1 would indicate a date in the late 5th century for the erem's finishing, making it the oldest of the dated erems discovered so far at Naqlun.

The dating is further confirmed by the stratification of the deep storage pit discovered here. The first of the two floors which were introduced into the pit during its existence was made of bricks set on a layer of sherds belonging on the whole to early "chocolate" amphorae; the bricks were plastered on top. The second floor sealed the pit after it had been filled completely. The fill contained a large quantity of pottery, including locally produced vessels decorated with openwork: incense burners, chalices, small amphorae and bottles. The Greek papyri found in the fill date it to the late 6th century, as does a coin of Tiberius II (578-582).

Based on the evidence provided by the pit's fill, it should be assumed that a renovation took place in the erem sometime at the turn of the 6th century. The window was widened at this time to form a sort of passage into the small courtyard which preceded the entrance to unit B. The latter was turned into an oratory of sorts with a niche in the eastern wall decorated with fragmentarily preserved paintings. Unit D was also completed presumably at this time; to judge by the fine plastering of the walls and floor, it was intended for habitation. Pottery and a coin of Justin II (565-578) found in the donkey pen in the courtyard indicate that it was already in existence at this point. Unit A.1 underwent some changes as well with a large mudbrick bed with headrest being built just inside the entrance.

In the third stage of the erem's occupation, the structures in the courtyard were filled and discarded domestic pottery was dumped onto a heap accumulating against the northern wall of the pen. At this time unit A.1 served as a kitchen as well; the northern wall is black with soot and there are remains of what may have been a simple furnace. B.1 continued being used as an oratory, and indeed it must have remained accessible and in good condition for a long time to judge by the Coptic and Arab graffiti on its walls. Apparently, it was still visited by pilgrims in the 14th century.

Written documents found inside erem 89 include a few Greek texts on papyrus. Of the 6 recorded, 3 came from the storage pit. All are notary documents from the late 6th century. Nine Coptic texts were recorded, all in fragmentary condition, some on paper and some on papyrus. There were also 6 Coptic graffiti on the walls of B.1, mentioning, for instance, deacons who had visited the oratory. Among the preserved documents Arabic texts are the most numerous. There is a rare piece on papyrus and 8 written on paper. One of the latter is a grain contract dated to 400 AH, i.e. AD 1010, listing witnesses with the typically Arab name of Muhammad; on the back side of the card there is a letter written to one Theodore. Numerous Arab graffiti on the walls of B.1 mention the names of Barsum and Lutfallah which became popular only in the 14th century. The texts include a short prayer usually.

The pottery found in erem 89 is perhaps the most interesting in this assemblage. It consists of over 40 handmade vessels, more or less fragmentary, which have apparently never been used. Fragments of unfired clay decorations would suggest the vessels had been produced at the monastery, although so far no traces of a workshop or a kiln have been discovered. The vessels are decorated with ornamented openwork, impressed patterns or applied ones; the ornaments are painted in white. The incense burner is among the most frequent forms, but chalices, small amphorae and storage pots are also present.

Dating this group of vessels meets with some difficulty. The evidence from the storage pit fill (papyri documents and a coin) suggests the turn of the 6th century, but analogies with unglazed Early Islamic wares would rather point to the second half of the 7th century.

Other objects found in erem 89 reflect the everyday life of its inhabitant. There are pieces of textiles, shoes, glass and wooden objects, and large quantities of domestic pottery and table-wares.

S i t e   D

Excavations pursued on site D in the northern end of the monastic complex situated on the plateau uncovered further sections of an extensive building which had an upper floor and was enlarged several times in antiquity. The eastern side, which has been cleared, consists of a number of rooms clearly intended as residential or administrative in function. The upper floor was evidently residential, demonstrating rather high standards of decoration to judge by the remains found in the fill inside the rooms on the ground floor. The windows in the upper floor rooms had stucco grills and round panes. Some of the paned openings took on

the form of a Greek cross. Small unpaned openings
ensured ventilation. The walls were covered with
fine lime plaster and painted. Attempts to
reconstruct the decoration from preserved fragments
have resulted in frames and a throne being put
together, along with some human countenances
(including a representation of cherubins possibly).
In terms of style, these paintings are very close
to the murals uncovered inside the Church of
Archangel Gabriel at Naqlun, but appear to be a
little earlier, perhaps from the turn of the 11th
century.

A valuable recent find was a wooden casket
discovered in room D.9. The front was decorated
with an inlaid and gilded design of birds and other
ornaments. In style the decoration brings to mind
caskets produced in workshops of Late Fatimid times
or the Early Norman period in Sicily. The Naqlun
casket seems to have been put together from pieces
of two different earlier objects, for the back and
the sides are decorated with a "mosaic" ornament
quite obviously different from the bird motif on
the front.

Inside the casket there were 5 Arab books and some
documents on paper and parchment. One of these is
dated to 577 AH, i.e. AD 1181. All the documents
from inside the casket are definitely Muslim and
are mostly religious or mystic in character,
perhaps even magical. They could not have had
anything to do with the Naqlun monastery. It should
be assumed that the casket was abandoned in the
ruins of the monastery by someone who stopped there
sometime in the late 19th or early 20th century
(the date is suggested by a mechanically made
needle stuck into a bookmark in one of the books).

Church of Archangel Gabriel
The church which is still open today is doubtless
medieval in date. Peter Grossmann has even
suggested that it belongs to the early basilican
complexes of the 6th-7th century, but a date in the
9th or even 10th century is much more probable. It
is first mentioned at the turn of the 12th century
in a description of Naqlun written by Abu Saleh.

During a renovation of the church in 1991 murals
were discovered under layers of plain plaster on

the western and northern walls of the building.
Restorers who worked on the preservation of the
paintings in 1991 and 1992 were able to confirm
that the paintings in the present narthex come in
fact from two periods. On the northern wall there
is a frontal representation of a standing monk
dressed in a tunic and a phelonion with a hood on
his head. In his left hand he holds a staff topped
by a cross. Shown behind him is a niche with two
columns, one on either side, supporting a
horizontal beam above. Some of the features of this
representation recall illustrations in the codices
from Hamouli in the Fayum, which are dated to the
9th/10th centuries. The staff in the monk's hand
indicates that this is a representation of a holy
abbot, perhaps Apa Shenute himself.

Two other paintings on the western wall, which
have already undergone conservation, appear to be
later than the picture of the saint in monastic
garb. The monumental representation of Mother of
God with Child, seated on a throne between two
standing archangels in imperial dress, is a typical
Byzantine apse composition which is to be found in
churches in Sicily and southern Italy. It is
sometimes described as an enthroned Queen of Heaven
(O. Demus) or Maria Kaiserin (G.A. Wellen). In
Egypt it is known from Bawit and Saqqara, and also
appears in the Hamouli manuscript illuminations as
well as the medieval church of al Chohada in Esna.
This last painting is very close to the Naqlun
composition in terms of style and should presumably
be dated to the same period.

The position of the painting in the Church of
Archangel Gabriel at Naqlun is something of a
surprise. It is found on the western wall of the
southern aisle of the naos and the only reference
to an apse is the niche depicted behind the throne
of the Virgin. The presence of two doves is an
interesting iconographic element. The birds are
shown on the niche's arch, as in Byzantine
iconography, i.e. the silver plaques from Antioch
or the arcades with the concordances and letters of
Eusebius in the manuscripts containing books of the
New Testament; the only difference is that the
birds there are peacocks, not doves. An analogy of
sorts is provided by the doves shown above the arms

Fig.A. Mother of God with Child between archangels.
Mural from the Church of Archangel Gabriel in
Naqlun.

Fig.B. Mother of God with Child between archangels -
detail. Mural from the Church of Archangel
Gabriel in Naqlun.

of the man in a turban in the Capella Palatino in
Palermo. Both paintings draw upon a Late Fatimid
tradition. A throne with mashrabiyah decoration
appears in one of the illuminations from Hamouli,
while a similar floral decoration is to be observed
on the structural elements of the throne in the
Annunciation scene from Wadi an Natrun. The
characteristic way in which the wings of the
archangels are shown, their ornamental robes and
loros, all appear in the representations of
archangels in the al-Chohada church at Esna as well
as in the Church of Archangel Raphael at Tamit in
Nubia, where we are certainly dealing with a
painting by a master from Egypt.

Apart from this monumental composition there is
another large painting depicting two mounted
warrior saints. The horses are turned toward each
other. So far only the saint on the left has been
cleaned by conservators, and the legend next to the
rider has identified him as St. Pitchosh, a martyr
from the times of Diocletian who has not been
evidenced before. He is receiving his martyr's
wreaths from the hands of an angel on the right and
a hand appearing from the Heavens on the left.
Lying under the horse's belly is a man who points
with his hand to a small building with columns and
a dome, set in a palm grove. The painting
presumably reflects a hagiographic text describing
the saint's triumph over a pagan believer of
Apollo. By placing the small temple between the
hind legs of the saint's horse, the artist probably
meant to belittle the structure.

The representation of St. Pitchosh is kept in the
popular medieval tradition of mounted warrior
saints, such as St. Theodore and St. Claudius from
the al Chohada church at Esna and from the church
inside the Monastery of St. Anthony on the shores
of the Red Sea, and the wooden panel
representations of saints on the higab of the Abu
Sarqa church in Cairo. In the latter case there is
a saint identified as St. Mercurios who could in
fact be St. Pitchosh, considering the analogy
presented by the fallen man shown pointing to a
small structure between the horse's hind legs.

The paintings from the church at Naqlun are Late
Coptic and should be dated to the second half of

the 12th century. The murals from the al Chohada church at Esna are the closest analogy, although, artistically, the Naqlun frescoes are on a much higher level.

The results of the past few years of fieldwork at Naqlun have confirmed the importance of this medium-sized monastic complex for further studies on Egyptian monasticism. It is not only very complex from the architectural point of view, but it also is a source of written documents, objects of everyday life and works of art, especially murals. Taking everything into account, Naqlun remains a highly promising site for future studies.

B i b l i o g r a p h y   1989-1992

Preliminary excavation reports

Włodzimierz GODLEWSKI,Tomasz HERBICH, Ewa WIPSZYCKA, Deir el Naqlun (Nekloni), First preliminary report, Nubica I/II, Köln 1990, 171-207
Idem, Tomasz DERDA, Tomasz GÓRECKI, Deir el Naqlun (Nekloni) 1988-1989: Second Preliminary Report, Nubica III, 1993 (in press)

Preliminary archaeological announcements

Tomasz DERDA, Deir el Naqlun: The Greek Papyri, Polish Archaeology in the Mediterranean II, Warsaw 1991, 54-56
Włodzimierz GODLEWSKI, Archaeological research in Naqlun in 1991, Polish Archeology in the Mediterranean III, Warsaw 1992, 49-50
Idem, Deir el Naqlun 1990, Polish Archaeology in the Mediterranean II, Warsaw 1991, 48-53

General studies

Jarosław DOBROWOLSKI, Naqlun-Deir al Malak Ghubraᶜil: The Existing Monastic Complex, Nubica I/II, Köln 1990, 61-170
Idem, The monastic complex of Naqlun. Topography of the site, Bibliotheca Nubica II, 1993 (in press)

Włodzimierz GODLEWSKI, Deir el Naqlun. Quelques
  observations historiques, Actes du IVe Congrès
  Copte I, Louvain-la-Neuve 1992, 178-186
M.FATHY KHORSHED, Dedication of a sacred sanctuary
  (Haikal) of Archangel Gabriel in the Church of
  Archangel Michael at the monastery of al-Khashaba
  (Fayum) in the Mameluk Period, Actes du IVe
  Congrès Copte I, Louvain-la-Neuve 1992, 187-194
Peter GROSSMANN, Neue frühchristliche Funde aus
  Ägypten, Actes du XIe congrès international
  d'archeologie chrétien. II, Roma 1989, 1862-
  1865, fig.8

Texts

Tomasz DERDA, Inscriptions with the Formula θεοῦ
  χάρις κέρδος on Late Roman Amphorae, ZPE 94, 1992,
  135-152
Idem, P.Naqlun inv.no.35/88: A Papyrus from the
  recently excavated monastic center in Fayum,
  Proceedings of the 20th International Congress of
  Papyrology, Cairo 1992, 603-611
Idem, P.Naqlun inv.no.53/86: A Letter from Bishop
  Nicolaos to Comes Basileios, JJP XXII, Warsaw
  1992, 11-19
Olaf E.KAPER, Arabic Papyri and Inscriptions from
  Naqlun, Hermitage no.89, Polish Archaeology in
  the Mediterranean II, Warsaw 1991, 57-59
Adam ŁAJTAR, Two Greek inscriptions from Deir el-
  Naqlun, Nubica III, 1993 (in press)
Youssouf RAGHEB, L'inventaire des documents exhumes
  à Naqlun, 1991, Polish Archaeology in the
  Meditteranean III, Warsaw 1991, 57-58
Katarzyna URBANIAK, Drei Inschriften aus der Kirche
  des Erzengels Gabriel in Deir an-Naqlun im Fayum,
  BSAC XXXII, 1992 (in press)

RECENTLY DISCOVERED CHRISTIAN
MONUMENTS IN EGYPT

PETER GROSSMANN

My subject deals with the new discoveries in Egypt. In order not to conflict with the time, I shall limit myself to the discoveries of the last few years, about which no information has yet been published. A further reduction of my announcement (No 11 in the list of abstracts) is due to the fact that I did not succeed in getting the necessary material on all monuments in hand at the right moment.

The monuments mentioned here follow each other according to their geographical position from north to south.

1. *Sidi Mahmūd*: The church is situated at the south-western margin of an unidentified ancient settlement named after the neighbouring tomb of Sidi Mahmūd, in the vicinity of Burǧ al-Arab[1], which is itself a small modern Bedouin village on the Mediterranean Sea. It was excavated in 1985 by the pharaonic section of the Egyptian Antiquities Organization (EAO) and has a three-aisled naos with two apses at both ends (fig. 1). The eastern apse contains a *synthronon*, an altar, and a short distance in front of it there are also traces of a pulpit. Traces of a screen are not evident. The lateral side chambers of the apse are very different in size and they are both furnished with an additional absidiola. The western apse was screened. It has an inner curved bench, similar to the *synthronon* at the eastern end, but apparently no altar. Below the northern side of this apse a vaulted underground corridor is visible, which apparently gives access to an underground tomb. On both sides of the western apse two stairs descend westward to a crypt. It was styled as a small underground chapel with a rectangular niche (prayer niche ?) in the eastern wall. Its relationship with the underground burial-place below the western apse is not visible. To the south of the church a baptistry is extant, originally surrounded with four columns which apparently once carried a small dome thus forming a *ciborium*.

The church belongs to a small group of double apsed churches in Egypt. Other examples of this type are the church in the neighbouring town of Taposiris Magna, published in the last volume of the Bull. of the

---

[1] Named after the romantic British 19th cent. castle in the area.

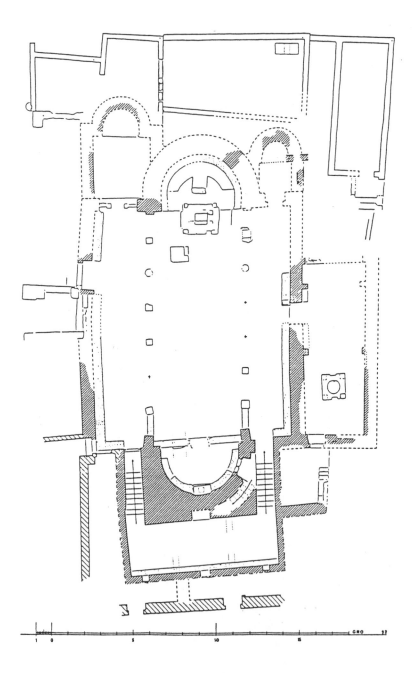

Fig. 1. The church of Sidi Mahmūd (Burǧ al-Arab)

Copt. Society[2] and the unfortunately totally destroyed church of Hermonthis[3]. The two northern churches which, with regard to their typological origin, have no tradition in Egypt (except perhaps for the example at Hermonthis), are apparently influenced from North Africa, where many examples of this kind are extant[4]. The date of the Burğ al-Arab church may be settled for the 6th cent. A.D.

2. *Abū Minā, Great Basilica*: The excavations in Abū Minā brought to light so many new observations that another communication could easily be filled. However, the results are published regularly, and the next report of our last season is already in print.

Today I want to call attention only to a rather unusual discovery in the sanctuary of the Great Basilica. Fig. 2A shows the center of the church with the apse, the two original underground burial chambers, the presbytery, and the four bases of the ciborium surrounding the original altar place. In addition to these features already known[5], there came to light between the altar and the apse remains of three concentrically curved rows of columns. The center of these curves lies roughly in the middle of the western pair of columns of the *ciborium*[6]. I cannot understand these three curved rows of columns other than as the supports for a higher, raised platform, similar to the tribunes which were used by the Emperors and their staff on official occasions in front of the public. A representation of such an Imperial tribune survives in a relief on the base of the obelisk in the hippodrom of K/pel probably of the 4th cent.[7]. Of course, the struc-

---

[2] P. Grossmann, *A new church at Taposiris Magna-Abusïr*. Bull. Soc. d'archéol. Copte 31 (1992) 25-30.

[3] E. Jomard in: *Description de l'Égypte* I (Paris 1921) 437ff. vol. I Antiquités pl. 97,6. 8; a revision of this plan was published by P. Grossmann, *Zum Grundriß der Basilika von Armant (Hermonthis)*, in: Studien zur spätantiken und byzantinischen Kunst, Festschrift F.W. Deichmann I (Mainz 1986) 143-153.

[4] Examples are mentioned in the article cited above.

[5] C.M. Kaufmann, *Die Menasstadt und das Nationalheiligtum der altchristlichen Aegypter. Ausgrabungen der Frankfurter Expedition am Karm Abu Mina 1905 -1907.* I (Leipzig 1910) 86ff. fig. 23 pl. 58; see also the new plan of H. Schläger, *Abu Mena. Vorläufiger Bericht.* MDAIK 19, 1963, 114-120 esp. 118 fig. 1.

[6] Three bases of the third row had already been discovered by Kaufmann, *loc.cit.* 86 pl. 58, who interpreted them, however, as candelabra or parts of a screen; see also Schläger *loc.cit.* 118 fig. 1 pl. 25a. G. und H.-G. Severin, *Marmor vom heiligen Menas.* Liebieghaus Monographie Bd. 10 (Frankfurt 1987) 30 fig. 18ff.

[7] G. Bruns, *Der Obelisk und seine Basis auf dem Hippodrom zu Konstantinopel* [Istforsch 7 1935], particularly informative is the relief of the south-west side which shows in the lower register a chariot racing, ibid. 53ff. fig. 64; the supporting elements of the tribune are, however, not shown.

200

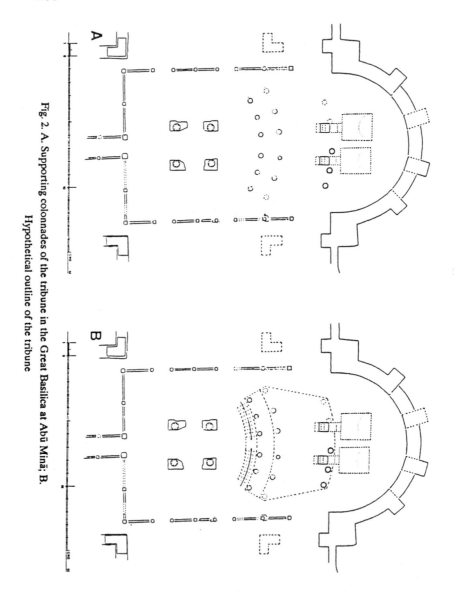

Fig. 2. A. Supporting colonnades of the tribune in the Great Basilica at Abū Mīnā; B.
Hypothetical outline of the tribune

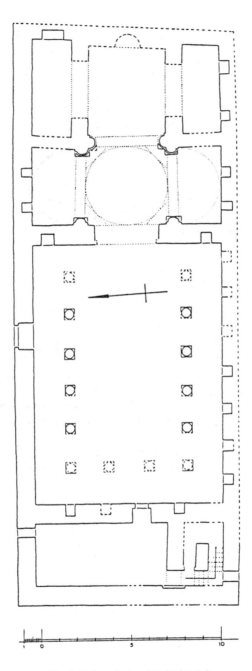

Fig. 3. Dair aṣ-Ṣyrian (Wadi Naṭrūn)

202

ture in the Great Basilica of Abū Minā has nothing to do with the Emperor, but it might have been used for a similar purpose such as to afford a place for a larger number of bishops, when several communities from the Delta-regions, together with their bishops, came to Abū Minā to join in the feast of the Saint. After the destruction by the Persian invasion in A.D. 619 it was replaced by an ordinary *synthronon* built of stone, which serves more or less the same purpose.

On fig. 2B I have drawn how the outline of the tribune in the Great Basilica of Abū Minā would have looked. The smaller space in front seems to be slightly lower in height than the rest. Unfortunately there are no indications of the position of the stairs. They might have been situated in front of the structure ascending from both sides to meet on top of a small central platform. The construction of the stairs would thus be similar to the construction of an ambo[8].

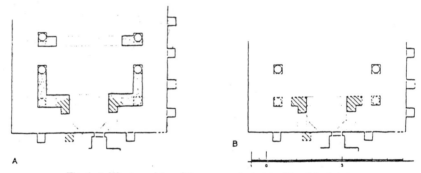

Fig. 4. A. Western niche of the nave, actual state; B. original state

3. *Dair aṣ-Ṣyrian (Wadi Naṭrūn)*: During the restauration work in the half dome of the western exedra in the al-'Adra'-church of Dair aṣ-Ṣyrian in Wadi Naṭrūn, which led to the discovery of the marvelous painting shown on the first day of our congress by Maggy Rassart Debergh, there was also an opportunity for a few archaeological investigations. These resulted in a new interpretation of the existing remains. Fig. 3 shows the original state of the building; fig. 4A gives the actual state, and fig. 4B the situation when the western exedra was first installed. The two original columns at the western end of the nave were replaced by two symmetrically arranged corner pillars. The final stage (fig. 4A) was reached, when the original wooden roof of the nave was replaced by a much heavier barrel vault for which additional supports became necessary and as a result the western intercolumnia were walled up.

---

[8] For examples see P.H.F. Jakobs, Die frühchristlichen Ambone Griechenlands (Bonn 1987) passim.

Concerning the date of this church, there is now almost no doubt that the major part of the church belongs to the rebuilding of the Patriarch Benjamin I (626-665)[9] as mentioned by Maqrizi shortly after the Arab conquest[10]. The hurus in front of the sanctuary cannot be dated earlier and a *terminus ante quem* is given by the date of the painting in the semidome of the western exedra which is settled by C. Innemée and P. van Moorsel[11] at around 700 A.D. Since this exedra for structural reasons could have been added only later the church itself must be a few decades earlier.

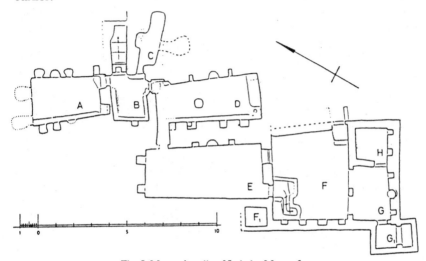

Fig. 5. Monastic cells of Imbaba-Manṣurīya

4. *Imbaba-Mansurīya*: In Imbaba-Manṣuriya, not very far from the western edge of Cairo, the Egyptian Antiquities Organization (EAO) discovered in 1991 a small hermitage dating back to the 7th cent. It consists of a group of underground cells (fig. 5), principally similar to those discovered by the IFAO in the neighbourhood of Iṣna in Upper Egypt[12]. The

---

[9] Dates according to A. Jülicher, *Die Liste der alexandrinischen Patriarchen im 6. und 7. Jahrhundert*, in: Festgabe Karl Müller (Tübingen 1922) 7-23, esp. 23.

[10] *Macrizi's Geschichte der Copten* (ed. with German transl. by F. Wüstenfeld, Göttingen 1845) 48.

[11] Personal communication; P. van Moorsel has, however, some scepsis; see also the recently published discussion of the paintings by P. van Moorsel, Une annociation faite à Marie au Monastère des Syriens, Bull. Soc. Fr. d'Égyptologie 124 (juin 1992) 5-20 spec. 15ff. Pl. 1-4.

[12] S. Sauneron - J. Jacquet, *Les ermitages chrétiens du désert d'Esna I-IV* (Cairo 1972) passim.

developement of the hermitage of Imbaba-Mansuriya started with the rather irregular rooms A, B, C, and the stairs situated to the east of B. They form the original nucleus of the complex, which was then progressively enlarged by adding rooms D and E, to serve as additional prayer-halls. The additions themselves were progressively more regular in size and richer in design. As in the first chamber A the furnishing consists in both cases of a semicircular niche in the eastern wall flanked on both sides with two slightly smaller rectangular niches. Room E was additionally decorated with a painted series of saints and monks. This room had its own entrance stairs from the south, thus giving a relative date for the blocking of the original entrance at the east of room B.

The remaining rooms to the south are erected above ground. F was apparently a court. The entrance is situated on the eastern side.

5. *Hermopolis Magna, South church*: Some very fine results were obtained in Spring 1991 with the excavation of the South Church at Hermopolis Magna[13]. It is situated upon the site of a temple of Ramesses II, restored under the Emperor Nero, for which reason this temple is often called «Temple of Nero».

As almost all monuments in Hermopolis Magna the church has been so seriously robbed that practically only the foundations remain in place (fig. 6). It has a three-aisled nave, with a western *return aisle* - typical for church architecture in Upper Egypt - and a tripartite sanctuary with a relatively narrow apse and the two usual lateral side chambers. Two inwardly placed columns are extant at the eastern ends of both colonnades, probably because of the rather narrow apse.

Along the south side of the church several rooms are lined up. The two western-most ones belong to a baptistery, of which the various elements are still in place: These include the upper basin to collect the water for consecration, the piscine with steps to the east and west, the water channel to remove the used water to a seepage shaft through which the water returns to the earth. The baptismal chamber proper was apparently of octagonal shape and thus very probably originally covered with a dome. The third room from the west is an underground burial chapel with an attached elongated chamber for the placing of the required sarcophagus; this is published already by D.M. Bailey.

---

[13] A preliminary description of this church before excavation was given by D.M. Bailey, *Excavations at el-Ashmunein. British Museum Expedition to Middle Egypt* IV. Hermopolis Magna: Buildings of the Roman Period (London 1991) 46-53 pl. 89ff.

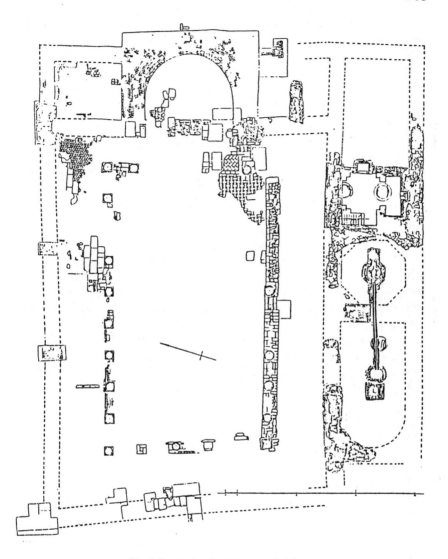

Fig. 6. South church of Hermopolis Magna

According to the pottery finds the construction of the church dates to the middle of the 5th cent. Its technical state is very bad due to the fact that it was built upon a rather fresh rubbish mount which was not strong enough and sufficiently settled to carry the weight of a big church. Problems on the static structure must have arisen already in antiquity, as demonstrated by a considerable number of ancient repairs; for example the stylobates for the colonnades were rebuilt on several occasions.

6. *Two chapels within the Roman settlement at al-Haiz (Baharia Oasis)*: The reopening of the excavation of A. Fakhry in the Late Roman settlement of al-Haiz in 1990/91 by the Egyptian Antiquities Organization (EAO) produced some interesting results and allowed a closer study of the two chapels in this area, known already from the time of A. Fakhry[14]. One of them is situated at the eastern side, the other in the north-west part of the settlement.

Both chapels appear as installations within already existing Roman structures. The original Roman parts of the eastern chapel consist of a series of rooms to the east and a kind of court to the west entered through three symmetrically arranged openings on the south side. On the plan (fig. 7) the elements added later to the chapel are shaded. They show a kind of single-aisled transversally extended nave, a hurus, entered from the nave through four differently sized doors, and an altar chamber, for which a small, already existing chamber, originally domed, was used, furnished with an altar and a painted cross on the eastern wall. Of the latter only traces remained in place. A. Fakhry saw the whole cross and published photographs and a drawing in his well known publication[15]. Remarkable is the decoration of the crossing point of the four arms, which shows a human face obviously representing Jesus Christ.

The north-western chapel (fig. 8) is constructed in the main room at the eastern side of a large court surrounded with single and double-aisled porticoes. It consists here of a tripartite sanctuary, characteristic for the Early Christian churches in Egypt, again a hurus, and a small broad nave. Our workers asured us that also here the central room of the sanctuary was furnished with an altar. However, we did not see it and A. Fakhry did not report it.

C.C. Walters dates both chapels to the very beginning of Christianity in Egypt[16], even before the official peace of the church, and the next example he mentions is the early 3rd cent. church at Dura Europos in Northern Syria. However, both of our chapels are originally furnished with a hurus which is not found before the second half of the 7th cent. Thus the 2nd half of the 7th cent. is the earliest possibility for the date of both chapels.

---

[14] A. Fakhry, *Baharia Oasis* II (Cairo 1950) 60ff.; republished with a shortened text and another photograph in: ibid., *The Oases of Egypt II. Bahriyah and Farafra Oases* (Cairo 1974) 114-124.

[15] Fakhry *loc.cit.* 64 fig. 43 pl. 38C; resp. 121f. fig. 57f.

[16] C.C. Walters, *Monastic Archaeology in Egypt* (Warminster 1974) 28f. «.. *possible ... an example of the primitive house-chapel as found at Dura.* ».

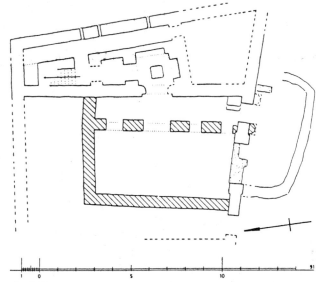

Fig. 7. East chapel at the Roman settlement of al-Haiz (Baharia Oasis)

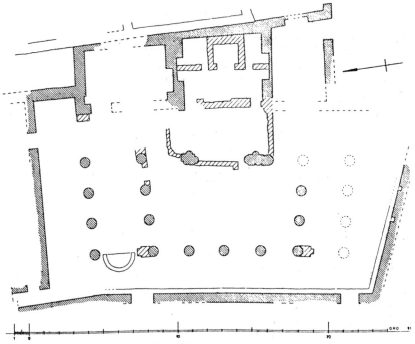

Fig. 8. North-west chapel

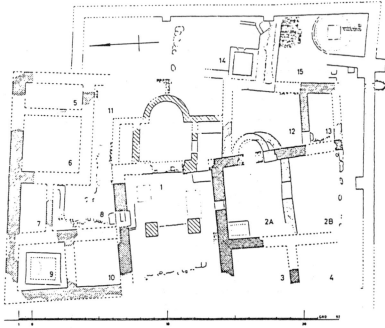

Fig. 9. Chapel of Tall al-Farama South (Pelusium)

7. *Tall al-Farama South*: At the end of my communication I like to show you something of the activities of the Egyptian Antiquities Organization in the area of Pelusium in North Sinaï which became urgently necessary because of the cultivation project in this region. I had the opportunity to collaborate with the Organization at a small site called Tall al-Farama South (fig. 9), which appears to be a former private house which was later turned into a small ecclesiastical complex. The first little church was built into room 1. It received two pillars in the nave, in which way a narthex was probably separated from the naos. To the east a tripartite sanctuary was added. Special attention should be devoted to the forechoir and the eastward projecting apse, two rather unusual features in Egyptian church architecture.

During a later period the neighbouring room 2A was turned into a chapel. It has two apses, of which the earlier one corresponds to the larger unit 2A/2B, when the inner partition wall was still not built. This wall came into being only when the later smaller apse was installed. According to the pottery finds both chapels must be dated to the time after the Persian invasion of 619.[17]

---

[17] For the dating of the pottery we have to thank Mme Pascal Ballet.

THE COMPOSITION OF THE *HISTORY OF THE CHURCHES AND MONASTERIES OF EGYPT*: SOME PRELIMINARY REMARKS

JOHANNES DEN HEIJER

A. Introduction.

The following paper is a small side-product of a larger project involving the famous *History of the Patriarchs of Alexandria* (henceforth *HP*, an Arabic text compiled in the late 11th century from older Coptic sources, by the Alexandrian notable and deacon, Mawhūb Ibn Manṣūr Ibn Mufarriǧ, and continued by other authors. At present, I am preparing a new critical edition of the primitive (or original) recension of this text[1]. One of the activities planned within the framework of this project is a systematical analysis of the quotations from this text in the works of later authors. One of the works studied in this respect is the *History of the Churches and Monasteries of Egypt* (henceforth: *HCME*), a most informative work

---

1 On the composition and the two recensions of the *History of the Patriarchs of Alexandria*, see J. den Heijer, *Mawhūb Ibn Manṣūr Ibn Mufarriǧ et l'historiographie copto-arabe. Etude sur la composition de l'Histoire des Patriarches d'Alexandrie* (= *Corpus Scriptorum Christianorum Orientalium*, Vol. 513: Subsidia, tomus 81), Lovanii 1989; idem, "History of the Patriarchs of Alexandria", *The Coptic Encyclopaedia*, New York 1991, (Vol. 4) 1238-1242.; idem, "Mawhūb Ibn Manṣūr Ibn Mufarrij al-Iskandarānī (c. 1025-1100)", *Coptic Encyclopaedia*, (Vol. 5), 1573-1574. The current project is sponsored by the Netherlands Organization of Scientific Research (NWO) and carried out by the present author at Leiden University, The Netherlands, and at the Institut français d'Archéologie orientale (IFAO) and the Netherlands Institute for Archaeology and Arabic Studies, Cairo, Egypt. The edition is to appear as a publication of the IFAO.

often consulted not only by students of Coptic and Coptic-Arabic
literature, but also (and perhaps even more) by archaeologists and art
historians, and by those interested in the historical geography and
toponomy of Egypt. This work is well known under the name of the
person to whom it is traditionally attributed, viz. the otherwise utterly
unknown Abū Ṣāliḥ al-Armanī (the Armenian). Re-reading what has
been written about the history of this text, I soon began to realize that
many essential points remain obscure, and that it would hardly make
sense to consult the *HCME* as a secondary witness of the *HP* before
at least a beginning to a comprehensive study on the *HCME* itself had
been made. Therefore, I will not discuss the quotations from the
History of the Patriarchs in the *HCME* in this paper, but instead,
present some very preliminary remarks on the *HCME* itself, in which
I rely, I must hasten to point out, on the available editions only.

In 1895, Evetts published his edition of the then only known ms. of
the *HCME* (kept in Paris)[2]. Since the cover of the ms. mentions the
name of Abū Ṣāliḥ al-Armanī, Evetts identified this person as the
author of the text. In 1984, Father Samuel of Dayr as-Suryān (now
Anba Samuel, Bishop of Šībīn al-Qanāṭir) produced a new edition[3], in
which Evetts's edition was completed by using another ms., which now
seems to be kept in Munich[4]. This second ms., according to Fr.
Samuel, contains the first and the third parts of the *HCME*, whereas

---

2 Abū Ṣāliḥ, *The Churches and Monasteries of Egypt and
some Neighbouring Countries attributed to Abū Ṣāliḥ the Armenian*,
edited and translated by B.T.A. Evetts, with added notes by Alfr. J.
Butler (= *Anecdota Oxoniensa*, Semitic Series, 7), Oxford 1895.

3 Abū l-Makārim, *Tārīḫ al-Kanā'is wa-l-Adyurah fī l-qarn
aṯ-ṯānī 'ašar al- mīlādī, li-Abī l-Makārim, alladī nusiba ḫaṭa'an ilā
Abī Ṣāliḥ al-Armanī*, i'dād wa-ta'līq ar-rāhib Ṣamu'īl as-Suryānī, ǧuz'
1-4, Dayr as-Suryān 1984. Recently, Bishop Samuel published an
English translation of Part I: Abu al Makarem, *History of the
Churches and Monasteries in Lower Egypt in the 13th Century*, Cairo
1992

4 Oral and written communications from several colleagues in
the field of Coptic studies.

the ms. published by Evetts represents the second part[5].

As an appendix to his edition, Fr. Samuel reproduces a hand-written essay by the well-known Egyptian scholar, Ğirğis Fīlūṭā'us 'Awaḍ, in which it is argued that the two mss. actually belong together[6]. And in fact, I do not see anything that would counter this assertion. One may well agree with Ğirğis Fīlūṭā'us 'Awaḍ that there is a logical distribution of contents between the three parts: Part I deals with Lower Egypt and a part of Cairo; Part II with other parts of the capital and with Upper Egypt, and very briefly with some places outside Egypt; and Part III deals with the Sinai, Greater Syria and Mesopotamia, Anatolia, and Rome.

Furthermore, Ğirğis Fīlūṭā'us 'Awaḍ convincingly argues that throughout these volumes, basically the same sources are quoted or referred to, and the formulas used to refer to them are often of the same type in all three volumes[7].

Having demonstrated that the whole text, now available in Father Samuel's three volumes, constitutes one book, Ğirğis Fīlūṭā'us 'Awaḍ then argues that this whole work must be attributed to a Coptic priest called Abū al-Makārim Sa'dallāh Ibn Ğirğis Ibn Mas'ūd, and that Abū Ṣāliḥ al-Armanī is merely the name of someone who once owned the ms., but this point is more problematic and calls for further investigation. What I propose to do in this paper is to re-examine the editorial notes and other indications scattered thoughout the text.

B. Dates

But before doing so, I should like to pay some attention to those events where the text provides dates for the events described. Limiting ourselves to the latter half of the 12th century and the beginning of the 13th, we can see that from 1153/4 [548 A.H.] up to 1186/7 [903

---

5 Abū al-Makārim, Tārīḫ, introduction.
6 Abū al-Makārim, Tārīḫ, III, 159-170.
7 Abū al-Makārim, Tārīḫ, III, 167.

A.M.], there is a remarkably high degree of continuity: with maximum intervals of three years, most years in this period are mentioned in events reported in the text. By contrast, in the stretch of 14 years between 1186/7 and 1200 (596 A.H.), only one date is mentioned, viz. the year 1191 (907 A.M.)[8]. Then, we have four accounts dated to 1200 (596 A.H.)[9], 1203/4 (920 A.M.)[10], 1208 (924 A.M.)[11], and 1208/9 A.D. (925)[12]. Moreover, there is an event which is datable to an even later period, since it mentions al-Malik al-Muʿaẓẓam[13], by which title the Ayyubid ruler of Syria, Šaraf ad-Dīn, may be indicated: his reign lasted from 1218 to 1227[14]. The gap between the two periods thus covered obliges us to consider the possibility that two layers can be identified in the composition of the text.

Particularly revealing are those passages where the author(s) or editor(s) refer to the time in which they wrote, by employing such phrases as "in our times" and the like. In one such passage, we read:

In this our own time, at the beginning of the year 564, (...) [A.H., = 1168 A.D.][15]

---

8 Abū al-Makārim, Tārīḫ, I, 16a – References to the different parts of the *HCME* will be given henceforth under the author names used in the editions: thus, Parts I and III (ed. Fr. Samuel) will be indicated as Abū al-Makārim, Tārīḫ, whereas Part II (ed. Evetts), will be referred to as Abū Ṣāliḥ, Tārīḫ. Both titles will be followed by the relevant folio numbers.

9 Abū al-Makārim, Tārīḫ, III, 112a.

10 Abū al-Makārim, Tārīḫ, I, 71a.

11 Abū Ṣāliḥ, Tārīḫ, II, 51b–52a.

12 Abū al-Makārim, Tārīḫ, III, 164b.

13 Abū al-Makārim, Tārīḫ, III, 146a.

14 C.E. Bosworth, *The Islamic Dynasties* (= *Islamic Surveys* 5), Edinburgh 1967, 59. Theoretically, the title in question could even refer to al-Malik al-Muʿaẓẓam Tūrān Šāh, who ruled in Egypt and Syria from 1249 to 1250.

15 Abū Ṣāliḥ, Tārīḫ, II, 1b.

This year belongs to the earlier period identified above. The later period, on the other hand, is clearly represented in the account dated to 1209:

(...) until the final stage of writing down (tastīr) this history (sīrah), in the year 925 of the Righteous Martyrs [= 1208/9 A.D.][16].

The passage mentioning the year 1208 appears to be crucial in this respect. First, a relatively early date is mentioned in the following words:

The monastery now, in our time, housed five monks in poor circumstances, until the end of Baramhāt, in the year 891 of the Righteous Martyrs [= 1175 A.D.] ....

A few lines further in the same account, an additional piece of information is dated as follows:

After that, Faḫr Ibn al-Qanbar (...) came to live there (...) and he dwelt there 20 years until he died on Monday (...) on the 23rd of Amšīr, in the year 924 of the Righteous Martyrs [= 1208][17].

This can only mean that initially this passage consisted of the first report, of 1175, only, and that at a later stage, in 1208, it was updated, so to speak. This fact strongly supports the idea of the two layers introduced above.

C. Editorial notes

With the last passage studied above, we have actually entered the domain of editorial notes. Let us have a closer look at these notes,

16 Abū al-Makārim, Tārīḫ, III, 164b.
17 Abū Ṣāliḥ, Tārīḫ II, 51 b.

paying particular attention to the question of the two layers. To begin
with, the earlier period is clearly represented in Part II, where the
compiler / editor refers to himself in the 1st person sg.:

> The compiler (ğāmi') of this book said: I had a meeting with
> Abū al-Qāsim Ḫalīl, the physician and philosopher of Ascalon
> (...). The meeting which I, the miserable one, the editor (nāẓim)
> of the book, had with this Abū al-Qāsim, was on Monday, the
> 27th of Šawwāl 568 [A.H. = 1173][18]

This compiler refers to himself by using two different terms:
ğāmi' (literally, "collector") and nāẓim ("arranger"). Basically, this
compiler may be Abū al-Makārim himself, whom we meet in two
passages in Part I.

> (....) The court of the well-known house was the dwelling-place
> of aš-Šaiḫ al-Mu'taman Abū al-Makārim Sa'dallāh Ibn Ğirğis
> Ibn Mas'ūd, the editor (nāẓim) of this book[19].
> (...) to the property of the noble lady, Sitt ad-Dār, (....) the wife
> of the above-mentioned Šaiḫ Abū al-Makārim, the compiler
> (muṣannif) of this book[20]

If this identification is correct, Abū al-Makārim's involvement in
the redaction can be dated to the earlier layer. There is a problem,
however, regarding this identification: the two passages mentioning
Abū al-Makārim refer to him in the third person, in a way I cannot
help suspecting of being written by somebody else. Abū al-Makārim, I
think, can hardly be expected to refer to himself as a "Shaikh" (Šayḫ),
and even less to use his honorific title (laqab) aš-Šayḫ al-Mu'taman.
Therefore, we cannot rule out the possibility that we are dealing with
two compilers here: an anonymous one who wrote in the 1170s, and
Abū al-Makārim, whose contribution then cannot be dated with any

---

18 Abū Ṣāliḥ, Tārīḫ II, 3b–4b.
19 Abū al-Makārim, Tārīḫ, I, 5a.
20 Abū al-Makārim, Tārīḫ, I, 18b.

degree of certainty.

Now, theoretically one could maintain, as Ǧirǧis Fīlūṯā'us 'Awaḍ and others seem to have done, that all "contemporary" contributions to the *HCME*, pertaining to a period as long as 60 or 70 years (from ca. 1150 to 1209 and even to ca. 1220), are to be attributed to one author or compiler, *i.e.* to Abū al-Makārim. This would imply that one person would have been responsible for the two layers, i.e. would have re-examined and re-arranged the text at least some 35 to 50 years after his initial editorial activity. Only if this were so, could Abū al-Makārim simply be considered the author of the *HCME*. But the fact of the matter is that things are slightly more complicated, as may be inferred from the two following notes:

Then, after his death, I found a leaf (*ruq'ah*) in [some] papers written by (*bi-ḫaṭṭ*) Anbā Mīḫā'īl, Metropolitan of Dumyāṭ, in which he says to the author (*mu'allif*) of this book – and perhaps it was an answer to his correspondence with him concerning Ibn Qanbar – : (...)[21].

I found a copy (*nusḫah*) written by (*bi-ḫaṭṭ*) Anbā Mīḫā'īl, metropolitan of Dumyāṭ, in [dated to?] the 22nd of Baramūdah of the year 900 of the Church [= 1184], (...) among that which was underlined by (*mimmā šaṭabahū*) the author (*mu'allif*) of this book, in addition to underlining (?) (*'alā šaṭb*) a copy (*nusḫah*) which witnesses the Virtues of Jerusalem, from the book written by (*waḍa'ahū*) 'Alī [Ibn] 'Ubayd, the Metropolitan of the Nestorians in Damascus (...)[22].

---

21 Abū Ṣāliḥ, *Tārīḫ* II, 14a. The leaf in question may have belonged to a treatise against the controversial Bishop Murqus Ibn Qanbar (d. 1208), written by Mīḫā'īl of Dumyāṭ (d. between 1208 and 1216): cf. G. Graf, *Geschichte der christlichen arabische Literatur* II (= *Studi e Testi*, 133), Città del Vaticano 1947, 333-335.

22 Abū al-Makārim, *Tārīḫ* III, 139b-140a. On the identity of 'Alī (or Elias) Ibn 'Ubayd of Damascus, see Graf, *Geschichte* II, 134.

Even though the latter note is somewhat obscure in its details, the two notes combined indisputably demonstrate that at least two persons were involved in composing the *HCME*: in both notes, it is evident that the author (*mu'allif*) is not the same person as the man who is writing here (and probably not only here).

These two notes also show that the author (*mu'allif*) was actually a compiler himself, who kept files containing documents which he could use as sources for his work. The first note is the most important one, for it shows the gap in time that must have existed between the activities of the author (*mu'allif*) and the editor writing here: one has the impression that the latter is reporting on research carried out on the files left behind by the former, probably after his death, or at least at a time when he was no longer available to inform the editor about the nature of the document by Anbā Mīḫā'īl: the editor cannot but conjecture that he is looking at a correspondence between the author and the metropolitan. Such a late datation of the editorial work reflected here is confirmed by the date 900 A.M. = 1183/4 mentioned in the first passage: this is obviously the date of Mīḫā'īl's treatise, which was already an archival item by the time our later editor discovered it, while the date of 1183 itself already belongs to very last years of the earlier layer, as we have seen above. All this, to be sure, corroborates my remark on the gap of time that can be observed in the dates of reported events.

By now, it seems tolerably safe to confirm that the text of the *HCME* contains two layers, attibutable to two or more different persons. I would venture to suggest, moreover, that the later layer is to be dated to 1208 or later, perhaps even to ca. 1220, in view of the dates mentioned earlier in this paper. I do not know, however, how to identify the editor responsible for this later layer. It is obvious that we cannot distinguish neatly between the author (*mu'allif*) on the one hand and the compiler (*nāẓim / ǧāmi'* and *nāẓim / muṣannif*) on the other, since both the author and the compiler or compilers have been shown to belong to the earlier layer: we are simply left to wonder whether these terms refer to one author (Abū al-Makārim), or to two or even more persons.

An additional complication faces us in two notes, which may be ascribed to one person, who does not write directly in the first person sg., but nevertheless does seem to refer to himself:

Abū Ǧamīl, the writer (kātib) of these .....[23].

This church was consecrated at the beginning of the patriarchate of Anbā Yūḥannā, the 64th in number, in the year 907 of the Martyrs [1191] on the first of Misrā, [the festival] of Abū Būlā the martyr, its patron, in the presence of the writer (kātib) of these letters (aḥruf)[24].

The problem is whether we are to understand this note as a late stage of the earlier layer, as an early phase of the later layer, or as an independant, intermediate layer. I just cannot tell. A final complication presents itself in the copyist's note at the end of Part II, the relevant parts of which run as follows:

(1) Here ends what was collected by (mā ǧama'ahū) the author of the history (ṣāḥib at-tārīḫ). For he was unable to make his work complete on account of the extent of the surface of the earth to the east and to the west; yet he collected (ǧama'a) matter which no other had collected (lam yaǧma'hū), and he devoted extreme care to his work (wa-htamma ǧāyat al-ihtimām). Nevertheless, he was concise in his exposition (qaṣīr al-'ibārah), because in his narrative he shunned all amplification that was not necessary.

(2) That poor, wretched, feeble slave, the copyist (an-nāsiḫ), has copied (naqala) what he found in [the] (?) copy (an-nusḫah) from which he was copying (al-manqūl minhā), without addition or deletion (bi-ǧayr ziyādah walā naqṣ).

(3) The work of copying it (nashiḫī) was finished on Wednesday, the second of the month of Ba'ūnah in the year 1054 of the Blameless Martyrs, which corresponds to the eighth

---

23 Abū al-Makārim, Tārīḫ I, 5b. At the end of this sentence, a word meaning "letters", "words" or "lines" is wanting.
24 Abū al-Makārim, Tārīḫ, I, 16a.

of Dū al-Qaʿdah of the year 739 (= 1338 A.D.). May God grant us a good end to this year.

(4) That poor slave the copyist (*an-nāsiḫ*) has attempted to abridge the book (*an yaḫtaṣir al-kitāb*), as it has been said, without detracting from the sense (*walā yaḫruǧ ʿammā fīhi min an-naṣṣ*), but the task has been too great for him. He prays all those who read the book will accept the apologies of him who offers them (...)[25].

At the beginning of this note (par. 1), we are once more informed about the work of the author or compiler. In par. 3, we see that the manuscript containing Part II was written down in 1338 A.D. The ms. of Part III must be somewhat more recent, for it contains a passage mentioning the year 750 A.H. = 1349 A.D. The problem for the history of the text is situated in the contradiction between paragraphs 2 and 4. What does the scribe mean by his attempt, mentioned in par. 4, "to abridge the book, without detracting from the sense", if he has stated in par. 2 that he has made his copy "without addition or deletion"? Whatever the answer may be, we cannot rule out the possibility that to the redactional layers already discerned, we must add a final stage in the textual history, in which a copyist (in the 14th century or perhaps earlier) left his trace by omitting words (or perhaps more) which he considered redundant.

D. Conclusion

As a result of the preceding observations, we can tentatively identify several layers in the composition of the *HCME*, and at the same time indicate various remaining uncertainties:

I. An earlier layer, compiled between, say, 1160 and 1187, in which the following persons are involved: (a) an anonymous compiler, who refers to himself in the 1 sg., and calls himself *ǧāmiʿ* and *nāẓim*; (b) an

---

25 Abū Ṣāliḥ, *Tārīḫ* II, 112b-113a.

anonymous author (*mu'allif*), actually also a *compiler*, who also speaks in the 1 sg. and therefore could be identical with the anonymous compiler (a); (c) Abū al-Makārim himself, who may be identical with the anonymous compiler (a), but this is not certain at all; he might also be identical with the anonymous author (b) provided (a) and (b) are two persons; or he may be a third person involved in the earlier layer; although, if he is not identical with (a) or (b), we have no information at all about the period in which he lived and worked.

II. An intermediate layer, added by a certain Abū Ǧamīl, around the year 1190; although this could be a later stage of layer I or an earlier stage of layer III, so that either I (a) or I (b) - if they are not identical - could also be due to this Abū Ǧamīl.

III. A later layer, added between 1200 and 1220, again by an anonymous compiler or scribe (*kātib*). If this compiler is not the aforementioned Abū Ǧamīl (II), it could theoretically also be Abū al-Makārim.

IV. On top of the aforementioned layers, there is the contribution of the anonymous scribe of 1338 and 1349, who apparently made some sort of abridgement of the text.

From these remarks, Abū al-Makārim emerges as just one out of several persons involved in compiling the *HCME*, and his contribution is hard to situate in time. Finally, it should be stressed that the involvement of at least two, perhaps even three or four, anonymous contributions to the history of the text does leave ample room for the enigmatic Abū Ṣāliḥ, who no longer necessarily has to be dismissed as a mere owner of a manuscript.

I am afraid that the outcome of this presentation is that very little is clear with regard to the way the *HCME* was produced. All I was able to do here is analyse the relevant passages and point to the various possible ways to interpret them. Suffice it to say, in conclusion, that, although the distinction between the two main layers (I and II) seems pretty well established, the history of the text is not a very transparent one, and we will just have to live with the frustration of being unable to solve all problems related to it.

ATTEMPTS TO REVIVE THE COPTIC LANGUAGE

IN EGYPT,

AND RELEVANT PROBLEMS

DR. KAMAL FARID ISHAQ (ISAAC)

In many Countries, the Coptic Language may have its importance from a theological, historical or archaeological point of view, but to Copts, it has the further value of being an identity

After the Arab Conquest of Egypt, the invaders succeeded in imposing their Arabic Language on the Egyptian tongue, but the Coptic Church had the honour of keeping the national language of Egypt in its books, prayers & rites.

The motive here was not religious, since one can pray in any language. It was a national motive, in order to save Egypt's Language and identity. We hope that someday all Egypt - not only the Copts & the foreign scholars - will take care of the Coptic Language. This can only occur if all the Egyptians - not only the Copts - might realize the fact that they are Egyptians, not Arabs.

It is not easy that a people changes its language, but if ruled for a lot of centuries by foreigners who speak only their language, one has to learn it, in order to deal with them, especially if they are cruel & violent.(1)

Also speaking Arabic became a must for anybody who would like to keep his job, according to the instructions of the Arab ruler.(2)

Later an Arab Fatimid Ruler called Al-Hakim prohibited speaking Coptic. He was a mad man & it was impossible to keep alive if you disobey him.(3)

The Coptic Language disappeared as a living language. The Copts kept it in dictionaries called " Al Sullam " & in grammar books called " Al Mokaddimah ", written in the period from the eleventh to the fourteenth century, anno domini.(4)

In the nineteenth & twentieth centuries, the Copts partially got rid of the yoke of discrimination & persecution. New books appeared in Egypt in order to teach the Copts their Language.

Also a lot of books appeared abroad, written by great foreign scholars of Coptology & Egyptology, which helped in reviving the Coptic Language in Egypt.

In Egypt , Ikladios Labib , in Cairo , compiled a Coptic – Arabic Dictionary & wrote a lot of grammar & teaching books. His family spoke Coptic.

Mr. Pissenty in Alexandria taught Coptic to his brothers & sisters , & brought up his nephews & nieces speaking Coptic as their mother tongue. Also Mr. Meawwad Abdel Nour speaks Coptic with his wife & students in Alexandria.

Dr. Imil Maher Ishaq in Cairo speaks Coptic with the students of his department in the Institute of Coptic Language. Also there is a group of graduates of the Institute of Coptic Studies, & students of the Institutes of Coptic Studies & Coptic Language whom I (Dr. Kamal Farid Ishaq) taught Coptic & we do speak Coptic in our monthly meeting.

The difficulties which face the attempts to revive the Coptic Language in Egypt include :

1. Difficulties in the vocabulary :
How to compensate for the lost words & how to suggest new words needed in modern life.

2. Difficulties in syntax & morphology :
Some expressions are not easy to express in Coptic. There is no perfect participle in Coptic. Adjectives are few , & a lot of verbs have no qualitative form. Some Greek loan words are too long to be accepted by the modern Copt who wishes to speak Coptic.
It is impossible for Coptic to be a living language if we confine ourselves to what we received in texts. We have to derive new words & expressions , on a scientific basis.

3. The lack of modern Coptic literature , the lack of teachers of the Coptic Language especially efficient teachers. Also the lack of suitable students of the Coptic Language. The majority of young people prefer to learn a living language , to help them in earning living.

4. Difficulties in Phonetics :
Some Copts began to pronounce the Coptic according to what Dr.Imil Maher Ishaq suggested. The majority refuse this , & stick to the current ecclesiastic pronunciation. This schism causes the disappointment of a lot of scholars , it is difficult for each group to understand the other pronunciation.

5. Social & Political Difficulties :
These difficulties arise from the name of the Coptic Language i.e.from the word " Coptic ".
The majority of the population of Egypt who are not christian misunderstand the word " Coptic ". They combine this word with the Christian Religion. They are not aware that

the word " Coptic " means " Egyptian " & that the Coptic Language is a heritage of all Egypt.

The Egyptian government does not encourage the suggestion of having a department of Coptology in any Egyptian University. Nobody is aware that it is a national duty to take care of the Coptic Language.

I have been trying to find solutions to the above-mentioned difficulties :

For example , in order to compensate for the defects in the vocabulary in the Bohairic Dialect – which is the Dialect used nowadays by the copts - I had to :

1. Borrow loan words from other languages.

e.g. ⲧⲥⲁⲓ or ⲧⲉⲓⲟⲛ for "tea",from modern greek (5), ⲣⲁⲁⲓⲟ for " radio " , from English & French.

2. Borrow words from other Coptic Dialects , & modify them – if needed – to Bohairic morphology.

e.g. I borrowed from the Sahidic Dialect the verb ⲝⲱⲁⲩ which means " to make merry " or similar meanings such as " to be merry " (6) & I changed it to the Bohairic form ⲅⲱⲁⲉⲩ. I used it in the meaning " to celebrate ".

N.B. : The word ⲅⲱⲁⲉⲩ has been also found in the Bohairic Dialect but only as a noun.

3. Derive new words from the Bohairic Dialect itself.

e.g.From ⲥⲱⲧⲡ " to choose " I derived ⲥⲱⲧⲡ˙ ⲛⲉⲏⲧ " to prefer ",literally " to choose by the heart "., in addition to ⲥⲱⲧⲡ ⲛ = , e.g. ϯⲥⲱⲧⲡ ⲛⲏⲓ "I prefer "(literally:" I choose for myself ") From ⲉⲙⲓ " to know ",I derived ⲉⲙⲓ˙ ⲛⲉⲏⲧ "to feel " ,Literally " to know by the heart ".

From ⲓⲱⲓ"to wash",I derived ⲣⲉⲥⲓⲱⲓ "washing-machine" cf. ⲣⲉϥⲓⲱⲓ " a man or woman who washes ".

N.B.:I derived the Syllable ⲣⲉⲥ on analogy of the syllable ⲣⲉϥ to express a neuter present participle.

From ⲓⲱⲧ "father" ,I derived * ⲓⲱⲧⲱ" grandfather ",and from ⲙⲁⲩ"mother",I derived * ⲙⲁⲩⲱ "grandmother" by adding ⲱ " great " to ⲓⲱⲧ or ⲙⲁⲩ (7).

4. I chose some Coptic words to express relevant meanings e.g. the word ⲧⲁⲧⲉⲟ which is found only as a noun or as a verb in the qualitative form (8). I used it also as an infinitive absolute form meaning " to impede or restrain ".

No doubt it was used thus by our ancestors , it is not logic to deny this only because we could not find it in an old text.

5. To form a Coptic word acting as a perfect or past participle ,I suggested putting a prefix before the verb,such as:

ϢⲀⲠ-(9) participium conjuctivum from ϢⲰⲠ "to receive".
ϬⲀI-(10) participium conjuctivum from ϬI " to take ".
ⲢⲀ-(11) a prefix most probably derived from ⲢⲀ " to do
",sometime used to indicate place (giving a local sense) ,and here
I mean to indicate the thing or person on which the effect of
the verb was done.
Example : (using the verb ⲔⲰϢ " to break " of which no
Bohairic qualitative form reached us.)In order to get a word
meaning " broken " I can use one of the above-mentioned
prefixes or I can derive a qualitative form , in addition to the
usual expression : ⲠⲈⳘⲞⲨ ⲔⲀϢϤ & ⲠⲈⳘⲀⲨ
ⲔⲀϢϤ & ϢⲞⲨ ⲔⲀϢϤ (12) , which can be used but
do not mean the word " broken " precisely.
So we have :
* ϢⲀⲠⲔⲰϢ,* ϬⲀIⲔⲰϢ,* ⲢⲀⲔⲰϢ,* ⲔⲎϢ (+),&
* ⲔⲞϢI.(+)
* ϢⲀⲠⲔⲰϢ & * ϬⲀIⲔⲰϢ   mean literally :
" receiver of breaking "
* ⲢⲀⲔⲰϢ   means the thing to which or in which breaking
was done.
* ⲔⲎϢ +(13) is a qualitative form derived on analogy of
ⲂⲎⲀ

* ⲔⲞϢI is a qualitative form derived on analogy of the
Sahidic qualitative form ⲔⲞⲞϢⲈ , but ⲔⲎϢ is preferred
because its construction is similar to the other Coptic qualitative
forms of this type of verb which has an absolute form
composed of 2 consonants & an omega between them.
N.B. : Sometimes the infinitive was used as a participle e.g.
ⲞⲨⳘⲒⲤⲒ ⲠⲈ , ⲞⲨⲐⲀⲨⲒⲞ ⲀⲚ ⲠⲈ " born , not
created " (14) and
ⲠⲒϢⲰⲠ ϧⲀ ⲈⲀⳘ "(the thing) bought by money "(15).
But this way to get past participles cannot be generalized ,
because what is meant by this way of expression can be
confused with other meanings of same word , because the
infintive is also used as a noun , e.g. from ⲤⲀϪⲒ " to speak "
we get ⲠⲒⲤⲀϪⲒ " the word " , so we cannot use the same
word " ⲠⲒⲤⲀϪⲒ to mean " the spoken " , for fear of
confusion , so the above-mentioned way of expression can be
used only in selected cases to express the past participle.
6. I restricted the use of some words to one meaning only
   among their several meanings.
   e.g. the word ⲞⲨⲰⲚⲈ ⲈⲂⲞⲀ has three meanings :
   " to appear " , " to confess " & " to thank "
   I restricted using the first part which is ⲞⲨⲰⲚⲈ to the
   meaning " to appear ".

Here ⲈⲂⲞⲖ is not added. I restricted the expression ⲞⲨⲰⲚϨ ⲈⲂⲞⲖ to the meaning " to confess ".

And I used the expression ϢⲈⲠ· ϨⲘⲞⲦ to mean " to thank " , which is the usual word used to express this meaning.

This differentiation helps us , to express precisely in speech.

Lastly , I would be grateful , if any Coptic scholar would like to participate , in suggesting , or approving or opposing the words & expressions suggested by me to compensate for the defects in the Coptic Language.

Please contact me at my permanent address published in the Newsletters of the IACS & the Congress members' List , or contact me any time during the Congress.

Dr. KAMAL FARID ISAAC (ISHAQ)
Professor of the Coptic Language
in The Institute of Coptic Studies,
& The Institute of Coptic Language
Cairo , Egypt

Permanent Address : 9 , Abdel Hamid Abu Heif Street ,
Heliopolis , Cairo , Egypt.

REFERENCES.

(1)   All books of history of Egypt in the middle ages,passim,e.g.
  (a) Stanley Lane-poole , A History of Egypt in the middle ages,third edition , 1924 , Methuem & Co , 36 Essex Street,W.C. London.
  (b) E.L. Butcher , The Story of the Church of Egypt , 1897 , smith Elder & Co , 15 waterloo Place , London.
(2) (a) Poole p. 27
  (b) Dr. Ahmed M. Omar

تاريخ اللغة فى مصر
سنة ١٩٧٠ الهيئة المصرية
العامة للتأليف والنشر
صفحة ٣٠ ، ٣٢ ، ٣٣

(3) Poole P. 118 ff.
(4)   Alexis mallon , Grammaire Copte , quatrieme edition , 1956,Imprimerie Catholique , Beirut ,p. 6

226

(5)   J.T. Pring , The Oxford dictionary of Modern Greek 1990,Clarendon press , Oxford.

(6)   W.E. Crum , A Coptic Dictionary , 1979 , Oxford Clarendon Press ,p. 768 b.

(7)   Crum , p. 253 a.

(8)   Crum , p. 439 b.

(9)   Crum , p. 575 a.

(10)   Crum , p. 747 b.
       & Mallon p. 137 § 276.

(11)   Crum , p. 287 a:
       cf. ⲣⲁϫⲱⲩⲓ : " joint " (a joined place) , and
       ⲣⲁϣⲁϫ : " loss,deficit (a lost money) "

(12) (a) ⲉϫⲟⲧⲕⲁϣ̄ϥ cf. Mallon p. 137 § 273.

     (b) ϣⲟⲧ ⲕⲁϣϥ cf Crum p. 600 b.cf ϣⲟⲧⲉⲣ
         ⲉⲡⲓⲑⲧⲓⲙ " επιθυμητος " & Crum 603 b. cf
         ϣⲟⲧϣⲟⲧⲱⲓ " sacrifice ,offering " (thing offered) "

(13)   Crum p. 130 b & Mallon p90 § 207.

(14)   The apostles' Creed , Kitab Alkhulagy al Mukaddas (Euchologion) , Cairo , all prints.

(15)   Mallon , p. 161 (Gen 17 , 12).

SOME REMARKS ON FALSE COPTIC MONUMENTS
(To the Problem of Coptic Forgeries)
Alexander Kakovkin

Art forgery is a phenomenon accompanying mankind through its whole history. Forgeries were made for various reasons, but most often for easy money. The increase of the number of forgeries (or imitations) is connected as a rule with the growth of interest on the part of the collectors, connoiosseurs of art, museums, etc. to this or thar group of artistic monuments. The same concerns Coptic art.[1]

By the end of the 1950s - beginning of the 1960s on the eve of several international exhibitions of Coptic Art (Essen, Zürich, Vienna, Paris),[2] the world antiquary market was flooded by various limestone artifacts, some of them painted, supposed to have come from Antinoüpolis (Sheikh Ibada).[3] Similar pieces were acquired by several museums and by some private collectors in Europe and North America[4] (Recklinghausen Ikonenmuseum[5]; The Brooklyn Museum (fig.1)[6]; Münchner Aegyptische Staatssammlung;[7] The Newark Museum;[8] The Art Museum, Princeton University (fig.2,3)[9]; Sammlung Senator W.Esch in Duisburg[10] etc.[11]) Moreover these objects were being acquired not just by some museum staff members, but by such experts in Coptic Art as J.Conney or P.Du Bourguet.

Some of those pieces, unfortunately, have been published as genuine.

First they were denounced as forgeries by J.Beckwith.[12] A group of similar forgeries has been exposed by G. Vikan.[13]

However, their opinion was ignored by specialists.

According to my estimation based on publications and on my own observations, we have now about thirty obvious forgeries and pieces of sculpture of doubtfull genuiness.

The main characteristic feature of such recently manufactured antiquities are: "flabby", glossy facture, rough applicative painting, non-canonical iconography of some scenes and personages.

Forgeries occur, unfortunately, not only in stone sculpture. J.Beckwith and R.Berliner noticed their presence among textiles.[14] There are obvious forgeries of wood, bone, clay.

Several factors provide the possibility of their large-scale production:
accessibility of materials, comparatively small dimensions and simple technique used in creating these monuments so close in spirit to folk-art.

The aim of my report is to attract the specialists' attention to this problem first arising about 40 years ago and no less actual in our days.

Modern forgeries can be exposed by the detailed comparison of their stylistic and technological pecularities with those of the original Coptic monuments from the collections created in the late nineteenth - beginning of the twentieth century (The Coptic Museum, Preussischer Kulturbesitz Museum für Spätantike und byzantinische Kunst zu Berlin, Louvre, Hermitage in St.Petersburg etc.) and, naturally, by all recently developed scientific research-methods.

The problem of forgeries is a delicate one for many reasons. In ideal it would be very good to survey each monument personally and to investigate it from all points of view. Now we want only to attract the attention of specialists to this problem and to advise them to be more careful when acquiring or attributing objects of art. It would be useful in our opinion to organize some international conference dedicated to the problem of Coptic forgeries to make an exhibition of obvious fakes and to renew the activities of the International Union of Museum Staff (1898-1936) dealing with the problem of fake works of art.

Coptic forgeries are represented in more than fifteen publications.

NOTES

1. The problem of the falsification of works of art, the nature of forgery and its history from ancient times to the present day is surveyed in detail in a series of articles comprized under the title "Falsification and Forgery" in the Encyclopedia of World Art, vol.V,1961, New York, Toronto, London, cols.333-350; bibliography - cols.349-350. Coptic forgeries are not considered there.

2. Koptische Kunst. Christentum am Nil. 3-5 - 15.8.1953 in Villa Hügel. Essen.; Christentum am Nil. Koptische Kunst. Mitte Nov. 1963 - Mitte Jan. 1964, Zürich; Frühchristliche und Koptische Kunst. Ausstellung (11.3 - 3.5.1964) in der Akademie der bildenden Künste. Wien; L'art copte. Petit Palais (17.6 - 15.9.1964), Paris. In our opinion, severeal forgeries were present at the abovementioned exhibitions.

3. First publications of these monuments: H.W.Müller. Grabstele eines Isismysten aus Antinoe. Mittelägypten. Eine neuerwerbung der Ägyptischen Staatssammlung München. Pantheon, XVIII. Jahr. Heft 6,1960; J.D.Conney. A Nameless Boy of Roman Egypt. Wadsworth Atheneum Bulletin. Hartford (Conn.), 5th series, No.9. Winter 1961.

4. In our opinion forgeries are present not only among the Sheikh Ibada Group.

5. I think that most pieces of "Coptic" sculpture in this collection are forgeries. See: K.Wessel. Koptische Kunst. Die spätantike in Ägypten. Recklinghausen, 1963, Abb.18,20,44,49,61 etc. Forgeries are present in other works as well: H.Zaloscher. Die Kunst im christlichen Ägypten. Wien - München, 1974, Abb.31,40,46,48; A.Effenberger. Koptische Kunst. Ägypten in spätantiker, byzantinischer und frühislamischer Zeit. Leipzig,1975, Abb.10,11, S.145.

6. J.D.Cooney. An Early Christian Sculpture from Egypt. The Brooklyn Museum Annual, 1960-1962, II-III.; Brief Guide to the Department of Ancient Art. The Brooklyn Museum, New York, 1970, p.100-103.

7. Staatliche Sammlung Ägyptischer Kunst. München, 1976. S.252 (ÄS 4860), S.253 (ÄS 5528).

8. S.H.Auth. Coptic Art. The Newark Museum Quarterly, vol.29, No.2 - Spring 1978, p.12-13, Nos.16,17.

9.Frances F.Jones. Six pieces of sculpture. Record of the Art Museum. Princrton University. Vol.XXI, No.2, 1962; J.H.Turnure. Princeton's "Enigmatic" Relief. Record of the Art Museum. Princeton University, Vol.XXII, No.2, 1963; P.J.Kellcher. The Uses of Sculpture in a Teaching Museum. University of Princeton Quarterly. Spring, 1971.

10. H.W.Müller. Stelle eines Jünglings mit christlichem Kreuz. Die Sammlung Wilhelm Esen, Duisburg. Werke altägyptischer und koptischer Kunst. Von seinen Münchner Freunden, 1961, S.35-39, Abb.23,24,25,27.

11. Several examples: Kestner Museum - Hannover Jahresbericht 1965-1966, S.292, No.3; Christie's, Dec.2, 1970, p.55 Nos.193,194; Sotheby, March 23, 1971, p.52, No.158; Werke aegyptischer Kunst. Auktion 46, 28 April 1979 (Basel), S.84, No. 156, Taf.39; The Temple Gallery, 1990, p.66, No.16; p.73, No.21. Almost all works of Coptic art presented at the following two exhibitions were forgeries: Coptic Stone Sculpture. The Early Christian and Late Classic Art of Egypt. Dec. 4 to 29, 1962, New York: Andre Emmerich Gallery, 1962.; A Catalogue of Egyptian and Other Near Eastern Antiquities by J.M.Eisenberg. Catalogue No.42. Dec.1962. Royal Athena galleries, New York.

12. In his review of the book by A.Effenberger, Koptische Kunst... Bibliotheca Orientalis, XXXIV, nos.5-6, Sept-Nov. 1977, p.399.

13. Questions of Authenticity among the Arts of Byzantium, Washington, D.C.,1981, p.8-9; The so-called 'Shekh Ibada Group' of Early Coptic sculptures. Third Annual Byzantine Studies Conference Abstracts of Papers, Columbia University, New York City, 3-5 Dec. 1977, p.15-16.

Also see: G.Koch. Ein ungewöhnliches 'Koptisches' Grabrelief im Getty Museum. Studien zur frühchristlichen Kunst. Wiesbaden, 1986, p.25-30.
14. The veil representing the Virgin with Christ enthroned between two angels is obviously also a forgery - D.G.Sheperd. An Icon of the Virgin , a Sixth-century Tapestry Panel from Egypt. The Bulletin of the Cleveland Museum of Art, Vol.LVI, No.3, March 1969, p.90-120, on forgeries and changes introduced into ancient monuments see also: R.Berliner. A Coptic Tapestry of Byzantine Style. Textile Museum Journal. Nov.1962, Vol.I, No.1, p.3-22.

Fig. 1

Fig. 2

Fig. 3

DJİNKİM

SUR TEL GRAPHÈME NASAL OU VOCALİQUE
DE LA LANGUE COPTE BOHAÏRİQUE

Rodolphe Kasser

Les connaissances de la coptologie dans le
domaine de l'emploi du djinkim[1] en bohaïrique (B5)
classique avaient fait, il y a bientôt un demi-
siècle, un progrès décisif grâce à un excellent
travail du regretté H. J. Polotsky. Cet auteur
avait montré (POLOTSKY 1949, p. 26) que si l'usage
du djinkim en bohaïrique très tardif est fort abon-
dant et complexe (il y apparaît dans pas moins de 6
cas systématiques), cette pléthore était encore in-
connue "à la date après laquelle le témoignage des
manuscrits bohaïriques, pour ce qui est de la langue, cesse en général d'avoir beaucoup d'autorité,
à savoir à la fin du XIVe siècle". Et précisant sa
pensée, il ajoutait ceci: "personne ne l'ignore,
c'est un système beaucoup plus simple que l'on
trouve employé dans les manuscrits antérieurs à
cette date. Des six cas énumérés ci-dessus[2] il n'y
en a que deux, 1[o] et 2[o], où le djinkim figure dans
l'orthographe qui seule mérite l'épithète de tradi-
tionnelle"[3]. Ces cas sont donc les suivants[4]:

---

(1)   Signe supralinéaire en forme de point ou d'accent, grave
ou aigu, placé systématiquement au-dessus de certains graphèmes
en langue copte bohaïrique (ou en dialecte mésokémique, ou ex-
ceptionnellement encore dans un manuscrit fayoumique).

(2)   Voir POLOTSKY 1949, p. 25-26.

(3)   POLOTSKY 1949 a donc démontré que les règles N° 3, 4, 5 et
6 d'usage du djinkim (usage cette fois non pas proprement phonologique comme dans les règles 1 et 2, mais plus largement
grammatical, cf. ad loc.) ne sont pas en usage en B avant le
XVe siècle. Dans l'ensemble, le résultat de sa démonstration
peut être accepté, même si LAYTON 1987, p. XXV et LXIV, a si-
gnalé deux manuscrits de la British Library, de la fin du XVe
siècle, n'utilisant encore que les règles 1 et 2, non les règles
3 à 6. Cette découverte de témoins isolés, archaïsants, dont les
scribes sont restés fidèlement attachés à des procédés graphi-
ques devenus surannés à leur époque, est certes fort intéressan-

236

reçoivent le signe supralinéaire "1º chaque voyelle formant syllabe à elle seule: ⲀϤⲒ ⲈⲂⲞⲖ 'il sortit', ⲀⲚⲞⲘⲒⲀ 'péché'; 2º les lettres Ⲙⲓ et Ⲛ quand elles sont des éléments grammaticaux (prépositions, marque du génitif, négation) et comme première radicale devant une autre consonne... : ⲠⲈⲘⲚ̇ⲬⲎⲘⲒ 'égyptien', ⲘⲀ Ⲛ̇ⲤⲰⲚⲌ 'prison', Ⲙ̇ⲦⲞⲚ 'repos', Ⲛ̇ⲐⲞⲔ 'toi'". Ainsi, comme l'a démontré Polotsky, mais dit en d'autres termes: le djinkim du bohaïrique classique (généralement non postérieur au XIVe siècle) signale dans ses textes, à l'usage des lecteurs, toute voyelle et toute sonante autosyllabiques[5].

te; toutefois, elle n'est pas de nature à affaiblir le résultat obtenu par Polotsky dans ce domaine de l'orthographe bohaïrique. De telles survivances, à vrai dire sporadiques, n'ont rien de surprenant en elles-mêmes. Plus curieuse est la découverte faite par QUECKE 1970, p. 361 etc., d'un manuscrit saïdique de la fin du IXe siècle (M 574, de la Pierpont Morgan Library), lequel, avec d'autres témoins S à peu près contemporains, utilise un système de surlignes combinant les usages de S classique (IVe–VIIe siècles au moins) aux usages (djinkim, non surligne!) de B tardif (règles 1–2 et aussi 3–6 de POLOTSKY 1949), en les soumettant à quelques modifications systématiques fondamentalement peu importantes. Ainsi (p. 370–371): "Abschliessend noch kurz ein Wort zum Alter dieses Systems der Bezeichnung von Buchstaben durch den übergesetzten Strich (bzw. Punkt). Schon eingangs wurde Polotskys Meinung angeführt, dass das in jüngeren bohairischen Handschriften und Drucken gebräuchliche System vermutlich erst seit dem Ende des 14. Jahrhunderts in Gebrauch ist. Ich kann diese Angabe nicht eigentlich bestätigen, sondern nur sagen, dass eine Prüfung des mir zugänglichen beschränkten Materials keine älteren bohairischen Texte zutage gefördert hat, die schon dieses System anwenden. Nun steht das oben beschriebene System von M 574, das in vielen anderen saïdischen Handschriften der Zeit Parallelen hat, diesem späteren bohairischen System trotz einiger Unterschiede äusserst nahe. Grob gesprochen handelt es sich um ein und dasselbe System. Das System ist also auch in dem Fall, dass es sich wirklich nicht in älteren bohairischen Handschriften finden sollte, dennoch um ein halbes Jahrtausend älter als seine Bezeugung in den jüngeren bohairischen Handschriften und kann nicht als für letztere typisch angesehen werden". Cette observation tendrait à prouver que l'usage du surlignement "grammatical" s'étant imposé en B (toujours B5) au XVe siècle seulement, a été pratiqué, et peut-être même créé, par certains grammairiens de l'aire saïdique au moins un bon demi-millénaire plus tôt.

(4)   POLOTSKY 1949, p. 25.

(5)   Toute voyelle: entendre, tout phonème vocalique rendu par un seul graphème vocalique, et non par la combinaison de deux graphèmes, comme c'est le cas avec ⲞⲨ /u/. En ce qui concerne les sonantes (POLOTSKY 1949, p. 27), elles sont, en B, beaucoup

Polotsky fait remarquer ensuite (p. 29) que, par le phénomène de la "liaison étroite" avec tel élément grammatical la précédant, telle voyelle autosyllabique initiale cesse d'être initiale et donc aussi d'être autosyllabique, perdant du même coup la faculté d'avoir son graphème surmonté du <u>djinkim</u>, et il en est de même en ce qui concerne les sonantes nasales /ɱ/ et /ɳ/. La liaison étroite se produit après l'article défini "faible" au singulier, m. ⲡ- et f. ⲧ- , après les préfixes verbaux du présent I formés d'une seule consonne, et après la particule relative ⲉⲧ- , dont le ⲧ se lie étroitement à la voyelle ou à la sonante suivante[6], isolant ainsi le ⲉ qui le précède et qui devient du même coup autosyllabique, porteur du <u>djinkim</u>. Exemples: ⲁ̀ⲃⲱⲕ /a bŏk/ "corbeau", ⲡⲓⲁ̀ⲃⲱⲕ "le corbeau", mais ⲡⲁⲃⲱⲕ /pa bŏk/; ⲁ̀ϣⲁⲓ /a šaj/ "se multiplier", ⲁϥⲁ̀ϣⲁⲓ "il s'est multiplié", mais ϥⲁϣⲁⲓ /fa šaj/ "il se multiplie"; ⲁ̀ⲅⲁⲑⲟⲥ /a ga thŏs/ "bon", ⲟⲩⲁ̀ⲅⲁⲑⲟⲥ ⲛ̇- "un bon ...", mais ⲡⲁⲅⲁⲑⲟⲥ /pa ga thŏs/ "l'(homme) bon" ; ⲉ̀ⲥⲱⲟⲩ /ə sŏw/ "mouton", ⲡⲓⲉ̀ⲥⲱⲟⲩ "le mouton", mais ⲡⲉⲥⲱⲟⲩ /pə sŏw/; ⲉ̀ⲡⲓⲥⲧⲏⲙⲏ /ə pis tĕ mē/ "connaissance, science", ⲧⲉ̀ⲡⲓⲥⲧⲏⲙⲏ "la connaissance", mais ⲧⲉⲡⲓⲥⲧⲏⲙⲏ /tə pis tĕ mē/; ⲏ̇ϫⲓ /ē či/ "poireau", ⲡⲓⲏ̇ϫⲓ "le poireau", mais ⲡⲏϫⲓ /pē či/; ⲏ̇ⲡⲁⲣ (ou ⲍ̇ⲏⲡⲁⲣ) /ē par/ "foie", ⲡⲓⲏ̇ⲡⲁⲣ (etc.) "le foie", mais ⲡⲏⲡⲁⲣ /pē par/; ⲓ̇ⲛⲓ /i ni/ "(ap)porter", ⲧ̇ⲛⲁⲓⲛⲓ "j'(ap)porterai", mais ϥⲓⲛⲓ /fi ni/ "il (ap)porte", ⲉ̇ⲧⲓⲛⲓ ou ⲉ̇ⲧⲛⲓ /ə ti ni/ "qui (ap)porte"; ⲓ̇ⲇⲟⲥ /i dos/ "objet", ⲟⲩⲓ̇ⲇⲟⲥ "un objet", mais ⲡⲓⲇⲟⲥ /pi dos/ "l'objet"; ⲟ̇ϩⲓ /ŏ hi/ "se tenir (debout)", ⲉϥⲟ̇ϩⲓ "se tenant (debout)", mais ϥⲟϩⲓ /fŏ hi/ "il se tient (debout)"; ⲟ̀ⲃⲟⲗⲟⲥ /o bo lŏs/ "obole", ⲡⲓⲟ̇ⲃⲟⲗⲟⲥ "l'obole", mais ⲡⲟⲃⲟⲗⲟⲥ /po bo lŏs/; ⲟⲩⲣⲱ (normalement non ⲟⲩ̇ⲣⲱ)

---

moins nombreuses et abondamment utilisées, qu'en <u>S</u> etc. Ainsi <u>S</u> (et avec lui la plupart des idiomes de Haute et de Moyenne-Égypte) ont 5 sonantes (cf. KASSER 1981a, p. 34 et 40-41): /ḅ/, /ḷ/, /ɱ/, /ɳ/, /ṟ/ ; elles peuvent être autosyllabiques ou constituer le sommet de syllabes polyphonémiques. <u>B</u> au contraire n'a que les sonantes nasales, /ɱ/ et /ɳ/, et en <u>B</u>, elles ne peuvent être qu'autosyllabiques; elles sont donc toujours initiales.

(6) Elle devient alors la sonore correspondante, précédée d'un ⲉ anaptyctique.

/u rⱶ/ "haricot", etc.; OYPⱭNOC (normalement non
OẎPⱭNOC) /u ra nòs/ "ciel", etc. ; ⲰⲖⲒ
/ō li/ "prendre, ôter", ⲀϤⲰⲖⲒ "il a pris", mais
ϤⲰⲖⲒ /fō li/ "il prend"; ⲘBON /ṃ bòn/ "colère",
ⲠⲒⲘBON "la colère", mais ⲠⲈⲘBON /pəm bòn/;
ⲘⲘⲀⲨ /ṃ màw/ "là", ⲈϤⲘⲘⲀⲨ "étant là", mais
ⲈⲦⲈⲘⲘⲀⲨ /ə təm màw/ "(qui est) là"; ⲚⳬⲞⲦ
/ṃ šòt/ "s'endurcir", ⲀϤⲚⳬⲞⲦ "il s'est endurci",
mais ϤⲈⲚⳬⲞⲦ /fən šòt/ "il s'endurcit", ⲈⲦⲈⲚⳬⲞⲦ
/ə tən šòt/ "qui s'endurcit", ⲠⲈⲚⳬⲞⲦ /pən šòt/
"l'endurcissement, la dureté (de coeur)".

Celui qui observera l'orthographe des manuscrits
bohaïriques antérieurs au XVᵉ siècle constatera que
cette définition de l'usage phonologique et syllabique du djinkim établie par H. J. Polotsky est
certes globalement satisfaisante en théorie et pour
l'essentiel, puisqu'elle l'est pratiquement aussi
dans la plupart des cas (cf. supra). Il reste quelques cas "récalcitrants", cependant, qui ne se
laissent pas expliquer ainsi, du moins pas de
manière aussi évidente. Dans des mots tels que
ⲰⲈBⲒⲰ "changer", OYⲰⲦⲈB[7] "déplacer", ⲘⲈⲨⲒ
"penser", il paraît assez difficile d'affirmer tout
simplement, sans tenter de l'étayer par aucune
argumentation, que ces mots doivent être considérés
comme trisyllabiques, en sorte que ces ⲱ ou ⲓ
surmontés du djinkim sont autosyllabiques. En effet,
selon la phonologie communément appliquée en copte,
ces mots sont disyllabiques: /šə bjō/, /wō təb/[7] et
/mè wi/. Si cela, toutefois, se vérifie en syllabation rapide ou tachysyllabation (domaine exclusif
de la phonologie), il n'en est pas de même en
syllabation lente ou bradysyllabation, domaine à
l'intérieur et selon les règles duquel ont été
établis les divers systèmes orthographiques (dia-
lectaux etc.) de la langue copte (KASSER 1982d); et
là, ces ⲱ ou ⲓ sont effectivement autosyllabiques,
les mots '/šə bi ō/', '/u ō təb/' et '/mè u i/' y
étant trisyllabiques. Mais que dire d'un mot tel
que ⲘOⲨⲒ /mùj/ "lion" ? Son glide final /j/, qui
porte normalement le djinkim en B5, peut-il donc
devenir '/i/' en bradysyllabation, alors que le /j/

(7) DE LAGARDE 1867, p. VIII, le souligne avec raison (en
protestant contre la présence du djinkim qu'il constate
régulièrement, sur l'oméga de ce mot).

final de ΦⲀⲒ "celui-ci", ⲘⲈⲒ "aimer", ⲎⲒ "maison", ⲔⲞⲒ "champ", ΦⲰⲒ "le mien", ne porte jamais le djinkim en B5 ? Pourquoi cette différence de traitement? Quelle signification convient-il de lui attribuer?

En procédant à l'examen préliminaire de ce problème, l'on ne prendra pas en considération, ici, les plus anciens longs témoins qu'on peut qualifier de "bohaïriques", le P. Bodmer III (IVe siècle, B74-(B4))[8] et le Pap. Vat. Copto 9 (IVe siècle, B74, cf. KASSER-QUECKE-BOSSON 1992)[8], n'appartenant pas à la variété bohaïrique la plus courante, B5. De même d'autres témoins plus brefs, appartenant à B4 (non à B5)[9]. Les inscriptions coptes des Kellia (VIe-VIIIe siècles), en revanche, semblent bien faire partie de B5[10]; or la plupart d'entre elles n'ont pas de djinkim du tout, et quand elles l'ont, c'est pratiquement toujours et exclusivement sur les sonantes nasales (autosyllabiques) /ṃ/ et /ṇ/.

Dès le Xe siècle en tous cas[11], se met progressivement en place le système appelé ici celui de B5 classique, observable en particulier, avec toute la netteté désirable dans les Vat.Copt. 5 et 6 (XIIIe et XIVe siècles, Psaumes, inédits). Dans ces témoins, et dans beaucoup d'autres, contemporains, on peut voir le djinkim placé régulièrement sur tout graphème

(8) Le premier de ces témoins (éd. KASSER 1958) n'a d'ailleurs pas de djinkim du tout; le second, encore inédit, n'a le djinkim que sur les sonantes (nasales, autosyllabiques) /ṃ/ et /ṇ/.

(9) P. Mich. inv. 926 (éd. HUSSELMAN 1947) et P. Heid. Kopt. 452 (éd. QUECKE 1974a).

(10) On y lit ⲤⲚⲀⲨ (non ⲤⲚⲀ) "deux", dans l'expression quelque peu énigmatique ⲠⲒⲢⲞ ⲤⲚⲀⲨ (= "les biblingues" ?) au début d'une liste de personnages découverte en 1967 et encore inédite (Q. Îsâ 1). On y lit aussi ⲞⲨⲞⳞ (non ⲞⲨⲞ&ⲈⳞ) "et" en divers passages, par exemple GUILLAUMONT - KASSER 1969, p. 106, N° 26, ligne 5.

(11) Le seul grand manuscrit B5 connu du IXe siècle est le Vat. Copt. 1 (première main = 99% du tout); on y voit déjà, plus ou moins sporadiquement, tous les usages du djinkim du bohaïrique classique, sauf celui sur Ⲓ suivant ⲞⲨ (pour /ⱳi/ ou /uj/, cf. infra). Les usages du djinkim dans les témoins des Xe-XIIIe et XIVe siècles peuvent être observés en particulier dans les planches 23-25, 27-31, 33-34, 36-38, 41a, 42c, 43, 44a, 53a, 54a, 55a d'HYVERNAT 1888. Aux XIIIe-XIVe siècles, cependant, un usage prédomine nettement, celui de B5 classique (cf. infra).

rendant à lui seul un phonème autosyllabique[12], donc
sur M^{13} et N^{13} en fonction de sonante (nasale),
et (dans les mêmes conditions) sur divers ⲁ , ⲉ ,
ⲏ , ⲓ[13], ⲟ et ⲱ[14]. Exemples: ⲘⲂⲞⲚ "se fâcher";
ⲚⲐⲞⲤ "elle"; ⲀⲚⲞⲔ "moi", ⲆⲒⲀⲐⲎⲔⲎ "allian-
ce", ⲀⲚⲞⲘⲒⲀ "péché"; ⲈⲂⲞⲖ "dehors", ⳅⲒⲈⲂⲒ
"agneau", ⳝⲀⲈ "fin"; Ⲏ̇ⲬⲒ "poireau", ⲂⲞⲎⲐⲞⲤ
"auxiliaire"[15] ⲩⲒⲎ́ "longueur"; ⲒⲚⲒ "(ap)porter",
ⲞⲨⲒⲚⲀⲘ [15] "(main) droite", ⲘⲈⲨⲒ "pensée";
Ⲟ̇ⳅⲒ "se tenir (debout)", pl. ⳅⲒⲞ̇ⲘⲒ "femmes",
ⲦⲀⲒⲞ̇ "honneur"; ⲱ̇ⲖⲒ "ôter", ⲞⲨⲱ̇ⲦⲈⲂ "déplacer", ⲩⲈⲂⲒⲱ̇ "changer".

On a déjà remarqué précédemment que ces voyelles
peuvent être autosyllabiques même après les glides
/j/ et /w/ de tachysyllabation, par le fait que ces
glides deviennent glidantes '/i/' et '/u/' en
bradysyllabation. D'où, entre autres, on l'a vu,
l'apparition de finales B5 -ⲞⲨⲒ qui sont des /wi/
⟩ '/u i/'. Plus surprenantes sont d'autres finales
en -ⲞⲨⲒ valant, en phonologie, non pas /wi/ (susceptible de devenir '/u i/') mais /uj/, et contrastant avec tous les autres cas où ⲓ /j/ suivant une
voyelle autre que /u/, dans une même syllabe, ce
ⲓ ne porte néanmoins jamais le djinkim (cf. supra).
Cet -ⲞⲨⲒ /uj/ imitant -ⲞⲨⲒ /wi/ ⟩ '/u i/'
serait-il le résultat aberrant d'un jugement ortho-
graphique par analogie superficielle? Le moment est
venu, maintenant, d'examiner ce problème.

À ce sujet, une première hypothèse pourrait être
envisagée: celle, dans le djinkim bohaïrique classique, de la convergence de deux éléments hétérogè-
nes. Le djinkim sur ⲙ et ⲛ (nasales) sonantes
autosyllabiques, et sur les voyelles autosyllabiques, serait le "vrai" djinkim qu'on trouve déjà,

(12)   Est donc exclu ici /u/ rendu par la combinaison de
graphèmes ⲞⲨ.

(13)   Toujours à l'initiale en tachysyllabation de B5.

(14)   Cela, aussi bien dans les mots coptes autochtones que
dans les mots copto-grecs, ou même dans les noms propres. En
outre, en ce qui concerne ⲁ , ⲉ , ⲏ , ⲟ , ⲱ (et ⲓ seulement en bradysyllabation sauf à l'initiale), ces voyelles peuvent être autosyllabiques au début du mot, en position médiane
(ⲓ seulement après ⲞⲨ), ou à la fin du mot (ⲓ seulement
après ⲞⲨ).

(15)   Exemple, toutefois, de l'anomalie -ⲞⲨⲒ /uj/ où néanmoins l'iota porte le djinkim; cf. infra.

dans tel document B74 ancien et dans telle ou telle
inscription kelliote (cf. supra), sur les nasales
sonantes; le "vrai" djinkim qu'on trouve aussi dans
les manuscrits M, tous anciens (IVe-Ve siècles), en
M4 sur ces Ϻ , Ⲛ et Ⲉ , en M5 sur ces Ϻ , Ⲛ ,
Ⲉ et ⲇ . En revanche, le djinkim sur ι valant /j/
de tachysyllabation après /u/ serait un pseudo-
djinkim dérivé du demi-tréma, signe comportant un
seul point (ou une surligne très brève) comme le
djinkim, et qu'on trouve utilisé ici ou là en copte
ancien, dans les positions où l'on attendrait le
tréma (une fois sur deux environ dans le P. Bodmer
III[16], B74-(B4); régulièrement dans le P. Heid.Kopt.
452, B4, QUECKE 1974a); pour un motif encore inconnu-
nu, l'usage de ce demi-tréma aurait survécu en B5
classique uniquement dans les rares cas où /j/ suit
/u/ (le fait qu'ainsi le glide suive la glidante,
comme en -ⲞⲨⲓ /wi/ la glidante suit le glide,
pourrait avoir joué un rôle, encore obscur actuellement, dans ce choix d'usages orthographiques).
Hypothèse non dénuée d'intérêt, mais insuffisamment
convaincante.

Une autre voie à explorer semble conduire à des
résultats plus consistants. Elle implique un réexa-
men des problèmes de la syllabation copte, évoqués
ci-dessus. Premièrement, faut-il admettre que par-
tout les glides de tachysyllabation deviennent iné-
vitablement glidantes en bradysyllabation?[17] L'absence du djinkim sur le ι final de ⲪⲀⲒ , ⲘⲈⲒ ,
ⲎⲒ , ⲔⲞⲒ , ⲪⲰⲒ (voir ci-dessus) entame sensible-
ment la crédibilité de cette affirmation trop absolue. De même, l'orthographe de ⲞⲨⲰⲒⲚⲒ "lumière",
contrastant avec celle de ⲞⲨⲰⲦⲈⲂ "déplacer": si
ⲞⲨⲰⲦⲈⲂ , /wŏtəb/ dégage un ⲱ autosyllabique
en bradysyllabation[18], en revanche, ⲞⲨⲰⲒⲚⲒ ,

(16) Cela, beaucoup plus souvent que ne le laisse supposer
l'édition princeps de ce texte (KASSER 1958). Cf. l'article du
même auteur, "Le P. Bodmer III réexaminé, amélioration de sa
transcription", à paraître dans JCoptS, 3.

(17) Cette règle est présentée comme une loi absolue dans
KASSER 1982d, p. 28: "Il semble bien qu'un glide ne peut exis-
ter (en copte) qu'en tachysyllabation..., et s'il faut passer à
la bradysyllabation, on passe... obligatoirement du glide à la
glidante correspondante".

(18) '/u ŏ təb/' .

/wój ni/ n'en dégage aucun[19], parce que son ⲱ continue à constituer une syllabe avec ۱ /j/ qui le
suit. Il convient donc de nuancer la règle décri-
vant le passage du glide à la glidante en bradysyllabation: seul le glide prévocalique devient néces-
sairement glidante en bradysyllabation; le glide
postvocalique, lui (et à l'extérieur d'une seule et
même syllabe), reste glide en bradysyllabation[20].

Ce premier résultat étant acquis, le raisonne-
ment permettra, semble-t-il, une progression intéressante vers une solution acceptable du problème
posé antérieurement. Il est vraisemblable que, selon
leur position par rapport à la voyelle sommet de la
syllabe, la capacité ou l'incapacité, pour les glides /j/ et /w/, de devenir glidantes '/i/' et '/u/'
en bradysyllabation, doit avoir un rapport quelcon-
que avec la sonorité de ce qui, ainsi, devient ou
ne devient pas autosyllabique. En position prévocalique, le glide qui devient glidante dégage une voyelle comptant parmi les plus sonores, '/a/', '/e/',
'/ē/', '/o/', '/ō/' (pour autant que cette voyelle
soit totalement dégagée, n'étant pas bloquée encore
par la présence d'un glide immédiatement consécutif,
comme c'est le cas dans ⲞⲨⲰⲒⲚⲒ "lumière", non
ⲞⲨⲰⲒⲚⲒ , cf. supra); étant particulièrement
sonore, cette voyelle ainsi favorisée sera particulièrement bien disposée à devenir autosyllabique.
En position postvocalique au contraire, la bradysyllabation, si elle avait le même effet, transforme-
rait le glide en glidante, et dégagerait alors une
voyelle parmi les moins sonores[21], '/i/' ou '/u/',
voyelles particulièrement peu disposées à devenir
autosyllabiques. Ce contraste entre la sonorité
forte de '/a/' etc. et la sonorité faible des glidantes est surtout sensible quand le glide est en
position postvocalique et suit les voyelles remar-
quablement sonores que sont '/a/' etc. Ce contraste

(19) Dans '/u ój ni/', ⲱ '/ó/' n'est dégagé que sur son côté
antérieur, non sur son côté postérieur, ce qui, ainsi, ne suffit
pas à l'isoler syllabiquement.

(20) Cela, peut-être en français aussi: cf. le "pailleté"
/paj te/ > '/paj te/' plutôt que '/pa i te/' mentionné dans
KASSER 1982d, p. 25, fin de la note 9: là aussi, le glide est,
non pas prévocalique, mais postvocalique.

(21) Les glidantes sont les moins sonores des voyelles.

disparaît cependant si la voyelle précédant le glide est une glidante, elle-même à sonorité faible.
Ainsi, la différence de sonorité entre /a/, /e/,
/ē/, /o/, /ō/ d'une part, /u/ d'autre part, con-
frontés à /j/ consécutif, a-t-elle suffi, éventuel-
lement, à empêcher le dégagement de Ⲓ '/i/' autosyllabique à la fin de mots tels que ⲪⲀⲒ "celui-
ci", ⲔⲞⲒ "champ", etc., et à permettre au contraire le dégagement de Ⲓ '/i/' autosyllabique à la fin
d'un mot tel que ⲘⲞⲨⲒ "lion", en bradysyllabation. Voilà du moins la solution hypothétique présentée par l'auteur de cette modeste étude à la
critique de ses pairs.

S I G L E S   E T   B I B L I O G R A P H I E

B = "langue" (plutôt que "dialecte") bohaïrique; variété
supra-régionale et supra-dialectale de la langue copte,
dont elle est la "moitié" septentrionale; sa fonction a été
celle d'une langue véhiculaire: la koinè autochtone de tout
le Delta égyptien. Principaux (sub)dialectes de B: B4, B5,
B74.

B4 = (sub)dialecte du groupe dialectal B; sur le plan de
l'orthographe, seuls trois mots permettent de distinguer B4
de B5: "et" ⲞⲨⲞⲌⲈ B4, ⲞⲨⲞⲌ B5; "là" ⲘⲘⲀ B4, ⲘⲘⲀⲨ
B5; "deux" ⲤⲚⲀ B4, ⲤⲚⲀⲨ B5; les manuscrits de B4 actuellement connus sont tous anciens (IVe-Ve siècles).

B5 = principal (sub)dialecte du groupe dialectal B; B5 est
le bohaïrique classique enseigné dans les grammaires (cf.
STERN 1880, MALLON 1907) et attesté par presque tous les
manuscrits bohaïriques (du IXe siècle ou plus tardifs);
différences entre B5 et B4: voir B4.

B74 = (sub)dialecte du groupe dialectal B; en plus des caractéristiques orthographiques de B4, la spécificité de B74
est de n'utiliser jamais Ϭ /čh/, toujours remplacé par Ϫ
/č/ ; les manuscrits de B74 actuellement connus sont tous
anciens (IVe siècle).

BOSSON voir KASSER - QUECKE - BOSSON 1992.

DE LAGARDE 1867 = P. A. DE LAGARDE, Der Pentateuch
koptisch, Leipzig 1867.

GAWDAT GABRA 1986a = A. S. GAWDAT GABRA, "A New Manuscript
in the Coptic Museum (Psalms, Middle Egyptian or Oxyrhynchite Dialect)", IACS, Newsletter Nr 18, April 1986, p. 10.

GAWDAT GABRA 1986b = A. S. GAWDAT GABRA, "Zur Bedeutung
des koptischen Psalmbuches im oxyrhynchitischen Dialekt",
Göttinger Miszellen, 93, 1986, p. 37-42.

GUILLAUMONT - KASSER 1969 = A. GUILLAUMONT et R. KASSER,
"Les inscriptions coptes", dans F. DAUMAS, A. GUILLAUMONT,

avec la collaboration de J.-C. GARCIN, J. JARRY, B. BOYAVAL, R. KASSER, J.-C. GOYON, J.-L. DESPAGNE, B. LENTHÉRIC, J. SCHRUOFFENEGER, Kellia I, kôm 219, fouilles effectuées en 1964 et 1965, Le Caire 1969, p. 99-112.

HUSSELMAN 1947 = E. M. HUSSELMAN, "A Bohairic School Text on Papyrus", Journal of Near Eastern Studies, 6, 1947, p. 129-151.

HYVERNAT 1888 = H. HYVERNAT, Album de paléographie copte pour servir à l'introduction paléographique des Actes des martyrs de l'Égypte, Paris - Rome 1888.

KASSER 1958 = R. KASSER, Papyrus Bodmer III, évangile de Jean et Genèse I - IV,2 en bohaïrique, Louvain 1958.

KASSER 1981a = R. KASSER, "Voyelles en fonction consonantique, consonnes en fonction vocalique, et classes de phonèmes en copte", Bulletin de la Société d'égyptologie, Genève, 5, 1981, p. 33-50.

KASSER 1982d = R. KASSER, "Syllabation rapide ou lente en copte, I, les glides /j/ et /w/ avec leurs correspondants vocaliques '/i/' et '/u/' (et phonèmes appariés analogues)", Enchoria, 11, 1982, p. 23-27.

KASSER - QUECKE - BOSSON 1992 = R. KASSER, H. QUECKE, N. BOSSON, "Le second chapitre d'Aggée en bohaïrique B74", Orientalia, 61, 1992, p. 169-204.

KASSER voir GUILLAUMONT - KASSER 1969.

LAYTON 1987 = B. LAYTON, Catalogue of Coptic Literary Manuscripts in the British Library Acquired Since the Year 1906, Londres 1987.

M = dialecte copte mésokémique (appelé aussi "moyen-égyptien" ou "oxyrhynchite"; chef de groupe dialectal; subdialectes de M: M4 et M5.

M4 = subdialecte du groupe dialectal M; il est caractérisé particulièrement par le préfixe verbal du parfait II, ⲁⲙⲁ- , ⲁⲙⲁ⸗ etc.; en outre, c'est sur ⲙ, ⲛ et ⲉ autosyllabiques, qu'il utilise le djinkim; les manuscrits de M4 actuellement connus sont tous anciens (IVe-(Ve) siècles, pour l'un, éd. ORLANDI-(QUECKE) 1974, et cf. SCHENKE 1989; l'autre est encore inédit, cf. GAWDAT GABRA 1986a et 1986b).

M5 = subdialecte du groupe dialectal M; il est caractérisé particulièrement par le préfixe verbal du parfait II, ⲉⲙⲁ- , ⲉⲙⲁ⸗ etc.; en outre, c'est sur ⲙ, ⲛ, ⲉ et ⲁ autosyllabiques, qu'il utilise le djinkim; les manuscrits de M5 actuellement connus sont tous anciens (Ve siècle; éd. SCHENKE 1981a et SCHENKE 1991).

MALLON 1907 = A. MALLON, Grammaire copte, avec bibliographie, chrestomathie et vocabulaire, Beyrouth 1907.

ORLANDI - (QUECKE) 1974 = T. ORLANDI (avec la collaboration de H. QUECKE), Papiri della Università degli Studi di Milano (P. Mil. Copti), vol. V, Lettere di San Paolo in copto ossirinchita, edizione, commento e indici di T. Orlandi, contributo linguistico di H. Quecke, Milan 1974.

POLOTSKY 1949 = H. J. POLOTSKY, "Une question d'orthographe bohaïrique", Bulletin de la Société d'archéologie copte, 12, 1949, p. 25-35.

QUECKE 1970 = H. QUECKE, Untersuchungen zum koptischen Stundengebet, Louvain 1970.

QUECKE 1974a = H. QUECKE, "Ein altes bohairisches Fragment des Jakobusbriefes (P. Heid. Kopt. 452)", Orientalia, 43, 1974, p. 382-392.

QUECKE voir KASSER - QUECKE - BOSSON 1992.

S = "langue" (plutôt que "dialecte") saïdique; variété supra-régionale et supra-dialectale de la langue copte, dont elle est la "moitié" méridionale; sa fonction a été celle d'une langue véhiculaire: la koinè autochtone de toute la vallée du Nil égyptien en amont du Delta.

SCHENKE 1981a = H.-M. SCHENKE, Das Matthäus-Evangelium im mittelägyptischen Dialekt des Koptischen (Codex Scheide), Berlin 1981.

SCHENKE 1989 = H.-M. SCHENKE, "Mittelägyptische 'Nachlese' 1, Bemerkungen zum Adverb ϨⲒ ⲦⲢⲞⲨⲢ 'schnell' anlässlich der Edition von Restfragmenten der Mailänder mittelägyptischen Handschrift der Paulusbriefe mit einem neuen Beleg", Zeitschrift für Ägyptische Sprache und Altertumskunde, 116, 1989, p. 160-174.

SCHENKE 1991 = H.-M. SCHENKE, Apostelgeschichte 1,1 - 15,3 im mittelägyptischen Dialekt des Koptischen (Codex Glazier), Berlin 1991.

STERN 1880 = L. STERN, Koptische Grammatik, Leipzig 1880.

Vat. Copto 5, Psaume 27,3-5.

SHARING THE PAIN: SAINT AND SINNER IN LATE ANTIQUE EGYPT

Anitra Bingham Kolenkow

Early monastic growth occurred in a time of change -- from a time of Christian martyrdom to a time of Christian success. Why? There had been few people in the desert (marginal people -- hermits, failed martyrs, traders, bandits, miners, etc.). Now there are many. A certain few marginal persons (with the skills of the desert) organized the many. How did they build a sense of community among the many marginalized. How did they become the focus for forgiveness in the larger society. This paper hears the growth of and reasons for a "sense of sin" as described by religious writers in a time of political and social change. It also watches the organization of religious communities with an emphasis on forgiveness through shared ascesis (of both saint and sinner). This ascesis (multileveled and related to intercession and vision) became a model for forgiveness in a vindictive post-persecution world.[1]

----

1. Economic conditions (taxes, difficulty in supporting a wife, etc.) are often blamed for the crowds. However, although economics may drive people to the desert or against society (and although difficulty supporting a wife may make men come to monasteries in modern Egypt as well as ancient), this does not account entirely either for the group sense of sin or desire for virtue. There is almost a group fear of having survived -- and still being guilty when history said God was powerful (the more so for reasons described below). This paper thus has a more sociological-religious emphasis than those studies which have emphasized economics. The paper sees leadership-judicial participation in the punishment and blame which the society put on many people.

Economic problems continue before and after the period. Pachomius gives poor people food (SBo 8) but many stories (as SBo 39, Par. 21) of the early period suggest that diet is often better outside than inside the monastery (although one has later stories like those of the poor man who complains about Arsenius' pillow) until the monasteries become great landowners and food producers or monks get organized by helpful priests (HM 18:1-2, cf. HM 5 and Palladius HL 10). The Bible and visions be-

I. THE CRUCIBLE OF DIFFICULTY

The time of Constantine might be considered a time of fruition for Christianity. But in that time thousands came to the monasteries and there was a sense of sin. Hausherr talks of desert fathers as specialists in "penthos" and conscious of sins. Hausherr remarks that the growth of monasticism occurred at the same time as the introduction of "Kyrie Eleison."[2] Veilleux recognizes that "making penitence" was the meaning of becoming a monk.[3] Why this sense of guilt? One watches the build up of candidates for monastic life: the lapsed, the post-Constantinian apocalyptic fearers, those caught in social change -- and all those who either had wished to be among the martyrs or had watched (and even tried to harm) the martyrs.[4]

----

come not only the basis of teaching inside the monastery, but of fostering distribution of monastic gardens' produce outside (Besa VS 144-50).

2. I. Hausherr, The Name of Jesus (Kalamazoo, Mich.: Cistercian, 1978) 244-45. Hausherr argues that the monasteries are open to everyone -- even great sinners -- and asks "whether public penitents were permitted to become monks." He basically argues "yes" for the desert, "infrequently" for Pachomius, "yes" for Basil (244-45).

3. A. Veilleux La Liturgie dans le cénobitisme Pachômien au quatrième siècle (S.A. 57; Rome: Pontificium Institutum S. Anselmi, 1968) 342.

4. The first Greek life of Pachomius pictures the time of persecution as a time of test set by God for those with faith. It says faith in Christ increased after the time of martyrdom -- and that monasteries and places of asceticism began to increase (places famous for chastity and renunciation of possessions). The life then explicitly pictures pagans who saw the martyrs and who renewed their lives by askesis and reverence for Christ and the martyrs. In Chap. 2, the two founders of monasticism become examples of the two groups; St. Antony of the first and St. Pachomius of the second (SBo 2, G1 2). Cf. the apostle Paul faced by the death of Stephen. Cf. also the Arabic life 338-39 on those who look at the cross and see the martyrs. After the age of Diocletion and Maximus the people

TO WATCH THE MARTYRS

What it meant to watch the martyrs becomes clear as one reads the stories of these centuries. Perpetua is converted and feels she must become a martyr. She preaches that witnesses to her death are either condemned or blessed by their response (Mar. Fel. Perp. 19). (She also sees-accomplishes otherworldly healing.) In 252, Cyprian (Ep. Dem. 24) says that those who look on the martyrs will be looked on in eternal punishment by the martyrs. Cyprian urges repentance (and presumed martyrdom) while there is still time. In the martyrdom of Shenoufe, one reads:

> The tormenter answered and said, "When I die may the pupil of my eye be set under the hinge of the gate of Hell."
> The rest of the saints answered "Amen."[5]

Thus you are called to be a martyr or guilt-punishment is put on you by the martyrs' speeches; you are either guilty because you did not become a martyr or guilty because you did agree to or join in the persecution.

Eusebius tells how he saw "the outrages and agonies" in the Thebias, where martyrs speak boldly and others join in martyrdom (HE 8:9). The reader has a picture of the ten to one hundred martyrs a day (visible test cases) together with those who recant and those who smite. Guards vie with threats; all who wish insult the martyrs or smite them with rods and cudgels (HE 8:10.4).

APOCALYPTIC: Punishment

After the conversion of Constantine, a second aspect of the situation seems to be a post-Constantinian guilt-responsibility-belief that the world continued to exist because of the punishments which occurred. The conversion of Constantine was proof that the martyrs' threats of Hell would be valid. Constantine's coming put political reality

----

make penitence and continue to frequent the church.

5. E. Reymond, J. Barns, <u>Four Martyrdoms from the Pierpont Morgan Coptic Codices</u> (London: Oxford University, 1973) 202. These situations make people take sides even if some claim there is little evidence of popular hostility.

on top of latent guilt. Also in this time,
apocalyptic-eschatological threat is combined with
or replaced by teaching about earthly punishment
for known sins. Punishment allowed the world to continue. Eusebius presents internal church strife as
the cause of God's allowing persecution. Persecution was a punishment which when paid allowed the
world to continue (HE 1.34.56).[6] Lactantius moves
from apocalyptic threat to a description of the
punishment of the persecutors. Rufus of Aquila's HM
prologue says the world continued to exist by the
prayers of the martyrs. Suffering, prayers and
punishment kept the world going.

OUTSIDE THE DOORS
        Punishment also occurs in the churches. The
church put outside the doors those who had lapsed
during the persecution -- with the mortal sinners
(murderers, etc.). Both groups practiced fasting
and chastity outside the doors -- often for many
years or until death.[7] Although the rest of the
church took on more fasting before festivals
(Cassian Con. 18:5, like the ancient Egyptian
priests[8]), the sinners became the real ascetics.
The martyrs used to forgive more easily than the
priests, but they were now dead (or would be by the
end of the 4th century). Where was forgiveness?
Bishops have many on their hands whom they ask

----

6. Cf. on a lesser scale Ep. Amm. 10 on mercy in the
past and present and the monks, in comparison to the
world not destroyed before the coming of Jesus.

7. O.D. Watkins, A History of Penance (London:
Longmans, Green, 1920) 269, 298-300. Even if one
received eucharist, one was still forbidden marital
relations, etc. until death (320). This was not
only the lapsed but all mortal sinners. It was
easier to be a monk. Monastic life assumes forgiveness and gives one community. Note that there was a
real spectrum of time spans demanded by different
bishops -- and cf. Apollonius of Tyana and the
naked philosophers cited later.

8. A. Kolenkow, "Chaeremon the Stoic on Egyptian
Temple Ascesis" In V. Wimbush (ed.) Ascetic Be-
havior in Greco-Roman Antiquity (Minneapolis:
Fortress 1990) 387-395.

people like Pachomius to organize. Oxyrhynchus shows the city situation facing bishops -- a town full of monks to be organized (HM 5:1).

THOSE ALREADY IN THE DESERT

Flight had been fostered as a useable alternative to martyrdom (cf. Peter of Alexandria). Deserts had always been an Egyptian resource for quiet and escape. Deserts had also been an alternative to martyrdom. St. Paul the Hermit is said to have fled persecution by going to the desert. Chaeremon Bishop of Nilopolis (with his wife) also flees from persecution to the mountains. Eusebius speaks of the multitude who "wandered in deserts and mountain and perished by hunger and thirst and frost and disease and robbers. Such of them as survive bear testimony to their election." (HE 6:42:2-3) An old man, who had been bishop, sacrificed to the emperor, confessed his sins, went to the desert -- and spent 49 years there with the Lord sustaining the man's life by a palm tree which grew 29 days journey in the desert (Nau ROC 10 (1905) 412-413). In a papyrii, some persons (threatened by martyrdom) sacrifice, some withdraw from the city, some virgins flee two miles from the city and dwell together under a presbyter named John.[9] Bishop Nepos (who writes apocalypses) encourages an ascetic community (Eusebius HE 7:24). These people join the robbers and liminal people who already lived in the desert -- as the Life of Macarius tells.

SOCIAL CHANGE

After Constantine's conversion, there was also social change -- and especially a change of social ethics which fostered going to monasteries. Female children were not killed in Christian society[10] -- and eventually one sees twice as many female virgins as male in places like Oxyrhynchus (HM 5.1). Christians value purity over marriage[11] and Pachomius now

----

9. Reymond. Martyrdoms 16. A. Alcock "Persecutions under Septimus Severus," Enchoria 11 (1982) 2-3 [P.Oxy 4 1B 74/k(a)].

10. Groups of female virgins had long existed in the church.

11. Tertullian also sees the philosophers preaching chastity, but notes that a taint on Christian purity is considered worse than any death (Apol. 46, 50). Note the effective competition between Hellenistic

tries to bring many people "pure to God." (SBo 107).

Homosexuality had been a socially recognized sexual practice before late marriage. Pachomius sends passionate people by the hundreds to the desert beyond in the mountains, but he also struggles with a few in the monastery (SBo 107) where homosexuality can be a problem (Horsiesius Inst. 7). Where marriage had been fostered and divorce easy, now Constantine legitimized celibacy and required men to be chaste after divorce. E. L. Butcher saw the law of 320 (which freed childless persons and celibates from taxation) with exemption of monks from military service as causes for Egyptians undertaking monastic vows.[12] Families come when one member choses purity. Ascetic couples like Amoun and his wife become monks (Socrates HE 4.23; Palladius HL 8).

Harlots, soldiers (not allowed to marry) and theater people (often excluded from the church) are found in monasteries. Monasteries become a refuge of those sought for the army (as well as storage place for government recruits).[13]

SPECTRUM IN THE MONASTERY -- IDEALISTS AND SINNERS

They were also a refuge for idealists. Pachomius tells of the spectrum of people who came to the monastery and the desert (SBo 107, 40 "many kinds"): the pure, the passionate, the unknowing and the unstoppable.[14] Even Antony (one of those who had neither apostized or been martyred) felt the need of more ascesis. There are idealistic converts like Theodore of Alexandria and Bishop Ammon or born Christians like Theodore of Latopolis who decides the place of the outsider-pagan is also the place of

----

romances (defense of marriage pledge to the death) and the Christian Acts of Thomas, John, etc. which emphasize chastity above marriage.

12. E. L. Butcher The Story of the Church in Egypt (London:Smith, Elder, 1897) 193-94.

13. Is this the reason for the eight sleeping place room found by Father Samuel Syrien?

14. Cf. Pachomius and his monk Silvanos (Par. 2). Where Origen, Egyptian Church Order and Basil condemned soldiery, the empire continued to seek recruits.

salvation for Christians. Pachomius tells how murderers, adulterers and sorcerers come (Drag. 1:5) as
earlier they had come to the ancient temples. In
monasteries, as in the ancient temples, the askesis
of the criminal or liminal person is like that of
the ideal religious life. Saints and sinners moved
from the doors of the church to the doors of the
monastery. Monastic consecration assumes forgiveness and gives community. As Cassian knew (Conf.
18:5), those who wanted to keep the biblical stric-
tures of giving up property and marriage and kindred
left the churches. Basil's Ep. 90 tells of houses
of prayer empty and deserts full of mourners. The
deserts and the boundary like area of the monasteries are a new city-caravansary[15] for old and new
sinners, for those who strove and failed, those who
tried to find new ways of extra ascesis, those who
tried to save the world. How do you organize life
for saint and sinner together?

This time was a crucible of martyrs and
watchers, of apocalyptic and realized punishments,
of those who fled to the desert and those who waited
at church doors, of those made liminal by social
change and all the others commonly in the desert.
This meant ordinary people as well as great saints
and sinners. Martyrdom had been an opportunity for
salvation (cf. Pachomius and the would-be martyr, Gl
85). Guilt is focussed by martyrdom, Christian success and social disruption. Thousands came.

II. FROM INDIVIDUAL TO GROUP: THE ORGANIZATION OF LIMINALITY

With the great variety of persons coming to the
desert and monasteries, there developed dialogues:

1. between responsibility to seek only one's
own salvation (as in St. Basil) and responsibility
to seek the salvation of others.

2. Between a monastic vow which provided forgiveness for all previous sins -- and the need of
severer ascesis for great sinners.

Responsible fathers move toward sharing the penances
they give sinners -- and thus toward organization
and forgiveness.

----

15. On the refuge and caravansary aspect of churches
and monasteries, cf. P. Vinogradoff, "Social and
Economic Conditions of the Roman Empire in the
Fourth Century," Cambridge Medieval History
(Cambridge: Cambridge University, 1911) I 566.

VISIONS TOWARD UNDERTAKING RESPONSIBILITY

In the writings and lives of the desert fathers, one reads that if one went to the desert, the ideal was to seek individual salvation. This was in contrast to the picture of regular Christians (who had fed Pachomius, SBo 7) or the priests (who are expected to take care of the sick -- as you read in the life of Pachomius (SBo 9).

In the stories and visions of the monks, the reader meets remarkable people in the process of moving back from the ideal of ascesis-separation[16] to an emphasis on service reconciliation and the salvation of others. The ideal had been to seek one's own salvation in the desert. The problem of the "moving back to community" was whether the monk can reach the height of virtue if the monk helps others. Revelations and visions[17] answer this.

St. Bishoi (the famous Coptic carrier of Christ, like St. Christopher) asks this question:

And the Lord answered him, "He who struggles for himself is my disciple. But he who struggles for himself and for others is my son and heir." (Paisios 133)

In a similar story, a luminous man says to St. Pachomius, "God's will is to serve mankind and reconcile it to him." Pachomius protests indignantly, "I

----

16. The stories themselves are validation that this standard commonly existed and was being fought against; cf. Life of Antony 3 "intent on himself," "whoever wished to concern himself with his own destiny, practiced asceticism by himself." This is like Palamon, who however does his work to support the poor.

17. Visions have always been a way of validating the difficult and speaking to the needs of society through the perspective of something higher than normal usage. For this reason (regardless of ths social tendency to increase the number of visions) the visions illuminate the problems of the society. One may speak of the "use" of visions (and not just reception) because of the argument that visions should not be spoken of unless useful. Apparently, visions are an essential component of leadership or successorship in the Pachomian commonity, cf. SBo 121, "Indeed, because of his purity of heart, he used to have revelations and was qualified in every respect." said of Petronius in discussing his succession to Pachomius.

seek the Lord's will (i.e. personal salvation) and you say to serve mankind." The luminous man repeats himself three times.[18] Bishoi, Pachomius and others (Macarius, Or [HMBE 62-3, HM 2:2]) receive visions and then the reality of many coming to them for salvation (Paisios 17, SBo 8). Leaders had to arrange for the many who came.

III. FORGIVENESS AND ASCESIS IN THE MONASTERY

A common or official belief was that the monastic vow and taking of monastic dress (then and now) symbolized the forgiveness of all sins previous to the vows. The life of Antony 65 tells of Antony's vision that the Lord erases things done before becoming a monk, only taking account of things since the person became a monk. The Life of Pachomius tells of forgiveness in the 40 days, but shows a greater ambiguity of requirements -- beyond the ordinary rules of psalms and food. (Cf. Barsanuphius and John on forgiveness of sins from birth after 40 days.[19])

The monastic life (as the ancient Pythagorean) required putting "ponos" on yourself (as Palamon said, to take the kingdom of God by force[20]). Further, as the Life of Pachomius shows, each person was given the amount of ascesis required for the person's salvation (SBo 93). (The lives of

----

18. S1 6, cf. SBo 17 (where visions and decision are validated by the anchorite Palamon). Cf. the repetition of the struggle for the followers of Pachomius (Horsiesios Test. 8) as leaders who say to themselves, "What have I to do with other men. I seek to serve God and fulfill his commandments." On this and other arguments in the Pachomian community, cf. the author's forthcoming article, "To Teach the Young to speak." The saviour promises Bishoi double the wages for the labor he will undergo for the salvation of others as for that for himself (Paisios 25). On advice to individual's to work only for own soul's salvation, cf. Pachomius SBo 115.

19. "The great mediator Jesus tells me,'Thy sins which are many are forgiven from birth until the present. Show great and worthy works of patience and thanksgiving." (108-202)

20. SBo 10, cf. SBo 89 using Gal. 5:24, "crucified their flesh." Maximus the Confessor uses this reference.

Pachomius, Shenouda and John of the Ladder show what
a real benefit this was considered, a power like insight into hearts of the Pachomian tradition.[21])
The desert was the place of "ponos" (as Eusebius
knew). Everyone needed to put on "ponos" and take
off the veneer of civilization -- and especially to
receive the blessing of God and to focus on the possibility of the future.[22]

However, the great variety of persons meant the
need of options in working with individual strain
and guilt. The Life of St. Macarius talks of robbers and travellers in the same area as Macarius.
Pachomius knows that sinners come to the monastery
(Ep. Amm. 10, 12). Of course, life in the desert
equalizes.

There were, in fact, at least three basic
types of "struggle" or "pain" which were given or
shared. 1.) The first, of course, is the basic testing. The one who wants to become a monk joins his
father in ascesis. Pachomius joins in Palamon's ascesis. This is the ordinary preliminary of coming
to the desert "to labor until you know yourself"
(SBo 10) and whether you can live the life. In
Pachomius' monastery it is preliminary to the great
forgiveness of sins which occurs at passover (or in
the Forty days). There is the story of a young man
who practices ascesis but dies in the Forty days.
The brothers are upset and the Father has a vision
of angels baptising the young man.SBo 81. Cf. Par.
2:4 on angels taking Silvanos

The process of working with the person (inside
the monastery as well as in the desert) is shown in
the story of Silvanos, the boy who become negligent.
Pachomius asks an older monk to "suffer with the boy
until he is saved." So young and old work together
on mats, fasting and prayer (G1 105). These are the
ordinary stuggles and testing that occur in the
monastic life.[23]

----

21. SBo 29, G1 34. Cf. Besa VS 14-16 and the fate
of a murderer; Ladder 4:112 with confession and vision of sins crossed off.

22. This is like the strenuous life of modern Egyptian novices -- like "Outward Bound" -- organized
ascesis to unite, to empower, to enable all to live
together under difficulty. Leaders themselves maintain (or heighten) this life or may lose
credibliity. There may be envy or distain for the
less arduous life lived by monks after the
novitiate.

The second type is working with those who sin seriously after the monastic vows. In ordinary life one sins again. It becomes one of the commonplaces for monks to request or to share in the punishment of those who sin (John of the Ladder 4:18; cf. life of Pachomius SBo 115). There are also serious sins which take away the salvation given by monastic entry. John of the Ladder's prison is a place of extreme ascesis for those who have committed serious breaking of vows (5). There is no assurance of salvation. The monks hope to receive a vision of forgiveness and ask every form of punishment. John of the Ladder also recognizes that those who have fallen and suffered are actually more blessed than those who have never fallen.

There is a third, more complex category of working with those who join the monastery and are major sinners. The Fathers (like Pachomius, Shenouda and the Shepherd of John of the Ladder's prison, see above.) have eyes that are clear to see what behavior is necessary for a sinner to gain forgiveness (SBo 29, 107. cf. 112, Gl 34). Major sinners would require major askesis. The spiritual father of the monastery responded to some of these (even the most hardened) who came to the monastery.

For the hardest cases, Pachomius will send them to the desert as anchorites, but says Pachomius:

> For my part I sometimes accept one or two men of that kind and struggle with them until I save them from the enemies' grasp" He then goes to them night and day, until they are safe.
> He does this in order to fulfill the words of the Holy Apostle "Take pains with one another so that you may be saved."

The fathers share the weight of the great sinner's sins as their own ascesis intercedes for him -- and thus they shorten forgiveness times. The process is shown as Abba Lot tells a monk to sit in a cave and eat every two days and Lot "will carry half the fault." After three weeks, Lot was convinced that God had accepted the brother's repentance.[24]   A

----

23. Pachomius Ep. 5:11 "toil..carrying each others burdens ..lest in the age to come we be separated for our brothers who suffered afflictions;" cf. advice to Theodore (SBo 90).

24. AP Lot 2.   On short forgiveness times, cf. Poemen HM 12.99; AP Sisoes 20. One Abba Lot is a center of revelation against lack of obedience to the ways of the father -- and for forgiveness of

worried monk writes Barsanuphius wanting Barsanuphius to say Barsanuphius will carry all the monk's sin. Barsanuphius has said he will carry half (73 |168|-74 |169|).[25] Note also the guarantee elsewhere to lie in the same tomb with a brother and that brother's fear that one will be taken and the other left. (70 |165|, 61 |153|). Fathers like Theodore will undertake the ascesis (which they had given a brother) of not eating leeks (SBo 79), cf. Pachomius excommunicating himself (Drag. 1:1-6). Theodore fasts two days and does extra ascesis for three weeks when those under him fall (SBo *ii*); indeed, this is the way upper management gets middle management to take responsibility. The father may use his own fasting as a way to convince others -- as Pachomius makes vigil forty days and then fasts six days before God to bring about a change of heart in the older brothers (S Bo 92, Gl 100). One also hears how sick Pachomius became with ascesis (S Bo 48).

The ascetic fathers like St. Pachomius and St. Bishoi were thus building up their ascesis beyond the normal way of the monastery. St. Bishoi was told that his ascesis of twenty-two days was equal to the two days of a small struggler. There is indeed a two (or more) level ascesis building up. Ordinary monks may be required to live a regular life.[26] Pachomius wanted his cooks to keep an assortment of foods on the table.[27] Sinners (and cer-

----

brethren (Paradise II 207, 208).

25. Note also the guarantee to lie in the same tomb with a brother and that brother's fear that one will be taken and the other left. (70 |165|, 61 |153|).

26. AP Antony 8. Cf. Barsanuphius who says (85-181) it belongs to the perfect to partake everyday of the same cooked food without distaste. Barsanuphius also says that for the sick, the sickness takes the place of fasting. The body is weak of itself instead of made weak through fasting. Fasting is to make the body weak.

27. Macarius visits Pachomius' monastery and practices severe askesis. Pachomius asks him to leave (Palladius HL 18.15).

tain fathers) are admired for their stricter ascesis
(cf. SBo 107, as well as John of the Ladder on the
"prison") by the regular members of the monastery.

Further, the fathers' ascetic lives would be
recognized as a basis for their ability to see visions of heaven (and forgiveness or judgment, as
above). They also are considered able to gain the
forgiveness of heaven both for sins in community
even after a person's becoming a monk -- and for the
sins of those who have died. As part of Theodore's
assumption of leadership, Theodore makes a covenent
promise of forgiveness of sins after one becomes a
monk (SBo 192). Antony reveals the possibility of
forgiveness of sins up to Nov. 354 (Ep. Amm. 28-29).
An elder, worrying and fasting forty days for the
soul of an unrepentant monk in Hades, goes to St.
Bishoi. St. Bishoi prays and the savior appears
praising St. Bishoi for being willing to give up the
rewards of his own previous ascesis for the salvation of a sinner.[28]

There are those monks who complain when St. Barsanuphius assured a monk that the monk would go to
heaven (Life 10:15-22, 141ff.), but outside and inside the monastery, these fathers stood for forgiveness of post-baptismal sins -- a major problem "in
every place where the name of Christ is preached"
(Ep. Amm. 28, cf. 20). These Father's power becomes
support for those like Athansius against those who
believe otherwise. In both East and West, great
leaders seem willing to grant forgiveness (cf. S.
Severus [Martin 22], Hilary [Vie 3.476]).[29] Now it

----

28. Paisios 44-45. Note the ascetic lives of the
fathers before they become community organizers.
HM's Or, Apollo and John have been hermits before
organizing communities.

29. In both East and West, great leaders seem willing to grant forgiveness. Like Paul, ascetics also
receive heavenly reward from the number of those
they bring to God (HM 2, cf. the picture of
Pachomius with the soul of a brother which he gives
to God). Monastic forgiveness after a man became a
monk (officially a more difficult thing, as VA 65)
was now made easier -- and fostered belief in the
heavenly powers of the father. The ex-sinner was
under monastic control for the rest of his life.
Note the severe situation of those who break monas-
ticvows -- separation from the community and ascesis
in the Pachomian community, and the prison of John
Climacus' Ladder 4, 5. Macarius covers over short-
comings (Paradise II 204).

is the monks as well as martyrs who preserve the
world (as well as each other). Where HM Preface
said the martyrs were those through whom the world
is kept in being, now Apa Jeremias of Saqqara bows
"until he removes the sins of the whole world."[30]
In response to an earthquake, Pachomius prays and
tells Theodore, "Cry out unceasingly to God that he
may extend his mercies upon us, without which the
creation cannot exist" (Ep. Amm. 10).

Thus the social-religious feelings of apocalyptic guilt had been balanced by monastic leaders who
organized ways of life for those coming to the
desert. One of the methods was a development of special ascesis for major sinners. This ascesis was
shared by the leadership. Monasteries developed
double (or many) leveled ascesis. The higher level
of ascesis was that of great sinners and saints --
who then became symbols of forgiveness.

Where martyrs had served as givers of forgiveness for those who sought their support, now the
ascetic ones of the desert became purveyors of forgiveness in Constantine's great age of anxiety -- an
age where the Christian God had been shown powerful
-- and the world stood guilty and waiting at the
doors of church and monastery.

Note: The needs and solutions used for working with
people were not unique to the monastic world, only
the numbers were staggering. Pagans and Christians
knew the world of ascesis and vision; Pythagoreans
talked to spirits (Lucian Philops. 31-32). Gods
like Isis and Asclepius appeared to give authoriza-
tion and assurance of health and salvation. The Egyptian priests had long periods of fasting before
feasts (cf. Porphyry On Abstinence 4:7 on
Chaeremon the Stoic). Those who came to live with
them (like Apuleius' Lucius) apparently had con-
tinual fasting as or more severe than that of the
priests. The pagan could go to the temple on the
edge of the desert for a change of life. Ros-
tovsteff tells of Hephestion the soldier making a

----

30. J. Quibell Excavations at Saqqara (Cairo:1912)
4:55 # 188 quoted in P. Rousseau, Ascetics,
Authority and the Church, 57. Cf. also Qumran where
the Teacher of Righteousness and his community could
see themselves as suffering for the sins of people
who had excluded them.

change of life (like Pachomius later) from the
military. Apuleius' Lucius comes to live the life
of the priests after a multiformed life (Golden Ass
11). Worshippers of the God Suchos in the Fayyum
agree to pay rent to live in a temple -- in order to
get free from demons.[31]

The stories of sharing pain also have earlier
Christian parallels. Clement of Alexandria ends his
"Can the Rich Man be Saved" by telling of the
Apostle John who shares prayers and fasting with a
robber until the robber is restored to the church.

TEXTS AND TRANSLATIONS   The series of Migne, Loeb
Library, Sources Chretiennes, together with the
texts for Pachomius (Lefort, Halkin), Palladius
(Butler), Barsanuphius (Schoinas, thanks to Sava Zem-
billas of Oxford), F. Nau (ROC 10, 12-14, 17-18
(1905-13) have been used together with the English
and French translations (with abbreviations cited in
noted):
AP   The Desert Christian: Sayings of the Desert
Fathers (Trans. B. Ward) New York: Macmillan 1980.
Barsanuphius   Barsanuphe et Jean de Gaza Cor-
responence (trans. L. Regnault et al.) Solemes:1971
Besa VS   Besa The Life of Shenoute (trans. D. Bell)
Kalamazoo: Cistercian, 1983.
HM   The Lives of the Desert Fathers (trans. N. Rus-
sell) Kalamazoo: Cistercian, 1983.
HMBE Histoire des monastères de la Basse-Egypte
(trans. É. Amélineau) Annales de Musée Guimet 25;
Paris: Leroux, 1894.
Ladder   John Climacus The Ladder of Divine Ascent
(trans. L. Moore revised) Boston:Holy Transfigura-
tion Monastery, 1978.
Paisios   St. John the Dwarf of Egypt The Life of
Saint Paisios the Great (Trans. L. Papadopolos
and G. Lizardos) Jordanville, N. Y.: Holy Trinity
Monastery, 1983.
Paradise   The Paradise or Garden of the Fathers
(trans. E. Budge) New York: Burt Franklin, 1972.
SBo, S1, G1, Ep. Amm., Par. (Pachomius, Theodore,
Horsiesius) in Pachomian Koinonia 1-3 (trans. A Viel-
leux) Kalamazoo: Cistercian, 1980ff.
VA   St. Athansius The Life of Saint Antony (trans.
R. Meyer) New York:Paulist, 1950.

----
31. On these pre-monastic materials, see A. Kolenkow
"Chaeremon" 387-89 and a paper "Monasticism in an
Age of Anxiety" for the 1983 Claremont conference on
"The Roots of Egyptian Christianity."

THE VALLEY OF THE QUEENS IN THE COPTIC PERIOD

G. LECUYOT

Formerly known by the name *Ta set neferou*, the history of the Valley of the Queens covers two milleniums ; from the New Kingdom to the Coptic period.

During the New Kingdom it was one of the royal necropolises of Western Thebes. The cemetery was used as the burial ground for mummies of princes, princesses, queens and even high dignitaries. The most ancient tombs that have been dated go back to the reign of Sekenenrê-Taâ (VdR 47), Thoutmosis I (VdR 9 and 46) and Thoutmosis II (VdR 12). These are very simple "pit-tombs" comprising a vertical pit dug into the mountain and leading to one or more burial chambers.

In the XIXth and XXth dynasties more elaborate "syringes" were excavated : these had wall decorations and were accessible by a ramp or stairway[1].

From the Third Intermediary Period certain tombs were reused and sometimes transformed and adapted to receive the remains of people of simpler condition : low ranked clergymen.

In the Roman Period, between the IInd and IVth centuries A.D., the tombs were reused en masse and each served as a burial place for hundreds of mummies of the deceased from the region of the Memnonia and even as far away as Hermonthis[2].

In the first half of the IInd century A.D. a sanctuary was built at the entrance to the Valley on the site of what was probably an unfinished Pharaonic tomb (VdR 95) dating from the Twentieth Dynasty, and we know it was still in use in the IVth century. It is on this site that we can see today the ruins of the Deir er-Roumi.

In the IVth century A.D. the Necropolis still represented a place of pagan worship. This situation explains perhaps, on the one hand, the violent destruction of the sanctuary as can be seen in the burnt and broken ruins and, on the other hand, the settling

---

[1] Ch. Leblanc, Architecture et évolution chronologique des tombes de la Vallée des Reines, *BIFAO* 89, Cairo, 1989, p. 227-247 and pl. XXX-XXXI.

[2] Cf. G. Wagner, Ch. Leblanc, G. Lecuyot and A.-M. Loyrette, Documents grecs découverts dans la Vallée des Reines, *BIFAO* 90, Cairo, 1990, p. 370.

here of a monastic community which put an end to pagan practice. Up to the very end of its service, the Valley of the Queens seems to have acted as a burial place exclusively for pagans. It is interesting to remark that a Christian cemetery has been identified not very far from here, north of Medinet-Habou, and it seems that the two cemeteries coexisted for some time. Nevertheless, we can suppose that the monks from the Deir were buried close to their monastery, though no trace of their tombs has yet been found.

For many years now the Franco-Egyptian team of the CNRS and the CEDAE has been studying the Valley of the Queens. Since 1984, thanks to the generous donation of Mme G. Ford de Maria for "the Renovation of the Valley of the Queens", we have been in a position to undertake a systematic exploration of the different parts of the site and thus to obtain a clear all-round view of its history.

Some traces of the Coptic occupation have been known about for some time but haven't yet been sufficiently studied. Even the little monastery at the entrance to the valley[3], which had been excavated by Schiaparelli's Italian mission, received no more mention than two brief references in their published account[4].

---

[3] At the beginning of this century this place was known by the name "Bab el-Hagi Hamid", cf. J. Bonomi cited by P. Newberry, Topographical notes on Western Thebes collected in 1830, *ASAE* 7, 1906, p. 82 n° 45 : "the abode of a man from Bairat who lived in the building called Dêr er-Rumi, at the entrance of the valley of the tombs of the Queens". J. Černy̒, Ch. Desroches Noblecourt and M. Kurz, *Graffiti de la Montagne Thébaine*, I, Cairo, 1969-70., pl. VI and LXXIX-LXXX ; H. Winlock and W. Crum, *The Monastery of Epiphanius at Thebes*, Part I, The Metropolitan Museum of Egyptian Art Expedition, New York, 1926, p. 7-8 ; O. Meinardus, *Christian Egypt Ancient and Modern*, Cahiers d'Histoire Egyptienne, Cairo, 1965, p. 313 ; Ch. Leblanc, *Taset Neferou une nécropole de Thèbes-ouest et son histoire*, I, Cairo, 1989, p. 6-8, 13 fig. 9 and pl. XXIV-XXVII.

[4] F. Ballerini, *Notizia sommaria degli scavi della missione archeologica italiana in Egitto*, 1903, p. 38 ; E. Schiaparelli, *Relazione sui lavori della missione archeologica italiana in Egitto, anni 1903-1920, Valle delle Regine*, Turin, 1924, p. 126. S. Curto, Un egittologo comasco : Francesco Ballerini, *Rivista Archeologica dell'Antica Povincia e Diocesi di Como*, 135, Como, 1953, p. 46.

In 1974 M.P. Grossmann, who was interested in the monument, published a short report in the German review M.D.A.I.K[5].

In 1988 I commenced a new investigation of the site[6]. I found the Deir in very dilapidated condition ; in fact it was completely covered over with rubbish. It was in clearing the site that I discovered, under the Coptic structure, the not yet known remains of a Roman sanctuary. A dedication sculpted on the lower part of a door jamb which lay on the floor in the church and which originally stood at the entrance to the tomb indicates that the sanctuary dates from the time of Antoninus Pius. Ph. Derchain[7] had already identified the name of this emperor on one of the other decorated fragments he found in the rubble, but he did not imagine that it belonged to a monument *in situ.*

The Coptic occupation of the Valley is not restricted to the Deir, other remains going back to the same time have been identified in the necropolis : in particular, at the heart of the principal ouadi, in and around the tomb VdR 60 ; and also in the side ouadi, La Vallée de la Corde[8], La Vallée des Trois Puits[9] and the Ouadi of Prince Ahmès.

Now let us look individually at the different remains.

The Deir er-Roumi is situated at the entrance to the Valley of the Queens, half way up the southern slope of the Theban

---

[5] P. Grossmann, Untersuchungen im Dair ar-Rumi bei Qurna in Oberägypten, *MDAIK* 30, 1974, p. 25-30 and pl. 4-6 ; art. Dayr al-Rumi in *The Coptic Encyclopedia*, 3, New York, 1991, p. 856-857.

[6] G. Lecuyot, Deir Roumi monastère copte de la Vallée des Reines, *Dossiers Histoire et Archéologie*, 136, Dijon, March 1989, p. 60-63 ; Un sanctuaire romain transformé en monastère : le Deir er-Roumi, Acts of the VIth International Congress of Egyptology, Turin, September 1991, in press; Le Deir er-Roumi, *Le Monde Copte*, 1992, in press.

[7] Ph. Derchain, Une porte d'Antonin le Pieux et l'Osiris d'Erment à Medinet Habou, *CdE* 34, n° 67, January 1959, p. 21-23.

[8] J. Černý, Ch. Desroches Noblecourt and M. Kurz, *Graffiti de la Montagne Thébaine*, I, Cairo, 1969-70, p. 38-39 and pl. XCV-XCIX.

[9] *ibid.*, p. 36-37 et pl. LXXXVI-XCIV.

mountain between the Vallée de la Corde and the Vallée des Trois Puits (Pl. Ia).

On the site of a ancient tomb and the Roman sanctuary, the Deir - which is partly concealed by a rocky spur - comprises two parts on either side of a long vestibule running east-west, the entrance of which is situated to the south (Pl. II). The floor of the vestibule was paved with fragments of red bricks and a bench occupied most of the space along the bottom of the northern and southern walls. In the eastern part of the vestibule the same walls, on the north and on the south side, had many built-in niches. In front of the main entrance door, another door gave access to a space situated to the east of the Deir. This area, which was probably used for domestic purposes, contains some wall ruins and the remains of a small arched granary constructed with mud bricks.

A series of four rooms running east-west are located on the south side, along the rocky spur. The biggest of these, which is slightly below the vestibule, has two big arched cavities in its side walls, to the east and west. A small bench was built along the foot of the western wall. The preserved height of these walls leads us to believe that there was an upper floor to this room. Its ceiling was flat as can be deduced from the preserved holes that once supported wooden beams. The most western of these rooms, which has a circular mark on its floor, may have contained an oven[10].

To the north another series of rooms lie alongside the church. In the eastern room a big jar decorated with a cross in raised relief has been found at the middle of the eastern wall embedded in a mass of plastered masonry. This jar and the location of this room at the south-east corner of the church are somewhat reminiscent of a baptistry[11]. The stairway leading to the upper floor of the Deir was probably situated to the west, along the church wall.

The church was built along the face of the mountain in front of the entrance to the tomb. Facing east-west it has its entrance at the middle of the southern wall and contains an apse at its eastern side (Pl. Ib). The apse, which is topped by an arch *cul*

---

[10] For an example of an oven cf. Winlock, *op. cit.*, p. 53-54 fig. 13.

[11] W. Godlewski, Faras VI, Les baptistères nubiens, Warsaw, 1979.

de four style, is flanked by two stone columns with very simple capitals[12]. A bench was constructed along three sides of the church : north, south and west. This bench was covered over with the same plastering as was put on the floor. The interior of the apse and the space immediately in front of it were paved with sandstone tiles. The church, as P. Grossmann has observed, was surmounted by a dome on pendentives as can be deduced in observing the broken north-east angle of the building. The walls were plastered and some rare traces of red and yellow colour indicate that they must have been decorated at least in part. Though very faint, a plant motif can still be seen on the eastern wall, left of the apse. To the north, the Phraonic tomb which probably represented the heart of the sanctuary in the Roman period, was once again reused, as an annex. Its opening, which is situated in the axe of the main entrance to the church, was narrowed and closed by a door. To the west there was another annex dug into the mountain and its walls were covered over with *mouna.*

The Deir is built with secondhand material : with stones but also with red bricks and mud bricks. The base walls of the church were constructed with stones, the rooms alongside the church mostly with red bricks, and the southern part containing the vestibule with crude bricks. The stones used in the walls and in the foundations came from Pharaonic monuments and, of course, from the Roman sanctuary.

It would seem that the southern part of the monastery including the vestibule is posterior to the northern part ; it was not built before the end of the VIth century A.D.

Abundant pottery has been found on the site : Roman pottery, going back to the time of the sanctuary, but mostly Coptic pottery comprising many fragments of ringed amphoras in brown baked clay[13] (Pl. IIa), household dishes and fine

---

[12] For comparison cf. : Ch. Bachatly *et al., Le monastère de Phoebammon dans la thébaïde*, I, Cairo, 1881, p.l. XCI (C and D) ; W. Godlewski, *Deir el Bahari V, Le monastère de saint Phoibammon*, Warsaw, 1986, p. 115 cat. n° 3 and fig 71 p. 117.

[13] For comparison cf. Winlock, *op. cit.*, p. 79 fig. 32 and pl. XXVIII ; Bachatly, *op. cit.*, pl. LVI(B) and LVII(A) ; Godlewski, *op. cit.*, p. 126-127.

tableware[14] of the O and W types - as categorized by Rodziewicz[15] - some decorated vases and numerous stamped bottle tops in mud earth[16].

Some broken ostraca have also been found scattered in the rubbish. Their inscriptions are in Demotic, in Greek[17] and in Coptic[18]. Most often the inscriptions we find represent accounts, notes and short letters, documents which tell us a lot about daily life in the monastery. It is probable that the monastery's archives have yet to be located.

Among the rare artefacts found let us mention : fragments of a wooden frieze decorated with a stylized vine[19] (Pl. IIIb), fragments of wooden lathwork[20], and also a fragment of a jar stand in stone on which the head of a lion and a cross were sculpted.

Some decorated pottery has also been discovered below the Deir on the eastern slope of the Vallée de la Corde.

In two pit-tombs, VdR 22 and 79, two decorated vases have been exhumed, but no clear explanation has yet been given for their being here.

Some other tombs bear the traces of Coptic occupation.

Tomb VdR 1 : It is located at the entrance of the Valley of the Queens in front of the Deir er-Roumi and seems to control

---

[14] For comparison cf. Winlock, *op. cit.*, pl XXXII(B), dish with stamp.

[15] M. Rodziewicz, *La céramique romaine tardive d'Alexandrie*, Warsaw, 1976.

[16] For comparison cf. Winlock, *op. cit.*, p. 80 fig 33 and pl. XXIX (B).

[17] G. Wagner *et al.*, *op. cit.*, p. 368-369, 376-380 and pl. XVIII.

[18] M. Pezin is working on the Coptic ones.

[19] A similar fragment, which was burned, was found by M. Nelson outside the tomb VdR 60. For comparison cf. Godlewski, *op. cit.*, p. 119 cat. n°17 and fig. 86 p. 121.

[20] For comparison cf. Winlock, *op. cit.*, p. 57 fig. 18 and pl. XV (C).

the access to the valley[21]. In fact this tomb may not have been an excavated chamber but simply a natural cavity adapted for burial. An alcove containing a niche in which a lamp may have been placed was situated at the eastern side of the tomb. The rocky walls and the ceiling were covered over with *mouna*. The northern wall, in which a door was cut, was built with rubble stones held together by dried mud. From the door, a few steps lead up to the small courtyard preceding the cell. The north-west corner of the courtyard's surrounding wall still exists today.

In two tombs dating from the reign of Ramses II - VdR 73 of Henout-taouy[22] and VdR 60 of Nebet-taouy - the pagan paintings were covered over by a coat of *mouna*.

In tomb VdR 60 the antechamber was transformed by the Coptic monks and two red crosses were painted on the eastern wall[23]. Only the painted decorations in the first room were covered over. The other parts of the tomb must have been in too poor condition and probably were not reused, with the exception perhaps of the small eastern annex where one of the two crosses was painted above the entrance. Also in the first room, a niche was cut into the eastern wall, a trench was dug in the floor between the western pillar and the southern wall - it may have served to support a dividing wall - and the floor, which was covered over with *mouna*, was perhaps partially paved as some remains in the south-eastern angle indicate. We may also mention that the capital of a column was found on the floor of this room.

Outside this tomb, which is situated in the heart of the main *ouadi*, some building ruins have been identified by Monique Nelson. These remains may be the same as those observed by R. Hay de Linplum at the beginning of the last century (1824).

The objects found during the excavations of the tomb and the stairway - *ostraca*, fragments of liturgical texts, bone pendants pierced with a hole and decorated with engraved

---

[21] Ch. Leblanc, *op. cit.*, pl. XXXVIII-XXXIX.

[22] Ch. Leblanc, *op. cit.*, pl. CLXXXVIII-CXCI ; Henout-Taouy et la tombe n° 73 de la Vallée des Reines, *BIFAO* 86, Cairo, 1986, p. 208.

[23] Ch. Leblanc, *Taset Neferou*, Cairo, 1989, pl. CXLVII(A) and CXLVIII(B).

concentric circles[24] - these things show that the tomb must have had a special status.

Greek and Coptic *papyri* fragments have been found, including a fragment of Coptic parchment probably dating from the VIth century. Some are documentary in nature, others liturgical, and these can be dated from the second half of the Vth century. Some fragments must be dated later : G. Wagner's paleographic study proposes the VIth and even the beginning of the VIIth century. The six *ostraca* discovered by Ch. Leblanc and studied by G. Roquet are written in sahidic and date perhaps from the VIIIth century[25]. Let us mention another fragment, a jug stand in baked clay which is decorated with a cross.

And there are findings of architectural interest : the angle of a building north of the tomb, a suite of two rooms to the south-west and, in particular, the remains of an important construction in front of the entrance to the tomb. Two building phases have been identified. In the first phase the stairway leading to the tomb was reconstructed and the lateral walls were extended towards the south. The space thus created was paved with small stone tiles (Pl. IVa). In the second phase, which is not earlier than the end of the VIth century, the floor was raised by 20cm, the level area was extended westward, and a new floor was laid, this time with red bricks. Unfortunately, these ruins being incomplete, it is not possible to state exactly the size of this construction or courtyard. A water pot of a *noria* covered with a plate (group O) was found just under the brick floor.

Other objects found in these ruins have to be mentioned : some *ostraca*, fragments of ringed amphoras in brown baked clay, cooking pots. Another find, the upper part of a vase, may have been manufactured in the workshop discovered in the Temple of Gournah, dating perhaps from theVIIth century.

---

[24] Two small plaques come from VdR 58 and four from VdR 60; the hole in one of them was still blocked by the knot of a leather strap, cf. *ASAE* 69, p. 39 fig. 3. These elements have been identified by M. Pezin as page markers.

[25] Ch. Leblanc, Les tombes n° 58 et n° 60 de la Vallée des Reines : *ASAE* 69, Cairo, 1983, p. 38-39, 43-44, 49-52 and pl. IV-V et *ASAE* 70, Cairo, 1985, p. 68 and pl. II.

The discovery of a large jar, deeply embedded in the floor of the presumed site of the Ramesside *Whyt* of the Valley of the Queens, leads us to believe that certain houses in this hamlet were reoccupied.

To the north of the stairway leading down to tomb VdR 53, a circular oven was built with red bricks[26], some of which were reused in the second pavement of the floor in front of tomb VdR 60. The oven dates back to the first phase of the coptic modifications of this tomb, that is to say between the end of the Vth century and the end of the VIth.

Some traces of occupation of the side *ouadi* have been remarked for some time now : the *ouadi* of Prince Ahmès, the Vallée des trois Puits[27] and the Vallée de la Corde.

The Vallée de la Corde owes its name to a rope which, up to only a few years ago, hung in a split at the back of the *ouadi*. This rope was probably used to climb up to the top of the cliff.

At the bottom of the Vallée des Trois Puits some hermit shelters with *graffiti* have been located, as has been another shelter on the western slope. This cavity is marked by the remains of a wall, some traces of *mouna* and some pieces of pottery which lay outside[28].

But it is at the top of the *Ouadi* of Prince Ahmès that the most important remains have been found[29]. On the western slope a series of cavities were more or less adapted as living quarters. Four in number, they run in an east-west line along a terrace the floor of which was covered over with *mouna*. Only the two

---

[26] Ch. Leblanc, *Taset Neferou*, Cairo, 1989, pl. CXXXII.

[27] J. Cerny, Ch. Desroches Noblecourt et M. Kurz, *Graffiti de la Montagne Thébaine*, I, Cairo, 1969-70, pl. XCII-XCIV.

[28] Other hermit shelters have been located and recorded all over the Theban Mountain. Cf. Winlock, *op. cit.*, p. 3-24 and pl. I ; R. Coque, F. Debono, Ch. Desroches Noblecourt, M. Kurz and R. Said, *Graffiti de la Montagne Thébaine*, I, 4, Cairo, 1973., p. 22 and pl. CCLVI ; *Graffiti de la Montagne Thébaine* I,3, Cairo, 1972, p. 50-51 and pl. CCXXXVI.

[29] Cf. Ballerini, *op. cit.*, p. 32 ; Ch. Leblanc, *Ta set neferou*, Cairo, 1989, p. 9-11 and pl. XXXV-XXXVII. This area was cleared and studied by Th. Zimmer in 1986 during an short excavation campaign.

central cavities underwent major conversion ; the other two simply received a coat of *mouna*.

The two central cavities open on to each other. The most southern cavity is in the shape of a yard : its south-east angle opens on to the terrace and its north-west angle to the second room. There is a *mastaba* alongside its northern wall. The second room, located slightly below the first one, opens on to the terrace by means of a narrow passage in its eastern wall. This room, square in shape, was surmounted by a dome, today collapsed, which rested on four brick arches built against the walls. There must have been *mastaba* under the arches to the north and to the west (Pl. IVb).

Only a few objects have been discovered in excavating this site. However some *ostraca* (fragmentary letters) were found in the rubbish below the terrace.

It is probable that all these elements that I have described belong to the same monastic settlement. The Deir obviously enjoyed a dominant position in relation to the other associated monuments, and together with its church it represented the principal edifice of the valley. The laura thus conceived with its central element and its surrounding cells, presents the same pattern as the other monasteries which abounded on the Theban mountain between the Vth and the VIIth centuries[30].

The destruction of the Roman sanctuary is, no doubt, an illustration of the struggle between the last pagans and the first Christians, and the establishment in the necropolis of this monastic community was perhaps also a manner of exorcising the demons.

CNRS Paris, August 1992.

---

[30] On Deir el Bahari cf. W. Godlewski, *op. cit.*, p. 16 fig. 2 and p. 28 -32 fig. 9-13. On St Epiphanius and St Cyriacus, cf. Winlock, *op. cit.* On St Marc, cf. G. Castel, Etude d'une momie copte in Hommage à S. Sauneron II, *BdE LXXXII*, Cairo, 1979, fig. 1 and pl. X. On St Phoebammon, cf. Ch. Bachatly *et al.*, *Le monastère de Phoebammon dans la thébaïde*, I-III, Cairo, 1981, 1965, 1961.

Pl. Ia - Valley of the Queens, general view with the ruins of the Deir er Roumi (Photo G.L.).

Pl. Ib - Deir er-Roumi, eastern side of the church with the apse (Photo M. Kurz)

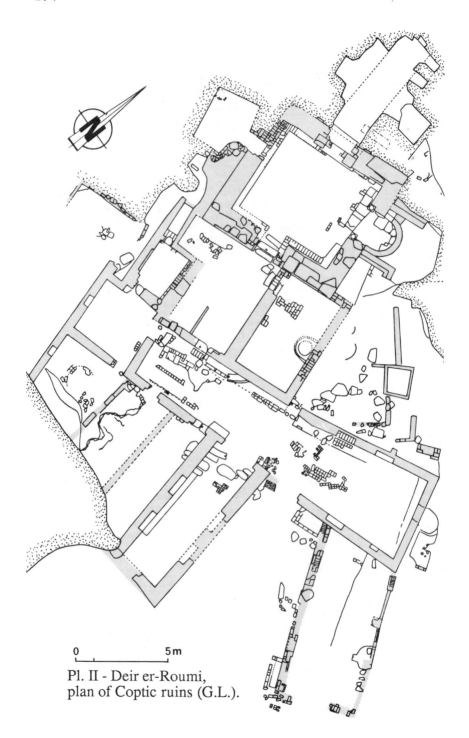

Pl. II - Deir er-Roumi,
plan of Coptic ruins (G.L.).

0   5m

Pl. IIIb - Deir er-Roumi, fragments
of a wooden frieze (Photo G.L.).

Pl. IIIa - Deir er-Roumi, Coptic amphora in brown
baked clay (Photo M. Kurz).

276

Pl. IVb - Ouadi of Prince Ahmès, hermit shelter originaly covered by a dome (Photo F. Bellay)

Pl. IVa - Valley of the Queens, Coptic ruins in front of VdR 60 (Photo Ch. Chapoton).

Riproduzione anastatica: 10 dicembre 1993
Tipografia Poliglotta della Pontificia Università Gregoriana
Piazza della Pilotta, 4 – 00187 Roma